THEORY OF PRODUCTION

RAGNAR FRISCH

THEORY OF PRODUCTION

D. REIDEL PUBLISHING COMPANY / DORDRECHT-HOLLAND

RAND McNALLY & COMPANY / CHICAGO

Innledning til Produksjonsteorien
First published as
'*Memorandum fra Universitetets Sosialøkonomiske Institutt*', Oslo, Norway
Translated from the Norwegian by R. I. Christophersen

SOLE DISTRIBUTORS FOR U.S.A. AND CANADA
RAND McNALLY & COMPANY, CHICAGO

1965

All rights reserved
No part of this book may be reproduced in any form, by print, photoprint, microfilm, or any other means without permission from the publisher

Printed in The Netherlands

PREFACE

In this feverish world of ours, where one wants the economic analyses to produce easily understandable results quickly and at the least possible cost, some of us have fallen into the habit of assuming for simplicity that the hundreds and sometimes thousands of variables that enter into the analyses are linked together by very *simple* relationships. Frequently we even go so far as to assume linear relationships. Only in this way have we been able to feed our problems into the electronic computers and get mechanical answers quickly and at low cost.

I would be the last to deny that there are instances where this is a most useful and convenient procedure. I am myself interested in this type of work. (I shall return to this point at the end of the preface.) But, in our enthusiasm for the powerful, modern means of calculation, we have run the risk of neglecting something essential which the good old 'traditional' ways of reasoning brought home to us. These good old types of analyses we shall however never be able to dispense with. We will in the end always need to fall back on them.

The danger of losing something essential in this feverish world of ours is particularly acute in the theory of production. The classical authorities on this subject, Ricardo, von Thünen, Justus von Liebig, John Clark, Léon Walras, Knut Wicksell and others devoted much of their time and energy to discussions that were *not* centred around this or that simple type of mathematical relationship, but proceeded directly from *the fundamental logic of the laws of production*. It is in the same spirit that the present work is conceived.

I began thinking about these problems long before the advent of electronic computers. To be precise: Already in the fall term of 1926 I delivered lectures in the Oslo University on the theory of production. And in 1962 the ninth edition of my Norwegian lectures on this subject was published.

I have retained my admiration for the classical ideas also after I started to devote a good part of my time and energy to mathematical programming. I have felt it a mission to safeguard the classical ideas, to systematise and develop them, and to endeavour to present the whole *in a coherent and logical form*.

This book is based in its substance on my Norwegian lectures. I had neither the time nor the space in this book to go into the several specialised subjects, which I had initially proposed to discuss. I can only hope that my choice has been judicious, and will result in bringing to light that which constitutes the essence of the classical thought and the modernized formulation of it.

I have had the good fortune, during my career, to be called upon to lecture on certain aspects of the theory of production elsewhere than in Oslo – at the Sorbonne, at Yale and at the University of Minnesota. The obligation to expound my thoughts in these various quarters has, I hope, helped to improve on the clarity of the presentation.

The fundamental concepts of product, production factor, marginal productivity, etc. apply, in their abstract sense, not only to the problems of a concern producing and selling goods, but to practically every conceivable sphere of human activity: to political action, to social reforms, to the speeding up of economic growth in an underdeveloped country, to improvement of breeding stock, to games of chance, etc. In many cases, it would suffice to change the names of the objects under consideration to return to an analytical formula common to all.

This, clearly, is due to the fact that the fundamental concepts of the theory of production which I have just mentioned – product, production factor, marginal productivity, etc. are not derivatives of concrete objects, but rather spring from the peculiar way in which the human brain functions. This is also the reason why I have not considered it necessary to bring up to date certain rather old data which I had used to illustrate my earlier lectures.

If it is true that the concepts themselves are extremely general as far as applications are concerned, and that it is quite possible to deal with them in a completely abstract jargon, it is much easier to follow the reasoning if we use a more concrete terminology. And, on the other hand, nothing is really gained in explicative power by using the abstract jargon. I have, therefore, in this book, expressed myself most frequently in terms applicable to the case of a concern producing and selling goods.

The need to take into account relationships that are very far from linear, was amply brought home to me when in the last decades I was engaged in developing the principles of macroeconomic planning and programming. Therefore, I found it necessary to orient a large part of the activity of the Institute of Economics of the University of Oslo towards the working out of a method of mathematical programming where the preference function may be non concave and the admissible region non convexe and where the number of variables may be very large. Previously my multiplex method had worked well in the case of a concave preference function and linear bounds, and to begin with I tried to extend this method to the very general problems with which we were now concerned. To day our programming work does not, however, proceed along these lines, but is based on an entirely different approach, using what I call the nonplex method. I hope to be able to report on the results in the not too distant future.

Many are the students and associates of mine from the Institute of Economics at the University of Oslo who, at different times and in different ways, have stimulated my work and contributed to building up my theory of production. Several of them have later been called upon to fulfil important functions in the service of Norway's economic life. In a general way I am greatly indebted to all of them, but it would be impossible to mention them all by name here.

As far as the contents of the present book are concerned, I owe a particular debt of gratitude to my colleagues at Norwegian universities, in particular to professors Johan Einarsen, Trygve Haavelmo, Gunnar Boe (for some years Minister for Prices and Wages), Preben Munthe and Ole Myrvoll. I must also mention Mr. Petter Jakob Bjerve, director general of the Norwegian Central Statistical Bureau (and former Minister for Finance).

I am particularly grateful to my friend and colleague, associate professor Per Meinich, who has devoted so much of his precious time to the checking and correcting of the 8th and 9th Norwegian editions, the English edition and the French edition. (In the Spanish edition none of my associates were able to help.)

On the technical side, Mr. Antonius Reidel and his collaborators, have performed a most excellent job and have done all that is materially possible to satisfy my wishes as regards typographical composition. I am particularly grateful to them for their extreme patience with an author who, because of many activities, has been nearly criminally slow in returning proof sheets.

Oslo, March 1965   RAGNAR FRISCH

CONTENTS

Preface   V

PART ONE

BASIC CONCEPTS OF PRODUCTION

Chapter 1. What is Production?   3

1a.   Production in the technical sense. Production factors and products   3
1b.   The distinction between a scientific statement and a value judgment   5
1c.   Production in the economic sense. Evaluation coefficients   8
1d.   Single production, assorted production, and joint production   10
1e.   The technical, financial, and political organisation of production. Horizontal and vertical concentration. State control   11

Chapter 2. Production Factors   14

2a.   Specified and implied factors. Controllable and non-controllable, economic and free factors   14
2b.   Fixed and variable factors. Capacity. Short-term and long-term factors   15
2c.   Special and general factors. The problem of association between given input elements and given output elements   17
2d.   Definition of the term factor quantity and product quantity. Elementary factors   18
2e.   Factor complexes. Equivalence factors and aggregated factors. Shadow factors   21

Chapter 3. Production Technique, Constant Technique and Variable Technique   24

3a.   Definition of constant technique   24
3b.   Changes in the nature of factors   25

CONTENTS

3c. Changes in the production function (changes in the production table) ... 25
3d. Changes in the factor quantities under a constant production function (production table) ... 26

Chapter 4. Various Types of Production Theory ... 29

4a. Momentary production and time-shaped production. Static and dynamic theory of production ... 29
4b. Number of stages and stage tempo. Input curves and step diagram ... 30
4c. The stage interval. Time-rigid and time-elastic production process ... 34
4d. Mean production period and average liquid capital in a closed production process ... 35
4e. Risk and anticipation in the theory of production ... 38

PART TWO

MOMENTARY SINGLE PRODUCTION USING ONLY CONTINUITY FACTORS

A. TECHNICAL SECTION

Chapter 5. Various Methods of Describing a Continuous Production Law ... 41

5a. Production function, product table, and isoquants ... 41
5b. Marginal productivities ... 51
5c. Product accelerations ... 58
5d. Average productivities ... 61
5e. Marginal elasticities ... 62
5f. The passus coefficient ... 65
5g. Further consideration on proportional factor variation ... 68
5h. Passus equation ... 73
5i. Further details concerning isoquants and isoclines ... 78

Chapter 6. The Technical Optimum Law when Considering Partial Variation of a Factor or a Group of Factors ... 83

6a. History of some basic concepts ... 83
6b. Detailed analysis of the technical optimum law as it appears when we consider the partial variation of a single factor ... 88
6c. The technical optimum law for variation of a partial factor complex ... 98

Chapter 7. The Pari-Passu Law — 99

7a. Definition of a pari-passu law — 99
7b. Special properties of the pari-passu law — 102
7c. Further observations on the pari-passu law in two factors — 105
7d. The pari-passu law in three factors — 113
7e. The substitution region in a pari-passu law in n factors — 115

Chapter 8. The ultra-passum law. The regular ultra-passum law — 120

B. ECONOMIC SECTION

Chapter 9. The Strategic Types and the Aims of Economic Adjustment — 135

9a. The necessity of taking into consideration other forms of market than free competition and absolute monopoly — 135
9b. Quantity adjustment — 138
9c. Stochastic price adjustment — 139
9d. Elasticity-influenced price-quantity adjustment — 140
9e. Option fixation — 140
9f. Option reception — 140
9g. Aims and conditions for an adjustment process — 141

Chapter 10. Economic Adjustment to Fixed Prices — 144

10a. Introduction — 144
10b. Cost minimisation under a given product quantity — 147
10c. Product maximisation with given total cost — 151
10d. The in-every-respect economic substitution. The substitumal — 154
10e. Co-variation between costs and product quantity along the substitumal. The economic optimum law — 164
10f. Profit maximisation — 175
10g. Profit optimisation — 186
10h. The general demand functions for the factors and the general supply function for the product — 186
10i. The effect of a change in the product price — 187
10j. The effect of a change in one of the factor prices — 190
10k. Capacity adjustment — 194

Chapter 11. Economic Adjustment under Elasticity-Influenced Price-Quantity Adjustment — 196

11a. Introduction — 196

11b. Cost minimisation under a given product quantity and variable factor prices ... 201
11c. Product maximisation under a given total cost and variable factor prices ... 203
11d. The in-every-respect economic substitution under variable factor prices. The substitumal under variable factor prices ... 205
11e. The covariation between costs and product quantity along the substitumal corresponding to the given factor supply functions. The economic optimum law under variable factor prices ... 208
11f. Product maximisation under variable product price ... 217

PART THREE

MOMENTARY SINGLE PRODUCTION WITH LIMITATION FACTORS

Chapter 12. Technical analysis of limitation laws ... 225
12a. The simple minimum law ... 225
12b. Marginal definition of minimum, maximum, and limitation factors. General definition of the limitation law ... 227
12c. The production law in the case of technically given but not constant limitation-fabrication coefficients. Independent limitation factors ... 230
12d. Separate factor rings ... 231
12e. Mixed factor rings ... 232
12f. Confluence analysis, all-region analysis and delimitation analysis. Basis variables ... 235
12g. The marginal productivity concept when the production law contains limitation factors ... 237
12h. The delimitation definition of the confluence region. The relationship with the substitution region. The limitation law as an extreme case of the optimum law ... 242
12i. The delimitation problem. A method of constructing the confluence region ... 244
12j. Basis factors and shadow factors. Product shadows and factor shadows ... 249

Chapter 13. Economic Analysis of Limitation Laws ... 252
13a. The economic production concepts within the confluence region ... 252

13b. The substitumal within the confluence region — 255
13c. Step-by-step adaptation taking marginal rentability and marginal profit into account — 256
13d. Further application of the arrow of rentability: adaptation to equivalence and to production laws with complicated factor bands — 262

PART FOUR

MULTI-WARE PRODUCTION

Chapter 14. Technical description of the Production Law for Multi-Ware Production — 269

14a. Connected products. Assortment and coupling — 269
14b. Factorially determined multi-ware production — 270
14c. One-dimensional assortment. Single product freedom — 276
14d. Multi-dimensional assortment. Multiple freedom of products — 278

Chapter 15. Economic Adaptation Under Multi-Ware Production — 282

15a. Product value and costs under multi-ware production — 282
15b. Economic adaptation under factorially determined multi-ware production — 282
15c. Two-stage economic adaptation under one-dimensional or multi-dimensional assortment — 286
15d. Direct analysis of the economic adaptation in the general case — 287

PART FIVE

ELEMENTS OF A DYNAMIC THEORY OF PRODUCTION

Chapter 16. A Survey of the Problems of a Dynamic Theory of Production — 293

Chapter 17. The Reinvestment Process in a Mass where each Capital Object has a Determined Life-Time — 295

17a. Reinvestment activity as a consequence of a primary investment dose where the distribution of durability is discrete — 295
17b. Reinvestment activity as a result of a primary investment dose where the durability distribution is continuous — 301
17c. Reinvestment when new primary investment doses are injected at various points of time — 304

Chapter 18. The Reinvestment Process in a Mass where there is a probability Law for the Lifetime of Each Capital Object   309

18a. Departure gauges   309
18b. Maintenance equation and calculation of maintenance investment as a time series   310
18c. Breaking maintenance investment down into its component parts   312
18d. The segment method   316
18e. Maintenance investment when a considerable period of time has elapsed since starting   320
18f. The method of curve fitting. Maintenance investment when the departure distribution is almost normal (Gaussian)   321

Chapter 19. Depreciation Analysis   333

19a. Technical depreciation defined by the principle of remaining services   333
19b. Writing-off plan and actual writing-off   337

Analytical Summary   346

Index   367

PART ONE

BASIC CONCEPTS OF PRODUCTION

CHAPTER 1

WHAT IS PRODUCTION?

1a. Production in the technical sense. Production factors and products

For the term *technical production* we intend to adopt a wide definition. By it we mean any *transformation process* which can be directed by human beings, or which human beings are interested in, viz. a transformation which a certain group of people consider desirable. The term transformation indicates that there are certain things (goods or services) which enter into the process, and lose their identity in it, i.e. *ceasing to exist* in their original form, while other things (goods or services) come into being in that they *emerge* from the process. The first category may be referred to as *production factors* (input elements), while the last-named category are referred to as *products* (the output or resultant elements). The grain put into the ground, manure, etc., are production factors, while the harvest is the product. Wooden materials and the carpenter's work are production factors, while the chairs and the tables are products.

The transformation which we call production in the technical sense of the word need not alter the actual material qualities of the things concerned. Often it need only be a *movement* or a *selection* or a *conservation* ('a movement in time'). Logs lying in the forest are not the same things as logs at the sawmill. The process of hauling the logs to the river, floating them down, and getting them to the sawmill is just as much production in the technical sense of the word as the business of felling the trees and stripping the bark off the stems. The same is true of the selection and conservation e.g. of vegetables and fruit. From the purely technical point of view production in the sphere of trade consists to a large extent of selections or movements in time and place.

Note that here we are only speaking of the facts that affect the process of transformation, which can be described quite objectively in *technical* terms, e.g. 'a table executed by a carpenter', 'logs lying at the sawmill,' 'apples in January', etc. When speaking of production in the technical sense, we are in fact not always concerned with the extent to which it is possible to measure the 'value' or 'use' which production creates. Thus if, for example, a product suddenly becomes valueless, owing to the state of the market, we can nevertheless say that the process that produced it was a production in the technical sense of the word. Nor do we in this connection try to find out whether the transformation is hygienic or morally justified or not. The process that takes place in a tobacco factory we should call production in the technical sense of the word, even though there are a great many people who consider that tobacco is harmful. Even the armaments industry constitutes production in the technical sense.

Originally the term 'technical production' was not as widely defined as has been done here. The *physiocrats*, for instance, maintained that only agricultural work possessed this quality, while *Adam Smith* enlarged the term, maintaining as he did that other kinds of work were also 'productive'. These somewhat philosophically inclined discussions on what was 'productive' have little direct bearing on the modern treatment of the problems of production, but should be mentioned here in order to complete our picture.

To a certain extent the distinction between production factors (input elements) and products (output elements) is conventional, depending at all times on the particular aspect of the problem we are interested in. Let us consider, for example, the production of woollen cloth. The wool passes through four stages: raw wool, tops (a preproduct of yarn), yarn, and cloth.

According to Hagström[1] the following data are available for the United States, 1912.

TABLE (1a.1)

In order to produce	There is required
1 metre of cloth (Fancy worsted suiting. Width 145 cm, weight 237 grams per sq. metre).	0.196 kg of yarn (worsted No. 45-2 (U-G)).
1 kg yarn (of the specified quality).	1.136 kg tops.
1 kg tops.	3.125 kg raw wool (fat, half-breed Ohio).

The figures in the column on the right in Table (1a.1) we call *coefficients of manufacture*. The coefficient of manufacture for a production factor ex-

[1] K. G. Hagström, *Ylleindustriens produktionsförhållanden*, Stockholm, 1924 (Statens offentlige utredninger 1924 : 35).

presses how much of the factor is on an average required in order to produce a unit of the product.

What appears as a product at one stage in the example given above, appears as a production factor in the next stage. If each stage is considered separately, tops, yarn, and cloth are all *products*. In fact, raw wool is also a product, i.e. of sheep breeding. If, on the other hand, the entire manufacturing process is considered as one, then the raw wool is the production factor, and the cloth the product, while the tops and the yarn are merely intermediate products.

In most practical cases no real difficulty is involved in distinguishing between production factors and products.

1b. The distinction between a scientific statement and a value judgment

For a rational approach to the theory of production, it is necessary to take as the point of departure the definition of production in the technical sense, such as set out in 1a. But this technical concept of production is only useful in so far as it furnishes a basis for further investigation. In any theory of production to be incorporated in a truly economic analysis, some form of *value judgment* must be included. A comparison must be made among the input elements, and between them and the output elements. And this can as a rule only be done on some basis of value judgments, which cannot be reduced merely to technical terms. This is a major problem which economics cannot overlook. This was the issue round which previous discussions centered in deciding the question of what sort of work should be considered 'productive'. The basis of these discussions, however, was not clear. We must in fact find a more precise formulation; and in order to do so we must review on a somewhat broader basis the distinction between scientific statements and value judgments.

A characteristic feature of all scientific research is that it attempts to obtain results which are objective, in the sense that they must be accepted by all those who have the necessary knowledge of the problems and methods involved. In this respect scientific research differs from the work that involves drawing up rules of conduct for practical application, and which, in their most far-reaching form, are expressed in political programmes.

In tackling scientific problems, in fact, the aim is to find solutions that can be subjected to the criterion of correct or false. In the case of practical rules of conduct, on the other hand, the question at issue is one of desirability and expediency – or belief in expediency – and this is based on a number of value judgment elements which must be considered in relation to the *practical or political object* in view, and on which it would naturally be impossible to expect unanimous agreement.

In purely scientific questions, too, differences of opinion can of course exist; but this applies in the main to cases in which the problem at issue has not been posed with sufficient precision, with the result that the various protagonists involved are talking of different things; or it applies in cases when the problem at issue has been precisely stated, but has not yet been exhaustively investigated, so that there is room for a difference of opinion as to what is *probably* the right solution. In principle those who are working on scientific problems will assume that something objective exists which must be recognised by all investigators, provided their analysis is penetrating and exact enough.

This applies more than anywhere else in a purely abstract science such as *mathematics*. Differences of opinion may exist as to what, from the purely logical point of view, is the most fruitful way of posing the problem of the fundamental mathematical operations – as is *inter alia* apparent in modern fundamental-logical research in mathematics, – but as soon as certain fundamental operations are accepted, a system is arrived at, in which every thesis is such that it must either be accepted or rejected by all those capable of following the analysis. Without investigating more closely just what this position involves from the point of pure cognition, it can be stated that we here possess a criterion that can be used to decide whether the result is *correct* or false in a definite, objective sense.

A similar situation applies in other sciences, including the empiric sciences. Every scientific analysis must operate with certain presuppositions which – provided they constitute a system free from contradictions – it accepts without any attempt at further 'proof' or justification.

Any attempt at such 'proof' or justification would merely lead into the realm of value judgment, where objectivity would be lost. The basic logical operations in mathematics are of this nature; and the same applies to the system of presuppositions in other sciences. In fact, in a scientific analysis we reason as follows: *if* we proceed from such and such fundamental axioms in collating our empiric material and in our logical operations, then we must arrive at such and such a result. *In the last resort this choice of presuppositions contains some element – be it large or small – of value judgment.* It is not until this evaluative point of departure is given, that the actual scientific analysis can commence. Thus the entire *type* of scientific analysis one obtains, depends in the last resort on what non-scientific value judgments one starts from.

The difficulties involved in maintaining complete clarity of thought in these questions vary considerably within the various sciences, with mathematics constituting one extreme. In the case of mathematics it is nearly always perfectly obvious what the presuppositions are, and when scientific objectivity prevails. From mathematics we can proceed via the *natural sciences* to the *social sciences*, where the difficulties become greater and greater, because the entire complex of ideas that constitutes the presuppositions of the science inevitably tends to become less and less clear-cut.

This applies to a very special degree to the social sciences and not least to *economics*, where the scale of possible presuppositions, and consequently also of possible types of scientific investigations, is very wide.

Admittedly there are, in the science of economics, certain problems in which the investigator's attitude to his object is essentially the same as that of the natural scientist's attitude to *his* object. This applies *inter alia* to the technical sections of the theory of production, and to large parts of the doctrine concerned with the regularities occurring in consumption.

But in a great many other spheres of economics the position is far more difficult. Even the attempt at an actual *description* of the phenomena dealt within economics involves the element of appreciation (evaluation), in so far as the bulk of the details constituting economic and social reality cannot be included in a scientific presentation. A *selection* must be made. And this selection or this basis of interpretation will not only depend on what, in a certain objective sense, is 'correct', but it will also to a considerable extent depend on the *purpose* for which the results *are to be used*, i.e. on a certain measure of value judgment.

The selection made in this respect by economists will, owing to the influences they have on public opinion and the political situation, inevitably affect *major human welfare interests*. For this reason it has often been coloured by the economic struggle for power in the community, and has in turn often reacted on this struggle, *inter alia* by helping to mould an economic-political ideology.

This does *not* mean that the economist, like the scientist, should fail to preoccupy himself with problems involving value judgments. This would prevent him from making *his* contribution to a solution of the major economic questions of his age. It merely means that he should always endeavour to draw the line of demarcation as clearly as possible. He should bear in mind the extent to which the results of his analysis are dependent on the non-scientific presuppositions from which his analysis proceeds. To the extent that he succeeds in making a clear and definite distinction between what is a scientific statement in the proper sense and what is a value judgment, he will be able to preserve his *objectivity*. And this is, in fact, the only way in which it can be preserved. It was the German economist and sociologist Max Weber who first clearly pointed this out.

It is no use denying that the difficulties in this respect are very considerable. It takes a real effort to spot the value judgements behind things that are *apparently* 'objective', 'unpolitical', etc. The more comprehensive the problem dealt with, and the more entangled it is with the economic interests of individuals or groups and ideological cross-currents, the more *detailed* must be the specification of the non-scientific presuppositions, in order to ensure the conditionality necessary to an objective result. A detailed specification of the presuppositions will naturally make it more difficult to present the results lucidly and comprehensively. In the case of limited *special* problems it is comparatively easy to give an exact specification of the presuppositions and in such cases an economic analysis will as a rule give an objective and lucid solution. In the case of *general* problems, on the other hand, where major principles of value judgment are involved and cut across one another in various ways, the difficulties are very considerable. Between these two extremes there is a wide range of intermediate cases.

1c. Production in the economic sense. Evaluation coefficients

The fundamental question of the place of value judgment in the analysis is encountered in every aspect of the theory of production, as soon as we proceed beyond the purely technical description of the production process. By production in the *economic* sense we mean the attempt to create a product which is *more highly valued* than the original input elements. Examples of this come readily to mind.

When a farmer has to decide whether he is to produce grain or potatoes in his fields, he does so – assuming that he belongs to the great majority who are primarily concerned with economic gain – by comparing the prices of grain and potatoes with the costs involved in these two kinds of production. In other words, in his case the basis of value judgment is simply provided by the market prices. Market prices provide the *evaluation coefficients* on which he bases himself, i.e. the coefficients he uses to reduce goods and services to a common denominator, so that they are capable of comparison. On this basis there is a comparison which enables him to define the concept of *economic* production.

But agricultural production can also be evaluated in other ways. A nutrition expert, for example, will reckon in terms of calories and vitamins and other basic constituents of foodstuffs, and this yardstick is in no way less realistic than the price gauge. We have only to remind ourselves of the way in which the various branches of agriculture are evaluated when a country's state of war-preparedness is discussed. In comparing the cost of living of a working family at various stages, we often take as a basis the nutritional equivalent of the foodstuffs concerned. There are many other examples where the price gauge is not the only element of interest. The prices of products, as well as of production factors, are almost certainly bound to be *changed* if a whole branch of industry changes its production policy. Consequently this policy cannot be discussed merely on the basis of prices, at any rate not on the basis of constant prices. The relativity inherent in the system of value judgment coefficients becomes still more marked in the case of social reforms or economic reforms with a social effect, since we must bear in mind the fact that the subjective value of money is different to the poor and the rich, as well as the fact that from the point of view of the community a great many *indirect* effects must be taken into account. For this reason productivity in the social sense is not the same as it is from the point of view of private economy or enterprise. For example, in a country short of foreign currency, and with considerable unemployment and a not very highly developed industry, it would be more 'productive' – all things being equal – from the point of national economy to initiate a programme of roadbuilding than shipbuilding, as the former would employ more hands and impose less strain on the import budget. The comparison between the output elements, taken in a very broad sense, and the input elements in a case of this kind must go much deeper into the question of evaluation coefficients than simply to consider market prices.

In some cases the basis of value judgment may be of a *quasi-technical* kind, i.e. it will appear in the form of something technical and objective, but will nevertheless in the last resort contain elements of value judgment. This applies, for example, when index computations are carried out on production *volume*, e.g. when formerly sailing ship tonnage was converted to steam ship tonnage, according to the efficiency of the two kinds of ship, or if we work out the number of 'computed cows' as an expression of the entire stocks of domestic animals[1] at a farm, or if we calculate the number of consumer units in a working family, etc.

To sum up we might say: the technical analysis of production is based

[1] In Norwegian statistics, livestock totals have been reckoned as follows: 1 head of cattle = ½ horse = 6 sheep or goats = 2 pigs = 4 reindeer. For a criticism of this method of computation see *Jordbrukstellingen i Norge 20. Juni 1929*, Vol. IV, p. 292, Oslo, 1932.

exclusively on terms and criteria which can be formulated technically and objectively. In other forms of production analysis we must presuppose a system of value judgment coefficients – for example, market prices – whereby the various goods and services occurring in the analysis, either as production factors or as products, can be reduced to a common denominator for the purpose of comparison. Depending on the nature of this system, one can speak of a market price analysis, a macro-economic decisional analysis, a quasi-technical analysis, etc. It is not the concern of objective research to decide which of these systems of value judgment is the 'right' one. Most frequently we shall use prices, as this is pedagogically simplest; but the nature of the argument leading up to an *economic optimum* will remain the same for other kinds of coefficients.

1d. Single production, assorted production, and joint production

If a production process is such that it results in a single, technically homogeneous kind of goods or services, we call it *single* production. If we consider the entire activity taking place within one whole, industrial establishment, i.e. within a production organisation of the kind which is nowadays generally coordinated under one technical management (a 'factory', or 'plant'), single production is a comparatively rare occurrence, though it does exist, at least approximately, e.g. the manufacture of matches.

A single stage in the production activity of an establishment will however often appear as a single production, e.g. the production of corn on a particular piece of land on a given farm, the production of a special sort of chocolate in a chocolate factory, etc. The most essential feature of each single one of these production stages is as a rule apparent if we presuppose that the result is a technically homogeneous product, whose *size* is measured by the number of units produced. This measurability assumption can also at times be justified in a macro-analysis, e.g. when studying in general outline what determines the actual magnitude of a nation's total production ('production volume', computed on the basis of some sort of volume index). For this reason it is appropriate that a great deal of the theory of production should be concerned with single production.

In a great many cases, however, the actual problem posed is more complicated. We may, for example, wish to investigate under what circumstances it would be profitable in agriculture to change from one kind of crop, e.g. grain, to another kind, e.g. potatoes. The core of the problem here is that a number of the existing production factors can be applied *alternatively* for the production of either product. Similar situations occur in industry and perhaps, even more clearly, in handicrafts. There are, for example, small universal cabinetmaker's machines which can be used alternatively for a great many different kinds of work. In such cases we should talk of *assorted* production and assorted products.

Finally we have the case of *joint* production and joint products. In this case the technical process itself contains an element which makes it impossible (or very difficult) to produce one product without at the same time producing one or more other products. Gas, coke, and tar are in this sense joint products, and the same is true of wool and mutton, etc. According to the value that the various products represent out of the total production value, we speak of main products, bi-products, and waste products. A change in the price situation may result in the bi-product or even the waste product being elevated to the status of main product.

The relative quantities of joint products produced are not always determined strictly on technical grounds, but are capable of being varied, at any rate, within certain limits. Thus, by changing over from one breed of sheep to another, one might get more wool and less meat, or vice versa. As a rule any change of this kind will involve costs (measured in terms of prices or other value judgment coefficients), and the question of which relative quantity to aim at will therefore be one of profitability. If there is a comparatively wide sphere within which variation is technically possible – and assuming that one is prepared to accept the costs involved, – one approaches the type of production which was referred to above as *assorted*, and whose characteristic feature is precisely that it was technically possible to produce either one or another product. In practice an intermediate form of this kind – a semi-rigid coupling between products – often occurs.

The theory of joint production (including the semi-rigid type) is an important part of the theory of production, but is naturally more complicated than the theory governing single production.[1]

1e. The technical, financial, and political organisation of production. Horizontal and vertical concentration. State control

When we speak of the *organisation* of production, we are thinking of the way in which men, machines, natural resources, etc. (or groups thereof) operate together in order to obtain production results. In describing this system, an essential point is *who* decides how the various operations are to be carried out, and on *which criteria* he bases his decision (e.g. prices or

---

[1] In Part Four of this book the main features of the theory of multi-ware production are discussed.

other value judgment coefficients). This *question of steering* is the fundamental question of organisation. We find it emerging everywhere, both in the micro-cosmos and in the macro-cosmos. Take for instance a factory, either privately owned or part of a socialistic community: the factory has a technical manager, who decides all the important questions on current production. He must confine himself to the most important matters: some of his authority he delegates to departmental chiefs or foremen who decide on details. The manager's task is first and foremost the most effective way of *sorting his problems*, i.e. how to distinguish between the problems that can be decided by departmental chiefs and the problems which should be submitted to his own personal judgment. In other words, he must decide on the degree of self-government to be carried out in the various departments, and the forms in which these should be coordinated into the complete system. The hallmark of the great organiser is his knack of solving these questions, and his ability to choose the right people.

But the factory management is responsible to someone. The main outlines of the manager's policy are directed in a society based on private capitalism by the person or persons owning the factory, and in a socialistic community by the supreme authorities within the industrial branch concerned. The entire productive activity in the community is also carried out within a system of organisation containing groups and cells superior or subordinate to the management, and where there are a great many technical dependencies between the various groups in the form of deliveries of finished products, transport services, and the like. The further down the scale we go, the more *technical* efficiency and responsibility is demanded of the management; the higher up the scale we go, the greater is the *financial* and *political* contribution.

The organisation of production in a present-day community is naturally the result of a long *historical* development; and in this development all three leading elements – the technical, the financial, and the political, – have played their part and mutually influenced one another. A detailed description of this development is outside the framework of the theory of production. It belongs rather to the sphere of *economics history, business economics* and *the history of ideologies*. Here we learn how the political attitude through the ages vacillated between laissez-faire and state control, and how in the last few generations – not least owing to the influence of technical progress, mass production, and specialisation – a *tendency towards concentration* has made itself felt in a great many fields. That is to say, concerns which severally constituted an independent unit, both financially and technically, are now to a large extent under a joint management, and are referred to as cartels, trusts, central planning boards, etc., according to the actual form of such combines. Concentration has been of a financial, political and also of a technical nature. Technically it has for instance taken the form of production quotas, specialisation of certain kinds of production in certain factories, etc. And it has been in some cases *vertical*, that is to say between establishments manufacturing products at various stages (forests, paper factories, newspapers), and in some cases *horizontal* (between establishments operating within one and the same branch).

Certain aspects of these diverse manifestations of concentration raise questions of considerable theoretical interest, both with regard to production and from the point of view of the mechanism of price formation. Some of these will be dealt with below.

CHAPTER 2

PRODUCTION FACTORS

2a. Specified and implied factors. Controllable and non-controllable, economic and free factors

If we go into details we shall find that the number of circumstances which in one way or another can influence a production result is endless.

Take for instance such a comparatively simple thing as the craft of producing silver spoons. If we were to draw up an accurate list of the production factors in the technical sense in this case, we should naturally first and foremost have to include the raw material, i.e. the silver, and then the various kinds of work, the work of forging, filing, polishing, etc., as well as the wear and tear on tools, light and fuel (including charcoal for firing), the room in which the work is carried out, etc. These are the sort of things we should primarily think of. But they only constitute a fraction of all the circumstances which in reality have operated. We must also include the atmosphere surrounding the workshop building, the sunlight, the forces of gravity, etc. In order to realise the importance of these factors, we have only to consider what good ventilation and good daylight mean to the work, or consider how inconvenient the work would have been if no natural force existed to keep all loose objects firmly fixed to one of the six surfaces forming the sides of the room, viz. the floor. We can in fact go even further. One of the most important production factors are the molecular forces. Production would be quite impossible if the various substantial materials were one day to start falling apart and dissolving into their individual particles.

No analysis, however completely it is carried out, can include all these things at once. In undertaking a production analysis we must therefore *select* certain factors whose effect we wish to consider more closely. We call these the *specified factors*. The others are the *implied factors*.

The principle according to which the selection is made will be different in the different cases, and will depend on the *aim* of our analysis. In some cases we may limit ourselves to a study of the effects of the *controllable factors*, those which human beings can control. But we cannot always do this. In agriculture, for example, many of the important production problems are connected with such factors as sunlight, precipitation, and temperature. There may exist artificial controllable replacements for these factors, but, at any rate in their natural form, these factors are not yet controllable.

In other cases one may perhaps select for an analysis of production technique the economic factors, while taking the *free* factors for granted, i.e. those which are available cost free in, practically speaking, unlimited quantities. At times it may be expedient to confine the analysis to the economic factors, but frequently this is not particularly rational. Even though we are mainly interested in the question of profit, it may often prove necessary to study the technical effect of a controlled change in the quantity of a free factor. We have only to consider the use of air in many chemical processes.

On practical grounds it may often be desirable to divide a certain production process into a number of separate analyses, according to which factors are included as specified in each case. We shall look more specifically into this question.

2b. Fixed and variable factors. Capacity. Short-term and long-term factors

At times the distinction between specified and implied factors will have a certain connection with the question of whether the factors can *vary*, depending on whether larger or smaller quantities of the product are to be produced. For instance many industrial production processes necessitate the use of large machines, containers, transport facilities, etc., which in a fairly precise manner define the technical *capacity* of the particular concern.

Moreover this capacity cannot be altered except at great cost and after a considerable period of new constructional work. In all such cases it is obvious that it may be of interest to study how the quantity of the product, the profitability, etc., vary, if the factors determining capacity remain *constant*, while certain *other* factors – labour, raw materials, use of electric or other forms of power, etc. – vary. The last-mentioned factors are then called *variables*, while the first are called *fixed*. In such an analysis the variable factors are specified, while those determining capacity are implied. The distinction between fixed and variable factors is of great importance *inter alia* with regard to the application of the theory of production to the doctrine of distribution. Among other things the distinction is connected with the concept of *quasi-rent*.[1]

---

[1] Cf. Alfred Marshall's theory of value. Marshall considers normal surplus as part of the fixed expenses (fixed factors).

Which factors are to be regarded as fixed, and which as variable, depends as a rule on the *length of time* one considers. Only if there is a demand, over a longer period of time, for a production of much larger quantities than an establishment has been designed to produce, will capacity be extended. On the other hand, if we investigate the *technical details* of the concern, we shall at practically every turn come across factors which must be considered as more or less fixed, if a variation in the rate of production is only foreseen to last for a short period. If, for example, the particular product needs burnishing before being placed on the market as a finished product, and if, for example, one possesses five burnishing machines which can turn out a total of a thousand finished units a day, by running these machines extra hard, and by using double shifts, etc., then production might probably be carried out at this high pressure for some time if only one single order were involved. But if there is a prospect of production being subject to this pressure over a long period of time, it would be reasonable to suppose that more machines would be acquired.

Instead of fixed factors it would therefore be more correct to talk of temporarily *fixed* (i.e. step-wise changing) factors or short-term and long-term factors. And one gets a hierarchy of production analyses according to whether a larger or smaller group of factors is retained as fixed factors of the first, second order, etc.

Classical examples of this are to be found in Alfred Marshall's analysis of fisheries (cf. his *Principles of Economics*, Book V, Chapter V, Section 4) and those mentioned by J. M. Clark, for instance with regard to railway management (cf. his *Studies in the Economics of Overhead Cost*, Chicago 1923, Chapter IX).

The more fixed a factor is, the more *irreversible* are the changes which in fact occur from time to time. A raw material such as copper or iron, for instance, is a typical variable factor. Its quantity is changed, practically speaking, in proportion to the product quantity; and its application is to a very high degree reversible, i.e. not only does an establishment procure more of this factor if the product quantity is to be increased, but *the reverse* can also be done. The establishment can without any difficulty limit the use of this factor, if this should be indicated; it can simply buy a smaller quantity, or if too much has been purchased the excess quantity can as a rule be sold without any difficulty, as iron and metals are staple articles commanding a world market.

In this sense copper as a raw material is a reversible factor; the unskilled labour, too, is from the point of view of the establishment reversible in this sense of the word. But with regard to certain categories of worker, who need specialist training, this is no longer the case. An establishment will often retain the services of specially trained hands, even though for the moment no employment can be found for them. Large fixed plants have to an even greater extent the character of irreversible factors. Once the plant has been constructed for a certain capacity, it is impossible simply to change one's mind and reduce capacity.

2c. Special and general factors. The problem of association between given input elements and given output elements

As far as a raw material is concerned, there is as a rule no difficulty in deciding – at any rate in principle – in what particular product unit a particular factor-unit is incorporated. We can, for example, say that this particular ton of iron plates, part of a consignment received on such and such a day, has been used in the building of such and such a ship. Correspondingly, as far as the bulk of manual work is concerned, providing the necessary notes were kept, one could say which particular product units every single working hour was used for. In such cases we talk of a *special factor* ('effect-individualisable factor'). We call the corresponding costs special costs. Every contributory element can here be *associated with a particular product unit*. More generally we speak of a special factor (special expense) in all cases where the factor contributions (expenses) can be *divided into categories according to their place in the production process*. The principle for doing this may vary; for example, according to the *type of goods* being produced, or the *place* in the concern where the costs are incurred, etc. In business economics these principles are studied in greater detail. Alfred Marshall uses the term special, direct, or prime cost to describe what we have here called special cost.

If a distributive principle of this nature cannot be used, if in other words the contributory factor (cost) must be interpreted as applying to the production process *taken as a whole* (the concern's main administration, the writing off of non-specialized buildings, etc.), we talk of a *general factor* (general costs). Marshall uses the term supplementary cost.

In many cases where the contributory factors (costs) can in principle be distributed, but where such distribution would involve unnecessary work (e.g. the distribution of telephone bills to the various departments of an establishment) a special factor (special cost) will for practical reasons figure in the accounts as though it were a general factor (general cost).

If the contributory factors are divided on the basis of their association with the individual units produced, the term special factor will coincide with the term variable factor, and a general factor will be identical with a fixed factor (at least as long as capacity is constant). But if the principle of distribution is different, e.g. the *place* in the concern, there will be no necessary connection between the speciality and the variability of a factor.

2d. Definition of the term factor quantity and product quantity. Elementary factors

Strictly speaking every contributory element is *unique*. We never get two pieces of coal with precisely the same heating capacity, or two working hours of exactly the same kind. But a great many of these differences are without any practical significance to the theory of production. As a rule what is important to the problem will emerge most clearly if we combine certain contributory elements into a generically defined factor, whose quantity is measured in terms of a certain *technical unit of measurement*. For practical purposes it is, for instance, sufficient to distinguish between certain sorts of coal, anthracite, brown coal, etc., and for each of these kinds simply to measure the factor quantity by the number of units of weight. This presupposes that all weight units of a definite kind of coal are similar in all respects (heating effect, handiness, etc.) relevant to the problem we are dealing with.

The term factor quantity which is arrived at in this way is of fundamental significance in the theory of production. To a large extent this theory deals with variations in these quantities. Unless the quantity concept is properly established, a great deal of the theory will have no valid foundation.

It is obvious that the entire approach will be greatly simplified by combining large groups of input elements. The further we can proceed in this direction, the simpler our analyses will be. But we should proceed with caution. *Per se* there need be nothing wrong in proceeding to a heavy aggregation of input elements. A *macro*-analysis of this kind, providing us with a good overall view of the general outlines of a problem, can often be just as helpful as a more detailed analysis. The danger, however, lies in the temptation to effect an aggregation of this kind without clearly visualising *how* one is to measure the quantity of the production factors arrived at in this way.

In this particular field a multitude of sins have been committed in the theory of production. Theorists have willy-nilly used such factorial terms as e.g. 'land', 'work', and 'capital', assuming that their quantities can be measured in technical units, i.e. without having recourse to prices or other evaluation coefficients as a basis of comparison. This last-mentioned condition is important, particularly the spheres of application of this theory to explain prices and the distribution of values. In such cases one has not infrequently *assumed* that the 'quantities' of these three factors were measurable in a definite technical sense, and then attempted *inter alia* to show how the corresponding three 'prices' were formed. A procedure of this kind is not satisfactory. If the object is to base far-reaching conclusions on the results arrived at by studying the *quantitative* variations in factors, one should first specify how these quantities are to be defined. And the same need for a quantitative definition arises, of course, with regard to the product or products.

If the theory is built up with a view to enabling statistical data or other concrete evaluations and measurements to be incorporated into the theory, thus providing a numerical characterisation of the relations studied in the theory, then the quantity concepts must be defined very explicitly. Due attention will be paid to all the practical details which are bound to arise in the course of one's observations. Everyone who has endeavoured to combine an economic theory with statistical or other data, will know how carefully and circumstantially one frequently has to proceed in order to obtain meaningful results.

If an immediate numerical application is not envisaged – that is to say, not initially, – the quantitative definitions need not be stipulated in exactly the same way. But in this case too, in order to be precise, the definitions should be elaborated by referring to a system of observations. These, however, need now not be concrete, they can be *imaginary*. Basing quantitative definitions on a system of imaginary observations of this kind is of great value as an aid to concise thinking. This applies to all the empirical sciences. The time concept in the theory of relativity, for example, is defined by the aid of certain light signals which are not capable of being carried out concretely in the form in which they are presented in the actual definition, but are still of fundamental importance. The same applies in economics. In choice theory, for example, one defines the elasticity of demand by imaginary questions to the individual whose needs are being discussed. And in the theory of production this method finds its application in the definition of factor- and product-quantity. Subsequently a more or less direct connection can be established between the imaginary quantitative observations and actual measurements. Let us take some examples from the production theory.

First of all let us imagine that, by carrying out our technical description in sufficient detail, we finally achieve such an accurate specification of every single factor, that its 'quantity' can be measured in terms of the technological system of measurement – i.e. can be given in terms of metres, kilos, hours, or other technological units derived from these, – without any major difficulties. These factors are called *elementary factors*, or, more precisely, absolute elementary factors. The simplest examples are raw materials. Every material of this kind must be exactly specified, if we wish to get down to elementary factors. It is, for example, insufficient merely to state that 'yarn' is a production factor in a certain textile manufacturing process. The quality, thickness, etc., in fact the make, too, of the yarn must be specified. Not till we have done this have we reached a point where the factor quantity can be measured in purely technical units in a perfectly unambiguous manner.

The same applies to the various kinds of work. Here the difficulty of specification may be even greater. The simplest cases are those entailing a monotonous kind of work, such as rinsing and labelling bottles in a brewery. In a case of this kind the rhythm of work is to a large extent mechanically determined, and this makes it comparatively easy to measure the working factor in terms of hours. In principle it is not sufficient to measure it in terms of the number of bottles rinsed or labelled, as this – at any rate in relation to the factor 'labour' – constitutes *the product itself*, and not a factor. Another point is that it may be desirable to regard the entire brewing process as one combined process, and in such cases 'rinsing and labelling bottles' – measured technically in terms of the number of bottles rinsed and labelled, – can be regarded as a factor, without specifying in further detail the concrete manner (manual labour and/or rinsing and labelling machine) in which this work is done.

A more complicated case is provided, e.g., by the work of a spoon-maker in a silversmith's workshop. He has a great many different manual processes to carry out: cutting, stamping, filing, etc. If we are to consider the number of hours as a measure of the factor involved in spoon-making, we must presuppose a certain average hour, made up of a representative *selection* of the working processes he has to carry out, and which is also characterised by a certain *average intensity*. In more complicated forms of work the average must be extended over longer periods in order to include what is typical.

Forms of work consisting mainly in *managing* others' work – typical examples are the work of the owner or managing director of a firm – are almost impossible to reduce to terms of elementary factors, at any rate unless we operate with a very artificial concept. In this case there are two alternatives available: If the analysis is to be carried out on an entirely technical basis, these factors must be treated as *qualitatively different* input elements. They will appear in the analysis as factors determining the *form* of the production functions (cf. Section 5a), but not as one of the specified variables entering into it as arguments.

The second alternative is to adopt an *economic* formula to the factor concept, i.e. introducing 'sum of money spent on management' as a variable. In this way practically every production problem can be reduced to a problem of quantitative factors; but one must remember that in such cases one is no longer dealing with a purely technical production law.

2e. Factor complexes. Equivalence factors and aggregated factors. Shadow factors

There are two cases in which it is possible to aggregate several elementary factors on a purely technical basis, so that the complex appears as a single factor for which a quantity concept still exists in the technical sense. This is when the elementary factors are either complete *equivalence factors* or completely *coupled factors*. The meaning of this is as follows: Let us imagine, for example, that there are two elementary factors and that their quantities, each measured in the technical units of each factor concerned, are designated v_1 and v_2. Let us assume, for instance, that factor No. 1 constitutes brown coal nuts and factor No. 2 anthracite coal. Suppose that the heating effect of factor No. 1 is $a_1 = 4850$ calories per kilo, and of factor No. 2 $a_2 = 7800$ calories per kilo. If we are interested only in the heating effect, it makes no difference whether we use only factor No. 1 or only factor No. 2, or a *mixture* of the two elementary factors. In other words, in this case we would not be interested in the size of v_1 or v_2 separately, but merely in the size of the sum $a_1 v_1 + a_2 v_2$. More generally we may say: if we have n fuel stuffs, whose quantities are $v_1, v_2, ..., v_n$, and if their thermic equivalent figures are $a_1, a_2, ..., a_n$, then we can combine them in a single factor called 'fuel stuff', whose quantity can be measured technically by the figure v defined by the formula

(2e.1) $$v = a_1 v_1 + a_2 v_2 + ... + a_n v_n .$$

In this case we may say that the factors under consideration are equivalence factors, and that the complex constituted *by aggregating these equivalents* is reduced to a simple factor which also has the property that its quantity is technically defined. A combination of this kind can be carried out in all cases where we have technical equivalence figures for all the factors constituting the complex, and we are interested only in the quality expressed by their equivalence figures.

To what extent the sum (2e.1) is the only matter of interest to us naturally depends to a certain extent on *the purpose of our production analysis*. It is, for instance, not always only the heating effect that we are interested in. The work of stoking, the smoke nuisance involved, etc., may vary for the various elementary factors, and we may wish to take this into account. If this can be done merely by making a constant *correction* to the equivalence figures, we can still make a technical aggregate, but now on the basis of the new equivalence figures. But if the way in which these other circumstances operate cannot be described merely by using a constant (fixed) correction of the equivalence figures (which would, for instance, be the case if the *variation* of the wage rate – and hence of the cost of stoking, etc., – is an essential element in the problem involved), then an aggregate of form (2e.1) – even with corrected coefficients a_1 – cannot be made, and we must carry out a technical analysis using all of, or at least many of, the single elementary factors.

The other case where an aggregation on a technical basis is possible, is where *the quantity relationship between the factors* is determined on technical grounds. If, for example, a farmer wishes to use a certain quantity of fertiliser on a piece of ground, it is not sufficient merely to procure the fertiliser, it must also be spread, and the quantity of work involved in this depends in a very definite way on the quantity of fertiliser that has to be spread. (We are not taking into account minor variations due to the various methods in which spreading can be carried out.) If v_1 is the quantity of fertiliser and v_2 the work of spreading, then v_2 is a technically determined function of v_1. That is to say, it is not possible to apply a given quantity of factor 1 without at the same time using a corresponding quantity of factor 2. We say that 1 and 2 are *coupled factors*. We can also say that 2 is a shadow factor, as it has to follow factor 1 'like a shadow'.

In this case, too, the aggregate formed by the two factors can on technical grounds be regarded as a single factor; and the quantity of the aggregate can be measured either by v_1 or by v_2, i.e. by a technical yardstick. In principle it does not matter which of the two we choose if v_2 as a function of v_1 is monotonic. But in practice – especially in a statistical analysis – one may for obvious reasons be preferred to the other; in the example given, for instance, fewer random irregularities are liable to blur the statistical picture if we measure the quantity of the aggregate in terms of v_1 than if we do it in terms of v_2, and for this reason v_1 should be selected.

Note that the coupling referred to in this example is only a coupling describing the nature of the factors. It is a *factor coupling* pure and simple (cf. the section on limitation factors in Part Three.) We are not for the moment interested in describing the quantity of the product and its variation (as we were in the case of joint products, cf. 1a). No matter what the reasons for the functional relationship – the coupling – between the factors may be, provided merely it is constant during the analysis, it can be used as a starting point for a technical aggregation of elementary factors.

If the factors are neither equivalence factors nor coupling factors, an aggregation can only take place by constructing a *volume index* for the factors in the complex – which would make the aggregated quantity concept semi-technical –, or by going the whole length, and instead of the quantity of the complex, considering its value in terms of money or in terms of some other gauge of value. In such cases, however, one is no longer operating on a technical basis.

For the aggregation of product quantities the same rules apply as in the case of factors.

These problems of the aggregation of factors or products in complexes are of considerable importance especially with regard to the application of the theory or its expression in terms of statistical data.

CHAPTER 3

PRODUCTION TECHNIQUE, CONSTANT TECHNIQUE AND VARIABLE TECHNIQUE

3a. Definition of constant technique

Let us now examine the actual technique of production a little more closely. The technical conditions for the processes of production are constantly developing, and new inventions are opening up new fields for technical production. At any moment, however, the technical conditions applicable to any production process are given. There is a definite *socially given technique*, a certain system of technical inventions available to the factory owner or manager. But the *individual factory technique* is not only dependent on the socially given technique. Just what technical alternatives at any moment are to be exploited in any particular factory depends on a great many factors – the size of the market, the availability of capital, etc. At times social, national, and/or military considerations also apply.

In studying laws of production it is important to realise clearly the various ways in which a change in individual factory technique can take place. Only in this way is it possible to give a precise definition of the concept of *constant technique*, and without this concept the analysis of the laws of production is bound to lose its way in a haze of speculation.

Terminology on this subject is highly varied. Some authors consider that any change in production process is a change in technique, whilst others associate a 'change in technique' with major inventions, industrial revolutions, and the like. Between these two extreme views are to be found a great many divergent opinions, more or less clearly formulated.

In defining the concept constant technique in a precise way the best approach would *prima facie* appear to consist of a detailed description of the actual *method* of production, the nature of the different handicraft manipulations or machine processes, etc., in order to decide which changes should be permitted within the framework of 'constant technique', and which should not be permitted. A detailed description of this kind, however, makes it very difficult – or rather impossible – to achieve a clear-cut and theoretically precise definition.

A theoretically more satisfactory procedure for defining what in principle should be considered as essential for the concept 'constant technique', is *first* to define quantitatively what should in the analysis be considered as 'factors' and as 'product' (or 'products'), and next to postulate that *the technique is constant as long as the functional relation(s) expressing the dependence of product quantity(-ies) on factor quantities remain(s) the same.* In the case of multi-ware production there are several products, and therefore several functional relationships involved.[1] This in essence covers the main points of our definition. We intend, however, to clarify it by drawing a sharp line of demarcation between constant technique in the sense defined and other changes in the production process which we shall not consider as changes in technique.

3b. Changes in the nature of factors

In formulating a production law a number of specific factors must be introduced and described. Let us imagine that a change in the production process takes place which is such that the *list* of these specific factors has to be changed. In such cases a *transition* takes place from certain kinds of production factors to others. Manual power may be replaced by electric power, or the entire process may be changed, and a new method of production introduced. In this case we say that a change in the nature of a factor has taken place. And this is obviously, according to our definition, *a change in technique*.

3c. Changes in the production function (changes in the production table)

Let us imagine that the specific designation of production factors remains unchanged, while the *law* connecting the factors and the product is changed. In other words the same *kinds* of factors are used as before, but the internal technical coordination of these factors is arranged in a different way from what it was before, with the consequence that to one and the same factor combination will now correspond a different quantity of the product.

This can be illustrated by a simplified example. Let us assume that there are two substances which are going to be added in a certain chemical process, and that the effect on the product quantity is originally as given in Table (3c.1).

The added quantities of the two substances are here called v_1 and v_2. Certain other things are also required in order to carry out the process, but we presuppose that these are constant. Let us now assume for instance that

[1] Cf. Part Four.

TABLE (3c.1)
Product quantity using the first method

Quantity of factor 1	Quantity of factor 2		
	$v_2 = 1.6$	$v_2 = 1.7$	$v_2 = 1.8$
$v_1 = 2$	100	103	106
$v_1 = 3$	102	106	110
$v_1 = 4$	104	109	115

TABLE (3c.2)
Product quantity using the second method

Quantity of factor 1	Quantity of factor 2		
	$v_2 = 1.6$	$v_2 = 1.7$	$v_2 = 1.8$
$v_1 = 2$	101	105	109
$v_1 = 3$	103	108	113
$v_1 = 4$	105	109	118

according to the first method substance No. 1 is added first, and subsequently substance No. 2. This is the assumption on which Table (3c.1) is valid.

Let us next assume that we *change the sequence* in which these additions are made. Now substance No. 2 is added first, and substance No. 1 next. Let us assume that the effect on the product quantity in this case is as given in Table (3c.2). It is seen that for all factor combinations the latter method is better than the former. Once this discovery is made, the question of using the old method no longer arises. The transition from the first method to the last is *permanent*. As an example of a permanent improvement of this kind (but without changing the nature of these factors) can be mentioned rationalisation of a business organisation which, for example, may result in a reduction in the time during which one category of workers has to wait for another, etc.

A permanent change of this kind in the coordination between factors can be interpreted as a *transition from one production table to another*, while retaining the same table heading and the same rubric column. If a transition of this kind occurs, we say that a *change of production function* or a change of production table has taken place. This, too, is, according to our definition, to be interpreted as a change in technique.

3d. Changes in the factor quantities under a constant production function (production table)

Finally, let us examine the case when purely quantitative factor changes occur *within one and the same production table*. This will lead to changes which, according to our definition, are *not* changes in technique. In the case discussed in 3b the concept production table does not exist at all, because the things which should be listed in the heading and the rubric column of the table undergo a change during the course of the argument. In the case discussed in 3c the concept production table does actually exist, the heading and the rubric column of the table are unchanged, but the *contents* of the table undergo a change during the course of the line of argument. We switched from one table to another. In example 3c, for instance, corresponding to the factor combination ($v_1 = 3$, $v_2 = 1.7$), at the beginning of our reasoning we had a product quantity of 106, and at the end of our reasoning a product quantity of 108. In the case we shall now consider, 3d, on the other hand, there exists a single, determined production table, whose contents remain constant. In other words now, throughout our whole line of argument, one and only one definite product quantity corresponds to a definite factor combination.

The fact that the content of the production table is constant, does not necessarily presuppose that the *internal organisation* between the factors is unchanged throughout the entire argument, nor that the manipulations and *processes* are always carried out in the same way. It does not even exclude a certain specialisation of work. *The point is that any change of this kind must occur hand in hand with any change taking place in the quantitative factor combination.* In other words, throughout the entire argument, a certain definite form of internal organisation must correspond to each factor combination. If changes of organisation do occur, they must therefore be changes of a reversible kind, in contrast to the changes in organisation mentioned under 3c, which are of a permanent nature. If, thus, a certain change in factor combination involves a certain change in the internal organisation of the factors, then this change – if it is to belong to type 3d – must cease as soon as we return to the original quantitative factor combination. Supposing, for example, that the second method in the example in 3c does not give the product quantity shown in Table (3c.2) but that shown in Table (3d.1).

TABLE (3d.1)
Product quantity by the second method

Quantity of factor 1	Quantity of factor 2		
	$v_2 = 1.6$	$v_2 = 1.7$	$v_2 = 1.8$
$v_1 = 2$	99	101	105
$v_1 = 3$	101	105	111
$v_1 = 4$	103	110	120

TABLE (3d.2)
Permanent law of production

Quantity of factor 1	Quantity of factor 2		
	$v_2 = 1.6$	$v_2 = 1.7$	$v_2 = 1.8$
$v_1 = 2$	100	103	106
$v_1 = 3$	102	106	111
$v_1 = 4$	104	110	120

From Table (3d.1) compared with Table (3c.1) we see that the new method is more advantageous than the old in the 'large' factor combinations (3, 1.8), (4, 1.7), and (4, 1.8), viz. the three factor combinations bottom right. In other factor combinations the old method is to be preferred. It is obvious that in this case we should use the new method only for the three combinations mentioned. Thus we can set up a new production table (3d.2), identical with Table (3d.1) as far as the three mentioned combinations are concerned, and otherwise identical with Table (3c.1). *This table, (3d.2), now remains unchanged throughout the entire argument.*

All the same, certain changes in method may occur. These changes, however, are related to the quantitative factor combination in such a way that we can describe the relationship between factor quantities and product quantity in its entirety using an unchanged production table, viz. (3d.2). If we do not wish to take into account the fact that small production quantities in the example are produced with the aid of the first method and large production quantities with the help of the second method, we can merely ignore the whole question of 'method' and internal organisation between factors, and only use Table (3d.2). Since *the permanency of a production table is our definition of constant technique*, we must say that in this case too we have 'constant technique'.

As a concrete example the following may be adduced: If it is a question of increasing the production of grain, this can in some cases be carried out by increasing the number of workers, while the land area remains constant. It will then be possible to specialise the work allotted to the workers. If this specialisation *disappears* when production is again reduced, and the number of workers returns to its original, then the change that has taken place in the production process has been of type 3d. If, on the other hand, an increase in the number of workers results in specialisation, but conversely a reduction does not result in a suspension of specialisation, then we are dealing with an example of a change of type 3c. And if specialisation goes so far that we get an entirely new kind of specialist worker, then we have a change of type 3b. In this last case we thus get various kinds of worker (i.e., various kinds of production factors), who have no common sphere of labour where their working performance can be technically compared.

CHAPTER 4

VARIOUS TYPES OF PRODUCTION THEORY

4a. Momentary production and time-shaped production. Static and dynamic theory of production

In reality all production takes time. From the time the seed is placed in the soil until the crop has been harvested, from the moment when materials arrive at a factory and until the time when the finished products leave it, etc., a certain *production period* elapses.

If we were to formulate an entirely general theory of production, all factor inputs would have to be regarded as more or less continuous time functions, and the product quantity (or, in the case of multi-goods production, the product quantities), would likewise have to be considered as more or less continuous time functions. This would involve a study of how a *change in the shape of* one or several of the factor time curves, would influence the shape of the production time curve or the production time curves. The cases where *inputs* were markedly concentrated in time but the product time curve or the product time curves were more extensive in time, or vice versa ('point input' with continuous output as opposed to continuous input with 'point output'), could be regarded as special cases.

However, in adopting such an entirely general point of view, the relationships become so complicated that it is difficult to formulate conclusions that are generally valid and at the same time easy to apply. One would run the risk of becoming involved in rather formalistic statements which tell us little about problems that are important in practice. Frequently a more practical approach is to consider *other* aspects of the matter than the time shapes. For example the fact that 0.196 kilos of yarn are necessary for a metre of cloth, and 1.136 kilos of tops per kilo of yarn (see Table (1a.1)), are production facts which are practically unaffected by the length or the brevity of the time consumed in production, at any rate within the limits that are actually of interest to us. And what is expressed by these fabrication coefficients provides very relevant data in the study of the process. Consequently, in many cases we are justified in studying the production process *as though* it took place in a single moment of time. In developing a theory of momentary production, we do so, not because a major portion of production actually takes place in this way, but because this theoretical approach throws light on many important aspects of the problem, without involving us in unnecessary details and complications.

In some problems, however, the actual time shapes are important, because the sequence of the various stages in the production process and the speed at which they occur are essential. In order to throw light on such processes, a theory of time shaped production must be developed. This theory will prove of importance e.g. in production processes where work is carried out with large fixed capital plant, and where effective exploitation thereof depends on certain partial processes *being correctly coordinated in time*, e.g. that certain raw materials should be made available at the right moment, and that semi-finished products should be moved at the right speed (conveyor belt system), etc.[1] This kind of theory is also significant when dealing with processes in which the *quality* of the product depends on the rate of production. For example, wood with a tight grain, i.e. of slow growth, is firmer than wood with a wide grain, i.e. of quicker growth. In casting large mirrors for giant astronomic telescopes the cooling takes months, or even years, if the product is to be flawless.

A distinction between momentary and time shaped production coincides almost exactly with the distinction between *static* and *dynamic* theories of production.

In the ensuing Sections 4b–4e we shall pay some attention to factor variations in time-shaped production, but the bulk of Parts One and Two will deal with questions in which the time relationship is not essential. In Part Five, certain problems in the dynamic theory of production are discussed.

4b. Number of stages and stage tempo. Input curves and step diagram

If the problem is posed in such a way that special attention must be paid to the distribution in time of input elements, the concept of factor quantity becomes somewhat complicated.

Let us first consider an example: let us consider the work of *harvesting* in connection with the growing of potatoes. As an expression of the factor quantity which we term labour, let us take the number of working hours (man-hours) per week required during harvesting. If we consider the factor labour only from the point of view of *momentary* production, we know that an increase in this factor – that is to say an increase in the average number of

[1] The PERT system aims at studying such problems through mathematical programming.

man-hours per week – may mean two things: either that the entire size of the production process has been increased (the total number of working hours required for harvesting is, for example as a rule greater on a very large farm than on a smaller farm), or that cultivation has become more labour intensive, i.e. more work is used for each land unit. If we consider the problem from the point of view of the *time-shape* of production, we even get a third interpretation of the quantity of labour. It may be that an increase in the number of working hours per week required for picking potatoes *merely implies that it is desired to get this part of the work done in a shorter time.* In other words, the same total number of working hours will be used per acre, but the work will be concentrated in a shorter time.

This can be shown graphically in the following manner: we draw a time curve showing how the number of man-hours used every week changes with time. As a rule the work of picking potatoes in East Norway does not start until some time near the end of September; in other words, until this date the factor we are here considering is equal to nought. From a certain time in September it suddenly – in fact quite discontinuously – starts to rise, probably remains at a high level for some weeks, and gradually declines, reaching zero towards the end of October, when potatoes have been picked and garnered. We call this curve the *input curve* for the factor labour during potato digging. See Figure (4b.1). The area below the curve represents the total quantity of labour applied during potato picking.

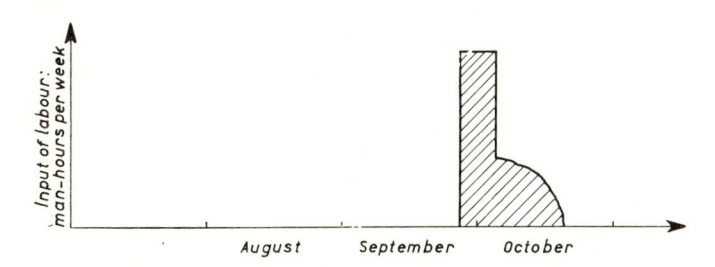

Fig. (4b.1). Input curve for labour during potato digging.

An increase in the factor representing the quantity of labour involved in digging potatoes without any change in time shape merely appears as a change in the vertical scale of Figure (4b.1). This would naturally also cause a corresponding increase of the area beneath the curve.

The change in the factor labour which occurs when we want to complete the potato picking in a *shorter* time, without an increase in the total quantity of labour, on the other hand, is expressed by the input curve becoming *higher and narrower, but retaining its area.* We can say that potato digging has now been *time-concentrated*. See Figure (4b.2).

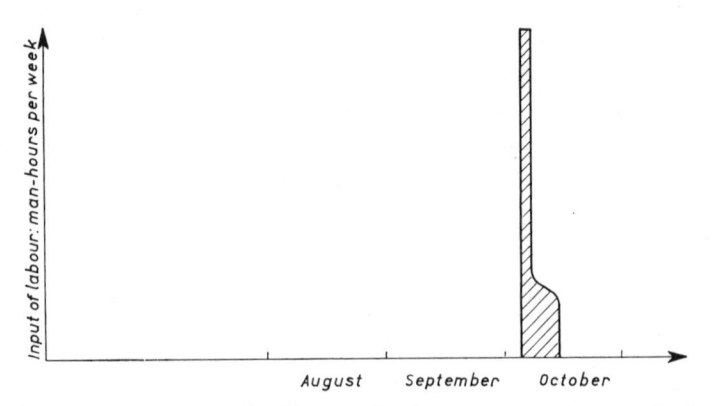

Fig. (4b.2). Input curve for labour under time-concentrated potato digging.

Something similar applies to every factor. In considering the theory of time-shaped production, therefore, we shall have to consider, in the case of every factor, not only the total quantity of the factor and the degree of intensification of this factor, but also its degree of time concentration.

The above example applies only to a single *stage* in the cultivation of potatoes. Let us now consider the other stages. First of all we have the *preliminary work of preparing the land* – ploughing, harrowing, etc. Some of this – maybe half of it – will be carried out in the autumn, and the rest in spring. For the sake of simplicity let us here only consider that part which takes place during the spring. The next stage is *work during the period of growth* – e.g. hoeing, etc. The third stage is the *work of harvesting*. There are also various other tasks to carry out. The relative importance of the various types of work during the major seasonal processes can be seen in Table (4b.3) for a number of important types of crop.

For the sake of simplicity let us consider only the three main tasks listed in the first three lines of the table for potato cultivation. For each of these tasks (stages) we have an input-time curve for labour (reckoned in terms of man-hours). Figure (4b.4) gives the curve based on concrete figures from a farm in East Norway. This diagram we call the *stage diagram*.

Similar curves can be drawn for the other variable factors.

The speed at which a stage in the process is carried out we call the *stage tempo*. This can be read off from the stage diagram. The stage tempo will be large if the input curve for this stage is tall and narrow.

VARIOUS TYPES OF PRODUCTION THEORY

TABLE (4b.3)

Number of working hours (man-hours) per hectar for various kinds of crop[1]

	Number of working hours (man-hours) per hectar			
	Seed crops	Turnips	Potatoes	Artificial pasture
Sowing, etc.	9.5	35.9	106.6	1.4
Work during the period of growth	0.3	268.0	72.3	0.7
Harvesting	50.8	224.5	289.4	63.1
Ploughing and harrowing	29.1	23.3	20.6	9.0
Manuring	21.6	41.7	41.7	15.7
Maintenance of fences and roads	9.3	9.3	9.3	9.3
Improvement of land	3.3	3.3	3.3	3.3
Care and maintenance of horses	25.8	40.8	57.4	14.7
Threshing and storing work	55.7	—	54.0	—
Other work	37.8	37.8	37.8	37.8
Total	243.2	684.6	692.4	155.0

[1] Data collected from nine East-Norwegian farms. See Paul Borgedal, *Intensitetsproblemet i det norske jordbruk*, Fredrikstad, 1926, p. 240.

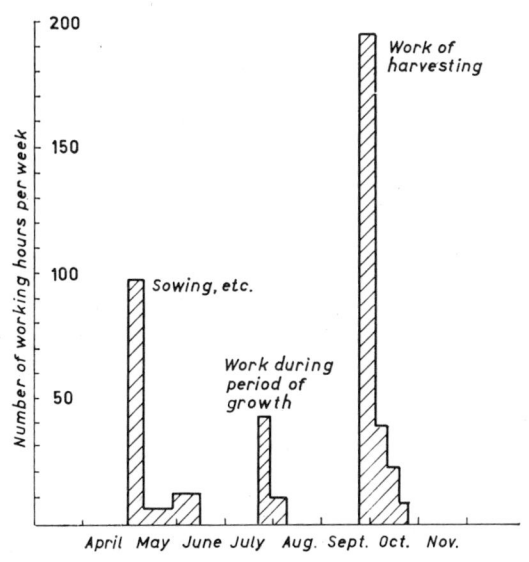

Fig. (4b.4). Labour-input curve during three production stages in the cultivation of potatoes at a farm in East Norway.

The stage diagram also provides information about the *number of stages*, i.e. the number of production stages in the whole process, and of the *stage interval*, i.e. the way in which the various stages are distributed over the total production period.

4c. The stage interval. Time-rigid and time-elastic production process

The stage interval is an important concept, which we should examine a little more closely. For the sake of simplicity we shall only consider the input of a single factor, for example labour, but the same arguments will apply to the other factors.

In the example taken from potato cultivation it will be possible to increase the tempo in every single stage, but the average *time lapse* between stages – the stage interval – cannot in practice be altered, as it depends on the process of growth, and this in turn depends on the various climatic factors, over which one has no control.

The stage-tempo can be schematically exhibited as in Figure (4b.1). In the lower part of Figure (4c.1) every single 'peak' has been made narrower and taller than in the upper part, but the average time lapse between them is practically speaking unchanged. Each stage-tempo has been increased, but it has not been possible to increase the *tempo of the entire process*; in such

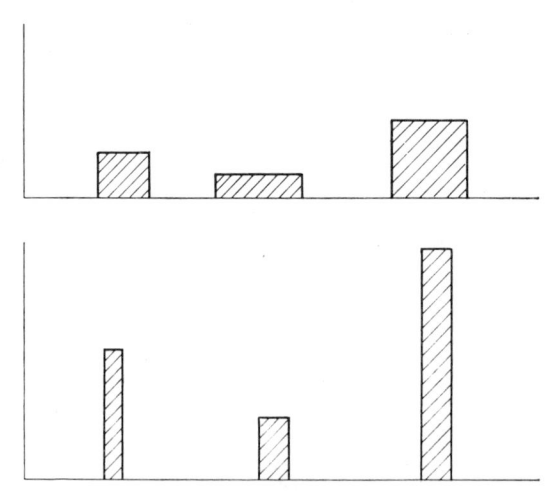

Fig. (4c.1).   Increase in stage tempo while retaining the same stage interval.

cases we say that the entire process is *time-rigid*. An increase in the stage tempo of a single stage may of course be desirable, even though the process as a whole is time-rigid. It may, for example, be desirable owing to prevailing weather conditions (getting the harvest in before the rain comes, etc.), or because one wants to achieve an efficient total distribution of labour over time. For instance it might be possible to employ the available labour force for other current tasks (the necessity of completing one seasonal work in due time, in order to be able to start another, etc.).

Most production processes outside agriculture are less time-rigid, i.e. more time-elastic. By increasing the stage tempo it may be possible at the same time to reduce production time for the whole process. The manufacture of motorcars is a good example. Thanks to effective rationalisation the tempo in the individual stages has historically been increased tremendously; and *at the same time* it has been possible to dovetail the various stages: as soon as one group or category of workers has completed its task, another group or category can take over. Coordination between stages has even been mechanised by using a conveyor belt. This belt conveys the various parts of the engine, etc., from one stage to the next. The speed at which the conveyor belt moves determines not only the speed of the individual stage, but also that of the process as a whole. In this case an increase in the tempo will appear not as shown in Figure (4c.1), but as shown in Figure (4c.2).

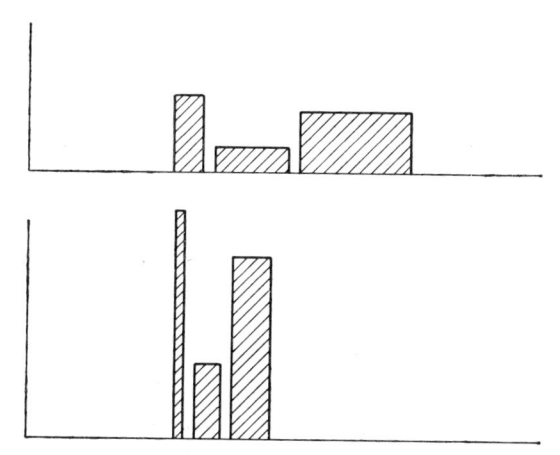

Fig. (4c.2). Increase of stage tempo in conjunction with a reduction of time-lapse between stages.

4d. Mean production period and average liquid capital in a closed production process

It is an advantage to provide a measure showing the length of the total production process. We shall do this for a *closed* process, i.e. one in which it is possible to say that such and such productive inputs are associated with a definite product quantity. For example certain production inputs may be associated with a definite crop of potatoes at a certain farm, or with a particular consignment of motorcars from a certain factory, and so on. In the case for instance of an automobile factory the tools and machines used have of course themselves been produced by means of other processes. We are, however, for the moment not concerned with this, but only with the production of motorcars as it goes on within a given factory.

The set-up may be so simple that it is possible to specify both a natural *beginning* and *end* of the process. This is for example the case with the cultivation of potatoes. It is fairly obvious that it starts with autumn ploughing and comes to a conclusion when the potatoes have been picked and stored during the following autumn. In a case of this kind it is easy to define the *total* production period. It is simply the lapse of time from the very beginning to the very end of the whole process.

In a great many other cases, however, the situation is different. Frequently there may for instance be various input elements which are carried out *a long time* before the final result is available, and which are of somewhat *incidental and subordinate* to the actual result. Let us imagine, for example that a motorcar factory lays in a supply of small tacks, to be used for fastening the upholstery in cars, and that these tacks are kept on the premises for a great many years before they are all used up. They would obviously give an entirely false picture of the activities carried out in the factory if all these years are counted in full as part of the production period. If we confine ourselves to a consideration of the inputs that really mean something substantial, we clearly get a much shorter total production period.

Generally speaking we must focus our attention on the time that *on an average* elapses between the moment when the various input elements take place and until the product emerges in its final form. And this average must be computed as a *weighted* average, using the *importance* of the input elements as weights. The total production period referred to in the first example was only significant because the general set-up in this case was such that the *total* period – i.e. the lapse of time from the very beginning to the very end – gives a fairly serviceable expression for the mean production period.

How, then, are we in the general case to define the mean production period? Let us first consider a single factor. Let us call it No. 1, and let v_1 be the quantity of it used per *time unit*. This input per time unit can of course vary with the time. For this reason it would be better to use the more precise notation, v_{1t}, which specifies how much of factor No. 1 is used per time unit at time t. In practice factor inputs will often vary almost continuously, but as a rule it is easier to state a case if we imagine that production is divided up into single time units, for example weeks, years, or the like, and if we assume that the input in each such time unit occurs *at the beginning* of this time unit, i.e. v_{1t} will denote an input made in the beginning of the time unit No. t.

Let T be the emergence point, i.e. the point of time when the finished product emerges (the beginning of the Tth time unit), and let us consider the input which takes place τ time units earlier, in other words at the point of time $T-\tau$. If this were the only input, the production period (whether mean or total) would simply be τ. If there are inputs at other time points too, the input at τ will only be a component in determining the mean production period, and it will act with a *weight* which is the input quantity effected at this point of time, viz. $v_{1,T-\tau}$. In other words we must take the average over $\tau=0, 1, 2, \ldots$, with the weights $v_{1,T-0}, v_{1,T-1}, \ldots$ etc. Thus the mean production period with respect to *a single factor, viz. No.* 1, is

$$(4d.1) \qquad \frac{1 \cdot v_{1,T-1} + 2 \cdot v_{1,T-2} + \ldots}{v_{1,T-1} + v_{1,T-2} + \ldots} = \frac{\sum_{\tau} \tau v_{1,T-\tau}}{\sum_{\tau} v_{1,T-\tau}}.$$

This is the mean production period (with respect to factor No. 1) for that part of the product which emerges at the point of time T. As we can see, this is *nothing but the moment of the input curve* taken about the output point of T. In many cases it may be of interest to compute this magnitude separately for the various factors. It will tell us something about *when* in the whole process this factor is on the average applied. In the special case where there is only one magnitude for τ we return to the simple example mentioned above, where the mean production period was simply this particular value of τ (reckoned from the emergence point T).

If we want a mean average expression for the production period for all factors taken together, we must introduce a system of evaluation coefficients which will reduce the various factors to a common denomination. We can, for example, choose prices. Generally speaking these will change with time. Let q_{it} be the price and v_{it} the input quantity for factor No. i at the point of time t. The total value of the input at the point of time t will then be

$$(4d.2) \qquad b_t = q_{1t}v_{1t} + \ldots + q_{nt}v_{nt} = \sum q_{it}v_{it}.$$

The mean production period for the whole input complex will now have to be computed on the same lines as for the single factor No. 1, but with this difference: that we shall now be using as weights the total input value b instead of the input quantity v_1 of the special factor. In other words, the average length of the production period, taking all inputs into consideration, will be

$$(4d.3) \qquad \frac{1 \cdot b_{T-1} + 2 \cdot b_{T-2} + \ldots}{b_{T-1} + b_{T-2} + \ldots} = \frac{\sum_\tau \tau b_{T-\tau}}{\sum_\tau b_{T-\tau}}.$$

This is the all-factor mean production period for that part of the product which emerges at the point of time T.

The value of the input elements is in (4d.3) shown *without interest rate*. This must be done if we are to compute the mean production period for those input elements which come *from outside*, and which are not created by 'inner growth' in the capital mass which is gradually accumulated by supplies from outside. It is also possible to set out a formula leading to identically the *same* mean production period, and *including* an interest rate, but if so, this formula will not contain the input element b (which denotes an input coming exclusively from outside), but another input concept. This was discussed in my lectures on macrodynamics, autumn semester 1940.

4e. Risk and anticipation in the theory of production

Practically all decisions associated with the process of production are based on anticipation, i.e. the assessment of probabilities with regard to future development of various circumstances. In some cases it is necessary to pay special attention to the *way* in which the element of probability operates. In most cases, however, it is sufficient to take into account the mathematical expectations that emerge after the element of probability has been taken into account. For instance, in a technical description of a production process, it is frequently sufficient to reckon with a certain *average* reject percentage; thus it is not necessary to proceed to a more detailed analysis of the deviations around this average. In the same way it will often be sufficient to consider that under certain external conditions (a certain price situation, certain market conditions, etc.), a certain category of producers will on the average act in such-and-such a way. It is not necessary to analyse in detail the role played by anticipation and risk elements in their motivations and the role these elements play in creating the average behavior. We do not intend to devote special attention to the element of risk and anticipation. We shall as a rule assume that this has already been included in the average regularities of a technical or psychological nature with which our theory is concerned.

PART TWO

MOMENTARY SINGLE PRODUCTION USING ONLY CONTINUITY FACTORS

A. TECHNICAL SECTION

We shall now proceed to a description of the actual laws of production, i.e. the way in which the *product* or *products* react(s) to changes in factor quantities. In the whole of Part Two we shall base our arguments on the following presuppositions:

(1) *Single-ware production*. This assumes that a single uniform article or service is produced (cf. Section 1d).

(2) *Momentary production*. This assumes that all essential points are covered if we base our reasoning on the assumption that the resultant product comes into existence at the same moment as the production factors are applied to the production process. This is only an 'as though' assumption which in fact cover many practical problems (cf. Section 4a).

(3) *Technical measurability*. We assume that both product quantity and the quantities of the production factors that are used can be measured in technical units (or at any rate in quantitative indices) (cf. Section 2d).

(4) *Constant technique*. The changes in factor quantity which are considered are assumed to take place under a constant technique. Consequently a uniform and definite product quantity corresponds to a definite factor combination (cf. Section 3a).

(5) *Continuity factors*. We assume that all the specified production factors are continuity factors. In (5b.8) a definition of the term continuity factor is given.

CHAPTER 5

VARIOUS METHODS OF DESCRIBING A CONTINUOUS PRODUCTION LAW

5a. Production function, product table, and isoquants

We are now concerned with a momentary production where a single product is produced, of which the quantity can be measured in technical units (or at any rate in quantity indices). Each factor quantity can also be measured technically. Let x be the quantity of the product and $v_1, v_2, \ldots, v_n$ the factor quantities. We assume that the technique is constant during all the variations of factor quantities under consideration. In that case, corresponding to given magnitudes of $v_1, v_2, \ldots v_n$, we have only one definite magnitude of x. We say that x is a function of the n variable $v_1, \ldots, v_n$, and call this the *product function*.

Using symbols we can set down the product function as follows

(5a.1) $$x = f(v_1, \ldots, v_n)$$
or
(5a.2) $$x = x(v_1, \ldots, v_n).$$

In (5a.1) x stands for a magnitude, but f represents the form of a relationship of dependence, viz. the relationship which expresses how x depends on $v_1, \ldots, v_n$. Equation (5a.1) is the most unambiguous way of expressing the relationship. In (5a.2) x has two different meanings. On the lefthand side it stands for a magnitude, as previously, while on the righthand side it stands for the *form* of the relationship of dependence. However, using x in this way to represent two different things will hardly cause any confusion. And on the other hand (5a.2) possesses the very great advantage that the magnitude which the relationship of dependence expresses is immediately apparent from the notation. As a rule, therefore, we shall generally use Equation (5a.2).

Throughout Part Two, for the sake of ease of analysis, we shall assume that the product function is continuous with continuous partial derivatives of the first and second order.[1] In the world of reality this is clearly not always

---

[1] The concept of continuity is discussed in R. Frisch, *Tetthet og masse ved en statistik fordeling*. Memorandum from the University Institute of Social Economics, Oslo, 8 February 1951, Section 21b.

the case, but we often get a sufficiently accurate result by reasoning *as though* continuity existed.

In a given case the form of product function can be represented either *analytically*, or *numerically in the form of a table*, or *graphically*. Let us consider these three methods of representation a little more closely.

ANALYTICAL METHOD OF PRESENTATION

The following are some analytically formulated product functions:

(5a.3) $$x = 100 \frac{(v_1 v_2 v_3)^2}{v_1^4 + v_2^4 + v_3^4}\left(\frac{1}{v_1} + \frac{2}{v_2} + \frac{3}{v_3}\right),$$

(5a.4) $$x = 24 v_1 v_2 - 10 v_1^2 - 8 v_2^2,$$

(5a.5) $$x = a_0 + a_1 v_1 + a_2 v_2 + \ldots + a_n v_n,$$

(5a.6) $$x = A v_1^{\alpha_1} v_2^{\alpha_2}, \ldots, v_n^{\alpha_n}.$$

Here $a_0, a_1, \ldots, a_n$ as well as A and $\alpha_1 \ldots \alpha_n$ are constants.

The functions (5a.4)–(5a.6) are mathematically simple to deal with, but – as we shall show below – they do not have all the varied properties which a product function ought to have (e.g. the optimum law). Function (5a.3), on the other hand, will – as a numerical example – satisfy all these requirements.

The function (5a.6) is occasionally used as an approximation formula. It is, for example, used by Paul Douglas in his *Theory of Wages* (New York, 1934, p. 133) and is therefore called the Douglas or Cobb-Douglas function. It does not have all the properties we must require.

NUMERICAL METHOD OF PRESENTATION

If the way in which a product quantity depends on the factor quantities is specified *numerically*, we can present this relationship in the form of a *product table*. Already in Chapter 3 we considered a few small stylised examples of a table of this kind. We shall present here a few others, which are more detailed and are based partly on concrete data and partly on constructed data. Table (5a.7) shows feeding results for bulls in the United States. Since we are only using the figures by way of example, pre-war data serve our purpose just as well as up-to-date data.

Table (5a.8) shows the effect of a special work factor and the addition of a special raw material in the manufacture of chocolate.

Finally Table (5a.9) shows the results of an experiment in planting sugar beet for feeding stuffs.

DESCRIBING A CONTINUOUS PRODUCTION LAW

TABLE (5a.7)
Average increase in weight per bull per day over a period of 138 days*

v_1 = Maize feeding per animal per day (in English pounds)	v_2 = Hay feeding per animal per day (in English pounds)			
	8 lbs	12 lbs	16 lbs	20 lbs
10 lbs	1.61 lbs	1.81 lbs	1.98 lbs	2.13 lbs
15 lbs	1.96 lbs	2.16 lbs	2.33 lbs	2.48 lbs
20 lbs	2.27 lbs	2.47 lbs	2.64 lbs	2.79 lbs
25 lbs	2.41 lbs	2.61 lbs	2.78 lbs	

* Average for 67 farms. Nebraska, U.S.A., 1920–1921. The initial weight of animals on an average of 847 English pounds. From Tolley, Black and Ezekiel, *Input as Related to Output in Farm Organization and Cost of Production Studies*. U. S. Department of Agriculture. Bull. No. 1277, September 1924, p. 25.

TABLE (5a.8)
Number of kilos of finished nut chocolate = x*

v_1 = Application of moulding and cooling work (shown in terms of its value in kroner)	v_2 = Addition of pure cocoa fat (shown in terms of its value in kroner)			
	5 kr.	10 kr.	15 kr.	20 kr.
100 kr.	352 kg	396 kg	402 kg	403 kg
150 kr.	500 kg	562 kg	577 kg	589 kg
200 kr.	625 kg	725 kg	760 kg	783 kg
250 kr.	738 kg	858 kg	930 kg	957 kg

* Data from Freia Chocolate Factory, Oslo, 1935. (Cf. Ragnar Frisch, 'The Principle of Substitution. An Example of its application in the Chocolate Industry', *Nordisk Tidsskrift for Teknisk Økonomi*, September, 1935, p. 24).

TABLE (5a.9)
Root pulp in kilos per dekar*

v_1 = distance between plants	v_2 = amount of seed			
	13.3 g/m^2**	26.7 g/m^2	53.3 g/m^2	106.7 g/m^2
25 cm	863	857	792	717
30 cm	809	796	779	708
37.5 cm	744	688	751	687

* An experiment in planting sugar beet feed (Pajbjerg Korsroe) under glass at Vestmyra 1946. Source: Øivind Nissen, 'Comparison of cultivation costs and cropping of various root crops, planted and sown'. Norges Landbrukhøgskoles Akervekstforsøk. Report No. 133, 1947.
** g/m^2 = represents grammes per square meter.

Let us now consider two constructed examples. They are given in Table (5a.10) and (5a.11). Table (5a.10) shows an example given in Thv. Aarum's theory of production.

Finally, in Table (5a.11), we have a constructed example – based on Formula (5a.3) of a product table for a production law in which there are three production factors.

TABLE (5a.10)
Number of hectoliters of the product*

$v_1 =$ Number of working days						
10	103	113.3	125	138.5	149.9	156
9	102	111.6	122	131.5	138.2	140
8	100	108.6	116	122	124	122
7	97	102	107.5	108.5	108.5	101
6	90	92.2	93.7	93	88	82
5	78	77.8	76.2	72.6	67.5	61
4	61	58	56.2	51.5	47.5	44
3	41	37.8	36.2	33.6	30.8	28
2	22	20.6	19.4	17.3	15.8	14
1	7	6.7	6.3	5.7	5.3	5
$=10$	$\frac{100}{9}=11.1$	$\frac{100}{8}=12.5$	$\frac{100}{7}=14.28$	$\frac{100}{6}=16.66$	$\frac{100}{v}=20$

$v_2 =$ number of dekars of land

* The figures are, after some conversion, taken from the example in Thv. Aarum, *Teoretisk Socialøkonomik*, Kristiania, 1924, p. 183. In order to relate this as closely as possible to the graphic presentation of isoquants, defined in connection with Figure (5a.14), the figures in the rubric column of the present table are set out in descending order, and instead of a heading in the table a bottom line is used.

TABLE (5a.11)
Constructed example based on Formula (5a.3)

		$v_1=1$	2	3	4	5	6	7	8	9	10
	$v_2=10$	4	15	32	54	80	107	132	151	162	165
	9	5	18	39	66	96	126	149	163	167	162
	8	7	23	49	82	117	146	164	169	163	152
	7	9	31	64	104	141	165	171	165	150	134
	6	12	42	86	133	165	175	166	148	128	109
$v_3=1$	5	18	61	119	166	180	167	144	119	99	82
	4	28	94	163	187	168	134	108	85	69	56
	3	51	153	199	167	123	90	68	52	41	34
	2	111	218	159	100	65	46	34	26	20	16
	1	200	122	58	33	21	14	10	8	6	5

Table (5a.11) (continued)

		$v_1=1$	2	3	4	5	6	7	8	9	10
$v_3=2$	$v_2=10$	11	35	72	121	179	238	291	331	354	360
	9	13	44	90	150	216	280	330	359	366	356
	8	17	56	114	188	263	327	365	374	362	336
	7	23	74	150	239	320	371	384	368	335	298
	6	31	101	202	306	378	398	376	334	288	246
	5	45	146	278	384	415	384	330	274	226	188
	4	70	222	381	436	392	318	252	199	160	131
	3	116	340	455	394	295	217	163	126	100	81
	2	170	400	361	244	164	116	85	65	51	41
	1	100	194	141	88	58	40	30	23	18	14
$v_3=3$	$v_2=10$	20	61	122	202	294	389	474	538	574	583
	9	24	75	152	249	357	459	539	585	596	579
	8	31	96	193	312	435	537	598	613	591	548
	7	41	126	262	396	527	610	616	605	552	490
	6	55	171	333	503	620	655	620	553	478	408
	5	76	237	446	617	676	634	549	457	379	315
	4	107	326	568	680	636	529	425	338	272	223
	3	133	394	600	594	480	367	280	218	173	141
	2	110	319	425	367	274	202	151	117	92	75
	1	43	129	166	138	102	74	56	43	34	28
$v_3=4$	$v_2=10$	30	90	179	292	423	557	677	767	818	829
	9	37	112	221	358	510	655	768	834	850	826
	8	47	141	277	444	617	761	849	873	844	785
	7	60	180	353	554	738	858	895	862	790	703
	6	77	233	450	680	849	910	875	789	687	590
	5	98	294	555	788	896	871	775	656	549	460
	4	112	339	615	800	816	722	602	489	399	329
	3	103	313	543	646	605	503	402	321	258	211
	2	64	200	340	388	326	282	222	176	141	115
	1	23	76	131	150	134	108	85	68	54	44
$v_3=5$	$v_2=10$	42	122	238	386	556	730	887	1005	1074	1091
	9	51	149	290	467	663	850	999	1088	1114	1087
	8	63	182	355	566	786	973	1093	1132	1104	1033
	7	76	223	433	678	911	1075	1138	1113	1032	927
	6	91	266	512	783	1002	1108	1098	1013	898	780
	5	100	296	563	830	1000	1031	963	842	720	611
	4	95	285	536	760	863	838	745	630	527	441
	3	72	220	412	568	620	580	500	417	346	287
	2	40	128	241	330	355	328	281	233	192	160
	1	14	48	93	129	140	130	111	92	76	61
	$v_2=10$	54	153	294	474	679	892	1085	1235	1325	1352
	9	64	181	349	559	793	1019	1205	1323	1365	1342
	8	75	213	410	653	909	1137	1293	1360	1344	1272
	7	85	244	470	739	1006	1211	1316	1319	1249	1141
	6	92	265	509	789	1041	1202	1242	1189	1083	961

Table (5a.11) (continued)

		$v_1=1$	2	3	4	5	6	7	8	9	10
$v_3=6$	5	89	260	490	761	972	1074	1070	981	869	755
	4	74	220	423	637	794	849	820	734	639	548
	3	51	155	300	450	553	582	550	491	422	361
	2	27	87	171	257	316	331	312	277	239	204
	1	10	33	67	102	126	133	126	112	97	83
	$v_2=10$	64	178	340	544	779	1024	1251	1433	1548	1594
	9	73	203	389	621	881	1139	1358	1509	1578	1572
	8	81	227	434	690	967	1224	1419	1523	1536	1480
	7	86	242	452	732	1011	1249	1400	1449	1414	1321
	6	84	240	460	722	981	1181	1282	1285	1216	1110
$v_3=7$	5	74	214	412	644	863	1016	1080	1050	973	873
	4	57	182	325	508	674	782	818	783	716	637
	3	37	113	221	347	460	530	534	524	477	422
	2	20	62	124	214	262	303	313	299	272	241
	1	7	24	49	79	106	124	129	123	112	100
	$v_2=10$	72	195	369	589	842	1110	1365	1576	1722	1793
	9	78	213	404	644	916	1193	1440	1624	1727	1750
	8	81	225	427	679	958	1230	1455	1600	1655	1632
	7	80	224	427	677	947	1199	1388	1489	1501	1446
	6	77	206	395	626	870	1085	1233	1295	1297	1210
$v_3=8$	5	60	172	332	527	730	901	1016	1045	1018	951
	4	44	129	251	400	553	680	.760	776	749	696
	3	28	85	167	269	372	458	508	520	501	464
	2	15	47	94	152	213	263	292	299	289	268
	1	5	18	37	62	87	109	122	125	121	112
	$v_2=10$	75	202	380	604	864	1143	1415	1652	1829	1931
	9	78	211	398	632	902	1183	1446	1660	1800	1860
	8	77	210	398	633	900	1171	1413	1593	1694	1715
	7	72	198	376	599	848	1094	1304	1447	1512	1505
	6	62	173	331	527	745	956	1128	1236	1274	1252
$v_3=9$	5	49	139	268	428	605	774	912	986	1008	982
	4	35	101	197	318	450	575	676	728	741	719
	3	22	66	130	211	301	386	451	489	497	482
	2	11	36	72	120	172	222	261	823	289	280
	1	4	14	29	49	71	93	110	120	122	119
	$v_2=10$	75	200	373	592	848	1127	1406	1660	1864	2000
	9	74	200	375	595	851	1125	1392	1624	1797	1898
	8	70	190	359	571	815	1073	1317	1520	1659	1726
	7	63	171	325	518	739	969	1182	1351	1459	1500
	6	52	144	375	440	629	823	1000	1135	1216	1240
$v_3=10$	5	40	113	217	349	500	654	798	897	956	970
	4	28	81	158	256	368	482	587	660	702	711
	3	18	52	104	169	245	323	392	444	472	478
	2	9	29	58	97	141	187	228	259	276	280
	1	4	11	24	40	59	79	97	110	118	120

Graphic method of presentation

A table can only show the magnitude of the product function at certain points. By choosing more and more tight sets of magnitudes of the factor quantities figuring in the table, the information provided by the table will of course be more and more detailed, but *continuous* variation in the real sense of the word cannot be presented in this way. This, however, can be done by a graphic presentation.

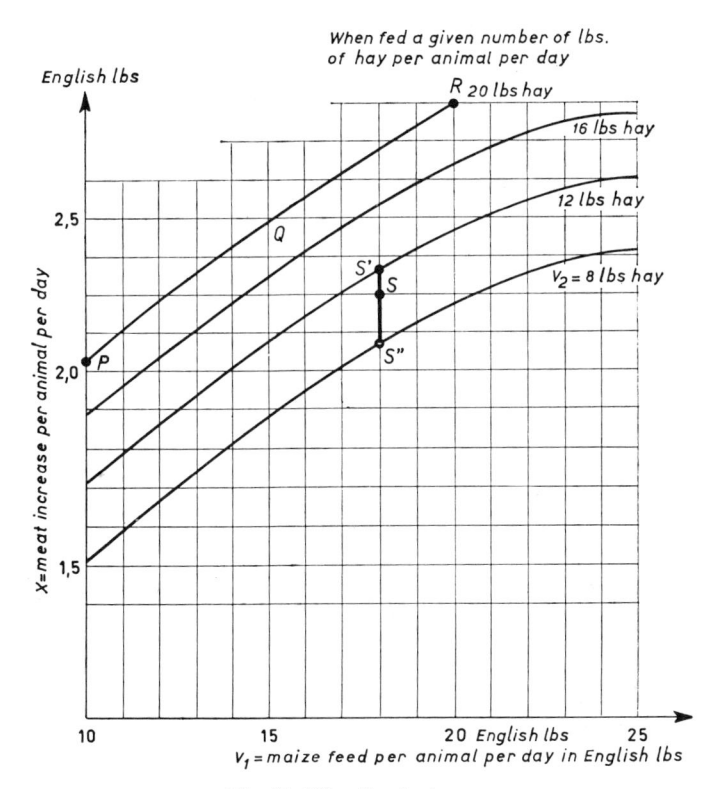

Fig. (5a.12). Product curves.

We can do this, for example, with a set of *product curves*. In Figure (5a.12) the maize feedstuff dealt with in Example (5a.7) is measured along the horizontal scale, and along the vertical scale the daily meat increase. Points P, Q, and R represent the three figures in the last column of (5a.7), viz. in the case of hayfeed a constant equal to 20 lbs per day. A curve drawn freehand through these three points will with a certain degree of accuracy show what the increase in meat would have been per day if *intermediate* amounts of maize feeds had been used, but the same amount of hayfeed = 20 lbs. We can, for example, read off by the eye the fact that for a value for maize feed of 12 lbs per day, the increase in meat will be approximately 2.17 lbs per day. In the same way we can draw curves for the other columns in Example (5a.7). In this way we obtain a whole set of product curves, and this set of curves provides a good expression of the character of the variations involved.

If we have given certain intermediate magnitudes of *both* factors, e.g. $v_1 = 18$, $v_2 = 11$, the interpolation in Figure (5a.12) can take place as follows: draw a perpendicular line for $v_1 = 18$, and consider the segment $S'S''$ of this line between the product curves for $v_2 = 8$ and $v_2 = 12$ respectively. Obviously the point we are looking for must lie somewhere here. In the present case where the curves run smoothly, an interpolation by 'proportional parts' will give a sufficiently accurate result. As $v_2 = 11$ is situated

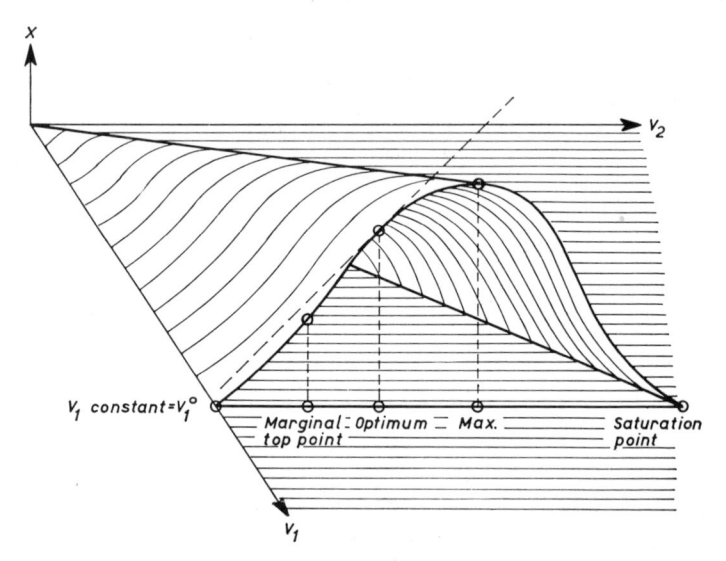

Fig. (5a.13). Product surface over the factor diagram. (The significance of the points *marginal top point*, *optimum*, *maximum*, and *saturation point* are explained in Chapter 6.)

one-quarter of the way between $v_1 = 12$ and $v_2 = 8$, we mark off a point S lying one-quarter of the way from S' to S''. This enables us to read off by the eye $x = $ a meat increase of about 2.3 lbs per animal per day.

In Figure (5a.12) the factors are not dealt with symmetrically: one is meas-

DESCRIBING A CONTINUOUS PRODUCTION LAW 49

ured along the horizontal axis, while the variation of the other is represented by moving from one curve to another in the sheaf of curves. In order to obtain a representation which is symmetrical with respect to the two factors the natural approach is to take our point of departure in a diagram where the quantity of factor No. 1 is measured along the horizontal axis and that of factor No. 2 along the vertical axis. A diagram of this kind is called a *factor diagram*. A point in the factor diagram is called a *factor point*. It

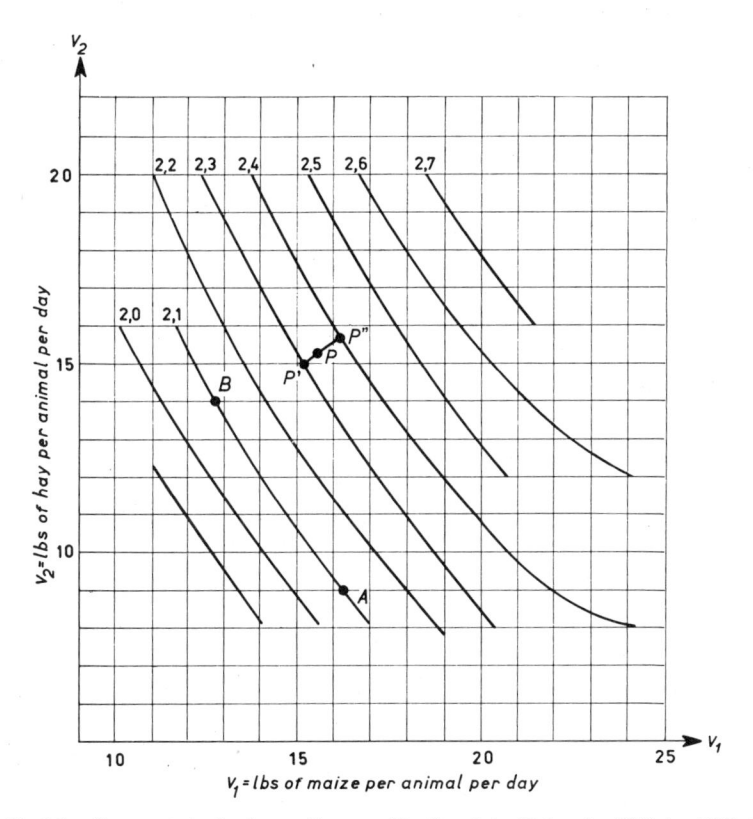

Fig. (5a.14). Isoquants in the factor diagram. Feeding data, Nebraska, U.S.A., 1920–1921 (cf. Table (5a.7)).

represents a certain total *factor* application. If on any factor point we construct a perpendicular, the length of which represents the magnitude of the product quantity corresponding to the factor combination concerned, we get a surface which will look something like the surface in Figure (5a.13). We call this the *product surface*.

50 MOMENTARY SINGLE PRODUCTION

It is, however, not so convenient to operate with stereometric figures of this kind, and for this reason we proceed as in the case of *map drawing*; viz. onto the horizontal plane – here the $(v_1 v_2)$-plane – we project the curves representing one and the same *altitude* above this plane, i.e. one and the same magnitude of the *product quantity*. These projected curves we call *isoquants*. An isoquant, in other words, is the curve which is drawn through the factor diagram and is such that the product quantity remains constant along this curve. Figure (5a.14) shows the isoquants for the example in (5a.7). For example, points A and B on the third lowest curve represent respectively the

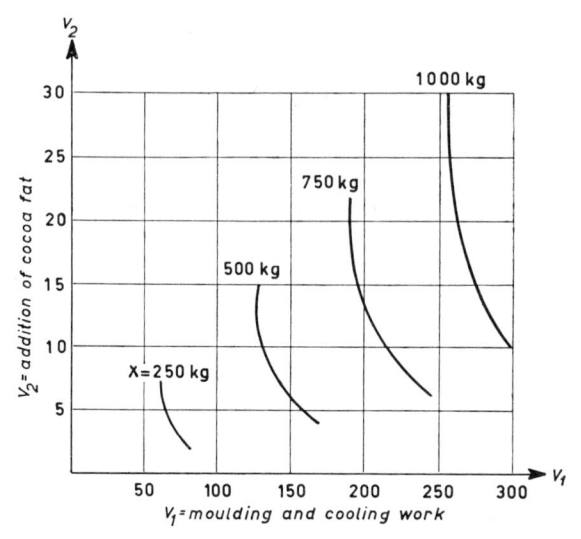

Fig. (5a.15). Isoquants in the factor diagram. Manufacture of nut chocolate, Freia, 1935.

factor combinations 16.2 lbs maize/9 lbs hay and 12.7 lbs maize/14 lbs hay. These two points are situated on one and the same isoquant, and therefore correspond to one and the same product quantity. This product quantity, as we can read off from the figure marked in the diagram, is equal to 2.1 lbs of growth per animal per day.

An interpolation on the isoquants can as a rule be undertaken without any difficulty. Let us imagine, for example, that we wish to find out the product quantity corresponding to 15.5 lbs of maize/15.1 lbs of hay, viz. factor point P. This lies between the isoquants $x = 2.3$ lbs and $x = 2.4$ lbs. In other words, the product quantity we are looking for must lie between these magnitudes. Point P lies, as we can see, *closer* to the 2.3-isoquant than to the 2.4-isoquant. In this case, where the isoquants run so smoothly, we can obtain a fairly accurate result by an interpolation with 'proportional parts'. We draw a straight line through P, running as far as possible perpendicular to both the isoquants concerned. This will determine points P' and P''. If we place a millimetre-rule on the figure, we shall find that the distance $P'P$ is approximately 31 per cent of the total distance from P' to P''. Hence we ought to proceed approximately 31 per cent of the distance from $x=2.3$ to 2.4, i.e. the product quantity we are looking for can be put equal to $x=2.331$.

Figure (5a.15) represents isoquants for the example (5a.8) taken from the manufacture of chocolate.

The three different methods of presentation make it possible to study not only what happens when one factor varies at any one time, but also the effect of *simultaneous* factor variations. This is important, as *the problem of production cannot be solved by considering it n times as a problem involving one single factor, but it must be dealt with as* one *problem involving n simultaneously variable factors.*

5b. Marginal productivities

The concept marginal productivity is defined as follows: *In momentary single production marginal productivity with respect to factor No. i is the partial derivative (the partial degree of accretion) of the product function with respect to the quantity of factor No. i,* viz.

(5b.1)
$$\text{Marginal productivity with respect to factor No. } i = x_i' = \frac{\partial x(v_1, ..., v_n)}{\partial v_i} = x_i'(v_1, ..., v_n).$$

x_i' on the lefthand side of (5b.1) is a magnitude, while x_i' on the righthand side of (5b.1) is a *function symbol* which denotes the nature of the dependence between x_i' and $v_1 ..., v_n$. Marginal productivity with respect to a certain factor will as a general rule not be constant, but will be dependent on all factor quantities.

If we choose to use f as a symbol for the product function, it will be natural to use f_i' as a symbol of marginal productivity functions. As a general rule, however, we prefer to retain the notation x and x_i'.

If we have n production factors, the product function gets n partial derivatives, and we consequently get n marginal productivities. Each of the n factors has its marginal productivity.

In any factor point the sign (plus or minus) of the marginal productivity for a given factor will indicate whether the product quantity will rise or fall, if we start at the factor point concerned, and with this as our basis increase the quantity of the relevant factor while keeping all the other factors constant. We say that factor No. k is sub-maximal, maximal, or super-maximal in the factor point concerned, according to whether x_k' is positive, zero, or negative in the factor point concerned. This criterion can be used for any factor in the factor point concerned. The exact meaning of sub-maximal, maximal, and super-maximal will be dealt with in 6b.

Marginal productivity, as here defined, is a purely *technical* concept. To emphasise this the term marginal *efficiency* has sometimes been used instead of marginal productivity, but the latter term is most frequently used.

We shall here indicate the expressions for the marginal productivity for some of the analytically specified product functions given in 5a.

Whenever we have a production law conforming to (5a.4), we get, by differentation with respect to v_1

(5b.2) $$x_1' = 24v_2 - 20v_2$$

and by differentiation with respect to v_2

(5b.3) $$x_2' = 24v_1 - 16v_2.$$

The marginal productivities in the production law (5a.6) can be found in a corresponding manner by differentiating (5a.6) partially with respect to v_i

(5b.4) $$x_i' = \alpha_i A v_1^{\alpha_1} v_2^{\alpha_2} \ldots v_i^{\alpha_i - 1} \ldots v_n^{\alpha_n} = \alpha_i \left(\frac{x}{v_i}\right) \quad (i = 1, \ldots, n).$$

In the case of both these production laws, marginal productivities depend on all specified factor quantities. If we had the linear product function (5a.5), we would have had constant marginal productivities, since differentiation of (5a.5) with respect to v_i gives us

(5b.5) $$x_i' = a_i \quad (i = 1, \ldots, n).$$

If the relationship between product quantity and factor quantity is given numerically in the form of a product table, marginal productivities can be calculated *approximately*.

As an example, we shall take Table (5a.10). We can, for example, keep the number of working days constant, equal to 7, and vary the area of land. In changing over from $v_2 = 11.1$ to $v_2 = 12.5$, the increase of the product is $107.5 - 102 = 5.5$. The corresponding increase in the area of land is $12.5 - 11.1 = 1.4$.

DESCRIBING A CONTINUOUS PRODUCTION LAW

We thus have the marginal productivity with respect to factor No. 2 =

$$x_2' = \frac{107.5 - 102.0}{12.5 - 11.1} = \frac{5.5}{1.4} = 3.93.$$

This is the average magnitude of marginal productivity when v_2 varies in the interval from 11.1 to 12.5 and v_1 is kept constant at 7. As the interval is relatively small, we can take 3.93 as an approximate expression of marginal productivity with respect to v_2 *at the point* ($v_2 = 11.1$, $v_1 = 7$).

Let us start from the same point ($v_2 = 11.1$, $v_1 = 7$), and investigate the marginal productivity with respect to factor No. 1 (labour). This marginal productivity we shall call x_1'. We shall now keep v_2 constant at 11.1 and increase v_1. This gives us

$$x_1' = \frac{108.6 - 102}{8 - 7} = \frac{6.6}{1} = 6.6.$$

In this case the marginal productivity is exactly equal to the absolute increase in product – namely 6.6 –, because the increase of the factor concerned is equal to 1.

In the same way we can proceed from any given combination ($v_1 v_2$) we like in Table (5a.10), and determine both the marginal productivity with respect to factor No. 1 (labour) and with respect to factor No. 2 (land). On the basis of Table (5a.10) we can thus construct two new and entirely corresponding tables. One of these two tables will show how marginal productivity with respect to factor No. 1 (labour) varies when land and labour vary. The other will show how marginal productivity with respect to factor No. 2 (land) varies when land and labour vary. Marginal productivity with respect to factor No. 2 (land) is thus a function of two variables, both of v_2 (area of land) and v_1 (quantity of work). The same applies to marginal productivity with respect to factor No. 1. Marginal productivity with respect to labour changes not only if the land remains constant and the quantity of labour varies, but it will change even when the quantity of labour is kept constant and only the land factor varies.

Let us, for instance, keep v_1 (labour) constant = 8, and investigate how marginal productivity with respect to factor No. 1 (labour) varies when the quantity of factor No. 2 (land) varies. This is done in Table (5b.6).

Marginal productivity does not need to be a positive magnitude. It can be negative or zero. In the example, for instance, in the combination ($v_2 = 14.28$, $v_1 = 7$) x_2' is zero and x_1' is positive, while in the combination ($v_2 = 14.28$, $v_1 = 6$) x_2' is negative. This means that a further increase in land area will

TABLE (5b.6)

When the quantity of factor No. 2 (land) equals:	Then x_1', marginal productivity with respect to factor No. 1 (labour), equals:
10	$\dfrac{102-100}{1} = 2$
11.1	$\dfrac{111.6-108.6}{1} = 3$
12.5	$\dfrac{122-116}{1} = 6$
14.28	$\dfrac{131.5-122}{1} = 9.5$

lower the total product quantity, if we start from the combination ($v_2 = 14.28$, $v_1 = 6$). Concretely speaking the work will then be spread over too large an area.

The term marginal productivity is defined by a partial variation, viz. when one factor varies at a time. But when each marginal productivity has been defined (and, if possible, measured concretely) in this partial way, we can subsequently use these magnitudes to calculate the variation that takes place in the product quantity when an *arbitrary simultaneous* variation of all factor quantities takes place. If we assume that $dv_1, dv_2, \ldots, dv_n$ are arbitrary, infinitesimal increments of the factor quantities, and dx the corresponding increment in the product quantity, then, by retaining merely the linear terms of the marginal increment formula, we get

(5b.7) $\quad dx = x_1' dv_1 + x_2' dv_2 + \ldots + x_r' dv_n$ or more briefly, $dx = \sum\limits_{i=1}^{n} x_i' dv_i$.

The concept *continuity factor* mentioned in the preamble to Part Two, may be defined as follows:

DEFINITION (5b.8)

A *continuity factor* is a factor whose marginal productivity in any point is a continuous function of all factor quantities.

The validity of the marginal increment formula (5b.7) is dependent upon the fact that all the factors are continuity factors in the factor point considered. If they are, it is always possible to render the factor increments dv_1, ..., dv_n small enough to make the discrepancy between the *actual* product increment dx and the right member of (5b.7) as small as we please.

The fact that merely continuity factors occur in a production law, is the same as the fact that in each factor point the product function has continuous partial derivatives of the first order with respect to each factor.

The definition (5b.8) provides a more precise formulation of the assumption made in our preamble, to the effect that throughout Part Two we shall confine ourselves to an investigation of production laws where only continuity factors occur.

If, taking as our starting point a definite factor combination, we can *alternatively* increase the product quantity, either by increasing the quantity of a given factor (e.g. No. *h*) and keeping the quantities of all the other factors constant, or by increasing the quantity of another given factor (e.g. No. *k*) and keeping the quantities of all the other factors (now including No. *h*) constant, then we say that the two factors (No. *h* and No. *k*) are in a *substitution relationship* to one another in the factor combination concerned. It is possible for two factors to be in a substitution relationship to one another in one factor combination, but not in another.

This formulation of the substitution concept means that two factors are in a substitution relationship to one another in a definite factor combination when – and only when – *the marginal productivities of both factors are positive* in the factor combination concerned.

The region of the *n*-dimensional factor diagram where any pair of factors are in a substitution relationship to one another, is called the *substitution region*. Thus, according to this definition, the substitution region consists of those – and only those – points in the *n*-dimensional factor diagram where all marginal productivities are positive.

Any point where all marginal productivities are non-negative and one or more of them are *zero*, is said to lie on the *boundary of the substitution region*. From the formal point of view it is practical to include this boundary, too, in the substitution region. That is to say, the substitution region is then defined as *the comprehension of all factor points i.e. the point set where all marginal productivities are non-negative*.

In many cases we are more interested in the relative than in the absolute marginal productivities, for example in the relationship x_1'/x_2'. This expresses the *relative* marginal productivity between factor No. 1 and factor No. 2. If these two marginal productivities are continuous, we can call this quotient *the substitution ratio* between the two factors. The substitution ratio tells us in what proportion the two factors are capable of *replacing* (*substituting*) one another, if we insist that the product quantity be unchanged. If, for example, the quotient concerned is $x_1'/x_2' = 2.5$, this means that we must add 2.5 units of No. 2 in order to *compensate the loss* of one unit of No. 1, or vice versa: one unit of No. 1 can compensate the loss of 2.5 units of No. 2.

The increment formula (5b.7) shows that this is the significance of the ratio. This formula is valid for any kind of factor change, partial or simultaneous. Thus, it also applies especially to the kind of factor change we are now considering. In this present case all factors are bound to be constant, except Nos. 1 and 2. In other words $dv_3 = 0, \ldots, dv_n = 0$. And the two increments dv_1 and dv_2 must be such that the product quantity remains unchanged, in other words such that $dx = 0$. Therefore, between dv_1 and dv_2 the following relation must exist:

(5b.9) $$x_1' dv_1 + x_2' dv_2 = 0,$$

hence

$$\frac{dv_2}{-dv_1} = \frac{x_1'}{x_2'} = \text{the substitution ratio}.$$

Since relative marginal productivities play such an important role, it is obvious that it would be of interest to investigate *along what curves in the factor diagram* these relative marginal productivities are constant. A curve of this kind is called an *isocline*.[1]

When there are only two factors 1 and 2, there is only one *relative* marginal productivity, viz. the ratio x_1'/x_2' (the reciprocal ratio x_2'/x_1' naturally provides us with no new information). At what point in the factor diagram will this fraction possess a prescribed magnitude, for example 2.5? In other words: where do those points lie which are such that the same quantity is required, viz. 2.5 units of No. 2, in order to save one unit of No. 1?

As a rule we shall find that this is the case along a certain curve which, generally speaking, *is rising* in the factor diagram, i.e. something like the central curve in Figure (5b.10). (In an important special case – the pari-passu law, which we shall subsequently discuss – every isocline will be a straight line through the origin.[2] The equation for the curve considered can be set out in the form

(5b.11) $$\frac{x_1'(v_1, v_2)}{x_2'(v_1, v_2)} = 2.5.$$

---

[1] This name is an allusion to the inclination or slope, and is associated with a graphic representation of marginal productivity with the aid of arrows in the factor diagnose.
[2] Cf. (7b.1).

DESCRIBING A CONTINUOUS PRODUCTION LAW

Here, on the lefthand side, occur those *functions* which tell us in what way the marginal productivity for factor No. 1 and factor No. 2 respectively are dependent on the two factor quantities v_1 and v_2, i.e. (5b.11) is an equation between the two variables v_1 and v_2, that is to say it is an equation for a curve through the factor diagram.

If we had prescribed another magnitude for relative marginal productivity, for example 2.0, we should have had another curve, for example the highest curve in Figure (5b.10). This is, therefore, the isocline for the relative marginal productivity 2.0. In the same way the lowest curve will constitute the isocline for relative marginal productivity 3.0, etc. *Thus the factor diagram is filled with a set of isoclines.*

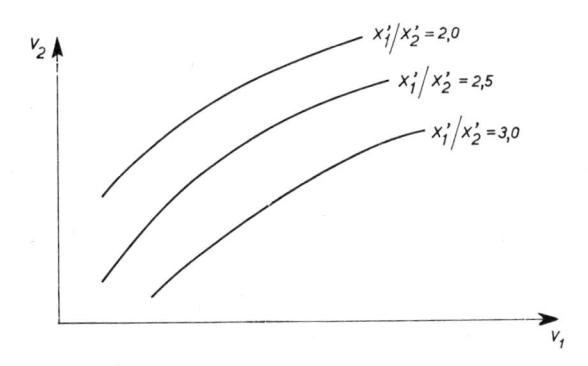

Fig. (5b.10). Isoclines.

In the case of two factors, an isocline is defined by prescribing one magnitude, namely that for the relative marginal productivity x_1'/x_2'. In the case of *three* factors an isocline is defined by prescribing the magnitude of two such relative marginal productivities and in the case of n factors it is defined by prescribing $(n-1)$ relative marginal productivities. (Note that we are now speaking of the relationship between the *marginal productivities*, not of the relationship between factor increments). In the case of n factors, the equations defining the isocline will be more symmetrical if they are written down in a slightly different form from that in (5b.11). We first determine n figures $c_1, c_2, \ldots, c_n$, which are such that the relations between them represent the relations required between marginal productivities. In the example (5b.11), for example, we can put $c_1 = 5$, $c_2 = 2$, so that the relationship between these two figures is 2.5. We can then say that productivities must be proportional to these n figures, viz.

$$(5b.12) \qquad \frac{x_1'(v_1, \ldots, v_n)}{c_1} = \frac{x_2'(v_1, \ldots, v_n)}{c_2} = \ldots = \frac{x_n'(v_1, \ldots, v_n)}{c_n}.$$

The formula (5b.12) defines $(n-1)$ equations between the n factor quantities $v_1, \ldots, v_n$. Thus there remains exactly one degree of freedom, and (5b.12) consequently represents a one-dimensional curve in the n-dimensional factor diagram.

In dealing with the economic adaptation processes, cf. especially 10d, it will be shown that with given factor prices, one particular isocline will acquire special significance (the substitumal).

5c. Product accelerations

Product accelerations are partial derivatives of the second order of the product function, viz.

(5c.1) Product acceleration for factors

$$\text{No. } i \text{ and No. } j = x_{ij}{''} = \frac{\partial^2 x(v_1, \ldots, v_n)}{\partial v_i \partial v_j} = x_{ij}{''}(v_1, \ldots, v_n).$$

As a general rule product acceleration for two definite factors will thus depend on all factor quantities. The symbol $x_{ij}{''}$ on the right side of (5c.1) is a function symbol denoting the form of this relationship. The symbol $x_{ij}{''}$ on the left stands for a magnitude.

Product accelerations may be conceived of as the partial derivatives of the first order of marginal productivities. Thus we get

$$(5c.2) \qquad x_{ij}{''} = \frac{\partial x_i'}{\partial v_j} = \frac{\partial x_i'(v_1, \ldots, v_n)}{\partial v_j}.$$

As mentioned in Section 5b, with n factors we get n marginal productivities, and each of these marginal productivities can be differentiated with respect to each of the n factors, so that we get a total of n^2 accelerations. These can be recorded in a table (matrix) which has the appearance as shown in Table (5c.3). The magnitudes in the descending diagonal of Table (5c.3) viz. $x_{11}{''}$, $x_{22}{''}$, ..., $x_{nn}{''}$, are called *direct accelerations*; the other magnitudes are called *cross accelerations*.

TABLE (5c.3)

Partial derivative of	With respect to factor No.			
	1	2		n
x_1'	x_{11}''	x_{12}''	....	x_{1n}''
x_2'	x_{21}''	x_{22}''	....	x_{2n}''
...				
...				
...				
...				
x_n'	x_{n1}''	x_{n2}''	....	x_{nn}''

If we assume that the product function is continuous with continuous partial derivatives of the 1st and 2nd order, the acceleration table will be symmetrical, viz.:

(5c.4) $$x_{ij}'' = x_{ji}'' \qquad (i=1, ..., n);\ (j=1, ..., n).$$

The reason for this is simply that a partial derivative of an arbitrary order has a value independent of the sequence in which the derivations are made, provided only that the function and its partial derivatives, up to and including the order considered, are continuous.[1]

For this reason we only get

$$\binom{n}{2} = \frac{n(n-1)}{2}$$

different cross accelerations. It is therefore sufficient to consider the diagonal and either the north-east or the south-west triangle in the acceleration table (5c.3). To obtain a good overall view, however, it is often useful to have the entire table filled out.

Direct accelerations show how the marginal productivity of a factor is changed whenever the quantity of this factor is changed. When $x_{ii}'' > 0$ in any given factor point, marginal productivity (marginal returns) with respect to factor No. *i* is *on the increase* at this factor point, and when $x_{ii}'' < 0$ in any definite factor point, marginal productivity (marginal returns) with respect to factor No. *i* is on the *decrease* at this factor point.

Cross-accelerations show how the marginal productivity of a certain factor is changed when the quantity of *another* factor is changed. A change of this kind is exemplified in Table (5b.6).

---

[1] These definitions apply to continuity factors. In dealing with *limitational factors* in Part Three the definitions will have to be stated with greater precision.

With the aid of cross-accelerations we can define the terms *complementary* and *alternative* (competitive) production factors. We shall say that two continuity factors, No. i and No. j, are *complementary* if $x_{ij}'' > 0$, that is to say if an increase in the quantity of one factor *increases* the marginal productivity of the other. On the other hand, we say that the two factors are *alternative* (competitive) if $x_{ij}'' < 0$, that is to say if an increase in the amount of one factor *decreases* the marginal productivity of the other. If $x_{ij}'' = 0$, we say that the two factors are marginally *independent* of one another.[1]

The question here being discussed must not be confused with the question of whether the two factors stand in a *substitution relationship* to one another. The latter, as we noted in Section 5b, is a question of how large marginal productivities are in a given factor point (especially if they are positive), while the complementary – and alternative – relationship, on the other hand, is a question of how the marginal productivities *change* in the neighbourhood of a given factor point, viz. a question of how large the accelerations are.

As accelerations depend on which factor combination we are considering, cf. (5c.1), it may happen that two factors are complementary in one factor point and alternative in another. The commonest case in continuity factors is that they are complementary in the substitution region. (cf. 7c). In examples (5a.8) and (5a.10) this is the case. Calculate, for example, the difference between the figure on one line and the corresponding figure on the line above, and investigate how this difference changes as we go to the right or the left. Or take the difference between two figures in two adjoining columns, and see how this difference alters as we proceed up or down.

Finally we shall give an example of how accelerations can be found when the product function has a specified analytical form. Let us turn to the special product function in (5a.4). By differentiating with respect to v_1 twice, we get

(5c.5) $\qquad\qquad\qquad x_{11}'' = -20.$

By differentiating with respect to v_2 twice, we get

(5c.6) $\qquad\qquad\qquad x_{22}'' = -16.$

By differentiating with respect to v_1 once and v_2 once, we get

(5c.7) $\qquad\qquad\qquad x_{12}'' = 24.$

---

[1] The figures in Table (5a.7) have been *smoothed* in such a way that the factors are marginally *independent*.

DESCRIBING A CONTINUOUS PRODUCTION LAW

In this special case we had $x_{12}''>0$ throughout, and the two factors are therefore complementary at every point.

As a general rule the situation will be more complicated.

5d. Average productivities

By average productivity for a factor we understand the product quantity calculated per unit of the factor concerned. Viz.:

Average productivity for factor

$$(5\text{d}.1) \quad \text{No. } i = \bar{x}_i = \frac{x}{v_i} = \frac{x(v_1, \ldots, v_n)}{v_i} = \bar{x}_i(v_1, \ldots, v_n).$$

When there are n production factors, we get a total of n average productivities, in other words one for each factor. Each one of these n average productivities will in general depend on all the factor quantities.

We shall give an example of average productivities for one of the product functions, with a specified analytical form such as that given in Section 5a, viz. (5a.4). By dividing (5a.4) by v_1, we get:

$$(5\text{d}.2) \quad \bar{x}_1 = \frac{x}{v_1} = \frac{24v_1v_2 - 10v_1^2 - 8v_2^2}{v_1} = 24v_2 - 10v_1 - 8\frac{v_2^2}{v_1}.$$

By dividing (5a.4) by v_2, we get:

$$(5\text{d}.3) \quad \bar{x}_2 = \frac{x}{v_2} = \frac{24v_1v_2 - 10v_1^2 - 8v_2^2}{v_2} = 24v_1 - 10\frac{v_1^2}{v_2} - 8v_2.$$

Both $\bar{x}_1$ and $\bar{x}_2$, in fact, depend as we see on which factor point we are in.

Average productivity for a given factor expresses the average returns of the factor concerned. If the average productivity for factor No. i *increases* when the quantity of factor No. i increases – and all other factors are constant – we say that there exists an *increasing average return of factor No. i*. Conversely, we say that there is a *decreasing average return of factor No. i*, whenever the average productivity of factor No. i decreases with an increase in the quantity of factor No. i. Note that we are now speaking of *average* productivity, while in the text following (5c.4) we spoke of *marginal* productivity.

The condition for the existence of an increasing average return with regard to factor No. i is that $\partial \bar{x}_i/\partial v_i > 0$. Decreasing average return with respect to factor No. i is characterised by $\partial \bar{x}_i/\partial v_i < 0$.

The nature of $\partial \bar{x}_i/\partial v_i$ can be found in the following way:

(5d.4) $\quad \dfrac{\partial \bar{x}_i}{\partial v_i} = \dfrac{\partial (x/v_i)}{\partial v_i} = \dfrac{v_i x_i' - x}{v_i^2} = \dfrac{1}{v_i}\left(x_i' - \dfrac{x}{v_i}\right) = \dfrac{1}{v_i}(x_i' - \bar{x}_i)$.

As v_i by its very nature will always be positive, we get

(5d.5)
$$\dfrac{\partial \bar{x}_i}{\partial v_i} > 0 \quad \text{when, and only when} \quad x_i' > \bar{x}_i :$$
$$\dfrac{\partial \bar{x}_i}{\partial v_i} < 0 \quad \text{when, and only when} \quad x_i' < \bar{x}_i .$$

We therefore have the following:

PROPOSITION (5d.6).

When, and only when, the marginal productivity is greater than the average productivity, there exists an increasing average return for factor No. i (i.e., average productivity increases). When, and only when, the marginal productivity is less than the average productivity, a decreasing average return exists for factor No. i (i.e., the average productivity sinks).

The *fabrication coefficient* for factor No. i is the quantity of factor No. i which on an average is incorporated in each unit of the product, i.e. the quantity of factor No. i divided by the product quantity, viz.

(5d.7) $\quad \bar{v}_i = \dfrac{v_i}{x} = \dfrac{v_i}{x(v_1, \ldots, v_n)} = \bar{v}_i(v_1, \ldots, v_n)$.

Thus the fabrication coefficient $\bar{v}_1$ is the inverse of the average productivity $\bar{x}_i$, i.e.

(5d.8) $\quad \bar{v}_i = \dfrac{v_i}{x} = \dfrac{1}{x/v_i} = \dfrac{1}{\bar{x}_i}$.

5e. Marginal elasticities

The marginal elasticity of a factor is equal to the partial elasticity of the product function with respect to the quantity of the factor concerned, that is to say:

(5e.1) The marginal elasticity of factor

$$\text{No. } i = \varepsilon_i = \text{El. } x \cdot v_i | \, v_1 \ldots)v_i(\ldots v_n = \dfrac{\partial x(v_1, \ldots, v_n)}{\partial v_i} \dfrac{v_i}{x(v_1, \ldots, v_n)}$$
$$= \varepsilon_i(v_1, \ldots, v_n) .$$

When we have n production factors, we have n marginal elasticities, one for each factor. Each of these will as a general rule depend on all the factor quantities.

The marginal elasticity of factor No. i is, in other words, defined in the same way as marginal productivity (by means of a partial factor variation), but with this difference alone: that we now consider the relationship between the *relative*, instead of the relationship between the absolute, increments.

The marginal elasticity can also be interpreted as the *ratio* between the marginal productivity and the average productivity for factor No. i. We have in fact

(5e.2) $$\varepsilon_i = \frac{\partial x}{\partial v_i} \cdot \frac{v_i}{x} = x_i' \cdot \frac{v_i}{x} = x_i' \frac{1}{x/v_i} = \frac{x_i'}{\bar{x}_i}.$$

In (5d.6) we noted that the ratio between the marginal productivity and average productivity for a given factor was decisive for the existence of decreasing or increasing average returns with respect to the factor concerned. On the grounds of (5e.2) we can now also use the marginal elasticity of the factor as a criterion for this. In fact, (5e.2) gives us

(5e.3)
when, and only when, $x_i' > \bar{x}_i$, then $\varepsilon_i > 1$,
when, and only when, $x_i' = \bar{x}_i$, then $\varepsilon_i = 1$,
when, and only when, $x_i' < \bar{x}_i$, then $\varepsilon_i < 1$.

If we compare (5e.3) with (5d.6) we get:

(5e.4)
If, and only if, $\varepsilon_i > 1$ there exists an *increasing* average return for factor No. i

If, and only if, $\varepsilon_i < 1$ there exists a *decreasing* average return for factor No. i

(5e.4) can also be found by using the partial *elasticity* of the average productivity instead of the partial derivative, as we did in Section 5d.

We first note – using ˇ as a symbol of elasticity – that

$$(\check{\bar{x}}_i)_i = \text{El. } \bar{x}_i \cdot v_i | v_1 \ldots) v_i, (\ldots v_n = \frac{\partial \bar{x}_i}{\partial v_i} \cdot \frac{v_i}{\bar{x}_i}.$$

As both v_i and $\bar{x}_i$ are always positive (in the relevant region), the sign – plus or minus – of $(\check{\bar{x}}_i)_i$ and $\partial \bar{x}_i / \partial v_i$ will always be the *same*.

The elasticity of the average productivity, however, is according to the rule for taking the elasticity of a fraction equal to

(5e.5) $$(\check{x}_i)_i = \left(\frac{\check{x}}{v_i}\right)_i = \text{El. } x - \text{El. } v_i = \varepsilon_i - 1$$

This proves the result (5e.4).

In the third place ε_i can be considered as the *virtual product share* of factor No. *i*, since it expresses the percentage of the total product quantity that factor No. *i would have* created, if all the units of the factor had created just as much as the 'last'. The 'last' unit having created x_i', the entire factor quantity would have created $x_i' v_i$, and this, calculated as a fraction of x, will be $x_i' v_i/x$, which is precisely ε_i (cf. (5e.2)).

In the fourth place marginal elasticities can tell us something about the question whether a certain factor point is to be found in the *substitution region* or not. The substition region is the region where all x_i' are non-negative, cf. the explanation given in the text between (5b.8) and (5b.9). But x_i' and ε_i always have the same sign when x and v_i are positive, cf. (5e.2). We can therefore define *the substitution region as the region in the factor diagram where all marginal elasticities are non-negative*.

Finally, as examples, we shall consider the product functions with a specified analytical form which were given in Section 5a, and find expressions for the marginal elasticities in these production laws.

Let us first consider (5a.3). Using the rules for partial elasticitation with respect to v_1 we get

(5e.6) $$\varepsilon_1 = 2 - \frac{4v_1^4}{v_1^4 + v_2^4 + v_3^4} - \frac{1}{v_1\left(\dfrac{1}{v_1} + \dfrac{2}{v_2} + \dfrac{3}{v_3}\right)}.$$

By partial elasticitation with respect to v_2 we get

(5e.7) $$\varepsilon_2 = 2 - \frac{4v_2^4}{v_1^4 + v_2^4 + v_3^4} - \frac{2}{v_2\left(\dfrac{1}{v_1} + \dfrac{2}{v_2} + \dfrac{3}{v_3}\right)}.$$

And by partial elasticitation with respect to v_3 we get

(5e.8) $$\varepsilon_3 = 2 - \frac{4v_3^4}{v_1^4 + v_2^4 + v_3^4} - \frac{3}{v_3\left(\dfrac{1}{v_1} + \dfrac{2}{v_2} + \dfrac{3}{v_3}\right)}.$$

It will be seen that in these examples every single marginal elasticity depends on all the factor quantities.

Next, let us consider (5a.4). By partial elasticitation with respect to v_1 we get

(5e.9) $$\varepsilon_1 = \frac{24v_1v_2 - 20v_1^2}{24v_1v_2 - 10v_1^2 - 8v_2^2} = \frac{2v_1(6v_2 - 5v_1)}{12v_1v_2 - 5v_1^2 - 4v_2^2}.$$

By partial elasticitation with respect to v_2 we get

(5e.10) $$\varepsilon_2 = \frac{24v_1v_2 - 16v_2^2}{24v_1v_2 - 10v_1^2 - 8v_2^2} = \frac{2v_2(6v_1 - 4v_2)}{12v_1v_2 - 5v_1^2 - 4v_2^2}.$$

Further, let us take the linear product function (5a.5). We then get:

(5e.11) $$\varepsilon_i = \frac{a_i v_i}{a_0 + a_1 v_1 + a_2 v_2 + \ldots + a_n v_n} \qquad (i = 1, 2, \ldots, n).$$

In the Cobb-Douglas function (5a.6) we get simply

(5e.12) $$\varepsilon_i = \alpha_i \qquad (i = 1, 2, \ldots, n).$$

While every single one of the marginal elasticities depended on all the factor quantities in the product functions (5a.7), (5a.8), and (5a.9), in the Cobb-Douglas function (5a.6) the marginal elasticities remain *constant* and independent of the factor point.

5f. The passus coefficient

The passus coefficient is the elasticity of the product quantity with respect to one of the factors, when all the factors vary *proportionally*.[1]

(5f.1) The passus coefficient $\varepsilon = \dfrac{d^{pr} x}{d^{pr} v_k} \cdot \dfrac{v_k}{x} = \dfrac{d^{pr} x / x}{d^{pr} v_k / v_k}$

(independent of k when the factors vary proportionally, viz. for d^{pr})

where $d^{pr} v_i$ ($i = 1, \ldots, n$) represents infinitesimal *proportional* factor increment (pr = 'proportional') and where $d^{pr} x$ indicates the corresponding infinitesimal increment in the product quantity.

In other words: we start at a given factor point, and give all factor quantities

---

[1] Erick Schneider uses the expression 'Niveauelastizität eines Prozesses' in his *Einführung in die Wirtschaftstheorie* (Tübingen 1958), and the term 'Ergiebigkeitsgrad der Produktion' in his *Theorie der Produktion* (Vienna 1934). W. E. Johnson uses the term 'elasticity of production' in the *Economic Journal*, 1913, and Sune Carlson uses the term 'function coefficient' in *A Study on the Pure Theory of Production* (London 1939). R. G. D. Allen, in his *Mathematical Analysis for Economists* (1947), p. 263, speaks of 'elasticity of productivity'.

one and the same infinitely small percentage increases. As a result the product quantity, too, will show a certain percentage increase. The *ratio* between the fraction by which the product has then increased, and the fraction by which all the factors have increased, is the passus coefficient.

The passus coefficient will be defined in any factor point and will depend on the factor point we happen to be in.

When all factor quantities increase in the same proportion, the relative factor combination is unchanged, but the production *scale* increases. Thus the passus coefficient provides an expression for the way the product quantity changes when an infinitesimal change occurs in the production scale. For this reason it may be called the *elasticity with respect to scale*.

In a factor point where $\varepsilon > 1$, the product quantity is changed *more rapidly* than the factor quantities with an infinitesimal increase in the production scale, and consequently we have *increasing* average returns (i.e. increasing average productivities) for the factor complex. In a factor point where $\varepsilon < 1$ we have, conversely, decreasing average returns for the factor complex. This is dealt with in greater detail in Section 5g.

In practice, when dealing with finite (as opposed to infinitesimal) increments, the passus coefficient, in the same way as the marginal productivity, should be calculated by *central placing* (a centrally placed divided difference). When dealing with the passus coefficient, which is an *elasticity*, i.e. the relationship between two *relative* increments, this central placing must also be made to apply for the magnitudes in relation to which the increments are expressed. Thus if, for example, factor No. k increases from 1510 to 1680 (and the other factors increase in the same proportion), while the product increases from 178 to 206, then we shall have to calculate the passus coefficient as follows: A production increase of 28 constitutes 15.7 per cent, calculated on the basis of initial quantity, but only 13.6 per cent calculated in proportion to the final quantity. The fact that these two percentages are different, is due to the fact that we are calculating in terms of finite instead of infinitely small increments. In arriving at an approximate expression of the infinitesimally defined passus coefficient, with the aid of finite figures, our natural approach is to make a *compromise*, by placing the observed product increment 28 in relation to, e.g., the arithmetical mean of the two product quantities, which in this case comes to 192. The product increment will then be 14.6 per cent. If we do the same with the factor increment, we shall find: 170 : 15.95 = 10.66 per cent. Thus the passus coefficient will be 14.60 : 10.66 = 1.369.

Generally speaking we can say: If the two magnitudes v^0 and v^1 are observed for one of the factors (and the other factors have changed in the

DESCRIBING A CONTINUOUS PRODUCTION LAW

same proportion) and the corresponding magnitudes of the product quantity are x^0 and x^1, then the passus coefficient – if the interval between magnitudes v^0 and v^1 are percent-wise not particularly large – can be calculated with sufficient accuracy as

$$(5\text{f}.2) \qquad \varepsilon = \frac{x^1 - x^0}{x^1 + x^0} \bigg| \frac{v^1 - v^0}{v^1 + v^0}.$$

where we may add any subscript $i = 1, 2, \ldots, n$ to the letter v.

Comparing *relative* increments of product quantity and factor quantity respectively, is the same as comparing *absolute* increments of *logarithms* of these two quantities (note e.g. the fact that we divide two figures by subtracting their logarithms). The passus coefficient can therefore also be defined as the ratio between the increment in the logarithm of the product quantity and the increment in the logarithm of one of the factor quantities (as all factor quantities change in the same proportion, their logarithms will show the same increments; for this reason it is the same whichever of the factors we take). In other words, we also have

$$(5\text{f}.3) \qquad \text{The passus coefficient } \varepsilon = \frac{d^{pr} \log x}{d^{pr} \log v_k} \quad (k \text{ arbitrary}).$$

To see that this is so, we first note that

$$(5\text{f}.4) \qquad \frac{d \log_a x}{dx} = \frac{1}{x} \frac{1}{\ln a},$$

where $\log_a$ is the logarithm of x, with a as a base, and where ln indicates the natural logarithm.

From (5f.4) we get

$$(5\text{f}.5) \qquad dx = d(\log_a x) \cdot x \cdot \ln a,$$

Correspondingly we get

$$(5\text{f}.6) \qquad dv_k = d(\log_a v_k) \cdot v_k \cdot \ln a.$$

If we substitute (5f.5) and (5f.6) in the expression (5f.1) for the passus coefficient, we get

$$\varepsilon = \frac{d^{pr} x}{d^{pr} v_k} \cdot \frac{v_k}{x} = \frac{(d^{pr} \log_a x) x \cdot \ln a}{(d^{pr} \log_a v_k) v_k \cdot \ln a} \cdot \frac{v_k}{x} = \frac{d^{pr} \log_a x}{d^{pr} \log_a v_k},$$

i.e., precisely the same as (5f.3).

This shows that another compromise formula, which can be used in practice for finite increments, is

(5f.7)
$$\varepsilon = \frac{\log x^1 - \log x^0}{\log v^1 - \log v^0}.$$

By calculating some numerical examples, it is easy to show that (5f.2) and (5f.7) will give practically speaking the same result. Thus, in the numerical example given above we get

$$\varepsilon = \frac{\log 206 - \log 178}{\log 1680 - \log 1510} = \frac{2.3139 - 2.2504}{3.2253 - 3.1790} = 1.361$$

as against formerly 1.369.

The v-point to which (5f.2) or (5f.7) refers can, by central placing be assigned as

(5f.8)
$$v = \frac{v^0 + v^1}{2}$$

or

(5f.9)
$$v = \text{antilog}\left(\frac{\log v^0 + \log v^1}{2}\right) = \sqrt{v^0 v^1}.$$

These two averages will not show much difference, unless the difference between v^0 and v^1 is great.

5g. Further consideration on proportional factor variation

The passus coefficient was defined by considering a proportional variation of all specified factors. Let us examine a little more closely the proportional factor variation.

When the factors are varied proportionally, certain *constant* relationships exist between the quantities of the factors. Let

(5g.1)
$$v_1^0, v_2^0, \ldots, v_n^0$$

be a given initial combination. This initial combination represents a given relative factor application and the proportional factor variation corresponding to this relative factor application is given by the equations

(5g.2)
$$\frac{v_1}{v_1^0} = \frac{v_2}{v_2^0} = \ldots = \frac{v_n}{v_n^0},$$

with $v_1, \ldots, v_n$ as running coordinates. This is tantamount to $(n-1)$ equations between the n factor quantities $v_1, \ldots, v_n$. There is thus one degree of freedom, and (5g.2) represents consequently a one-dimensional curve in the n-dimensional factor diagram. More precisely: we get *a straight line through origin* in the n-dimensional factor diagram. A line of this kind is called a *factor beam* and a proportional factor variation is therefore often referred to as a *variation* along a beam.

In the case of two factors, the graphic representation of a factor beam will be as shown in Figure (5g.3). For every given relative factor combination (v_1^0, v_2^0) in two variables, there is a corresponding factor beam like the one illustrated in (5g.3).

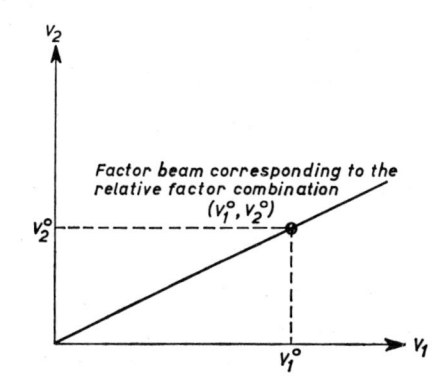

Fig. (5g.3). Factor beam in a two-dimensional factor diagram.

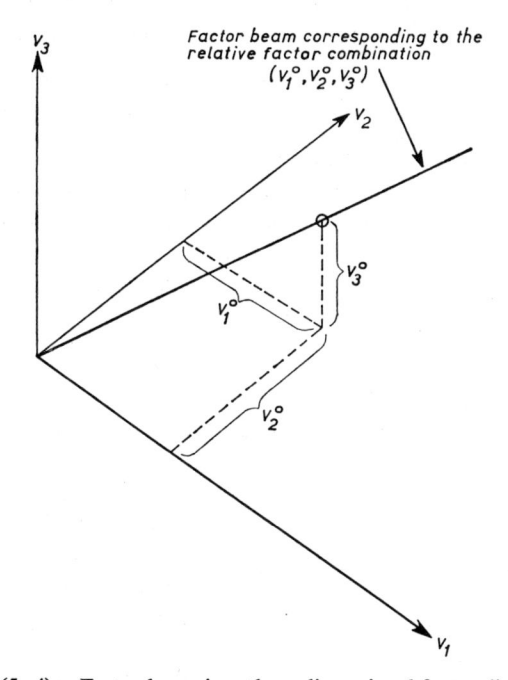

Fig. (5g.4). Factor beam in a three-dimensional factor diagram.

In the case of three factors, the graphic representation will be as shown in Figure (5g.4).

It is of interest for us to study how the product quantity varies along a given factor beam, for example the factor beam corresponding to the relative factor combination $(v_1^0, ..., v_n^0)$. We shall consider this variation as a *continuous process*, i.e. we imagine all factor quantities μ-doubled, as μ is a figure varying continuously between nought and infinity. The passus coefficient may be assumed constant or variable.

The variation of factor quantities in this process is given by the formula

$$(5g.5) \qquad v_i = \mu v_i^0 = v_i(\mu) \qquad (i=1, ... n,)$$

For the variation in the product quantity along this factor beam we shall get

$$(5g.6) \qquad x = x(v_1, ..., v_n) = x(\mu v_1^0, ..., \mu v_n^0) = g(\mu),$$

in which g is the function expressing the variation of the product quantity during the proportional factor variation we are considering.

The magnitude μ is a *scale factor* expressing our position on the given factor beam. Changing μ by 1 per cent, for example, is the same as changing all factor quantities by 1 per cent. The passus coefficient in any point along the factor beam we are considering can therefore be written as

$$(5g.7) \qquad \varepsilon = \frac{dg(\mu)}{d\mu} \cdot \frac{\mu}{g(\mu)} = \frac{d \log g(\mu)}{d \log \mu}$$

during proportional factor variation.

The passus coefficient can thus be regarded as the elasticity of the product quantity with regard to the scale factor μ, cf. what was said about this in Section 5f.

The passus coefficient depends on the factor point, i.e. it is a *local* expression of the existence either of increasing or decreasing average (returns) with an infinitely small change in the production scale. Let us look a little more closely at this question.

The elasticity of the average productivity $\bar{x}_i$ with respect to scale factor μ is

$$\text{El. } \bar{x}_i : \mu = \text{El. } \frac{x}{v_i} : \mu = \text{El. } x : \mu - \text{El. } v_i : \mu.$$

El. $x : \mu$ is according to (5g.7) equal to the passus coefficient and El. v_i is equal to 1, as we have

$$v_i = \mu v_i^0 \quad \text{and} \quad \text{El. } \mu v_i^0 : \mu = \text{El. } \mu : \mu + \text{El. } v_i^0 : \mu = 1 + 0 = 1.$$

Thus we get

(5g.8) $\quad\quad\quad\quad\quad\quad$ El. $\bar{x}_i : \mu = \varepsilon - 1 \quad\quad\quad\quad (i = 1, 2, ..., n)$

This is a preciser way of expressing the statement made in connection with (5f.1): in a factor point where $\varepsilon > 1$ the average productivities $\bar{x}_i$ will for any $i = 1, 2, ..., n$ according to (5g.8), *increase* during an infinitely small increase along the *factor beam*, through the factor point considered, and conversely. Note that *now* we are speaking of a proportional factor variation, whereas in Sections 5d and 5e we were speaking of a partial factor variation.

From (5g.8) it will be seen furthermore that when $\varepsilon = 1$ – and $\varepsilon > 1$ before the point and $\varepsilon < 1$ after the point – all average productivities will reach their *greatest* values during the proportional factor variation which is being considered. We say in such cases that *the production scale is technically optimal*. The way in which these situations are distributed under what we may call a regular ultra-passum law will be dealt with in greater detail in connection with Figure (8.5).

Let $v_1^0, v_2^0, ..., v_n^0$ be a given factor point, and let us see what happens to the product quantity when all factor quantities are multiplied by m, where m is a value of μ which is different from 1 by a finite amount. We still assume that the passus coefficient may be constant or variable.

We can consider ε as a function of μ along the factor beam under consideration. If $h(v_1, ..., v_n)$ is the function expressing the way in which ε depends on the factor point, we get

(5g.9) $\quad\quad\quad \varepsilon = h(v_1, ..., v_n) = h(\mu v_1^0, ..., \mu v_n^0) = \varepsilon(\mu)$.

By substituting (5g.9) in (5g.7) we get

(5g.10) $\quad\quad\quad\quad$ d log $g(\mu) = \varepsilon(\mu)$ d log μ .

If (5g.10) is integrated between $\mu = 1$ and $\mu = m$, we get[1]

$$\log g(m) - \log g(1) = \int_{\mu=1}^{m} \varepsilon(\mu) \, d \log \mu \, .$$

By taking the antilogarithm on both sides of the equation sign (assuming that we have used the natural logarithm system) we get

$$\frac{g(m)}{g(1)} = \exp \left(\int_{\mu=1}^{m} \varepsilon(\mu) \, d \log \mu \right),$$

i.e.

---

[1] As the indefinite integral is $\int d \log g(u) = \log g(u) + C$, where C is an arbitrary constant.

(5g.11) $$g(m) = g(1) \exp\left(\int_{\mu=1}^{m} \varepsilon(\mu) \, d\log\mu\right).$$

Bearing in mind (5g.6), we then get from (5g.11)

(5g.12) $$x(mv_1^0, \ldots, mv_n^0) = x(v_1^0, \ldots, v_n^0) \exp\left(\int_{\mu=1}^{m} \varepsilon(\mu) \, d\log\mu\right).$$

This is the first form of the *beam variation equation*. It applies irrespective of what factor point $(v_1^0, \ldots, v_n^0)$ we take as our point of departure. Furthermore, it is valid for any value of m. That is to say, it is an *identity* in $v_1^0, \ldots, v_n^0$ and m.

The average size of the passus coefficient in the interval between $\mu=1$ and $\mu=m$, $\bar{\varepsilon}$, is defined as follows:

(5g.13) $$\bar{\varepsilon} = \frac{\int_{\mu=1}^{m} \varepsilon(\mu) \, d\log\mu}{\int_{\mu=1}^{m} d\log\mu} \quad \text{(where the factor point } [v_1^0, \ldots, v_n^0] \text{ is given)}.$$

From (5g.13), noting that the indefinite integral

$$\int d\log\mu = \log\mu + D,$$

where D is an arbitrary constant, we get:

$$\int_{\mu=1}^{m} \varepsilon(\mu) \, d\log\mu = \bar{\varepsilon} \int_{\mu=1}^{m} d\log\mu = \bar{\varepsilon}(\log m - \log 1).$$

As $\log 1 = 0$, we get

(5g.14) $$\int_{\mu=1}^{m} \varepsilon(\mu) \, d\log\mu = \bar{\varepsilon} \cdot \log m.$$

From (5g.14) we get furthermore (still assuming that we are using the natural system of logarithms)[1]

(5g.15) $$\exp\left(\int_{\mu=1}^{m} \varepsilon(\mu) \, d\log\mu\right) = \exp(\bar{\varepsilon} \log m) = (e^{\log m})^{\bar{\varepsilon}} = m^{\bar{\varepsilon}}.$$

---

[1] Equation (5g.16) can be derived by using any system of logarithms, provided we keep the same system throughout. Here, however, we use the natural system of logarithms as this will be the simplest.

By substituting (5g.15) in the first form of the beam variation equation (5g.12), we get the important equation

(5g.16) $\quad x(mv_1^0, \ldots, mv_n^0) = x(v_1^0, \ldots, v_n^0) m^{\bar{\varepsilon}}$.

This is the *second form of beam variation equation*. It is an identity in $v_1^0, \ldots, v_n^0$ and m.

Thus, during a proportional factor variation, the effect of the passus coefficient on the product quantity will be expressed as an *exponent* on the *proportionality factor m* which expresses the proportion by which the factors increase.

In practice it will often be possible to make a rough estimate of the average magnitude of the passus coefficient over the interval of variation under consideration, and consequently with the aid of (5g.16) it will be possible to calculate what the effect of multiplying all factor quantities by m will be. If the average size of ε is not calculated exactly according to (5g.13), but in an approximate way, e.g. with the aid of formula (5f.2), the equation (5g.16) will no longer apply precisely, unless ε is a *constant* in the range of factor variation under consideration. In a great many cases, however, the difference will not be appreciable.

5h. Passus equation

From the general marginal increment formula, we get

(5h.1) $\quad dx = x_1' dv_1 + x_2' dv_2 + \ldots + x_n' dv_n$,

where $dv_1, dv_2, \ldots, dv_n$ are arbitrary small (strictly speaking infinitesimal) increments. In the special case involving proportional factor variation all dv_i/v_i are equal. In such cases (5h.1) may be expressed as follows:

$$dx = x_1' v_1 \frac{dv_k}{v_k} + x_2' v_2 \frac{dv_k}{v_k} + \ldots + x_n' v_n \frac{dv_k}{v_k} = (x_1 v_1 + x_2 v_2 + \ldots + x_n v_n) \frac{dv_k}{v_k}$$

where No. k is any arbitrary factor. From this we get

(5h.2) $\quad x \cdot \left[\dfrac{dx/x}{dv_k/v_k} \right] = x_1' v_1 + x_2' v_2 + \ldots + x_n' v_n$.

The square bracket on the left side of (5h.2) is as per our definition the *passus coefficient*, cf. (5f.1), so that we get

(5h.3) $\quad x_1' v + x_2' v_2 + \ldots + x_n' v_n = \varepsilon x$.

This is the *passus equation*. It is valid for every factor point, and provides a very important link between the passus coefficient and the marginal productivities. Note that it is a purely *technical* relation. Also note that it can be used in the study of all kinds of factor variations – proportional or non-proportional – since it is an identity in $v_1, ..., v_n$.

The numerical example in Figure (5h.4), with only two factors, will illustrate what is contained in the passus equation:

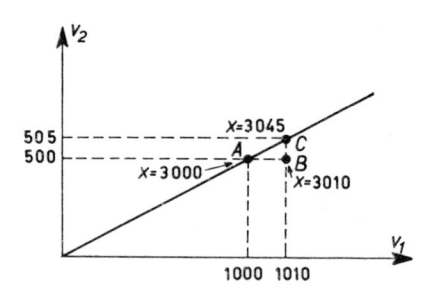

Fig. (5h.4). Passus equation.

From A to B the quantity of factor No. 1 is increased by 1 per cent. At C the quantity of factor No. 2 has also increased 1 per cent. The transition from A to C thus marks a *proportional* variation in the factor quantities, i.e. the relative factor combination is unchanged. This can be seen from the fact that A and C are situated on a factor beam running through origin.

In this transition from A to C the product quantity has increased by 1.5 per cent. Thus the ratio between the percentage increase of the product and the percentage increase of the factors, if we calculate in finite figures, is

$$\varepsilon = \frac{1.5\%}{1.0\%} = 1.5$$

This is the passus coefficient.

Let us now consider the marginal productivities. x_1' can be determined by the transition from A to B, as here only v_1 has been changed. We therefore get

$$x_1' = \frac{3010 - 3000}{1010 - 1000} = \frac{10}{10} = 1.$$

In order to determine x_2' we should consider the transition from B to C, as here only v_2 has been changed. We get

$$x_2' = \frac{3045-3010}{505-500} = \frac{35}{5} = 7.$$

The marginal productivities we have here arrived at do not correspond exactly to the initial combination A. But as the increases in the factors are relatively small, we can accept them as approximate expressions of marginal productivity in the initial combination.

Let us now collate the results:

Marginal productivities $\quad x_1' = 1, \quad x_2' = 7$
Factor quantities $\quad\quad\quad\; v_1 = 1000, \quad v_2 = 500$
Passus coefficient $\quad\quad\quad\; \varepsilon = 1.5$
Product quantity $\quad\quad\quad\;\; x = 3000.$

Thus we see that *the product sum of the factor quantities and the marginal productivities is equal to the passus coefficient multiplied by the product*, in other words

$$1 \times 1000 + 7 \times 500 = 1.5 \times 3000,$$

i.e.,

$$3500 + 1000 = 4500.$$

This is a numerical example of the passus equation.

Another way of arriving at the passus equation is to start from (5g.6). If this equation is differentiated with respect to μ, we get

(5h.5) $$\sum_{i=1}^{n} \frac{\partial x}{\partial v_i} \cdot \frac{dv_i}{d\mu} = \frac{dg(\mu)}{d\mu}.$$

From (5g.5) we see that we have

(5h.6) $$\frac{dv_i}{d\mu} = \frac{d(\mu v_i^0)}{d\mu} = v_i^0.$$

If (5h.6) is inserted in (5h.5), we get

$$\sum_{i=1}^{n} x_i' v_i^0 = \frac{dg(\mu)}{d\mu}.$$

By multiplying by μ on both sides of the equals sign, at the same as we both divide and multiply by x on the righthand side, we get

(5h.7) $$\sum_{i=1}^{n} x_i'(\mu v_i^0) = \frac{dg(\mu)}{d\mu} \cdot \mu = \left(\frac{dg(\mu)}{d\mu} \cdot \frac{\mu}{x}\right) x.$$

By substituting from (5g.5) and (5g.7), we get (5h.3).

A third method of deriving the passus equation is to start off with the first form of the beam variation equation (5g.12) and differentiate it with respect to m. In this way we get

$$(5\text{h}.8) \quad \sum_{i=1}^{n} \frac{\partial x}{\partial (mv_i{}^0)} \cdot \frac{d(mv_i{}^0)}{dm} = x \cdot \frac{d \exp\left(\int_{\mu=1}^{m} \varepsilon(\mu)\, d\log \mu\right)}{dm}$$

By inserting

$$d \log \mu = \left|\frac{1}{\mu}\right| d\mu$$

in the last term on the righthand side in (5h.8), this term becomes

$$(5\text{h}.9) \quad \frac{d\left(\exp \int_{\mu=1}^{m} \frac{1}{\mu} \varepsilon(\mu)\, d\mu\right)}{dm} = \exp\left(\int_{\mu=1}^{m} \frac{1}{\mu} \varepsilon(\mu)\, d\mu\right) \cdot \frac{1}{m} \cdot \varepsilon(m).$$

In Section 5g we found that the first form of the beam variation equation is valid for each and every value of m. Consequently it is also valid for $m=1$. Let us therefore substitute $m=1$ in (5h.8), while at the same time inserting (5h.9) and

$$\frac{d(mv_i{}^0)}{dm} = v_i{}^0$$

into (5h.8). When

$$m=1 \int_{\mu=1}^{m} \frac{1}{\mu} \varepsilon(\mu)\, d\mu = 0,$$

we thus get

$$(5\text{h}.10) \quad \sum_{i=1}^{m} \frac{\partial x}{\partial v_i{}^0} v_i{}^0 = x \cdot e^0 \cdot \frac{1}{1} \varepsilon(1) = x \cdot \varepsilon(1).$$

By putting

$$\frac{\partial x}{\partial v_i} x_i' \text{ and } \varepsilon(1) = h(1 \cdot v_1{}^0, \ldots, 1 \cdot v_n{}^0) = h(v_1{}^0, \ldots, v_n{}^0) \text{ (cf.(5g.10))}$$

in (5h.10), we get

$$\sum_{i=1}^{n} x_i v_i{}^0 = \varepsilon x,$$

DESCRIBING A CONTINUOUS PRODUCTION LAW

where all magnitudes now relate to the factor point $v_1^0, \ldots, v_n^0$. But this point is arbitrary. Thus we get the passus equation (5h.3).

Dividing by x on both sides of (5h.3), we get

$$\frac{x_1' v_1}{x} + \frac{x_2' v_2}{x} + \ldots + \frac{x_n' v_n}{x} = \varepsilon.$$

We know, however, that

$$x_i' v_i / x = \varepsilon_i \quad \text{(cf. 5e.2)}.$$

Therefore:

(5h.11) $$\varepsilon_1 + \varepsilon_2 + \ldots + \varepsilon_n = \varepsilon.$$

In other words, *in any factor point, the passus coefficient is equal to the sum of the marginal elasticities*. This is the passus equation expressed in the form of elasticities. It provides an important link between what happens during partial factor variations (represented by marginal elasticities) and what happens during proportional factor variations (represented by the passus coefficient).

Finally, let us turn to the product functions with a specified analytical form which we presented in Section 5a, and find the passus coefficient in these production laws. For this purpose we shall use the theorem that the passus coefficient is equal to the sum of the marginal elasticities, cf. (5h.11).

Let us first consider (5a.3). Bearing in mind (5e.6)–(5e.8), this will give us:

$$\varepsilon = \varepsilon_1 + \varepsilon_2 + \varepsilon_3$$

(5h.12) $$= (2+2+2) - \frac{4v_1^4 + 4v_2^2 + 4v_3^4}{v_1^4 + v_2^4 + v_3^4} - \frac{\frac{1}{v_1} + \frac{2}{v_2} + \frac{3}{v_3}}{\frac{1}{v_1} + \frac{2}{v_2} + \frac{3}{v_3}}$$

$$= 6 - 4 - 1 = 1.$$

Hence, in the production law (5a.3) the passus coefficient is equal to 1 for every factor combination.

Let us now turn to (5a.4). Bearing in mind (5e.9)–(5e.10), we get:

(5h.13) $$\varepsilon = \varepsilon_1 + \varepsilon_2 = \frac{(24v_1 v_2 - 20v_1^2) + (24v_1 v_2 - 16v_2^2)}{24v_1 v_2 - 10v_1^2 - 8v_2^2}$$

$$= \frac{48v_1 v_2 - 20v_1^2 - 16v_2^2}{24v_1 v_2 - 10v_1^2 - 8v_2^2} = 2.$$

In the production law (5a.4), in fact, the passus coefficient is equal to 2 in every factor point.

Next, let us consider the linear product function (5a.5). With the help of (5e.11) we get:

$$(5h.14) \qquad \varepsilon = \sum_{i=1}^{n} \varepsilon_i = \frac{a_1 v_1 + \ldots + a_n v_n}{a_0 + a_1 v_1 + \ldots + a_n v_n}.$$

If especially $a_0 = 0$, we get

$$(5h.15) \qquad \varepsilon = \frac{a_1 v_1 + \ldots + a_n v_n}{a_1 v_1 + \ldots + a_n v_n} = 1.$$

If the production function is linear, the passus coefficient is thus dependent on all factor quantities, unless the constant term is equal to 0. If the latter is the case, the passus coefficient is equal to 1 for every factor combination.

Finally let us consider the Cobb-Douglas function, (5a.6). With the help of (5e.12) we get

$$(5h.16) \qquad \varepsilon = \sum_{i=1}^{n} \varepsilon_i = \sum_{i=1}^{n} \alpha_i.$$

In this special case, the passus coefficient is always constant, and independent of the factor point which is being considered. It is simply the sum of the exponents constituting the function.

5i. Further details concerning isoquants and isoclines

In Section 5a we defined an *isoquant* as the locus of factor points where the product quantity has a constant magnitude. Thus, the equation for the isoquant corresponding to the product quantity x_0 will be

$$(5i.1) \qquad x(v_1, \ldots, v_n) = x_0.$$

(5i.1) is *one* equation between the n factor quantities $v_1, \ldots, v_n$. (5i.1) thus represents an $(n-1)$-dimensional manifold in the n-dimensional factor diagram. In a case involving only *two* factors, the isoquants will thus be *curves*, cf. Figure (5a.14), and Figure (5a.15); in a case with *three* factors they will be *surfaces*, and if there are more than three factors, they are 'hyper-surfaces'.

We shall now consider in greater detail the form of the isoquants in a case involving two factors. Equation (5i.1) then becomes

$$(5i.2) \qquad x(v_1, v_2) = x_0.$$

Equation (5i.2) defines *implicitly* v_2 as a function of v_1 along the isoquant for $x = x_0$, cf. Figure (5i.4).
Thus:

(5i.3) $$v_2 = v_2(v_1)$$

(along the isoquant corresponding to $x = x_0$).

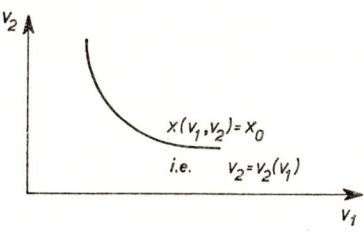

Fig. (5i.4).

We can thus write (5i.2) as

(5i.5) $$x(v_1, v_2(v_1)) = x_0 \, . \quad \text{(identically in } v_1\text{)}$$

As we are interested in the inclination existing along an isoquant, we must look at $dv_2(v_1)/dv_1$ along the isoquant in question. By total implicit differentiation of (5i.5), with respect to v_1, we get:

$$\frac{\partial x}{\partial v_1} + \frac{\partial x}{\partial v_2} \cdot \frac{dv_2(v_1)}{dv_1} = 0,$$

i.e.

$$x_1' + x_2' \cdot \frac{dv_2}{dv_1} = 0 \, .$$

Thus:

(5i.6) $$\frac{dv_2}{dv_1} = - \frac{x_1'}{x_2'} \quad \text{along an isoquant.}$$

(5i.6) applies to any isoquant.

In the interior of the substitution region (cf. Section 5b) both x_1' and x_2' are, as per definition, strictly positive. Consequently here $dv_2/dv_1 < 0$. *Thus in a case involving two factors the isoquants are on the decrease everywhere in the interior of the substitution region.*

From (5i.6), furthermore, we observe that the numerical value of the tangent steepness for the isoquant is equal to the substitution ratio, cf.

---

[1] If the two functional shapes $x(v_1, v_2)$ and $v_2(v_1)$ had been independent of each other, (5i.5) would have been an equation which defines a specific value of v_1. Actually this is not so, (5i.5) has a degree of freedom and serves to define the shape of the function $v_2(v_1)$ when the shape of $v_2(v_1)$ is given.

(5b.9). In other words: *the slope of the tangent to the isoquant through a given factor point expresses the substitution relationship in the factor point concerned.*

In Section 5b we defined an *isocline* as the locus for the factor points where the ratios between marginal productivities were constant. With the help of (5i.6), in the case involving two factors, we can construct a given isocline in the following manner: Select the tangent slope corresponding to the given proportion x_1'/x_2', plot its direction in the factor diagram, and construct a series of parallels tangential to the various isoquants. Mark the tangential points. With the slope selected in Figure (5i.7) we shall get the tangential points R, R', R'', etc. A curve running through these points is an isocline.

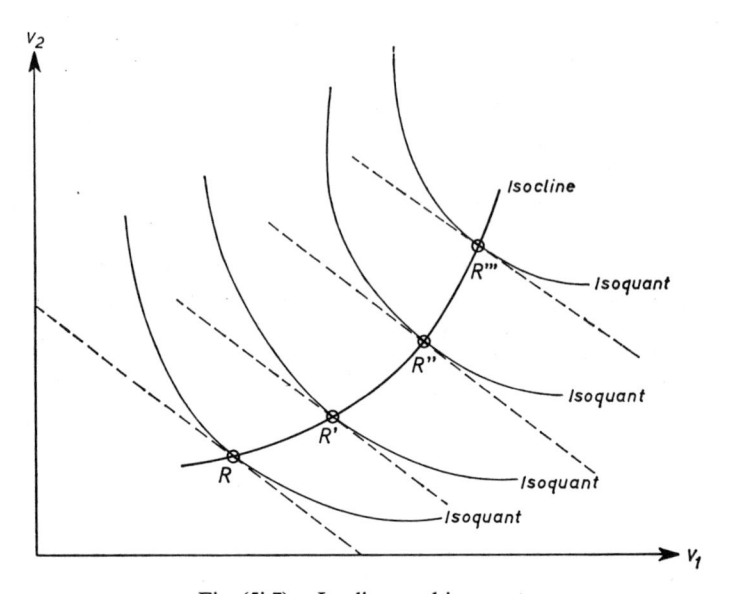

Fig. (5i.7). Isoclines and isoquants.

We are also interested in investigating the *curvature on the isoquants*. For this purpose we must consider $d^2 v_2(v_1)/dv_1^2$ along an isoquant. If this second derivative is positive, the isoquant curves towards origin. We get

$$\frac{d^2 v_2(v_1)}{dv_1^2} = \frac{d\left(\dfrac{dv_2(v_1)}{dv_1}\right)}{dv_1} = \frac{d\left(-\dfrac{x_1'[v_1, v_2(v_1)]}{x_2'[v_1, v_2(v_1)]}\right)}{dv_1}$$

$$= -\frac{x_2' \cdot \left(\dfrac{\partial x_1'}{\partial v_1} + \dfrac{\partial x_1'}{\partial v_2} \cdot \dfrac{dv_2}{dv_1}\right) - x_1' \left(\dfrac{\partial x_2'}{\partial v_1} + \dfrac{\partial x_2'}{\partial v_2} \cdot \dfrac{dv_2}{dv_1}\right)}{(x_2')^2}.$$

DESCRIBING A CONTINUOUS PRODUCTION LAW

By inserting from (5i.b) for dv_2/dv_1 we furthermore get

$$\frac{d^2 v_2(v_1)}{dv_1^2} = -\frac{x_2'[x_{11}''+x_{12}''\cdot(-x_1'/x_2')]-x_1'[x_{21}''+x_{22}''\cdot(-x_1'/x_2')]}{(x_2')^2}$$

$$= -\frac{1}{(x_2')^3}[(x_2')^2 x_{11}'' - x_1'\cdot x_2' x_{12}'' - x_1' x_2' x_{21}'' + (x_1')^2 x_{22}''].$$

Viz.:

(5i.8) $\qquad \dfrac{d^2 v_2(v_1)}{dv_1^2} = -\dfrac{1}{(x_2')^3}[(x_2')^2 x_{11}'' - 2x_1' x_2' x_{12}'' + (x_1')^2 x_{22}'']$

(along an isoquant).

Equation (5i.8) can also be written in the form:

(5i.9) $\qquad \dfrac{d^2 v_2(v_1)}{dv_1^2} = \dfrac{1}{(x_2')^3}\cdot D,$

where

$$D = \begin{vmatrix} 0 & x_1' & x_2' \\ x_1' & x_{11}'' & x_{12}'' \\ x_2' & x_{21}'' & x_{22}'' \end{vmatrix}$$

The correctness of (5i.9) will immediately be obvious if we expand the determinant D according to the first row.

We then get:

$$D = -x_1' \begin{vmatrix} x_1' & x_{12}'' \\ x_2' & x_{22}'' \end{vmatrix} + x_2' \begin{vmatrix} x_1' & x_{11}'' \\ x_2' & x_{21}'' \end{vmatrix}$$

$$= (-x_1')(x_1' x_{22}'' - x_2' x_{12}'') + x_2'(x_1' x_{21}'' - x_2' x_{11}'')$$

$$= -(x_1')^2 x_{22}'' + 2x_1' x_2' x_{12}'' - (x_2')^2 x_{11}''.$$

According to our definition, both x_1' and x_2' are positive in the substitution region. *Thus in the case involving two factors a necessary and sufficient condition for the isoquants being curved towards origin in the interior of the substitution area is that*

(5i.10) $\qquad D = \begin{vmatrix} 0 & x_1' & x_2' \\ x_1' & x_{11}'' & x_{12}'' \\ x_2' & x_{21}'' & x_{22}'' \end{vmatrix} > 0.$

In the general case involving n production factors, we get the following condition for isoquant 'surfaces' being curved towards origin in the interior of the substitution area:

(5i.11) $$(-1)^k \begin{vmatrix} 0 & x_1' & \ldots & x_k' \\ x_1' & x_{11}'' & \ldots & x_{1k}'' \\ \vdots & & & \\ x_k' & x_{k1}'' & \ldots & x_{kk}'' \end{vmatrix} > 0 \quad \text{(for all } k=2, 3 \ldots, n\text{)}.$$

The proof for (5i.11) has been omitted.

Finally, let us consider one of the production functions with a specified analytical form that we introduced in Section 5a, viz. (5a.4), and see whether the isoquants in this production law are curved towards origin.

By substituting for the accelerations from (5c.5)–(5c.7) we get the following expression for D, cf. (5i.10):

$$D = -(x_1')^2(-16) + 2 \cdot x_1' \cdot x_2' \cdot 24 - (x_2')^2(-20)$$
$$= 16(x_1')^2 + 48 x_1' x_2' + 20(x_2')^2 .$$

In the interior of the substitution region both x_1' and x_2' are positive. Consequently D is positive in the interior of the substitution region. Thus, in the production law (5a.4) the isoquants are curved towards origin in the interior of the substitution region (cf. (5i.10)).

CHAPTER 6

THE TECHNICAL OPTIMUM LAW WHEN CONSIDERING PARTIAL VARIATION OF A FACTOR OR A GROUP OF FACTORS

In the preceding chapter we have dealt with various methods of describing a continuous production law, but we have given no detailed account of *the shape it actually possesses*. This is the question we shall now deal with.

6a. History of some basic concepts

The beginnings of a production theory in the modern sense of the word are to be found in the investigations on *the diminishing returns from land*. These investigations have one feature in common with earlier discussions, viz. their object is in both cases to throw some light on the *distribution* of national income among the various groups of income earners. Both Ricardo (born 1772) and Von Thünen (born 1783) – two of the leading authorities in this field – dealt with the subject of production in connection with their attempt to explain the level of rent, wages, and interest.

In two respects, however, the new theory of production differs from the preceding one. In the first place the new theory aims at a far more exact and *quantitative* formulation of the regularities which apply. Investigators such as Ricardo and Von Thünen, for example, studied in great detail the way in which the actual size of the production result varied, when the size of the productive inputs vary, and they not only did this in the abstract, but based their finding on concrete observations. Von Thünen, for example, kept meticulous notes on crop returns, costs, etc., at his Tellow estate in Mecklenburg over a great many years. In this respect he is an outstanding representative of the 'econometric' treatment of economic problems.

In the second place Ricardo and Von Thünen introduced the *marginal* approach: they are particularly concerned with the *increase* in the product quantity which results whenever the magnitude of a certain productive input undergoes a certain *increase*. This approach is a very fruitful one, illuminating as it does a great many questions which would remain unanswered, as long as one merely considered each of the magnitudes involved *as a whole*. There is, for instance, little point in enquiring what the productivity of the land would be without work, or vice versa. But new and fruitful vistas are opened up when one enquires: By how much will the product quantity increase if – taking our starting point in a certain situation – we increase the application of work by a certain quantity. This leads us to the concept of marginal productivity[1], which plays such an important role in modern theory. The principle of marginal productivity has, it is true, been stretched too far by certain writers. Deductions based on it have been invested with a *universal validity*, which on closer inspection has proved non-existent. This, however, should not blind us to the fact that in a great many cases this principle is a very fruitful, nay indispensable, one.

Let us consider a few examples of Ricardo's and Von Thünen's application of the principle. In his observations on rent Ricardo[2] reasons as follows. Assuming that we have four portions of capital, and that by applying the first of these to a certain piece of land we achieve a product quantity of 100, by applying the second (on the same piece of land) we achieve a product increase of 90, from the third a product increase of 80, and from the fourth 70. In a case of this kind we are getting *diminishing* returns. The rent (calculated in product units) would in a case such as this be 60, according to Ricardo; since it is the difference between what in fact has been produced and what would have been produced if all four portions of capital had produced the same yield *as the last* (the marginal principle). In the example this difference is $30+20+10=60$. It can also be expressed as $340-280=60$.

Von Thünen went further than Ricardo, in so far as he studied the marginal productivity of labour and capital separately. As an example of the marginal productivity of labour, he shows how the crop yield from a field of potatoes can be increased by using more days' work for picking. See Table (6a.1).[3]

If the price of potatoes is 5, and the daily working wage 8, then, according to Von Thünen, it would be worth while making use of the eighth day's work, but not the ninth, as the eighth day's work produces an increase in the value of the product of $2 \times 5 = 10$, viz. more than a day's wage, while the ninth day's work merely produces an increase in the product value of $1.3 \times 5 = 6.50$, viz. less than a day's wage. Making a more exact adjustment, involving the use of fractions of a day's work, the application of labour must stop at a

---

[1] Cf. (5b.1).
[2] 'On the Principles of Political Economy and Taxation'. Here quoted from *The Works of David Ricardo*, McCulloch's edition, London, 1846, p. 42.
[3] Johann Heinrich von Thünen, *Der isolierte Staat in Beziehung auf Landwirtschaft und Nationalökonomie*, zweite Auflage, Jena 1921, p. 570.

THE TECHNICAL OPTIMUM LAW

TABLE (6a.1)

Number of days' work used for picking potatoes	The quantity of potatoes harvested	The last day's work has thus produced (marginal productivity)
4	80	
5	86.6	6.6
6	91	4.4
7	94	3.0
8	96	2.0
9	97.3	1.3
10	98.2	0.9
11	98.8	0.6
12	99.2	0.4

point where exact equality exists between a day's wage and the increase in the product value (marginal productivity) created by the work. According therefore to Von Thünen, the work has *its wage determined by its marginal productivity*.

In a similar way he analyses capital and its marginal productivity.[1] He gives the following example (see Table (6a.2)):

TABLE (6a.2)

Capital quantity applied (per worker)	Product quantity (per worker)	Marginal productivity of the capital	Total wages accruing to capital	Remainder (accruing to the worker in the form of wages)
4	247.6			
5	273.9	26.3	131.5	142.4
6	297.6	23.7	142.2	155.4
7	318.9	21.3	149.1	169.8
8	338.1	19.2	153.6	184.5

In the case of capital, too, the rule applies, he says, that its use must stop at the point where the price one has to pay for it is equal to its marginal productivity. Thus according to Von Thünen capital, too, has its reward determined by marginal productivity. There is an apparent contradiction between the *residual* determination of working wages and the *marginal*, which he develops with the aid of the example in Table (6a.1). Von Thünen, however, shows that the two methods of determination *are bound to lead to the same result*.

---

[1] *Op. cit.*, p. 507.

Von Thünen's reasoning is based on a definite presupposition, which can easily be explained with the aid of the passus equation (5h.3). Take for example factor No. 1. If the wage is determined *marginally*, it will be equal to x_1', calculated in product units per unit of the factor concerned, viz. altogether equal to $x_1' v_1$ product units as wages for factor No. 1. If the wages paid for the factor are determined *residually*, it will – still calculated in terms of product units – be equal to

$$x - \sum_{i=2}^{n} x_i' v_i,$$

provided that all the *other* factors have their reward determined marginally. The difference between the residual and the marginal determination of the reward for factor No. 1 will thus be

$$x - \sum_{i=2}^{n} x_i' v_i - x_1' v_1,$$

i.e. it will be equal to

$$x - \sum_{i=1}^{n} x_i' v_i,$$

which according to the passus equation (5h.3) is equal to $(1-\varepsilon)x$. Thus if all factors Nos. 2, 3, ..., n have their reward marginally determined, factor No. 1 will have the *same* reward marginally as residually, when – and only when – production ceases at a factor point such that $\varepsilon = 1$.

AGRICULTURAL CHEMISTS

In the course of the nineteenth century the decreasing yield of the soil has been studied in greater detail and experimentally by *agricultural chemists*, such as Justus von Liebig, Mitscherlich, and others. In these physical and chemical investigations the posing of the problems varied somewhat, as one tended to move away from the *macro* point of view, which was at the basis of Ricardo's and Von Thünen's analysis, viz. work and capital conceived as two large categories of productive inputs whose distribution quotas had to be determined, and over to the *micro* point of view, which operates with a great many production factors, each of them specified in technical detail, such as is necessary if these are to be included in exact physical-chemical experiments.

As an example we can take the following, which has been borrowed from Mitscherlich.[1]

[1] Here quoted after Paul Borgedal, *Intensitetsproblemet i det norske jordbruk*. Fredrikstad, 1926, p. 39.

TABLE (6a.3)

Addition of phosphorated lime (grammes)	Using 600 gr of water		Using 1200 gr. of water	
	Total yield of oats	Product increase per added gram of lime (marginal productivity for lime)	Total yield of oats	Product increase per added gram of lime (marginal productivity for lime)
0.000	4.9		9.2	
0.114	12.6	67.5	21.4	107.5
0.229	20.1	65.2	31.6	88.7
0.458	26.5	27.9	47.2	68.1
0.916	37.2	23.4	64.2	37.1
1.832	44.9	8.4	70.5	6.9
3.664	48.2	1.8	78.5	4.4

By reading down Table (6a.3) we can see how the yield of oats varies as the addition of phosphorated lime varies, while the other factor quantities remain constant. It will be seen that marginal productivity is decreasing. The table also contains interesting information with regard to another product factor, viz. water. The variation in the marginal productivity for lime is, as we can see by comparing the third with the fifth column, different according as the addition of water is large or small. If we compare the *figures horizontally* from the second to the fourth column, we shall see how the crop of oats changes as the addition of water is changed, while the addition of lime remains constant. This gives us the marginal productivity for water, while the vertical variation for the figures provides the marginal productivity for lime.

MULTI-DIMENSIONAL VARIATION AND THE OPTIMUM LAW.
ECONOMISTS ROUND THE TURN OF THE CENTURY

The example quoted from Mitscherlich illustrates two of the factors on which the crop of oats depends. Naturally there are in reality a number of other factors; and each of them can be subjected to a similar analysis, as was done in the case of lime in the example quoted above. Furthermore, it would also be of interest to investigate the changes that take place if several factors are varied *simultaneously* in certain prescribed manners. Generally speaking, as already noted at the end of Section 5a, this leads us to a consideration of *multi-dimensional* variations. This also applies even if we endeavour to define each factor as far as possible by the macro-approach. Even in this case, we get, as a general rule, several factors ('raw material', 'labour', 'consumption of energy', 'wear and tear of machinery', 'administration', etc.). The study of multi-dimensional variations of this kind constitutes the chief subject of the modern theory of production. The difficulty involved in these problems is nearly always to be found in the need for taking several factors into account simultaneously.

Of economists who have tackled production problems – especially those encountered in the doctrine of distribution – on the basis of a multi-factor approach, may be mentioned Philip H. Wicksteed[1], John B. Clark[2], Leon Walras[3], Knut Wicksell[4], and Alvin Johnson[5]. In most of these presentations recourse has been had to mathematics.

Through the investigations carried out by these authors and agricultural chemists, it has been shown that the law of diminishing returns is in fact only one *stage* in a more general law which states that to begin with one gets an increasing return, until a certain *optimum* is reached, and only then does one get diminishing returns. The more precise form of this law will be investigated below.

6b. Detailed analysis of the technical optimum law as it appears when we consider the partial variation of a factor

Empirical investigations into a number of different production processes shows that production as a rule passes through a stage of rising and then a stage of diminishing *returns*, if we vary a single factor while allowing the others to remain constant. Thus we shall get a typical *optimum law*. And it is possible to recognise this law in practically every sphere of agriculture as well as of industry.

As an illustration let us turn to Table (5a.10). If we keep land (factor No. 2) constant = 10 dekars, and increase the application of labour (factor No. 1), we shall get the sequence of figures given in the first column. This is graphically represented by the upper curve in Figure (6b.1). We have on purpose omitted the part of the curve which pertains to extremely small magnitudes of v_1, as it will in practice often prove difficult to decide how to interpret the product quantity and its variation if an extremely small quantity of a particular factor is applied. The product quantity rises to the point given by labour quantity = 10. Here the table ends. In Figure (6b.1), however, the curve has been continued in order to include an illustration of its remaining

---

[1] *An Essay in the Co-ordination of the Laws of Distribution*, 1894.
[2] *The Distribution of Wealth*, 1899.
[3] *Éléments de l'économie politique*, 4th edition, Paris, 1900. See especially pp. 371–385.
[4] *Föreläsningar i Nationalökonomi*, Häft 1, 3d edition, Lund, 1928, pp. 102–103.
[5] 'The Pure Theory of Utility Curves', *Economic Journal*, 1913.

course. Point $v_1 = 10$ is assumed to be the *maximum*, i.e. the greatest product quantity which can possibly be achieved by varying factor No. 1, while keeping the other factors constant. If more of No. 1 is added, the result will only be *detrimental*, and the total product quantity will start to decrease. In principle it is even conceivable that by adding a sufficient quantity of the factor it will finally be possible *to prevent all production*. In the example given it might be imagined that this has happened when so many workers are employed that there is not even sufficient 'standing room' left in the field. Similarly: if we are dealing with manure, it is undoubtedly possible to spread such a thick layer of a particular substance on the ground that all growth would be prevented. The point where a factor is added in such a quantity that no product is obtained, we call *strangulation point* for the factor concerned. The strangulation point is thus characterised by $x = 0$. In practice it will generally occupy an extreme position.

Let us consider a little more closely the *manner* in which the total product curve rises or falls. This will be characterised by *marginal productivity* x_1'.[1] The manner of variation for x_1', when v_1 increases (while the remaining factors kept are constant) is given by the dotted line in the top part of the figure. To start with there is a stage of *increasing marginal productivity*. That is to say, the total product is *progressively* increasing, and thus the acceleration x_{11}'' is positive.[2] In the curve for the total product this finds expression in an *upward* bend. This first stage lasts as far as to the *marginal top point* (see figure), i.e. the point where the marginal productivity reaches its maximum, thus where $x_{11}'' = 0$. From this point the marginal productivity x_1' begins to decrease, while total product continues to rise, though *degressively*. This continues as far as to the *maximum point*, viz. where total product assumes its greatest magnitude. Thus this point is characterised by x = the greatest quantity possible (when v_2 remains constant = 10 dekar and v_1 alone varies), and at the same time is characterised by the fact that the marginal productivity curve here passes zero, viz. $x_1' = 0$, after which it remains negative.

To the left of this point we say that the variable factor, here No. 1, is applied *technically submaximally*, in the point itself *technically maximally* and to the right of the point *technically super-maximally*; or we can say that the factor is *technically submaximal, maximal, or super-maximal*.

These concepts are here defined by considering the whole shape of the total product curve which we obtain by varying a single factor. It is, however,

[1] Cf. 5b.
[2] Cf. 5c.

obvious that the criterion we have used can also be formulated as a local criterion applicable to *any point whatever in the factor diagram*. If we quite generally take any point whatever $v_1, \ldots, v_n$ in the factor diagram, we can ask whether the product quantity in this point rises or falls with an increase in the quantity of a definite factor, e.g. No. k, all other factors remaining constant. The criterion for this is whether the marginal productivity x_k' is positive or negative in the factor point concerned. Cf. the explanation in connection with (5b.1).

Let us now turn back to Figure (6b.1). How will the marginal productivity

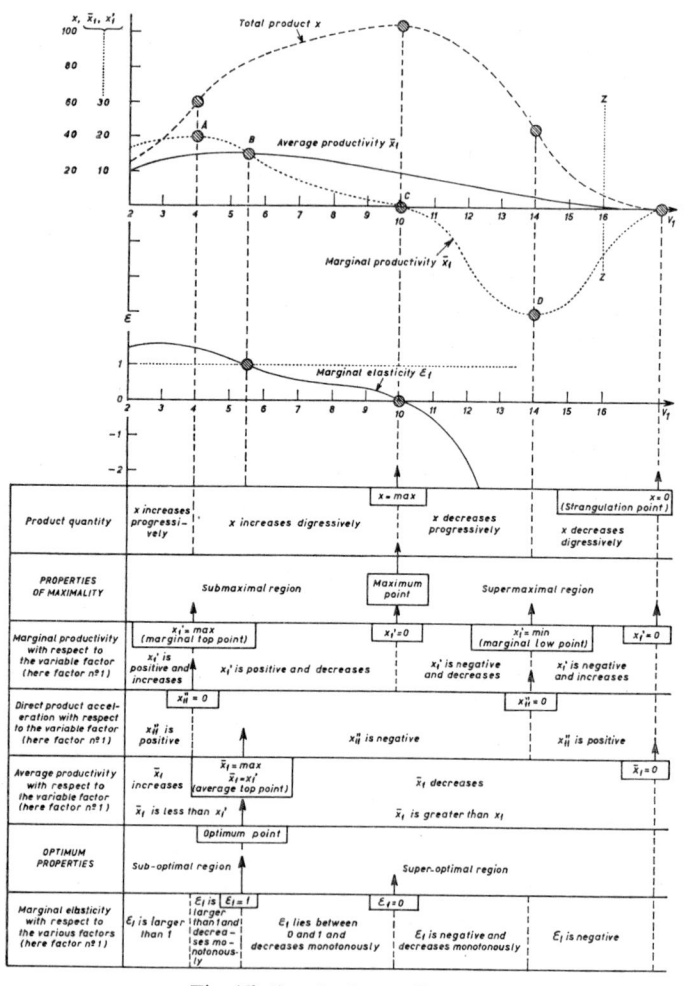

Fig. (6b.1). Optimum Curves.

evolve after the maximum point has been passed? This is tantamount to asking *how* the product quantity moves towards the strangulation point. In practice, this question is of minor importance, but it has a certain theoretical interest. As a rule it would not be plausible to assume that the product quantity could be negative; in certain cases it is possible that a concept of this kind could be entertained, but not as a general rule. If the product quantity is not to become negative, and if the movement is to take place in a continuous manner, it means that the product curve must approach the strangulation point in such a way that it here has a horizontal tangent. If the tangent in the strangulation point pointed downwards and at the same time the total product was not to be negative, the curve of total product would show a *break* at the strangulation point; i.e., if the transition is to be continuous, *the marginal productivity must again be zero in the strangulation point*. As the marginal productivity has been negative in a part of the super-maximal region (otherwise total product could never have been reduced to zero), this means that the marginal productivity in the latter part of this region must *rise* in order to reach zero. In other words, it must have had a low-point, which we call the *marginal low point* for the factor. See Figure (6b.1). It is hardly probable that in any concrete case it would be possible to have several rising and falling branches of the marginal productivity curve in the super-maximal region. As a rule the tendency will be towards the simple picture suggested in Figure (6b.1). Thus the total product in the supermaximal region will first decrease *progressively* and then *degressively*.

As both the region near the origin, viz. the region where only an infinitesimal quantity of the factor is used, and the region near the strangulation point are of little practical significance, and furthermore as we know very little about them, it would perhaps be more correct to exclude the extreme right portion of Figure (6b.1), e.g. after the line *ZZ*, and consider only what is left. This, in fact, is what we shall now do. We shall then see that the super-maximal region is to a certain extent a *catoptric or reflected image of the submaximal region*. This applies both to the total product curve and to the marginal productivity curve.

Let us then consider *the average productivity*[1] with respect to the variable factor in Figure (6b.1), viz. $\bar{x}_1 = x/v_1$. In the first stage, viz. where marginal productivity x_1' rises, average productivity $\bar{x}_1$ is also rising. And it continues to rise for a while even after marginal productivity has begun to fall. It is

[1] Cf. 5d.

immediately obvious that this must be so: it will be most easily understood if we consider an average magnitude in a statistical mass (e.g. the average size of persons in a population group). If we gradually add one unit at a time, and these units constantly have *increasing* magnitudes, it is obvious that this will constantly *raise the average*. In fact the average is bound to continue increasing even for some time after the newly added units have started to decrease, as the average will rise as long as only the last added unit *is larger than the average already existing*. In Figure (6b.1) this is expressed by the fact that the curve for average productivity continues to rise some time after the marginal top point has been passed. *The average productivity curve reaches its maximum precisely at the point where this curve and the marginal productivity curve intersect.* We call this point *optimum*, or more precisely, the optimum for factor No. 1. This point shows two marked characteristics: in the first place average productivity for No. 1, $\bar{x}_1$, is as great here as it can be when only No. 1 is a variable and v_2 remains constant (and equal to 10 dekars), and secondly in this point marginal productivity for No. 1 is equal to average productivity with respect to No. 1. In this point we may say that factor No. 1 is *technically optimal*, or, that it is *applied technically optimally*. See Formula (5d.4), which states that the necessary first order condition for the maximum of $\bar{x}_i$ with respect to a partial variation of v_i is $x_1' = \bar{x}_i$.

In practice there will practically always be a point possessing this property. The entire range will then be divided into two clearly separate regions:

I) In the left region the marginal productivity curve lies *above* the average productivity curve. Here, in accordance with (5d.6), there will exist an *increasing average return* of factor No. 1. We say that the factor is technically *sub-optimal*, or that it is applied technically suboptimally in this region. That a factor is applied technically suboptimally is thus tantamount to saying that there exists an increasing average return for the factor.

II) In the right region the marginal productivity curve lies *below* the average productivity. In accordance with (5d.6) there will be a *decreasing average return* with respect to factor No. 1 at this point. We say that the factor is technically *super-optimal* or that it is applied technically superoptimally in this region. The fact that a factor is applied technically superoptimally is thus tantamount to saying that there exists a diminishing average return for the factor.

We have defined what is meant by saying that a factor is submaximal or super-maximal. It is similarly of interest to express *to what extent* it is submaximal and super-maximal. If the position of the strangulation point were accurately known, this definition might be established by considering the deviation of the factor quantity from the factor quantity applicable in the maximum point, and then expressing this deviation as a percentage of the length of the distance between the maximum point and the strangulation point. But in practice, we shall never know the position of the strangulation point accurately; besides, a criterion of this kind, even if it could be obtained, would not express the situation in terms of how the product *varies at the various stages*, and this is fundamentally what is of greatest interest. A thought that immediately presents itself, consequently, is to use the *magnitude* of marginal productivity as a criterion, since we already took its zero point as a means of determining the actual maximum point. But this way, too, is not acceptable: in the first place because, as we can see from the figure, marginal productivity does not vary monotonically, and secondly because the question of units of measurement crops up. If, for example, we start measuring the quantity of factor No. 1 with another unit of measurement, the figure measuring marginal productivity will be altered.

We can avoid both difficulties by taking *marginal elasticity* (cf. Section 5e). In the first place it is independent of the unit of measurement; and in the second place it will as a rule have a monotonic course. Its course in Figure (6b.1) is given by the curve in the central portion of the figure. It constitutes throughout the ratio between the ordinate of the curve x_1' and the ordinate of the curve $\bar{x}_1$.[1] Thence it follows that ε_1 is, to start with, larger than 1, and that after a certain lapse of time it passes first 1 and then 0 (which characterises the location of the maximum point).[2] These three levels, which occur in a descending order, are immediately apparent from the assumption that the marginal productivity curve falls monotonically between A and D, and that the average productivity curve lies beneath the marginal productivity curve at A. On the basis of the assumptions referred to we can also make some other remarks.

Consider the formula

(6b.2) $$\frac{\partial \varepsilon_1}{\partial v_1} = \varepsilon_1 \left(\frac{x_1''}{x_1'} + \frac{1-\varepsilon_1}{v_1} \right)$$

which can easily be deduced by first elasticising the expression $\varepsilon_1 = x_1' v_1'/x$ partially with respect to v_1 and then multiplying the result by ε_1/v_1. This formula shows that between the marginal top point A and the optimum

---
[1] Cf. (5e.2).
[2] In the maximum point $x_1' = 0$. When $x_1' = 0$, it follows that $\varepsilon_1 = 0$, cf. the end of Section 5e.

point B, ε_1 must be monotically decreasing, as both terms in the square bracket above are negative. For a similar reason ε_1 must be monotonically decreasing between the maximum point C and the marginal low point D.

If we assume no more than that the marginal productivity for factor No. 1 is to be monotonically decreasing between marginal top point A and marginal low point D, and that the average productivity lies beneath marginal productivity in the marginal top point A, we cannot make any more detailed conclusion with regard to the course of marginal elasticity ε_1. It is, however, plausible to assume that ε_1 is monotonically decreasing also in the interval between optimum point B and maximum point C. In practice it is particularly this region which is of interest. That a supplementary presupposition of this kind in no wise runs counter to our other pre-suppositions, emerges from the fact that it is easy to construct examples embodying these properties. An example of this kind is found in Figure (6b.1). As a characteristic feature of the technical optimum law with partial variation of a factor, we shall therefore assume that marginal elasticity for the variable factor decreases monotonically between marginal top point A and marginal low point D. Taking marginal elasticity as a criterion, we can say that *a factor is strongly super-maximal when its marginal elasticity is negative and numerically large, and we say that it is strongly sub-maximal when it is positive and numerically large.*

The criterion for sub-optimality or super-optimality, too, can be expressed with the aid of marginal elasticity ε_1, and here it becomes still more evident that it is highly plausible to use marginal elasticity as a criterion for the various stages. In this case it is the magnitude in relation to 1 that is decisive.

In (5e.4) we saw that there exists an increasing average return for factor No. 1 when $\varepsilon_i > 1$ and that there exists a decreasing average return for factor No. 1 when $\varepsilon_i < 1$. The fact that an increasing average return for a factor exists is, however, tantamount to saying that the factor has been applied technically sub-optimally, and the fact that there exists a decreasing average return for a factor is tantamount to saying that the factor has been applied technically super-optimally. *Thus, whenever $\varepsilon_i > 1$, factor No. 1 is technically sub-optimal and whenever $\varepsilon_i < 1$, factor No. 1 is technically super-optimal.*

With the help of ε_1 we can also say something about the *extent* to which a factor is sub-optimal or super-optimal. If ε_i is *a great deal more than 1*, factor No. *i* is *applied strongly sub-optimally*. We then get *strongly* increasing average returns (with partial variation of v_i). Conversely, if ε_i is *a great deal under 1*. Remember that a *large* ε_i (not a small ε_i) shows sub-optimality –

because average yield would then be on the decrease. It is easy to make a mistake here.

We have thus expressed both the criterion of maximality and optimality by means of a simple parameter, whose concrete significance is easily understood. The shape of the ε_1-curve (in the central portion of Figure (6b.1)) thus contains *in concentrated form information on the various stages of production, both with regard to its point of maximum and its point of optimum*. The levels $\varepsilon_1 = 1$ and $\varepsilon_1 = 0$ are decisive.

Above, in Figure (6b.1) and the text dealing with it, we have characterised the optimum law by the shape of the curve for marginal productivity and average productivity, and assumed that marginal elasticity decreases monotonically in the entire region between marginal top point A and marginal low point D. If we wish to operate with a minimum of presuppositions, we need only presuppose that the marginal productivity curve falls monotonically in the interval between marginal top point A and *maximum point* C, and that the curve for average productivity lies beneath the curve for marginal productivity in A. In principle, however, it would be more natural to include in our analysis the entire interval between A and D. That this would be a more natural approach is evident *inter alia* in the discussion regarding the dual optimum law for one factor in the case of a pari passu law for two factors; cf. the end of Section 7c.

The production stages we have here described are ones we shall come across practically everywhere when *a single factor varies*, while the quantities of the other factors are kept constant. And we shall, as a general rule, recognise these stages within one and the same production, *no matter which factor is regarded as the variable. We can say that the optimum law cuts through the product function in every direction*, viz. in n directions if there are n factors. The example in (5a.11) is constructed in this manner. Let, for instance, $v_1 = \text{constant} = 5$ and $v_3 = \text{constant} = 1$, while v_2 varies. Marginal productivity will then first rise and then fall, finally becoming negative. The figures are 44, 58, 45, 12, -15, -24, -24, -21, -16. The average returns are 21, 32.5, 41, 42, 36, 27.5, 20.2, 14.6, 10.7, 8. Thus marginal top-point occurs at $v_2 = 3$, while there is an increasing average return for No. 2 all the way to $v_2 = 4$. If we choose $v_2 = \text{constant} = 7$, $v_3 = \text{constant} = 7$, and allow v_1 to vary, marginal productivity will be 156, 210, 280, 279, 238, 151, 49, -35, -93. In these cases we have been able to follow either a column or a line in the table. If v_3 is varied, we must start at one end of the table and move towards the other end, reading off the figures that correspond to each other. The optimum law for $v_1 = \text{constant} = 6$, $v_2 = \text{constant} = 4$ is for instance characterised by a product sequence 134, 318, 529, 722, 838, 849, 782, 680, 575, 482, and a corresponding marginal productivity sequence of 184, 211, 193, 116, 11, −67, −102, −105, −93. Thus in all three directions we get the typical course of marginal productivity which is given by the dotted line in the upper part of Figure (6b.1) and by the average return which is given by the fully drawn curve. And we shall find the same no matter which part of Table (5a.11) we choose (though for a few extreme magnitudes of the constant factors the table only gives a small portion of the curves). It is obvious that it is not possible to construct a three-dimensional table which possesses such a typical course in all directions, merely by writing down figures at random and attempting to 'fit them in'. It must be done systematically according to a formula which is known to give an optimum law in all directions. The table is constructed on the basis of (5a.3). Knowledge of formulas possessing these qualities is of importance for the smoothing of statistical production data. As already mentioned, the smoothing of the American feeding data in (5a.7) has been carried out by means of a formula that is too simple. It would probably have been more correct if it had taken place according to a formula constructed on the same lines as (5a.3), naturally with the sizes of the constants adapted to the material concerned.

Let us consider the product functions with a specific analytical shape which we gave in Section 5a, and investigate their optimum character.

As the numerical example in (5a.11) has been constructed on the basis of (5a.3), we get an optimum law in all three directions in (5a.3).

Let us next consider (5a.4). If we are to get a technical optimum law with partial variation of a given factor, we shall require the marginal elasticity for the factor concerned to be in excess of 1 to start with, and thereafter to pass first 1 and then 0, until it finally becomes negative. In the case under consideration, however, this condition is *not* fulfilled. Let us, for example, on the basis of (5a.9) construct a table to show how ε_1 varies when v_2 is kept constant = 10 and v_1 varies. We shall get

TABLE (6b.3)

v_1	1	2	3	5	6	7	8	9	10	11	12	13
ε_1	−0.36	−1	−1.93	−28	+36	+6.36	+4	+2.84	+2	+1.16	0	−2.36

This table shows that Formula (5a.4) is not capable of general use. But the formula may perhaps serve as an interpolation formula to cover certain short ranges.

Let us consider the linear production law (5a.5). According to (5b.5) all marginal productivities are constant and independent of the factor quantities in the production law (5a.5). The linear product function (5a.5) is thus no technical optimum law.

Finally, let us consider the Cobb-Douglas function (5a.6). From (5e.12) we can see that all marginal elasticities in (5b.6) are constant and independent of the factor combination under consideration. Thus the Cobb-Douglas function provides no technical optimum law.

To sum up we can say that with an optimum law we get *four fundamental points*, viz. (1) marginal top point, (2) optimum point, (3) maximum point, and (4) marginal low point. These four points can be completely characterised by means of the *two* concepts: *direct product acceleration* and *marginal elasticity* in the following way:

(1) Marginal top point: $x_{ii}'' = 0$
(2) Optimum point: $\varepsilon_i = 1$
(3) Maximum point: $\varepsilon_i = 0$
(4) Marginal low point: $x_{ii}'' = 0$.

In a case involving two factors these points can be graphically represented in a factor diagram as set out in Figure (6b.4). Considering a partial variation of v_1 while v_2 is kept constantly equal to v_2^0, is the same as making a movement along the straight line running parallel to the v_1-axis at a distance $v_2 = v_2^0$. Point A is the marginal top point, point B is the optimum point, point C is the maximum point, and point D is the marginal low point.

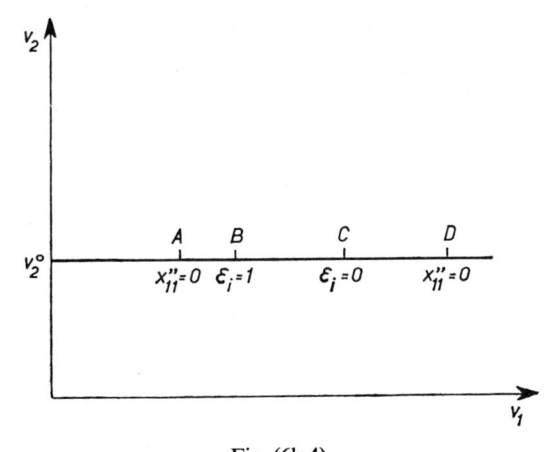

Fig. (6b.4).

Thus, by means of a movement from left to right, along the straight line, $v_2 = v_2^0$, ε_1 will generally show a monotonically decreasing course. To the left of point B $\varepsilon_1 > 1$, between points B and C we have $1 > \varepsilon_1 > 0$, and to the right of point C $\varepsilon_1 < 0$.

By a movement from left to right x_{11}'' will first be positive, until we reach point A. Between points A and D x_{11}'' is negative and to the right of point D x_{11}'' is once again positive.

We shall return to Figure (6b.4) at later points in the analysis.

6c. The technical optimum law for variation of a partial factor complex

As a rule, if we keep a complex consisting of some factors constant, and vary certain other factors proportionally, that is in such a way that the ratios between these factor quantities remain constant, or more generally, if we simply assume that the variable factors follow each other in a way that does not deviate much from proportionality, we shall have an optimum law of type (6b.1) in the complex which is variable.

The 'quantity' of the variable complex can be defined by some kind of quantity index. If the variable factors vary strictly proportionally, measuring the quantity of the complex will not present any problem; the variation in the complex can then simply be measured in terms of the variation in any arbitrarily chosen factor in the complex.

We shall state here the technical optimum law for variation of a partial factor complex, merely as a general rule to the effect, that if a complex varies the result will usually appear in the form of an optimum law. It is difficult to set out any necessary and sufficient conditions for the case where an optimum law of this kind will exist. But in special cases we can draw certain conclusions by making use of the passus character of the production law.[1] See for example Chapter 8.

---

[1] The concept 'passus character of the production law' is dealt with at the end of Section 7a.

CHAPTER 7

THE PARI-PASSU LAW

7a. Definition of a pari-passu law

In Section 5f we defined the term passus coefficient. *A pari-passu law is a production law in which the passus coefficient is equal to 1 for every factor combination.* Thus with the pari-passu law we have as per definition the identity

(7a.1) $$\varepsilon = 1,$$

for all values of $v_1, \ldots, v_n$.

From (5h.12) and (5h.15) we see that the production law (5a.3) and the linear product function (5a.5) without any constant term (viz. with $a_0 = 0$) are pari-passu laws, since the passus coefficient is equal to 1 in every factor point in both these production laws. From (5h.16), furthermore, we see that the Cobb-Douglas function (5a.6) is a pari-passu law when the sum of alphas is equal to 1. The production law (5a.4) on the other hand is not a pari-passu law, as here ε is equal to 2 in each factor point, cf. (5h.13).

The fact that (7a.1) applies is, as we shall see, the same as saying that the product function – assuming that it is continuous, and with continuous partial derivatives – satisfies the identity

(7a.2) $$x(mv_1, \ldots, mv_n) = m \cdot x(v_1, \ldots, v_n)$$

for all values of $v_1, \ldots, v_n$ and m.

The fact that (7a.2) is an identity in $v_1, \ldots, v_n$ and m means that the left side of (7a.2) is equal to the right side of (7a.2), irrespective of what values $v_1, \ldots, v_n$ or m assume.

A pari-passu law consequently has the property that *multiplying by m of the quantities of all the specified factors entails a multiplication by m of the product quantity*. If in a pari-passu law all factor quantities increase by the same percentage, e.g. 10 per cent, then the product quantity will increase by this same percentage, viz. 10.

When a function satisfies the condition (7a.2), we say that it is homogeneous to degree 1. Thus in the pari-passu law product function is homogeneous to degree 1.

The fact that (7a.1) follows from (7a.2) may be deduced as follows: By differentiating (7a.2) with respect to m, we get

$$\frac{\partial x}{\partial (mv_1)} \cdot \frac{d(mv_1)}{dm} + \frac{\partial x}{\partial (mv_2)} \cdot \frac{d(mv_2)}{dm} + \ldots + \frac{\partial x}{\partial (mv_n)} \cdot \frac{d(mv_n)}{dm} = x(v_1, \ldots, v_n).$$

Since

$$\frac{\partial x}{\partial (mv_i)} = x_i'(mv_1, \ldots, mv_n) \quad \text{and} \quad \frac{d(mv_i)}{dm} = v_i,$$

this gives

$$\sum_{i=1}^{n} x_i'(mv_1, \ldots, mv_n) \cdot v_i = x(v_1, \ldots, v_n).$$

This is an identity in m, in other words the left side is equal to the right side irrespective of the value of m. Let us put $m=1$. This gives us

$$\sum_{i=1}^{n} x_i'(v_1, \ldots, v_n) \cdot v_i = x(v_1, \ldots, v_n)$$

or in other words

(7a.3) $$\sum_{i=1}^{n} x_i' v_i = x$$

for all values of $v_1, v_2, \ldots, v_n$.

If we combine (7a.3) with the passus equation (5h.3) we get (7a.1). This shows that (7a.1) follows from (7a.2).

That, conversely, (7a.2) follows from (7a.1) can be shown in the following way:

In Section 5g we found that the second form of the beam variation equation (5g.16) applies in any factor point. In the pari-passu law, however, the passus coefficient is equal to 1 in any factor point. When ε is equal to 1 in any factor point, obviously $\bar{\varepsilon}$ – as defined in (5g.13) – is also equal to 1 in any factor point. If we substitute $\bar{\varepsilon}=1$ (in 5g.17), we get (7a.2). In other words necessary and sufficient for (7a.1) to hold it is necessary and sufficient that (7a.2) applies, and vice versa.

In the course of time several authors have maintained, or tacitly assumed, that it must *always* be so that an increase of all factor quantities in a production process by the same percentage gives an increase in the product quantity of this same percentage. The fact that the product does not change by the same percentage as the factors do, has often been taken as an expression of some 'change in technique'.

As the reader will recollect, we have another definition, viz. that the technique is constant as long as the product function is well defined and remains constant (cf. Chapter 3). The difference between the case where the product changes with the same percentage as the factors (when all the factors change in the same proportion) and the case where it does not do so, will according to our definition only be a difference between *two kinds of product function*. The first kind is a pari-passu law ('the product moves at the same rate as the factors'), and the second kind is an *ultra-passum law* ('the product moves at a different rate from the factors'). Cf. Chapter 8.

Experience shows that there are two misunderstandings which frequently arise with regard to the definition of the passus nature of the production law (i.e., as to whether a law is pari- or ultra-passum). The following explanations should help to clear up these misunderstandings:

(I) In order to be able to define the passus character of the production law, we must consider a special kind of factor variation, viz. the proportional one (all factors must change 'at the same rate').[1] It is impossible, for example, to define the passus character by referring to what happens in the case of a partial variation of *a single* factor. (A *calculation* may be made with the aid of the passus equation which comprises all specified factors, but this is another matter.)

(II) The fact that the production law is a pari-passu law does not prevent us from undertaking, whenever we so choose, factor variations which are *not* proportional. The fact that the production law is pari-passu can be expressed in the following terms: '*if* all factors vary by one and the same percentage, *then* the product quantity must also vary by this percentage'. This is obviously not the same as to say: 'It is never permissible to vary the factors in any other way than by changing them by one and the same percentage'.

Especially where practical applications are concerned, it is important to reckon with the possibility that the law may be ultra-passum. Admittedly, when we have an ultra-passum law in n factors, it will often be possible to explain this by pointing out that a certain factor, which was originally excluded from the analysis, actually did exert an effect, and actually did not follow the propositional variation which the n factors followed. In such cases

[1] Cf. some other form of variation which, in the sense of a necessary and sufficient condition, will reveal the same feature as the proportions factor variation.

we may perhaps – at any rate to a certain extent – re-establish the pari-passus character of the law by considering it as a law in the $(n+1)$ factors. But in many cases, it will only be possible to carry this kind of reasoning to its bitter end if we are prepared to admit for certain factors a most artificial definition of the factor concept. Basically the whole question then becomes little more than a question of *defining* quite conventionally the completeness of the factor list by saying that the list is complete when and only when the pari-passu law prevails in these factors.

As already mentioned above, the list of production factors can in reality never be exhaustive. However complete we try to make it, there will always be something left which we have omitted. To what extent we can then say that we 'ought to have' a pari-passu law, by including everything, is an abstract question of little interest. What is significant, is that in analyses of this kind that are really capable of being carried out, we very frequently *shall* come across the ultra-passum law. Pareto, Knut Wicksell, and Johnson were the first to insist on the need to study the ultra-passum law. In the following pages we shall devote a great deal of attention to this law. (Cf. conclusion of Chapter 8.)

7b. Special properties of the pari-passu law

Let us take (7a.2) as our starting point. By partial differentiation with respect to v_i, if m is an arbitrary constant parameter we get[1]

$$\frac{\partial x(mv_1, \ldots, mv_n)}{\partial (mv_i)} \cdot \frac{d(mv_i)}{dv_i} = m \frac{\partial x(v_1, \ldots, v_n)}{\partial v_i}$$

hence

$$x_i'(mv_1, \ldots, mv_n) \cdot m = m \cdot x_i'(v_1, \ldots, v_n) .$$

Thus for all values of $v_1, v_2, \ldots, v_n$ and m in the pari-passu law

(7b.1) $\qquad x_i'(mv_1, \ldots, mv_n) = x_i'(v_1, \ldots, v_n) \qquad (i = 1, \ldots, n)$;

i.e.: *In the pari-passu law marginal productivities remain unchanged during a proportional factor variation.*

Since marginal productivities are constant along a factor beam, the relationship between marginal productivities is of course also constant along a factor beam. A curve, along which the relation between marginal productivities is constant, is as per definition an isocline (cf. (5b.12). Hence, *in the pari-passu law isoclines and factor beams thus coincide, in other words the isoclines become straight lines running through the origin.*

[1] Use the rule for the differentiation of a function of a function.

Let us next differentiate (7b.1) partially with respect to v_j

$$\frac{\partial x_i'(mv_1, ..., mv_n)}{\partial(mv_j)} \cdot \frac{d(mv_j)}{dv_j} = \frac{\partial x_i'(v_1, ..., v_n)}{\partial v_j}$$

$$x_{ij}''(mv_1, ..., mv_n) \cdot m = x_{ij}''(v_1, ..., v_n).$$

Thus for all values of $v_1, v_2, ..., v_n$ and m in the pari-passu law

(7b.2) $\qquad x_{ij}''(mv_1, ..., mv_n) = \dfrac{1}{m} x_{ij}''(v_1, ..., v_n) \cdot \begin{bmatrix} i=1, ..., n \\ j=1, ..., n \end{bmatrix}$;

i.e.: *In the pari-passu law all accelerations are reduced to the mth part if all factors are multiplied by m.*

Let us next divide (7a.2) by mv_i

$$\frac{x(mv_1, ..., mv_n)}{mv_i} = \frac{m \cdot x(v_1, ..., v_n)}{mv_i} \, ;$$

in other words for all values of $v_1, v_2, ..., v_n$ and m in the pari-passu law

(7b.3) $\qquad \bar{x}_i(mv_1, ..., mv_n) = \bar{x}_i(v_1, ..., v_n) \qquad (i=1, ..., n)$;

i.e.: *In the pari-passu law all average productivities remain unchanged when a proportional factor variation takes place.*

Marginal elasticities can be conceived of as the quotients of marginal productivities and average productivities (cf. 5e.2). As both marginal productivities and average productivities remain unchanged in the pari-passu law by a proportional factor variation (cf. (7b.1) and (7b.3)), then consequently in this law *marginal elasticities must remain unchanged during a proportional factor variation*. Thus for all values of $v_1, v_2, ..., v_n$ and m in the pari-passu law

(7b.4) $\qquad \varepsilon_i(mv_1, ..., mv_n) = \varepsilon_i(v_1, ..., v_n) \qquad (i=1, 2, ..., n)$.

This can also be shown by partial elasticitation of (7a.2) for v_i.

In the pari-passu law $\varepsilon = 1$ in any factor point as per definition. The passus equation (5h.3) thus appears as (7a.3). Let us differentiate this equation partially with respect to v_k. For a term appearing in the lefthand side of (7a.3), where $i \neq k$, the derivative is equal to $x_{ik}'' \cdot v_i$. For the term in which $i = k$, we get

$$\frac{\partial(x_k' v_k)}{\partial v_k} = x_k' \cdot 1 + v_k \cdot \frac{\partial x_k'}{\partial v_k} = x_k' + x_{kk}'' v_k .$$

The derivative of the left member of (7a.3), $\Sigma\, x_i'v_i$, with respect to v_k, will consequently be equal to

$$x_k' + \sum_{i=1}^{n} v_i x_{ik}''.$$

This result can also be obtained in another way, by means of a technique which is often useful for the differentiation of product sums. Let e_{ik} be the unit numbers, i.e. 1 when $i=k$, but 0 when $i \neq k$. By direct differentiation of the summation sign in (7a.3), we get

$$\sum_{i=1}^{n} (x_i' e_{ik} + v_i x_{ik}'').$$

If a summation over i is here carried out, the first term will be reduced to x_k'. Thus differentiation of (7a.3) with respect to v_k gives

$$x_k' + \sum_{i=1}^{n} v_i x_{ik}'' = x_k'.$$

By subtracting x_k' from both sides of the equal sign we get

(7b.5) $$\sum_{i=1}^{n} v_i x_{ik}'' = 0 \qquad (k=1,\ldots,n).$$

This is an important formula for certain lines of reasoning.

From (7b.5) the following proposition can be deduced: *If a factor in a pari-passu law is complementary to all other factors in a factor point, then it must show decreasing marginal returns in the factor point concerned.*

Indeed when factor No. k is complementary to all factors, we have by definition $x_{ik}'' > 0$ for all i which are not equal to k as per definition.[1] As all factor quantities are positive, this is by (7b.5) sufficient for x_{kk}'' to be negative. The fact that x_{kk}'' is negative, however, is tantamount to saying that there exist decreasing marginal returns for factor No. k in the sense of decreasing marginal productivity (but not necessarily in the sense of decreasing average productivity).

Let us consider in more detail the special case with only *two factors*.

For $k=1$ we can then write (7b.5) as

(7b.6) $$x_{11}'' v_1 + x_{21}'' v_2 = 0.$$

And for $k=2$, we get

(7b.7) $$x_{12}'' v_1 + x_{22}'' v_2 = 0.$$

[1] Cf. Section 5c.

From (7b.6) and (7b.7), we get

(7b.8)
$$x_{11}'' \frac{v_1}{v_2} = -x_{21}'',$$
$$x_{22}'' \frac{v_2}{v_1} = -x_{12}''.$$

However, for continuity factors $x_{21}'' = x_{12}''$ in any factor point[1], and we consequently get the important formula

(7b.9)
$$x_{11}'' \frac{v_1}{v_2} = x_{22}'' \frac{v_2}{v_1} = -x_{12}'' = -x_{21}'';$$

i.e.: *In the pari-passu law for two factors the direct accelerations always have the same sign, and the cross-acceleration and direct accelerations always have opposite signs.*

7c. Further observations on the pari-passu law in two factors

Let us assume that we have a pari-passu law in two factors. Furthermore, let us assume that we get a typical *optimum law* (as described in 6b) by varying the quantity of factor No. 1, while keeping the quantity of factor No. 2 constant. We do not give any corresponding presupposition for a typical optimum law with variation of factor No. 2 with constant quantity of factor No. 1. (Below we shall see that in the case under consideration this will follow as a *consequence* of the two assumptions we have made.) Note that the assumption that we have a pari-passu law, and the assumption that we have an optimum law with partial variation of one factor, are *two quite different assumptions*. This can easily be shown by an example: Let us, for example, consider the Douglas function (5a.6), where the sum of the α's is equal to 1. In a case of this kind the Douglas function gives a pari-passu law. Cf. (5h.16). In order to investigate the optimum character for this special formulation of the Douglas function, we can consider marginal elasticities. On account of (5e.12) they are *constant* and independent of the factor point under consideration. We consequently get no optimum law with partial variation of a factor as specified in Figure (6b.1).

We shall now examine in a little more detail the structure of a production law in two factors where we have made the two above-mentioned assumptions, viz. that the law is a pari-passu law and that an optimum law exists in factor No. 1.

[1] Cf. (5c.4).

Let the quantity of factor No. 1 be kept constant and equal to $v_2{}^0$. We can then mark off the characteristic points in a two-dimensional factor diagram, as we did in Figure (6b.4). We have now done this in Figure (7c.1).

In (7b.1) we found that according to the pari-passu law the marginal elasticities remain unchanged during a proportional factor variation. A proportional factor variation is the same as making a movement along a

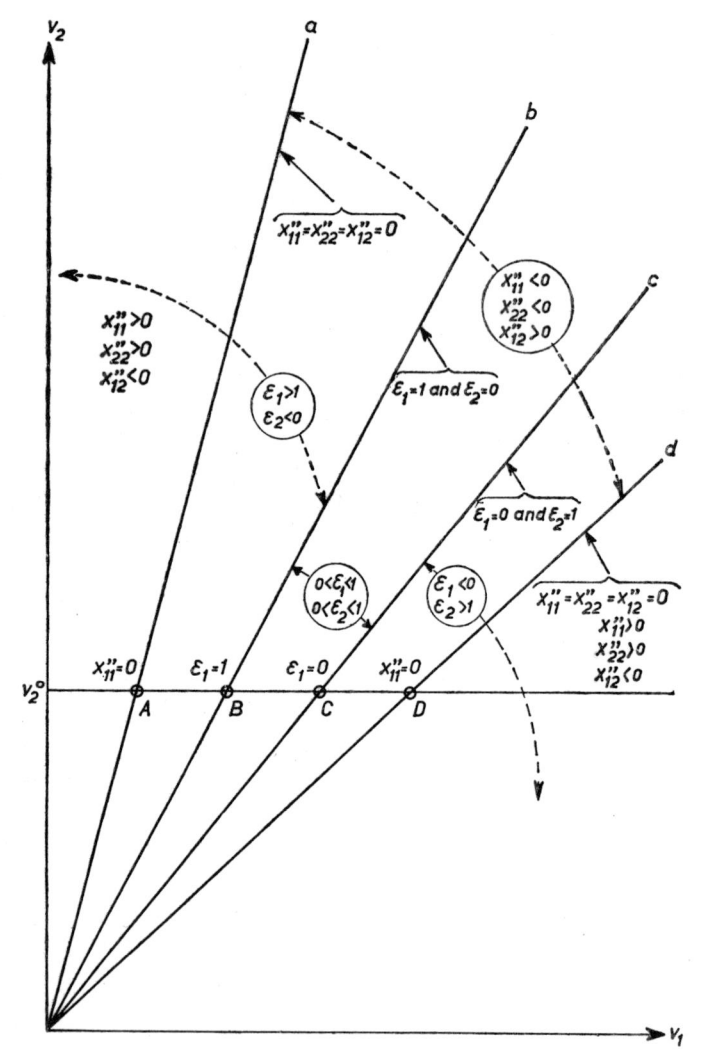

Fig. (7c.1). The pari-passu law in two factors.

factor beam. In all points on the factor beam b through point B we have $\varepsilon_1=1$, and in all points on the factor beam c through point C we have $\varepsilon_1=0$.

By considering all factor beams situated between beams b and c, we shall find that in the whole sector between b and c, ε_1 must lie between 1 and 0. To the left of factor beam b, $\varepsilon_1>1$, and to the right of factor beam c, $\varepsilon_1<0$.

After having noted this, we can now make certain conclusions with regard to ε_2. In a pari-passu law with two factors, $\varepsilon_1+\varepsilon_2=1$. Cf. (5h.11) and (7a.1). Along factor beam b, $\varepsilon_1=1$. Along this beam we must then have $\varepsilon_2=0$, i.e.: In a pari-passu law with two factors, factor No. 2 is applied technically maximally ($\varepsilon_2=0$) in all factor points where factor No. 1 is applied technically optimally ($\varepsilon_1=1$).

Along factor beam c, $\varepsilon_1=0$. We must then have $\varepsilon_2=1$ along this beam, i.e.: In a pari-passu law with two factors, factor No. 2 is applied technically optimally ($\varepsilon_2=1$) in all factor points where factor No. 1 is applied technically maximally ($\varepsilon_1=0$).

This can be summed up in the following proposition:

PROPOSITION (7c.2)

If we have a pari-passu law in two factors and one factor is applied technically optimally, then the other factor must be applied technically maximally, and vice versa: if one factor is applied technically maximally then the other must be applied technically optimally.

Since ε_1 in the region between factor beams b and c has a value between 0 and 1, and by the pari-passu law $\varepsilon_2=1-\varepsilon_1$, consequently ε_2 must also lie between 0 and 1 in this region.

In the region between the two factor beams b and c both marginal elasticities will consequently be positive. Furthermore we can see that it is *only* in this region that they can both be positive *simultaneously*, since to the right of c we have $\varepsilon_1<0$ and to the left of b we have $\varepsilon_2<0$. *The substitution in the case considered thus consists of the region which is limited by the two factor beams b and c* (both inclusive according to the definition given in Section 5e).

Furthermore we see that in the region between b and c, and *only* in this region, both marginal elasticities are less than 1 *simultaneously*, since to the left of b we have $\varepsilon_1>1$, and to the right of c we have $\varepsilon_2>1$. In the region between b and c – and only in this region – there exists, according to (5e.4), a decreasing average return for both factors simultaneously.

We can sum this up in the following proposition:

PROPOSITION (7c.3)

In a pari-passu law in two factors, the interior of the substitution region coincides with the region where there exists a decreasing average return for both factors simultaneously, in the sense that both for $i=1$ as well as for $i=2$ we have $\partial \bar{x}_i/\partial v_i < 0$, i.e. $\varepsilon_i < 1$.

From (7b.2) it follows that product accelerations do not change their *sign* as a result of a movement along a factor beam. In all points on the factor beam a, passing through factor point A in Figure (7c.1), we shall thus have $x_{11}'' = 0$, and in all points on factor beam d passing through factor point D in Figure (7c.1), we shall have $x_{11}'' = 0$. In the region between these two factor beams a and d we have $x_{11}'' < 0$, and in the regions to the left of a and to the right of b we have $x_{11}'' > 0$. This follows from the reasoning in connection with (6b.4) and from the assumption *that we have a* pari-passu *law*.

From (7b.9) we saw that in a pari-passu law in two factors, the two direct accelerations (x_{11}'' and x_{22}'') have the same sign. In the region between the two factor beams a and d, *both x_{11}'' and x_{22}'' are consequently negative*, and in the two regions on either side of the two factor beams a and d, *both x_{11}'' and x_{22}'' are positive*. In the region between a and b – and *only* in this region – there consequently exists a decreasing marginal return for both factors in the sense that $x_{ii}'' < 0$ both for $i=1$ and for $i=2$.[1]

From (7b.9) we saw furthermore that in a pari-passu law in two factors, the direct accelerations (x_{11}'' and x_{22}'') and the cross-acceleration ($x_{12}'' = x_{21}''$) have opposite signs. In the region between a and d, therefore, $x_{12}'' > 0$, and in the two regions on each side of a and d, $x_{12}'' < 0$. When $x_{12}'' > 0$, the two factors are *complementary*.[1] The region where $x_{12}'' > 0$ is therefore called the *region of complementarity*. The region of complementarity thus lies between the two factor beams a and d.

We therefore get

PROPOSITION (7c.4)

In a pari-passu law in two factors the region of complementarity coincides with the region where there exists a decreasing marginal return for both factors in the sense that both $x_{11}'' < 0$ and $x_{22}'' < 0$.

This common region must *comprise* the substitution region. Thus the substitution region is situated *within* the above-mentioned common region,

---

[1] Cf. Section 5c.

where we have decreasing marginal returns for both factors simultaneously, and where both factors are complementary to one another. This is due to the *sequence* between points *ABCD* which are given by the presupposition of the optimum character under partial variation of factor No. 1.

In a pari-passu law with two factors the substitution region will thus have the following properties (apart from the properties which are a direct consequence of the definition of the substitution region):

(I) In the interior of the substitution region there exists a decreasing average return for both factors.

(II) In the substitution region there exists a decreasing marginal return with respect to both factors.

(III) In the substitution region the factors are complementary.

REFLEXIVE PROPERTY OF THE OPTIMUM LAW (THE DUAL PRINCIPLE)

In 6b we mentioned that as a rule we shall get a typical optimum law as shown in Figure (6b.1), irrespective of which factor we vary. We shall now show that if we have a *pari-passu law* in *two factors*, and we have an optimum law in the first factor, the optimum law in the second factor is not a new presupposition but *a consequence*.

In the first place, it is clear that if in a pari-passu law with two factors the variation of the product quantity with respect to the variable v_1, and with $v_2 = \text{constant} = v_2^0$, is given, then we can deduce what the variation of the product quantity with respect to the variable v_2, and with $v_1 = \text{constant} = v_1^0$, must be. In other words, if we have given a function of one variable, viz. $x(v_1, v_2^0)$, we can deduce from it the form of another function of one variable, viz. $x(v_1^0, v_2)$. This is easily done with the aid of (7a.2), which we now write

(7c.5) $$x(v_1, v_2) = \frac{1}{m} x(mv_1, mv_2) .$$

If we here put $v_1 = v_1^0$ and $m = v_2^0/v_2$ we shall get

(7c.6) $$x(v_1^0, v_2) = \frac{v_2}{v_2^0} x\left(\frac{v_1^0 v_2^0}{v_2}, v_2^0\right),$$

where v_1^0 and v_2^0 are given constants. When the function $x(v_1, v_2^0)$ of v_1 is known, we can therefore find the value of the right side of (7c.6) for every given value of v_2.

But this means that we know the form of the function $x(v_1^0, v_2)$, which is now written on the left side of (7c.6)

Geometrically we can express the connection by saying that if in a two-dimensional factor diagram, such as Figure (7c.7), we know the product quantity in any point on an arbitrary *horizontal* line, as for example the one for v_2^0, then we can calculate from it the product quantity in any point on an arbitrary *vertical* line, as for example that for v_1^0. If, for example, we want to calculate the product quantity in P', we can draw a beam through P' and

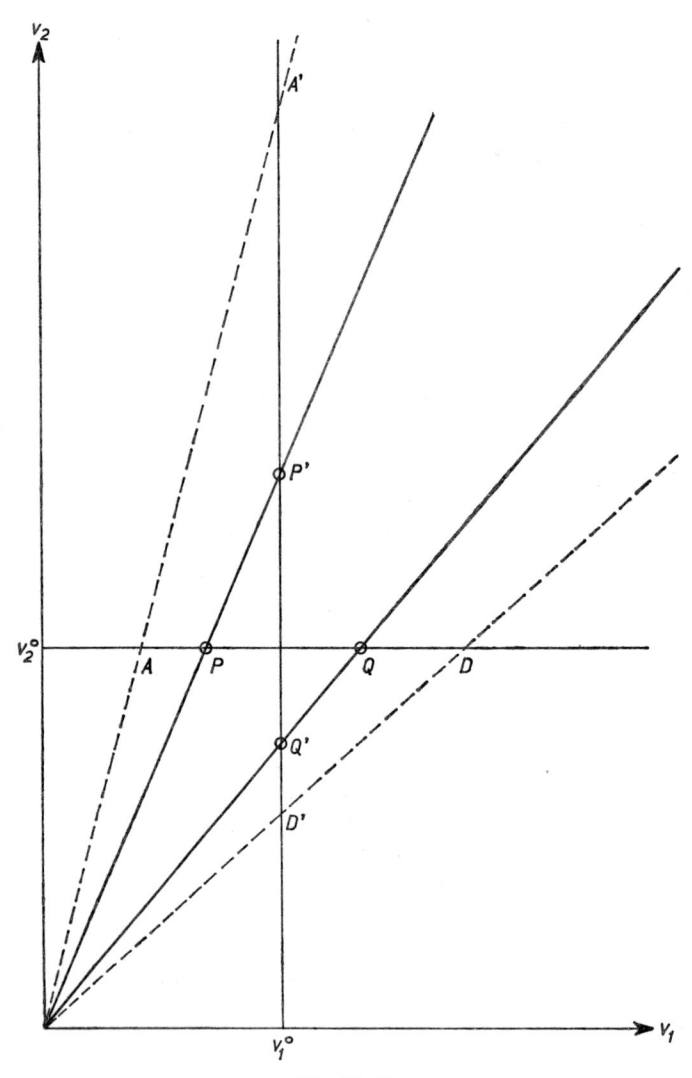

Fig. (7c.7).

determine its point of intersection P with the horizontal line v_2^0. According to our presupposition the product quantity is known in P. Furthermore we know the ratio between v_1^0 and the abscissa for P. If we multiply this ratio by the product quantity in P, by the pari-passu law we must get the product in P'. In the same way the product quantity in Q' can be calculated with the help of the product quantity in Q.

Correspondingly: If we know the variation of the product quantity along an arbitrary vertical line, we can by means of the pari-passu law deduce its variation along an arbitrary horizontal line.

This means that if we know the variations of a product quantity along one of these arbitrarily selected lines – i.e., if we know a function of one variable – then with the aid of the pari-passu law we shall be able to calculate the product quantity in every point in the entire factor diagram. That is to say, the fact that the law is a pari-passu law *takes out one degree of freedom* from the problem. The remaining degree of freedom can, of course, be covered also by taking as a datum the variation of the product quantity along some other curve in the factor diagram than a horizontal or a vertical straight line as discussed above, but it is not necessary to dwell on this here. We shall next show that, not only is knowledge of the variation of the product quantity along a horizontal line in the factor diagram sufficient to deduce the variation of the product quantity along any vertical line, but furthermore if the variation along a horizontal line has *optimum character* – as described in Figure (6b.1) – then the variation deduced from it along the vertical line must also have optimum character. In Figure (7c.8) points $ABCD$ and the beams $abcd$ are plotted precisely as in Figure (7c.1). Along these beams, and in the regions between the beams, the magnitudes of the marginal elasticities and the production accelerations are distributed as given in Figure (7c.1). In Figure (7c.8) however, only the magnitudes relating to factor No. 2 have been copied in. In this figure we now construct a *vertical* line, viz. with v_2 variable and $v_1 = v_1^0$. It intersects the beams $abcd$ in the points $A'B'C'D'$. From the distribution of the values of ε_2 which we have already studied (in Figure (7c.1)), we see that whenever we move up the vertical line, ε_2 will be greater than 1 below point C'. It will lie between 0 and 1 when we are between C' and B', and it is less than 0 when we are above B'. The direct product acceleration x_{22}'' will be positive below point D', negative in the interval between D' and A', and positive again above A'. We have thus proved that, whenever we are moving up the vertical line in Figure (7c.8), we get intervals typical of an optimum law. It now remains merely to show that marginal elasticity ε_2 decreases steadily when we move up the vertical line from D'

112   MOMENTARY SINGLE PRODUCTION

to A'. This follows from the fact that we have assumed ε_1 to decrease steadily as we move horizontally from A to D. For let P' and Q' in Figure (7c.7) be two arbitrary points in the vertical interval between D' and A', and let P be the point where the beam through P' intersects the horizontal line and Q the point where the beam through Q' intersects the horizontal line.

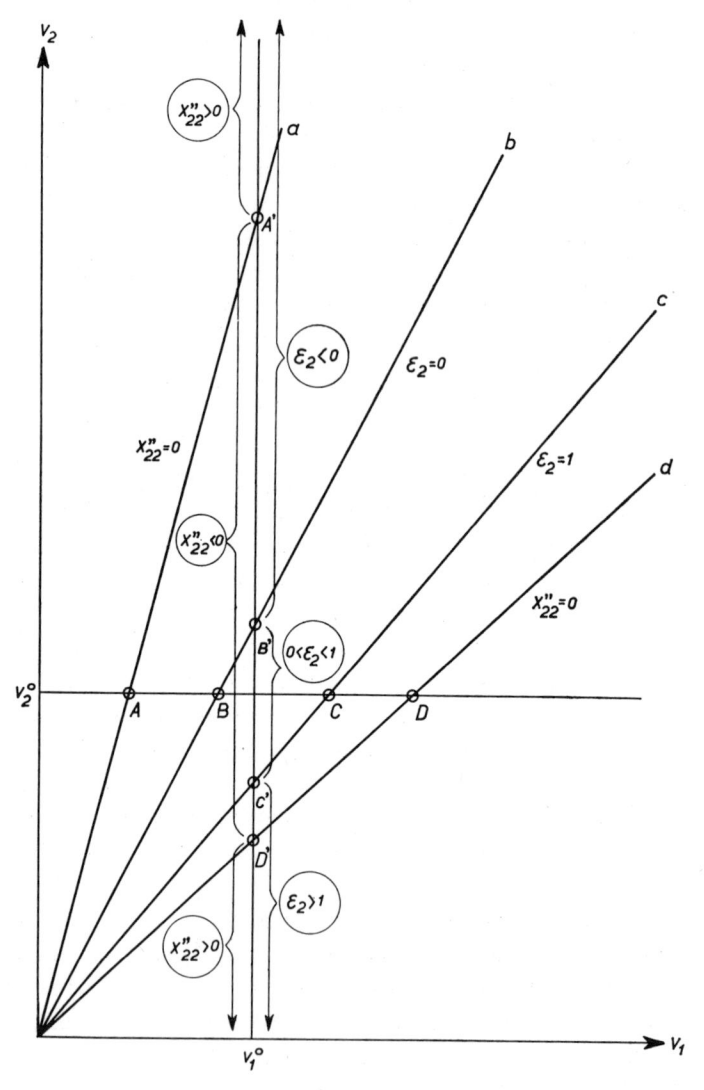

Fig. (7c.8).

If P' lies *above* Q' (i.e., P' corresponds to a greater value of v_2 than Q'), then P must lie to the left of Q (i.e., P corresponds to a lesser value of v_1 than Q). Now ε_2 is constant along any factor beam, cf. (7b.4). Consequently ε_2 in P' is equal to ε_2 in P and ε_2 in Q' is equal to ε_2 in Q. Since we have a pari-passu law, in any point $\varepsilon_2 = 1 - \varepsilon_1$, viz.

(7c.9)
$$\varepsilon_{2P'} = \varepsilon_{2P} = 1 - \varepsilon_{1P},$$
$$\varepsilon_{2Q'} = \varepsilon_{2Q} = 1 - \varepsilon_{1Q}.$$

Since we have assumed that ε_1 decreases steadily as it moves towards the right along the horizontal line, we shall have $\varepsilon_{1P} > \varepsilon_{1Q}$, i.e., in (7c.9) the topmost expression will be smaller than the lowest expression. As points P' and Q' were selected arbitrarily, it is thereby proved that ε_2 decreases steadily as we move up the vertical line between D' and A'. In other words, we have a typical optimum law with variation up the vertical line.

Generalisation in a case involving n factors and a production law which may not be a pari-passu law, is not very simple. The essential point is that when ε is given as a function of the factor point we have removed one and only one degree of freedom.

7d. The pari-passu law in three factors

In a pari-passu law in three factors, where we have an optimum law in every single factor, the substitution region will have the appearance suggested in Figure (7d.1). Let us first look at the surface marked 3 max. It may be conceived of as a triangular shield with its main vertex down and resting on the origin. The shield is hanging slantwise over the 'floor' (which is the $v_1 v_2$ plane). This shield represents the factor points where No. 3 is applied maximally ($\varepsilon_3 = 0$). The condition $\varepsilon_3 = 0$ gives *one* condition for the *three* variables v_1, v_2, v_3, and therefore represents a *surface* in the three-dimensional factor diagram (7d.1). The reason why the surface has the shape suggested is firstly connected with the presupposition of a pari-passu law in the three factors, and secondly with the presupposition that an optimum law applies in v_3. Because of the pari-passu law the region is bound to take the form of a conic surface with its apex at the origin; in other words it can be generated by means of a beam passing through the origin and running through various positions. This follows from the fact that marginal elasticities remain unchanged under a proportional factor variation. The fact that the shield 'leans forward' across the floor follows from the assumption of the optimum law in v_3. Indeed, if v_1 and v_2 are constant, i.e., if we are moving up a vertical line perpendicular to the 'floor' in (7d.1), then to start with ε_3 will be positive, subsequently passing through zero (where the vertical line intersects the shield), and being negative above. Owing to the pari-passu law, the point where the intersection occurs must lie the higher up, the further *out* across the floor the vertical line is placed.

In the same way a similar shield can be drawn for $\varepsilon_2 = 0$ and one for $\varepsilon_1 = 0$. This gives the two surfaces in the figure marked 2 max. and 1 max. In the

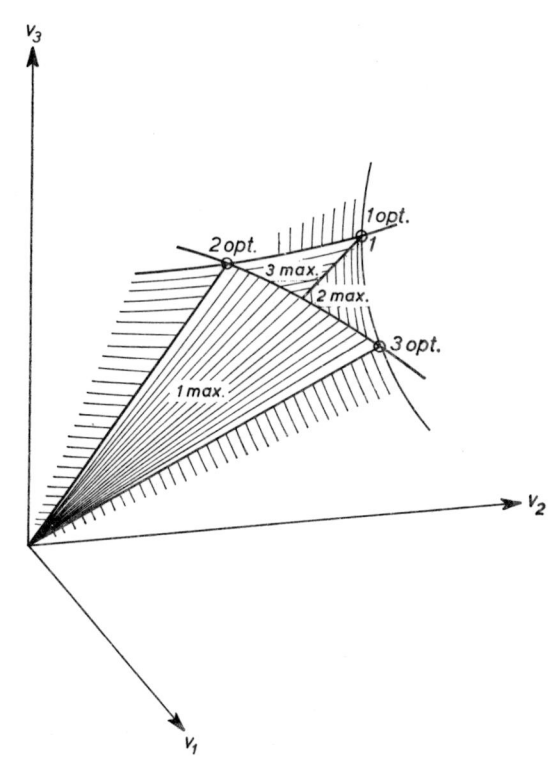

Fig. (7d.1). Substitution region in three factors under the pari-passu law.

first of these two surfaces No. 2 is applied technically maximally, in the last No. 1. The three surfaces considered above will intersect one another. As a general rule this will occur in such a way that a space exists *between them* where all three marginal elasticities are *simultaneously* positive. We thus get a sort of triangular 'dunce's cap' form as shown in Figure (7d.1). This is the *substitution region* in three factors under the pari-passu law. In this 'dunce's cap', and only here, all three marginal elasticities are non-negative.

The 'dunce's cap' has three bounding surfaces and three edges. In each of the *surfaces* one of the factors, according to our definition, is applied maximally. One *edge* is formed by the intersection of two surfaces. Thus, along an edge two factors are simultaneously applied maximally. Marginal elasticities for these two factors are then equal to nought. In the pari-passu law, however, the sum of marginal elasticities is equal to 1 in any factor point. Marginal elasticity for the remaining factor must therefore be equal to 1 along an edge of this kind, and this factor is consequently here applied technically optimally. Conversely, in the substitution region a factor is optimal anywhere along the edge concerned, and only there. In the substitution region, as we know according to our definition, all $\varepsilon_i \geqslant 0$, and if, therefore, one of the marginal elasticities in a pari-passu law is to be equal to 1 in the substitution region, the remaining factors must have marginal elasticities equal to nought (i.e., they must be situated on the boundary of the substitution region).

To sum up, then, we can say: each of the three bounding *surfaces* of the substitution area represents the factor points where one of the factors is applied technically *maximally* and each of the three *edges* of the substitution region represents the factor points where one of the factors is applied technically *optimally*.

It is only when we remain in the substitution region that the technically optimal factor points for a factor are situated on a *line*. If we do nothing more than to require that one of the factors, e.g. No. 1 be applied technically optimally ($\varepsilon_1 = 1$), i.e. if we only impose this single condition for the *three* variables (v_1, v_2, v_3), we get a surface in the factor diagram. This surface will naturally pass through the edge *of the substitution region* where No. 1 is technically optimal, but it will otherwise lie outside the substitution region. Correspondingly for factors No. 2 and 3. These surfaces are not fully drawn in Figure (7d.1).

In a similar way surfaces can be constructed for $x_{11}'' = 0$, $x_{22}'' = 0$, etc. In this way we get a *region where decreasing marginal returns exist* for all three factors simultaneously; we shall get a larger 'dunce's cap' which lies outside the substitution region (i.e., a case analogous to that with two factors). A *complementarity region* can also be constructed.

7e. The substitution region in a pari-passu law of n factors

We shall now consider a pari-passu law of n factors. In Section 7c we noticed that in a pari-passu law of two factors the interior of the substitution region will have the following properties:

(I) Decreasing average returns for both factors. Cf. theorem (7c.3).
(II) Decreasing marginal returns for both factors. Cf. text after (7c.3).
(III) The factors are complementary. Cf. theorem (7c.4).

We shall now examine whether these conclusions are connected with the special presupposition of only two factors, or whether they also apply in a general case with n factors.

It will be seen that (I) may be generalised. In the case of continuity factors we have the following proposition:

PROPOSITION (7e.1)

In the pari-passu law no factor can be applied technically optimally in the interior of the substitution region, on the contrary here every factor must be super-optimal, i.e. decreasing average returns must exist with respect to every factor.

In other words, for any factor, e.g. No. k, we must have ε_k less than 1, i.e. x_k' less than $x|v_k$. This follows from the passus equation when we write it in the form $\varepsilon_1 + \varepsilon_2 \ldots + \varepsilon_n = 1$. If all the ε, i.e., all marginal elasticities, are to be positive, and not zero, and the sum of them is to be 1, then any of them must be less than 1. (We assume that there are at least two factors.)

If we consider the substitution region, including its boundary, we get the following propositions:

PROPOSITION (7e.2)

If the production law is a pari-passu law and one factor – no matter which – produces increasing average returns i.e. $\varepsilon_k > 1$, then the factor point concerned must lie *outside the substitution region*, i.e., there must be at least one of the factors which in this point works with negative marginal productivity.

As a limiting case of (7e.1) and (7e.2), when the factor point lies on the boundary of the substitution region in $(n-1)$ of the factors, we can formulate the following proposition:

PROPOSITION (7e.3)

If in a pari-passu law all factors except one are applied technically maximally (i.e., their marginal productivities are nil), then the remaining factor must be applied technically optimally (i.e., its marginal productivity must be equal to its mean average productivity).

For if $\varepsilon_1, \varepsilon_2$, etc., except ε_k, are equal to nil, then according to the pari-passu law $\varepsilon_k = 1$, since the sum must be 1. In the pari-passu law, in other words, it is not possible to find any factor point where all factors are maximal (i.e., where all marginal productivities are nil). The same argument also shows that:

PROPOSITION (7e.4)

If in the pari-passu law one factor is applied technically optimally, and the point lies in the substitution region (including its boundary), then all other factors must be applied technically maximally.

Thus the point must lie on the 'outermost boundary' of the substitution region in all these other factors.

From the fact that a factor is applied technically optimally (and that we are in the substitution region) we can therefore draw a far-reaching conclusion, but from the fact that a factor is applied technically maximally, nothing in particular can be concluded about the other factors (unless there are altogether only two factors). If we are to be able to draw any conclusion on the basis of maximality, then we must have this information for *all* factors except one.

From (7e.4) it follows that in the substitution region of the pari-passu law it is *impossible for more than one factor at a time to be applied technically optimally*. The technical optimalisation is therefore *alternative* and not *simultaneous*. This point is not always clearly recognised. At times certain erroneous conclusions have been made with regard to this. It is, for example, tempting to argue as follows: let us start by varying v_1 until we find the technical optimum point, viz. the point where $\bar{x}_1$ is greatest (cf. Figure (6b.1)). Let the size of this factor quantity be v_1^0. Let us then keep v_1 constant at this 'optimum size', and vary the next factor, v_2. We know that by keeping all factors constant and varying v_2, we shall get an optimum law. Consequently, for this variation, let us look for the point where No. 2 is applied technically optimally. Let this point be v_2^0. We then keep v_1^0 and v_2^0 constant, and vary a third factor, etc. It would appear that in this way it would finally be possible to determine a combination $(v_1^0, v_2^0, ..., v_n^0)$ where all factors simultaneously were applied technically optimally. According to (7e.4), however, this must be wrong. The flaw in the argument is that when we start to vary v_2 (viz., when we follow the variation of the product quantity along a curve which has v_2 as its horizontal axis), then the originally determined factor quantity v_1^0 will *no longer be optimal with respect to No. 1*. The curve we originally used to determine v_1^0, and which we have now for a moment 'turned our back on', has taken this opportunity of *changing its shape*, so that v_1^0 is no longer an optimum point. This is a good illustration of the fact that the production problem cannot be discussed *merely* by considering one factor at a time. All factors must be borne in mind simultaneously.

The above – in common with everything in this chapter – refers to the case where the factors are continuity factors. If all factors, or some of them, are limitational factors, it becomes possible for several factors simultaneously to be technically optimal. This is dealt with in greater detail at the conclusion of Section 12h. Misconceptions with regard to simultaneous optimalisation are undoubtedly due to a failure to distinguish between continuity factors and limitational factors.

The generalisation of (II) is as follows:

PROPOSITION (7e.5)

If the production law is a pari-passu law and if an optimum law prevails for each factor as given by the curves in Figure (6b.1), then in any point lying in the substitution region for the n factors all the direct accelerations x_{kk}'' must be negative ($k=1, 2, ..., n$), i.e. for every factor there exist decreasing marginal returns.

This can be proved as follows: Let $(v_1^0, ..., v_n^0)$ be the given factor point, and let us investigate especially what x_{kk}'' is in this point. We keep all factors constant except No. k, which we allow to vary, both below and above the initial magnitude v_k^0. According to our presupposition we then get an optimum law as given in the upper part of Figure (6b.1). There are three possibilities here: (1) The initial magnitude v_k^0 is situated to the left of the optimum point for No. k, in which case No. k is sub-optimal and the factor point $(v_1^0, ..., v_n^0)$ must then according to (7e.2) lie outside the substitution region in the n-dimensional factor diagram. (2) If the initial magnitude v_k^0 lies to the right of the maximum point for No. k, x_k' will be negative (we are ignoring the region situated to the right of the vertical ZZ).

In this case, too, the factor point $(v_1^0, ..., v_n^0)$ must lie outside the n-dimensional substitution region. (3) Thus, if our position is to be in the substitution region in the n-dimensional factor diagram, v_k^0 in the optimum diagram for factor No. k must lie on the interval between optimum and maximum for this factor k. From the figure we can see that everywhere in this interval – including its terminal points – x_{kk}'' is negative, viz. marginal productivity with respect to factor No. k is diminishing. This argument can be applied for every factor. This gives (7e.5).

Under (3) in the reasoning above we merely state that *if* our position is to be in the substitution region for the n factors, v_k^0 must lie in the interval between optimum and maximum for factor No. k. But we do not say that this placing of v_k^0 is a *sufficient* condition for us to be placed in the substitution region for the n factors.

The proof of proposition (7e.5) can also be given in the following manner, which is more akin to the argument set out under proposition (8.9): Consider the optimum diagram (6b.1) for factor No. k. If we are to be in the substitution region, according to our definition v_k^0 must be situated in or to the left of point C. According to proposition (7e.2) we can furthermore conclude that if the point considered lies in the substitution region, including its boundary, then v_k^0 must lie either in or to the right of point B. However, in the whole interval BC the curve for x_k' is sinking, that is to say, x_{kk}'' is negative.

(III) cannot be generalised to cover the case involving several factors. If in a pari-passu law there are more than two factors, it may be possible for two factors to be alternative (i.e. not complementary) in one or more points in the substitution region.

It is easy to understand why (III) does not apply in the general case. The presupposition that an optimum law applies for every single factor is in its essence a law which merely tells us something about each factor *taken separately*. It says nothing about cross-accelerations between factors. Conclusions about cross-accelerations are deduced from the *passus equation*. It connects all the elements in the production law. The reason why we reached such a precise conclusion in the case involving only two factors, was that in this case only *one* cross-acceleration exists, viz. x_{12}'' (this is identical with x_{21}''). Between x_{12}'' and the direct accelerations the relationship contained in the passus equation then becomes a very sharp one, viz. as in (7b.9). When we get three factors, there are so many more possible variations, that the passus equation can no longer 'compel' all factors to be complementary in any point in the substitution region.

CHAPTER 8

THE ULTRA-PASSUM LAW. THE REGULAR ULTRA-PASSUM LAW

In Section 7a we defined the ultra-passum law as a production law in which the passus coefficient was not equal to 1 in every factor combination. In other words there exists at least one point where the passus coefficient is different from unity. For the sake of precision we shall call this a *general* ultra-passum law.

A special type of ultra-passum law is the regular ultra-passum law, which can be defined as follows:

DEFINITION (8.1)

A regular ultra-passum law is a production law which is such that if we move outwards along an arbitrary *rising* curve in the factor diagram (that is to say, a curve where all factor quantities *simultaneously* increase, or more generally no factor quantity diminishes and at least one rises when we move out along the curve), the passus coefficient ε will *diminish* steadily from values in excess of 1 to values less than 1 and finally to values less than 0, as suggested in Figure (8.2).

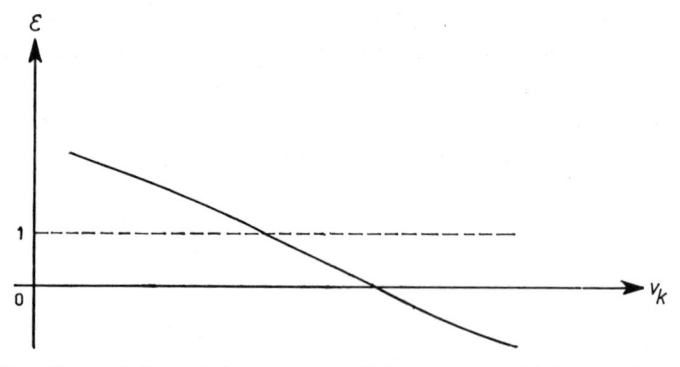

Fig. (8.2). The variation of the passus coefficient along a rising curve in the factor diagram (an arbitrary selected factor quantity taken as abscissae).

The 'rising curve' we are here considering is a generalisation of the conception of proportional factor variation. Along a generally rising curve, too, we can to a certain extent say that we have an increase in the scale of production. We must, however, remember that whenever we use the actual magnitude of the passus coefficient as a gauge to indicate *how* the product quantity increases with an increase 'in the scale', the scale variation must strictly speaking be defined by a proportional factor variation in the vicinity of the starting point considered.

In a case involving *two* factors we can depict the variation of the passus coefficient along a rising curve in a two-dimensional factor diagram, as shown in Figure (8.3).

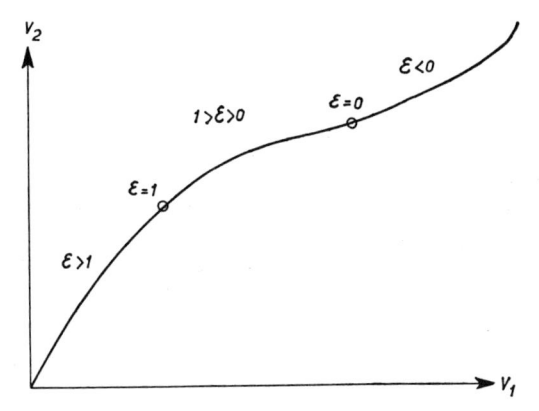

Fig. (8.3). Variation of the passus coefficient along a rising curve in the case of a regular ultra-passum law in two factors.

In Figure (8.3) we considered the variation of ε along a special rising curve. In a regular ultra-passum law, however, ε will, according to our definition, have a similar typical course with variation along any rising curve, viz. steadily diminishing values from values in excess of 1 to values less than 0. In Figure (8.4) we have drawn in the typical variation of ε along several rising curves. On any curve of this kind, in other words, there exists a point where $\varepsilon = 1$, and a point (which lies further out in the factor diagram) where $\varepsilon = 0$.

By connecting all the points on the various rising curves which have the same magnitude of ε, we get a set of *contour-lines* for ε as suggested in Figure (8.4).

By using a similar argument with regard to the form of the contour-lines for ε in two factors as we used in (5i.2) and (5i.6) with regard to the shape of the isoquants in two factors, we can show that the contour-lines for ε in two factors in a regular ultra-passum law are *falling*. For we can consider a curve where factor No. 1 is increasing while factor No. 2 is constant as a limiting case of a rising curve. From definition (8.1) we know that in a regular ultra-passum law the passus coefficient is bound to sink along a curve of this kind, i.e., we must have $\partial \varepsilon / \partial v_1 < 0$. In the same way we have $\partial \varepsilon / \partial v_2 < 0$.

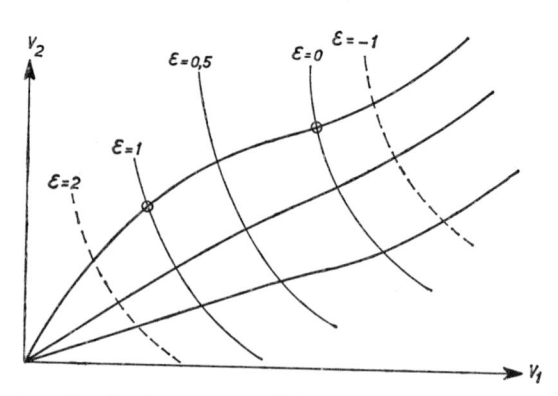

Fig. (8.4). Contour lines for the passus coefficient in the regular ultra-passum law in two factors.

By a reasoning analogous to that which led to (5i.6), we thus get along a contour-line for the passus coefficient

$$\frac{dv_2}{dv_1} = - \frac{\partial \varepsilon / \partial v_1}{\partial \varepsilon / \partial v_2},$$

which is a negative magnitude.

The shape of the contour-lines for ε in Figure (8.4) are only given as an example: other shapes, too, are conceivable, provided we do not introduce more assumptions than we have done in the preceding pages. We cannot, for example, make any definite statement about the curvature of the contour-lines for ε. The curvature in Figure (8.4) is only one possibility.

Once we have an idea of the distribution of ε-values in a regular ultra-passum law with the help of the contour-lines for ε, we can draw conclusions as to how the product quantity will change under a *proportional* factor variation starting from an arbitrary point, cf. Figure (8.5).

The contour-line for $\varepsilon = 1$ is called the curve of *technical optimal scale*. In the area to the south-west of this curve $\varepsilon > 1$, and we thus get here *increasing* average returns in the technical sense for all specified factors with an increase in the scale of production, and with a retention of the same relative factor combination, i.e. the reasoning associated with Formula (5g.8). This area is therefore called *the with respect to the scale technically pre-optimal region* or, more briefly, *the pre-optimal region*.

In the region north-east of the curve for the technically optimal scale $\varepsilon < 1$. Consequently we here get in a technical sense of the word *decreasing* average returns for all specified factors with an increase in the scale of production, retaining the same relative factor combination. This region is therefore called *the with respect to the scale technically post-optimal region*, or more briefly, *the post-optimal region*.

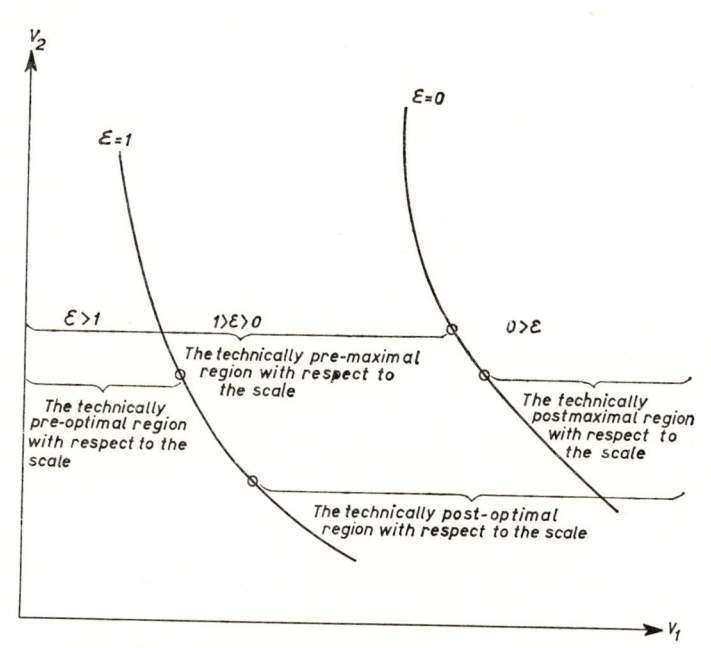

Fig. (8.5). The regular ultra-passum law in two factors.

The contour-line corresponding to $\varepsilon = 0$ is called *the curve for technically maximal scale*. Here the product quantity reaches its greatest value under a proportional factor variation. To the northeast of this curve $\varepsilon < 0$. Here the product quantity will *diminish* when all the factors increase proportionally. This region is therefore called *the with respect to the scale technically post-maximal region*. Correspondingly the region to the south-west of the curve for technically maximal scale is called *the with respect to the scale technically pre-maximal region*. Here the product quantity will increase when all the factors increase proportionally.

The case involving three or more factors should be dealt with in an analogous way. With three factors we get contour surfaces for ε. (The fact that ε must have a definite value gives only *one* condition for the *three* factor quantities.) Thus we get a surface for technically optimal scale, and a surface for technically maximal scale.

We shall consider a little more closely the shape of the substitution region and concomitant questions in a regular ultra-passum law. In doing so we presuppose that there exists a technical optimum law under partial variations with respect to each factor. This is a new presupposition which does not follow from the presupposition on the passus coefficient. We shall start by considering the case involving two factors.

Figure (8.6) gives a comprehensible picture of the distribution of the values of the passus coefficient and marginal elasticities under the presuppositions mentioned.

The geometrical locus for the points where a marginal elasticity with respect to a given factor has a constant value, will not necessarily be a straight line as in the pari-passu law, but a curved line (see Figure (8.6)). From the presupposition that there exists an optimum law in factor No. 1, it follows that by a movement from left to right along any horizontal line in Figure (8.6), we first have $\varepsilon_1 > 1$, then $\varepsilon_1 = 1$, and then $1 > \varepsilon_1 > 0$ and furthermore $\varepsilon_1 = 0$ and finally $\varepsilon_1 < 0$. The curve for $\varepsilon_1 = 1$ thus lies in its entirety to the left of the curve for $\varepsilon_1 = 0$. Similarly it follows from the presupposition

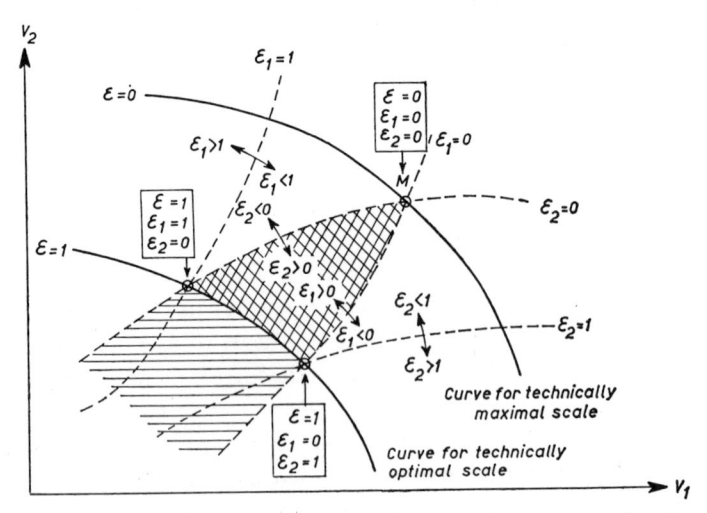

Fig. (8.6). The regular ultra-passum law in two factors with optimum effect in each one of the two specified factors.

on the optimum law in factor No. 2 that the curve for $\varepsilon_2 = 1$ lies in its entirety beneath the curve for $\varepsilon_2 = 0$.

The curve along which a factor is technically optimal, viz. the curve along which marginal elasticity for the factor is equal to 1, we call the partial optimality curve for the factor concerned, and the curve along which a factor is applied technically maximally, i.e. along which marginal elasticity equals 0, we call the partial maximality curve for the factor concerned.

In Figure (8.6) there are three sets of contour-lines, viz. for ε, ε_1, and ε_2 respectively. The way in which these contour-lines lie in relation to one another and the areas that are de-limited between them, describe the essentials of the structure of the production law. It is extremely important that in attempts at statistical verification of production laws the general structure which is exemplified in Figure (8.6) be kept clearly in mind. A closer study of the figure is therefore well worth-while.

In the region with *some* shading *between* the partial maximality curve for factor No. 1 and the partial maximality curve for factor No.2, both marginal elasticities are positive simultaneously. The *substitution region* is thus made up of this region with *some* shading and its boundary-lines.[1]

This substitution region has an entirely different form from the substitution region for two factors in the pari-passu law, cf. Figure (7c.1). In the latter the region was an open sector which opened up as we moved outwards in the factor diagram, and consequently the two boundary-lines never met. Here, on the other hand, it is only in part of the diagram (the part turning towards the origin) that the substitution region opens up; finally it must *contract* and the boundary lines meet at a point which in the figure is denoted M. In this point both marginal elasticities are simultaneously nil. Thus both factors are technically maximal at point M. At this point, therefore, the product quantity is as great as it possibly can be when v_1 and v_2 vary. Consequently we call this the *absolute maximum point* for the product in the $v_1 v_2$ diagram. A point of this kind does *not* exist in the pari-passu law (cf. the text prior to (7e.4)). In point M, on account of the passus equation, ε must obviously be equal to nil (disregarding the pathological case when the product quantity is nil in this point).

The interior of the substitution region with two factors must obviously in its entirety be situated in the area which is with respect to the scale technically pre-maximal, viz. where $\varepsilon > 0$ – that is to say, south-west of point M – cf. the definition of the with respect to the scale technically pre-maximal area

---

[1] An interesting numerical example is given by Healy and Pesek in *Econometrica*, October 1960.

in the text to Figure (8.5). This can easily be generalised for n factors in the following form:

PROPOSITION (8.7)

A point which is situated in the with respect to the scale technically post-maximal region, i.e., where $\varepsilon < 0$, cannot belong to the substitution region.

The correctness of (8.7) is evident from (5h.11), which in the with respect to the scale technically post-maximal region assumes the form $\varepsilon_1 + \varepsilon_2 + \ldots + \varepsilon_n < 0$. If this is to be so, then obviously at least one of the marginal elasticities must be negative.

In the pari-passu law in two factors the partial maximality curve for factor No. 2 coincided with the partial optimality curve for factor No. 1, cf. Figure (7c.1). In the ultra-passum law this agreement ceases. See Figure (8.6). The partial optimality curve for factor No. 1 will now no longer follow the upper limit of the substitution region, viz. the curve for $\varepsilon_2 = 0$, but in the region which is with respect to the scale technically pre-optimal it lies *within* the substitution region, and in the with respect to the scale technically post-optimal region it lies *outside* the substitution region. The same applies to the partial optimality curve for factor No. 2.

That the optimality curves run as mentioned above can be deduced in the following way: the curve for $\varepsilon_1 = 1$ is sure to run through the point of intersection between the curve for technically optimal scale and the upper boundary of the substitution region, viz. the point where we simultaneously have $\varepsilon = 1$ and $\varepsilon_2 = 0$. This follows from the passus equation for two factors $(\varepsilon_1 + \varepsilon_2 = \varepsilon)$. From this point the optimality curve for factor No. 1 can *not* lead *inwards* into the north-eastern section of the substitution region, viz. where the scale is technically post-optimal. For in any point in this region $\varepsilon < 1$, (as a consequence of the presupposition that we are in the with respect to the scale technically post-optimal region) and $\varepsilon_2 > 0$ (because of the assumption that we are in the substitution region), i.e. $\varepsilon_1 (= \varepsilon - \varepsilon_2)$ is undoubtedly less than 1. Nor can it lead into that part of the region which is technically pre-optimal for the scale which is situated above the substitution region, as here $\varepsilon > 1$ and $\varepsilon_2 < 0$, i.e. $\varepsilon_1 (= \varepsilon - \varepsilon_2)$ is undoubtedly greater than 1. The curve must therefore run as suggested in the figure. In the same way it can be shown that the optimality curve for factor No. 2 is bound to proceed as drawn in the figure.

While the boundary lines of the substitution region under the ultra-passum law finally converge when we move outwards in the factor diagram, the optimality curves will as a rule *spread* more and more. The partial optimality curves thus become less deformed in the transition from the pari-passu to the ultra-passum law than the curves determining the boundary of the substitution region.

The region where *decreasing average returns* for both factors exist is made up of the factor points where both marginal elasticities are simultaneously less than 1. From Figure (8.6) we can see that this condition is only fulfilled in the region between the two partial optimality curves.

Thus in the regular ultra-passum law for two factors, the region where there exist decreasing average returns for both factors simultaneously does not coincide with the interior of the substitution region as in the pari-passu case with two factors. Nor is it the case – as in the pari-passu law in three or more factors – that the substitution region lies within the region where there exist diminishing average returns for both factors simultaneously. But if we confine ourselves to considering that portion of substitution region which lies within the with respect to the scale technically post-optimal region[1], i.e., the double shaded region in Figure (8.6), we shall see that *this* region in its entirety lies within the region where there exist decreasing average returns for both factors simultaneously. Thus in every point of the portion of the substitution region which is with respect to the scale technically post-optimal, there will in a regular ultra-passum law in two factors exist diminishing average returns for both factors simultaneously.

This proposition can be generalised to cover the case involving n factors. For in the with respect to the scale technically post-optimal portion of the substitution region we have by definition $\varepsilon < 1$. Thus, on account of the passus equation, we have in this region

$$\sum_{i=1}^{n} \varepsilon_i < 1 .$$

On the other hand, by definition, all marginal elasticities are bound to be non-negative in the substitution region. When all ε_i are to be non-negative and at the same time the sum of them is to be strictly less than 1, then none of the marginal elasticities can be equal to or greater than 1. In other words:

PROPOSITION (8.8)

In the with respect to the scale technically post-optimal portion of the substitution region in a regular ultra-passum law for n factors, all factors

[1] We shall see below that it is as a rule in this portion of the factor diagram that the *economic* adjustment will take place.

must be technically post-optimal ($\varepsilon_i < 1$ for all i), i.e. decreasing *average* returns must exist for every factor.

When the course of the partial optimality curves for the two factors is known, it is not difficult to see precisely where the region in which diminishing *marginal* returns for both factors exist, is bound to lie. However, we will not go into greater detail about this, but merely state that in a regular ultra-passum law the entire substitution region will in general *not*, as is the case in the pari-passu law, be comprised in the region for decreasing marginal returns.

One special remark may be added: It is easy to prove that the with respect to the scale technically post-optimal part of the substitution region must in its entirety lie within the region where decreasing marginal returns exist simultaneously for both factors. This also applies in the general case of n factors. That is to say, we have the following proposition:

PROPOSITION (8.9)

In a regular ultra-passum law for n factors, where for each of the n factors an optimum law prevails as given by the curves in Figure (6b.1), there exist decreasing marginal returns for all n factors in the with respect to the scale technically post-optimal portion of the substitution region.

This can be proved as follows: From (8.8) it follows that in the with respect to the scale technically post-optimal portion of the substitution region, all factors will be applied technically post-optimally ($\varepsilon_i < 1$ for all i). Expressed in terms of Figure (6b.1), we thus know that for every factor we are placed *to the right* of point B, where the marginal productivity curve intersects the average productivity curve. At the same time we must be in or *to the left* of point C where marginal productivity becomes zero. This simply follows from the assumption that we are in the substitution region. In this interval between B and C, however, marginal productivity is on the decrease, as can be seen from Figure (6b.1).

The rules as to where in the factor diagram for two factors the factors are *complementary*, and where they are *alternative*, are not as simple as in the pari-passu case. Here we will merely state that even in the case involving two factors it is not certain that the two factors are complementary in the substitution region under the ultra-passum law.

It often happens that the regular ultra-passum effect in a given number of specified factors is the result of *a non-specified factor being kept constant*, while the production law would – at least approximately – have had the character of a pari-passu law, if this factor had been included in the variation (cf. conclusion of Section 7a). For example in the case of the regular ultra-passum effect in two factors, Figure (7d.1) itself – which gave the pari-passu effect in three factors – will give us a fairly good idea of the situation.

Let us, for instance in Figure (7d.1), keep v_3 constant and *study the production law as it then appears for the two factors* v_1 and v_2. In order to do this we must make a horizontal section through (7d.1). The result is shown in Figure (8.10). The section has here been projected down 'into the floor', which of course is the factor diagram for the two factors No. 1 and No. 2. What is now of interest is to see how the production law appears in this two-dimensional factor diagram, under the presupposition that v_3 is constant,

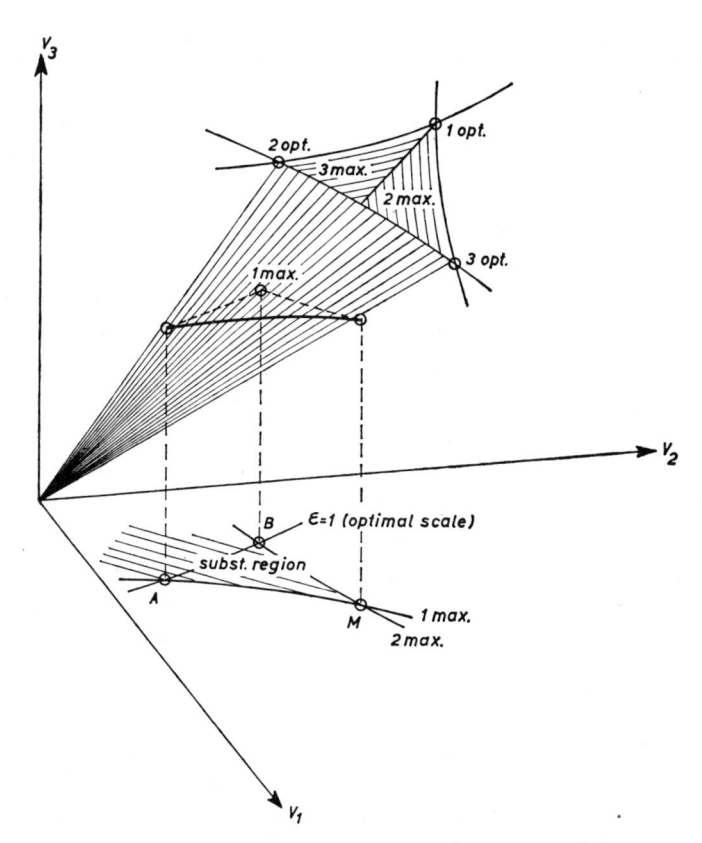

Fig. (8.10). The regular ultra-passum effect in two factors derived from a pari-passu effect in three factors.

that is to say equal to the magnitude corresponding to the horizontal section concerned.

Let us first consider the lines describing intersection between the $v_3=$ constant plane and the 'dunce's cap' surfaces 1 max. and 2 max. When projected down 'into the floor' these lines will appear as the two dotted lines AM and BM in Figure (8.10). Along one of these – namely AM which for most of its course lies closest to the v_1-axis – we have $\varepsilon_1 = 0$, and along the other – namely BM lying closest to the v_2-axis – we have $\varepsilon_2 = 0$. In other words, along one curve, factor No. 1 is maximal; along the other, factor No. 2 is maximal. See Figure (8.10). In the hachured area between these two curves both ε_1 and ε_2 are positive. This area, including its boundary, now becomes *the substitution region* in the (v_1, v_2) diagram. As we are for the moment only interested in the two factors v_1, v_2 – only these are now specified – there are only *two* conditions, $\varepsilon_1 =$ non-negative and $\varepsilon_2 =$ non-negative, we have to consider. In other words, we are for the moment not interested in the fact that a part of the projection is cut off by the third wall. The *substitution* region in $(v_1 v_2)$ is therefore all the hachured region in 'the floor', not only the portion of it cut off by the line AB, i.e. by the projection of the intersection line between $v_3 =$ constant plane and the 3 max. wall.

Thus the substitution region acquires the same typical appearance as in Figure (8.6). The curvature of the boundary lines is here of no avail.

The curve AB is interesting. If we consider it from the point of view of three factors, it is the partial maximality curve for factor No. 3. We cannot, however, now interpret it in this manner; we must, indeed now confine ourselves to the two-dimensional factor diagram $(v_1 v_2)$ and must therefore seek an interpretation on this basis. We can give an interpretation of this kind through the passus equation. In the three variables we have $\varepsilon_1 + \varepsilon_2 + \varepsilon_3 = 1$ (since we have assumed the pari-passu law in three factors). In the two variables 1 and 2 the passus equation is $\varepsilon_1 + \varepsilon_2 = \varepsilon$, where ε is the passus coefficient as it appears when the product quantity is conceived of as the function of only v_1 and v_2 (with $v_3 =$ the given constant magnitude).[1] If we compare these two equations, we see that we have

$$(8.11) \qquad \varepsilon = 1 - \varepsilon_3 .$$

The points where $\varepsilon_3 = 0$, must consequently coincide with those where we have $\varepsilon = 1$. In other words, from the point of view of two factors, AB is the curve for *technically optimal scale*. To the right of the curve AB, factor No. 3 is applied

---

[1] Since x_k' ($k=1, 2, 3$) are the same whether we consider the production law from the viewpoint of two or from that of three factors, the same applies to $\varepsilon_k = x_k' v_k / x_0$.

technically pre-maximally ($\varepsilon_3 > 0$). Then $\varepsilon < 1$ and the scale – from the viewpoint of two factors – is technically post-optimal. To the left of the curve AB, $\varepsilon_3 < 0$, and consequently $\varepsilon > 1$. Thus, in the area to the left of AB the scale is technically pre-maximal. In point M, $\varepsilon_3 = 1$, and consequently $\varepsilon = 0$. Here the scale is technically maximal from the viewpoint of two factors.

By comparing Figure (8.10) with Figure (8.6), we see that the two-dimensional production law which emerges when we keep one factor constant in the pari-passu law for three factors, *acquires the same characteristic properties as the regular ultra-passum law in two factors*. It is thus possible to visualise how the regular ultra-passum law in two factors has arisen by keeping one factor in a three-dimensional pari-passu law constant, and interpreting it as a production law in only the two variable factors.

By an analogous consideration, we may imagine that a regular ultra-passum law in n factors has arisen by keeping one factor in an $(n+1)$-dimensional pari-passu-law constant, and varying the other n factors. Or more generally: if we have a production law which is a pari-passu law in $(n+m)$ factors, and we then keep m factors constant, and analyse the effect of the production law in the remaining n variable factors, then this production law in n factors will as a rule be a regular ultra-passum law. It is, however, difficult to specify the necessary and sufficient conditions for this. We shall therefore confine ourselves to stating that as a general rule this will be the case. Even though there does not exist a pari-passu law in the $(n+m)$ factors, we shall have a regular ultra-passum law in the n factors, if the assumption of the technical optimum law with variation of an incomplete factor complex applies (cf. 6c).

As we mentioned in Section 7a, from a purely abstract point of view it would perhaps be possible to imagine that all production *would follow* the pari-passu law when the conception of the production factor is stretched to its uttermost limit. This, however, is of minor interest. In a concrete case it will prove necessary to confine our analysis to a larger or smaller *group* of more precisely specified factors, while all other factors are neglected. And in practice many of these neglected factors will remain constant. In studying the set-up of a concern it will, for example, often prove to be the case that the capacity-determining factors are kept constant, while only certain factors are varied. Cf. 2b and the text immediately following proposition (10e.19). The study of the regular ultra-passum law is consequently one of considerable interest.

B. ECONOMIC SECTION

CHAPTER 9

THE STRATEGIC TYPES AND THE AIMS OF ECONOMIC ADJUSTMENT

9a. The necessity of taking into consideration forms of market other than free competition and absolute monopoly

When the classical theorists investigated the question of how price formation found its own level, how national income was distributed, etc., they nearly always based themselves on the presupposition that free competition existed. This presupposition involves a number of elements, but the one which has the greatest bearing on the shape that the theory will assume, is the presupposition that none of the economic individuals operating in the market, in production, etc., plays such an important role that they are capable *on their own* of exercising a marked influence on the market situation. On the basis of this presupposition, it was natural that a theory was developed where, in practically every sphere, it was taken for granted that *every individual acts as though the general features of the market situation, especially prices, is given, and cannot be influenced by him.* Thus, the only course then left to the individual, was to adjust himself to the various given situations; the *consumers*, for example, adjusted their consumption, and *producers* adjusted their production to given prices, etc. The only exception was to be found in the very opposite extreme, viz. a single producer who exercised a monopoly.

It is obvious that the presupposition of free competition, or in an exceptional case of a complete monopoly, to a large extent helped to make the theory *simple and easy to grasp*, and there is no denying that this simplified theory was by no means out of place in the conditions obtaining in the last century, and therefore made a considerable contribution to clarifying problems of price formation and distribution.

But the development of social and economic institutions has rendered these two presuppositions – completely free competition on the one hand and complete monopoly on the other – less and less compatible with reality. We are now living in a period when many kinds of *concentration tendencies* are making their effect felt within the economic set-up. At the same time a great many public control measures of various kinds have been introduced. This has changed the overall picture in a great many ways. To some extent these elements have reduced competition, but this is by no means the case in every respect and in every sphere. At times competition has been sharpened; we have, for example, witnessed a life-and-death struggle between two or more large concerns ('Kampf der Giganten'). And the result of public measures aimed, e.g., at regulating production, and the like, has by no means always been to remove competition; it has merely assumed *other forms*.

In this somewhat confused situation it has proved necessary to develop an economic theory which not only considers the two extreme cases of free competition in the classical sense of the word and an absolute monopoly, but also a number of other forms of market and *other forms of economic strategy*.[1] This is of importance not least to the theory of production, as the production and price and sales policy of industry, etc., will also vary considerably according to the changing conditions, internally and externally. As far as possible a realistic theory must take this into consideration.

With this in mind, we shall undertake a classification of the most important *strategic types* with which we have to deal.

We distinguish first and foremost between two large groups, which we call *fixation strategy* and *negotiation strategy*. The difference between them can be described as follows: It must be possible to describe any economic situation which is to be analysed by a certain set of *attributes*. Many of these may be of a *quantitative* kind, occurring as variables or constants in the theory, e.g. the prices ruling in the market, the total quantities produced and consumed, and also such factors as the quantities produced by certain concerns or consumed by certain consumers. Some of the attributes may also be of a *qualitative* kind, viz. they are not expressed merely in figures. For the sake of simplicity we shall here merely consider the quantitative attributes, and we call them *parameters* characterizing the economic situation. The line of argument that now follows will, in actual fact, not differ markedly if we also take into consideration the qualitative attributes.

If the situation is such that it is possible to specify for a definite parameter a definite individual or organisation which has it in its power to *fix* the size of this parameter, and does actually in fact undertake this fixation, then we say that this is a fixation parameter or an action parameter for the individual or organisation concerned. It is assumed in principle that the individual or organisation concerned is entirely free to make such a decision. This, natural-

---

[1] The pioneering work in this domain was carried out by my late friend F. Zeuthen.

ly, does not imply that the decision is arrived at casually. In many ways it will have been *motivated* by a great many kinds of relations existing between the individual and other economic units; in fact, to a large extent the aim of the theory is to explain why the individual decides to choose a definite fixation of his parameter. But *if* the individual wishes to undertake a certain fixation, then this should be possible. This is the sense in which the individual is presupposed to be free to make his decision. As examples of fixation parameters (action parameters) can be mentioned: the quantity of a particular article that a consumer buys in the market, the price a monopolist sets for his product, etc.

If a certain sphere of economic life can be analysed with the help of fixation parameters and all other characteristics are dependent thereon, then we say that in this sphere there exists a *fixation strategy*.

This category includes not only the classical examples with completely free competition and an absolute monopoly, but also a number of others; for example, most forms of duopoly, polypoly, etc. There are, however, yet other strategic situations which are more complicated, and where the parameters that describe the constellation of the economy are not fixed at will by a definite party, but where more or less complicated negotiations take place. It is obvious, for instance, that in terms of the definition given above, we cannot describe a wage rate established by collective bargaining as a fixation parameter either for employees or employers. Both parties exercise their influence through the medium of negotiations. This is where negotiation strategy comes in. Proposals and counter-proposals, for example, are not always made because one expects the proposal to be accepted, but because one aims at achieving a certain effect on the subsequent course of negotiations. We can here distinguish between a *one*-move and a *two*-move strategy, etc.[1] All this tends to produce a theory which is essentially more complicated than the theory which can be formulated with the help of fixation strategy concepts. Below we shall not deal in detail with an analysis of production problems based on negotiation strategy, but shall consider certain simple problems involving fixation strategy.

The fixation-strategy type can be divided into two: the *autonomous* and the *conjectural*, according to whether the individual in his deliberations takes into consideration variations in other elements in the economic system, besides his own parameters of action. An individual may be said to act *autonomously*, or to carry out an *autonomous* adjustment, if in his deliber-

---

[1] The connection with the modern theory of games of strategy is obvious.

ations he assumes that the other parameters describing the constellation in the economic sphere concerned will not be changed because this individual decides to change *his* parameters. On the other hand, we say that the individual is acting *conjecturally*, or undertakes a conjectural adjustment, if in his deliberations he believes that a change in *his* parameters will probably induce a change in the fixation parameters belonging to *other* decision makers. The *strength* with which a person *believes* that the parameters belonging to others will be changed if he himself changes his parameters, can be described by means of certain *conjectural elasticities* for this individual. The size of these elasticities will have an essential bearing on the individual's own reaction and thus on the entire market situation and tendency of evolution. This is dealt with in my lectures on the theory of polypoly.

We shall now consider some of the most important special fixation strategy types and subsequently the aims and conditions of an adjustment process.

9b. Quantity adjustment

Let us consider an individual faced with a problem of evaluating two goods. These may be two direct goods, or one of the goods may be money. Let us imagine, for example, that our individual is given the opportunity of undertaking an exchange between the two goods in a certain given proportion, i.e., at a given price, but to an *extent* which the individual himself can decide. Any distinction between buyer and seller is quite unnecessary, since this difference can be described by calculating in terms of positive and negative quantities of goods. An individual placed in a situation of this kind is called a *quantity adjuster*, and the process is a quantity *adjustment*. The typical example of a quantity adjuster is the ordinary demander in a free market of goods. The presupposition is that he *believes* that the price will not be changed by the fact that he decides to buy a little less or a little more. This may be valid if he is not a *big* purchaser in relation to the whole market.

Another example of quantity adjustment is the speculator who acts as the seller of a staple article, for example wheat. If his transactions are not large in relation to the whole market, he will, and realistically so, believe that he is able to sell as much or as little of his quantity as he might want to at a price which is practically speaking equal to that quoted at the moment in question. But as soon as we turn to goods which by their nature are not staple articles, but more individually determined goods, it might be unrealistic for him to believe that the price is unaffected by his own action.

The ordinary supply and demand curves are based on the idea of quantity adjustment. If demand is more or less organised the concepts characterising 'demand' will be far more complicated and cannot be described by ordinary demand curves.

Not infrequently the supply curve is regarded as an expression of the price offered by sellers in order to place a certain quantity on the market. This is not correct if the demand curve is constructed as a quantity adjustment curve. Admittedly we could formally reverse the functional relationship between price and quantity, i.e. we could say that if a supply curve for the market exists, then the supply side of the market will react as though it required such and such prices in order to produce such and such quantities on the market. *But this does not mean that every single seller adjusts his price according to a quantity which has been decided from outside.* If the situation is such that a seller organises his affairs so as to adjust his price according to a given quantity, then the individual supply curve no longer exists, nor do the market supply curves in the ordinary sense of the word exist.

9c. Stochastic price adjustment

Situations occasionally arise where the individual is not faced with a given price, but with a given quantity. On the basis of this quantity the individual has to adjust the price. We may assume that the quantity is given in the sense that, *if* a deal is done, then it will be a deal for *this* given quantity. Whether or not a deal will actually take place, is assumed to depend on the price our individual fixes as corresponding to the given quantity. An individual in this situation is called a *price adjuster*; and the situation *stochastic price adjustment*. A *tender* is a typical example of a situation of this kind.

A stochastic price adjustment contains certain *probability considerations* which are not present in the case of what we have termed a quantity adjustment. The price adjuster in the case here considered quotes his price as he weighs the advantages of achieving a better price[1] against the increased risk he runs in failing to strike a bargain. There is a certain price which provides the maximum mathematical hope for his profit. It is also possible to construct a curve indicating the relationship between price and quantity to cover the case here considered. But this curve will be quite different from the ordinary supply-and-demand curve. It is called the *stochastic demand, respectively supply, curve*, in contrast to the ordinary demand, respectively supply, curve.[2]

[1] The expression 'better' price here means a higher price where the seller is concerned, but a lower price where the purchaser is concerned.
[2] This is dealt with in greater detail in my polypoly theory, 1932–1933, Section 7315.

9d. Elasticity-influenced price-quantity adjustment

Let us consider a demander whose business transactions are on a relatively large scale. In this case he will – realistically – *believe* that the market price will to a larger or lesser extent be affected by the quantity he takes. And he will take account of this. Let us assume that he thinks that *the price will vary continuously with the quantity* he purchases, and that he has formed an opinion on this functional relationship.

If we take the extreme case where our individual is the only demander, while suppliers constitute an organised body, this functional relationship will simply be expressed by the market supply curve, if he knows it.

As another example we can take a sales monopolist. As a rule he will know in general outline the elasticity of the demand curve that applies to his particular case, and will take this into consideration.

Such adjustments may be called *elasticity-influenced price-quantity adjustments*. In principle it does not matter whether we assume that the monopolist fixes his price or his quantity. The autonomous quantity adjustment discussed in Section 9b can be regarded as a limiting case of the above, viz. when the elasticity with respect to the quantity is infinite. In this limiting case there is, however, a definite distinction between the case where the point on the curve is determined by the individual fixing the price and that where he fixes the quantity. Indeed, no continuous principle exists capable of being used to calculate a price-change in terms of a corresponding quantity-change, when elasticity is infinite.

9e. Option fixation

The monopolist is only capable of determining *one* of the parameters – price and quantity. He has only a one-dimensional freedom of fixation. And in principle, as we have seen, it does not matter which of the two parameters we assume him to pick. A supplier who *vis-à-vis* the taker or takers can fix both parameters, will enjoy still greater powers. The question he puts to the takers is then simply: will you or will you not agree with these conditions? In other words he says: will you or will you not agree to this given price *and* this given quantity? It is in fact a question of 'take it or leave it'. An individual who has the power to conduct an economic policy of this kind is called an option fixer.

9f. Option reception

A person faced with a choice of 'take it or leave it' is called an *option receiver*. If he accepts, we call him an option accepter.

In the case of the option receiver a third supply, respectively demand, curve can be constructed, which can be called respectively the *forced* supply, respectively demand, curve.[1] In principle the forced demand curve may be assumed to have arisen as follows: First the seller as option poser is assumed to have posed an option containing a certain price and a certain quantity. If the option receiver does *not* accept, the option poser formulates a new choice, at a lower price but involving the same quantity. The option receiver still does not accept. A new offer is made, involving a still lower price, until a point is reached where the option receiver is on the *borderline* of answering Yes or No. This point of indifference is noted, and the attempt is repeated but with a new quantity specified, etc. In this way we shall in principle arrive at a relationship between price and quantity. This relationship is the forced demand curve for the option taker concerned. This curve is obviously different both from the ordinary[2] and the stochastic demand curve. Forced demand and supply curves can also be called *acceptance curves*. They are identical with the indifference curves of the theory of choice.[3]

9g. Aims and conditions for an adjustment process

The expressions 'best possible', 'most advantageous', etc., mean nothing unless one states precisely in the first place what *aim or object* is sought, and in the second place under what *conditions* (constraints) this aim is to be realised. In production the process of adjustment is therefore a question of how the person in charge of production *reacts* to a given situation taking account of the aims and the conditions. It may be the works foreman, if we are dealing with a stage in the joint activities of a larger concern, or the management, if we are dealing with a whole concern, or the head of the industrial branch, if we are thinking of a centrally directed production in a Socialist state. In every case the aim of adjustment and the situation involved, that is to say, the conditions, must be precisely stated before it is possible to say definitely how the adjustment must be carried out in order to be described as 'best possible'.

Aims may be of various kinds:

(1) *Costs minimisation.* Aim: To reduce costs as far as possible. In a case of this kind the conditions may, e.g., be given factor prices and a given

---

[1] The forced supply curve is dealt with in greater detail in my polypoly lectures, 1932–1933, Section 7316.
[2] The ordinary (direct) supply curve is dealt with in Section 10i.
[3] This shows the great power enjoyed by the option poser.

product quantity, or they may be a given level of employment for a certain factor (public works as a remedy for unemployment), etc.

(2) *Product maximisation*. Aim: To make the product as large as possible. In such cases the conditions may be, e.g., a constant given cost sum (given capital available, etc.), and given factor prices, or conditions may be simply 'at all costs', as for example during a war or crisis.

(3) *Profit maximisation*. Aim: To make *total* net profit (i.e., the money value of the product minus total costs) as large as possible.

(4) *Profit optimisation*. Aim: To make the *rate* of profit (i.e., the ratio between total net profit and total cost) as large as possible.

Conditions may be of various kinds. Apart from those already mentioned, there may be conditions with regard to prices or the nature of the price functions (given supply functions for factors, for instance), or conditions with regard to strategic types (cf. Chapter 9). What may be 'the best possible' under *one* set of conditions, may not be the same under another. Or there may be conditions with regard to factor variations, such as the following:

(A) *A single factor adjustment*. Condition: All factor quantities are constant except for one factor quantity which can be varied.

(B) *A group adjustment*. Condition: There is a group of factors whose quantities are each independently variable. All other factors are constant.

(C) *Complete adjustment*. Condition: All factor quantities are freely variable.

(D) *A general region-conditioned adjustment*. Condition: All factor quantities can be varied, but on condition that the factor point is to lie in a certain given region of the factor diagram. Conditions (A) and (B) are special cases of this.

In principle any of the above aims can be combined with any of the conditions mentioned; in this way we get a great many possible adjustment-types. Not all of them, however, are of equally great interest; we shall here select some of the most important ones and examine them.

It is especially in one respect that the selection we shall deal with is incomplete, viz. with regard to adjustment for the more complicated strategic types. A detailed study of this, however, would go well beyond the framework of the actual theory of production, and well into the general *polypoly theory*. This is another sector of the economic theory which undoubtedly has a great many points of contact with the production theory, but also has implications in other directions, e.g. connections with the general *localisation theory* and the modern theory of games, and which it would therefore be more convenient to deal with separately. The simpler

STRATEGIC TYPES AND AIMS OF ECONOMIC ADJUSTMENT

strategic types such as the quantity adjustment to fixed prices, or elasticity-influenced price-quantity adjustment under given supply-and-demand functions, will be dealt with below.[1]

---

[1] Cf. my polypoly lectures 1932–1933 or 1941.

CHAPTER 10

ECONOMIC ADJUSTMENT TO FIXED PRICES

10a. Introduction

We shall continue to base ourselves on the assumptions of the technical nature of production mentioned in the Introduction to Part Two. (Momentary single production with only continuity factors whose quantities – in common with the product quantity – can be measured in terms of technical units.)

Furthermore we shall presuppose that the adjuster – being a producer – acts as a *price-fixed quantity adjuster* (cf. Section 9b) both in the market for the finished product and in the market for the n variable production factors used in the manufacture of his product. (For the moment we shall not consider the fixed factors. Cf. Section 2b and the end of Section 10e.) In other words the decision maker will have to face 'outside' given prices for factors as well as for the product.

Let the price of the product be p and let the prices of the n production factors be $q_1, q_2, \ldots, q_n$.

The cost of production consist of the sum of the outlay for each production factor. The outlay for factor No. 1 is equal to the price of factor No. i, viz. q_i times the quantity v_i of factor No. i. Thus for the cost (of the variable factors) we get

(10a.1) Total cost (for the variable factors) =
$$b = q_1 v_1 + q_2 v_2 + \ldots + q_n v_n = \sum_{i=1}^{n} q_i v_i \,.$$

In the special case when there are only two production factors ($n=2$), we get

(10a.2) $\qquad\qquad b = q_1 v_1 + q_2 v_2\,.$

In (10a.2), q_1 and q_2 are given constants. If then the total cost for the variable factors are to assume a definite size, the equation (10a.2) will be a linear equation between the two variables v_1 and v_2. We call this equation the *cost equation*, graphically represented in Figure (10a.4). From (10a.2) we can get v_2 expressed explicitly as a function of v_1, viz.

(10a.3) $$v_2 = \frac{b}{q_2} - \frac{q_1}{q_2} v_2,$$

$(-q_1/q_2)$ is the angular coefficient of the line. If the price ratio between the factors is changed, the slope of the costs line will also be changed.

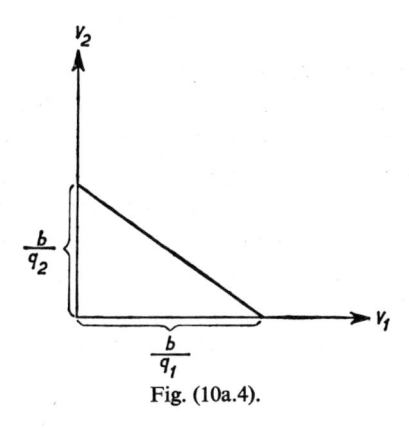

Fig. (10a.4).

The cost line cuts the v_1-axis where $v_1 = b/q_1$ (at this point the entire costs will be spent on factor No. 1). The line cuts the v_2-axis where $v_2 = b/q_2$ (at that point the entire costs will be spent on factor No. 2).

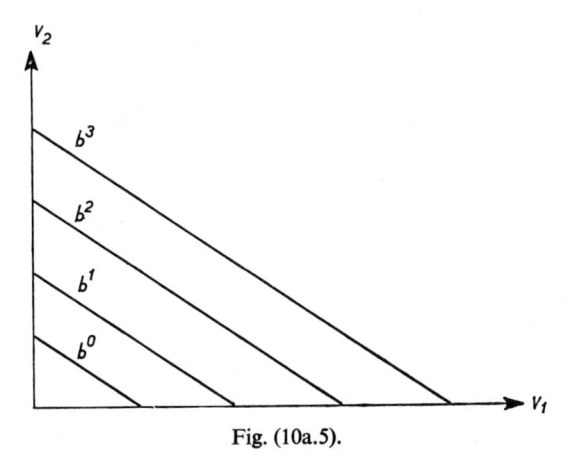

Fig. (10a.5).

The cost lines corresponding to various total costs for given factor prices are *parallel*. Obviously, when b is changed, the interception points of the cost line with the axes will be changed in the same ratio. If, for example, total costs are doubled, then both the two axis-cuts will be doubled. The cost lines therefore will be lying one after another towards the north-east. The whole factor diagram can be visualised as filled with parallel cost lines of this kind. In Figure (10a.5) the lines for total cost are drawn, equalling respectively b^0, b^1, b^2, b^3.

With three factors ($n=3$) the cost equation will be

(10a.6) $$q_1 v_1 + q_2 v_2 + q_3 v_3 = b.$$

If the q's and b are given, this is the equation of a plane. For every value of b, we here get a definite *cost plane* in the three-dimensional factor diagram. See Figure (10a.7). The axis cuts here, too, show how large a factor quantity will arise if the entire total cost is applied to a single factor. The cost planes corresponding to various total costs, with constant factor prices, are parallel. The situation is analogous to that involving two variables. If the ratios between the factor prices are changed, the slope of the cost plane will be changed.

For more than three variables we cannot use a direct graphic representa-

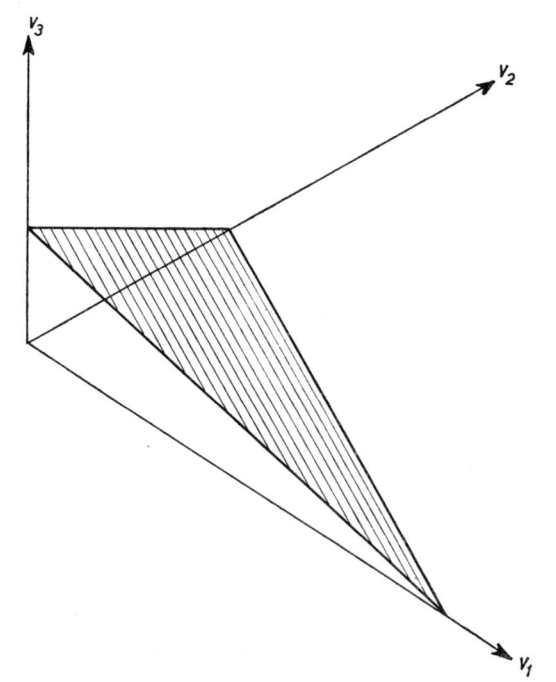

Fig. (10a.7). Cost plane in a three-dimensional factor diagram.

tion, but this does not prevent us, in a symbolical sense, from speaking of a 'costs plane', as this is a convenient form of expression.

The cost equation – with given factor prices and given total cost – is *one* equation between the *n* variable $v_1, \ldots, v_n$. The 'cost plane' will therefore be a $(n-1)$-dimensional 'hyper-plane' in the *n*-dimensional factor diagram.

10b. Cost minimisation under a given product quantity

We shall first take the case where the object of adjustment is to produce a given product quantity with the lowest possible costs.

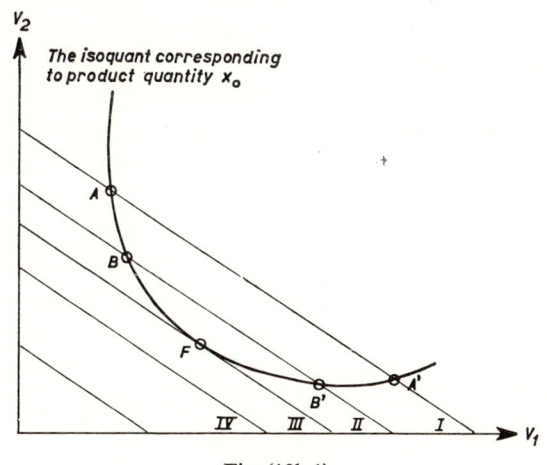

Fig. (10b.1).

The case involving *two* factors ($n=2$) can be dealt with in a graphic analysis of the kind suggested in the two-dimensional factor diagram (10b.1). We have here drawn in the isoquant corresponding to the given product quantity x_0. The equation for this isoquant is

(10b.2) $$x(v_1, v_2) = x_0.$$

We presuppose that the isoquant is curved towards the origin in the substitution region, as drawn in the Figure. Cf. (5i.10).

When the factor prices are given, a great many parallel cost lines can be drawn in the factor diagram of Figure (10b.1) in the same way as in Figure (10a.5).

The object is to find the factor point that can produce the given product quantity x_0 in the cheapest possible way. This is obviously solved by our moving along the isoquant for x_0 until we encounter a factor point on the lowest (most south-westerly) cost line which it is possible to reach as long as we are required to remain on the given isoquant.

Let us, for instance, take our point of departure in point A on the isoquant under consideration. Through point A runs the cost line I; it intersects the given isoquant also at point A'. It will then obviously be possible to find another point on the isoquant (for instance, point B) situated on a cost line lying south-west of cost line I. If this cost line, too, intersects the isoquant at two points, we can reach a still lower cost line. Not till we have reached a cost line which has only *one* point in common with the given isoquant, will the condition that we must remain on the isoquant prevent us from moving further south-west. Thus adjustment will take place in the factor point F, which is situated on cost line III. The fact that cost line III only has one point in common with the isoquant is expressed saying that cost line III *is tangential to* the isoquant. If the isoquant is curved towards the origine, as in Figure (10b.1), there will be one, and only one, such tangential point.

We shall now express this relationship analytically. In the tangential point the tangent steepness of the isoquant is equal to the steepness of the cost line. In the case of the tangent steepness of the isoquant we have seen, cf. (5i.6), that

(10b.3) $$\frac{dv_1}{dv_1} = -\frac{x_1'}{x_2'} \quad \text{along the isoquant.}$$

For the inclination of the cost line we found in (10a.3)

(10b.4) $$\frac{dv_2}{dv_1} = -\frac{q_1}{q_2} \quad \text{along the cost line.}$$

As we have, at the tangential point between the isoquant and the cost line,

(10b.5) $$\frac{dv_2}{dv_1} \text{ along the isoquant} = \frac{dv_2}{dv_1} \text{ along the cost line,}$$

the condition for cost-minimisation with a given product quantity in two factors will be

(10b.6) $$\frac{x_1'}{x_2'} = \frac{q_1}{q_2}.$$

Thus in the adjustment point considered *the ratio between marginal productivities must be equal to the ratio between factor prices.*

A simple rearrangement of (10b.6) gives

(10b.7)
$$\frac{x_1'}{q_1} = \frac{x_2'}{q_2}.$$

We can also express the condition by saying that at the adjustment point *marginal productivities are proportional to factor prices*.

Equation (10b.6) gives us an equation between two variables v_1 and v_2. (Both x_1' and x_2' are, indeed, functions of v_1 and v_2.) Furthermore we have the condition for the given product quantity, i.e. we have a total of two independent equations between the *two* variables v_1 and v_2. This determines v_1 and v_2.

If the factor prices are positive (i.e., not 'free' factors, cf. Section 2a) then according to (10b.7) marginal productivities must have the same sign. If both marginal productivities were negative, we could increase the product quantity by *reducing* the quantities of both factors. Obviously a point where this is so cannot be the factor point representing a given product quantity with the lowest costs. Consequently in the adjustment point both marginal productivities must be positive, or, in other words: *the adjustment point must be situated in the substitution region*.

We shall now consider the general case with n production factors. The problem consists in ascertaining the sizes of the factor quantities $v_1, v_2, \ldots, v_n$ so that

(10b.8)
$$b = \sum_{i=1}^{n} q_i v_i$$

is as small as possible, with the 'side-condition' (constraint)

(10b.9)
$$x(v_1, \ldots, v_n) = x_0.$$

This problem can be solved with the help of Lagrange's method. This consists of introducing an *auxiliary function* which is equal to the function to be minimized *minus* a temporarily undefined parameter λ times the function which, when it is made equal to 0, expresses the side condition. In the case under consideration this auxiliary function will be

(10b.10)
$$G(v_1, \ldots, v_n) = \sum_{i=1}^{n} q_i v_i - \lambda [x(v_1, \ldots, v_n) - x_0].$$

The necessary first order condition for a minimum of (10b.10) can be found by putting all the partial derivatives of the auxiliary function equal to 0, while the parameter λ is regarded as constant. This gives the n conditions

(10b.11)
$$\frac{\partial G}{\partial v_i} = q_i - \lambda x_i'.$$

Furthermore we have the condition (10b.9) for given constant product quantity, i.e. we have a total of $(n+1)$ equations. At the same time we have $(n+1)$ quaesitum-parameters, viz. the auxiliary parameter λ and the n factor quantities $v_1, v_2, ..., v_n$ (since marginal productivities are functions of the quantities). Thus in principle the system is determined.

The system (10b.11) can be written in the form

(10b.12) $$\frac{x_1'}{q_1} = \frac{x_2'}{q_2} = ... = \frac{x_n'}{q_n} = \frac{1}{\lambda}.$$

If we so desire, we can consider only the first $(n-1)$ of these equations. This is the same as eliminating λ. These conditions are quite analogous to the tangent condition (10b.7) which we considered in the case involving two factors.

The individual proportionality numbers in (10b.12) can be interpreted concretely by means of the concept of *partial marginal cost*. The partial marginal cost for factor No. k is simply the ratio between the change $q_k dv_k$ in total cost and the corresponding change $x_k' dv_k$ in the product quantity when factor No. k is given a small (infinitesimal) change and all the other factors remain constant. This ratio (under fixed factor prices) is the same as

(10b.13) The partial marginal cost with respect to factor

$$\text{No. } k = \frac{\partial \sum_{i=1}^{n} q_i v_i}{\partial v_k} \bigg/ \frac{\partial x}{\partial v_k} = \frac{q_k}{x_k'}.$$

Condition (10b.12) can then be expressed by saying that *all the partial marginal costs must be equal* and equal to parameter λ. 'A sufficient second order' condition for a regular minimum of (10b.8) with the 'side condition' of (10b.9) can in determinant form be expressed as[1]

(10b.14) $$\begin{vmatrix} 0 & x_1' & ... & x_k' \\ x_1' & G_{11}'' & ... & G_{1k}'' \\ .... \\ .... \\ x_k' & G_{k1}'' & ... & G_{kk}'' \end{vmatrix} < 0 \quad (k=2, 3, ..., n).$$

where

(10b.15) $$G_{ij}'' = \frac{\partial^2 G(v_1, ..., v_n)}{\partial v_i \partial v_j} \quad (i=1, ..., n; j=1, ..., n).$$

[1] A more complete study of 'second order' conditions is given in my book *Maxima et Minima*, Dunod, Paris, 1959, which will also appear in English at D. Reidel Publishing Company, Dordrecht, Holland.

This 'second order' condition can be connected with the *curvature* of the isoquants as follows.

By differentiating (10b.11) with respect to v_j we get

(10b.16) $\qquad G_{ij}'' = -\lambda x_{ij}''$.

And if (10b.16) is inserted on the left side of (10b.14) we get

$$\begin{vmatrix} 0 & x_1' & \dots & x_k' \\ x_1' & (-\lambda x_{11}'') & \dots & (-\lambda x_{1k}'') \\ \vdots & & & \\ x_k' & (-\lambda x_{k1}'') & \dots & (-\lambda x_{kk}'') \end{vmatrix}.$$

By dividing all the lines in this determinant except the top one by $(-\lambda)$ and then multiplying the first column in the determinant by $(-\lambda)$ we get

(10b.17) $\qquad (-\lambda)^{k-1} \begin{vmatrix} 0 & x_1' & \dots & x_k' \\ x_1' & x_{11}'' & \dots & x_{1k}'' \\ \vdots & & & \\ x_k' & x_{k1}'' & \dots & x_{kk}'' \end{vmatrix} < 0 \qquad (k=2, 3, \dots, n)$.

In the adjustment point both q_i and x_1' will be positive and λ – which is determined by (10b.12) – will consequently also be positive; that is to say the factor $(-\lambda)^{k-1}$ in front of the determinant in (10b.17) has the same sign as $(-1)^{k-1}$. In other words, the 'second order' condition (10b.14) is fulfilled if we have (5i.11), which is the condition that the isoquants are curved towards the origin in the substitution region. If this is the case, then consequently the sufficient 'second order' condition will be fulfilled, and we have a regular cost minimum.

10c. Product maximisation with given total cost

Let us now consider the case where the adjustment aim is to produce as much as possible for a given amount of cost. The producer may, for example, have a certain amount of money at his disposal when he has to procure the production factors.

Let us first make a graphic analysis to cover the case involving only two factors ($n=2$).

In the two-dimensional factor diagram (10c.1) we have drawn in the cost line corresponding to the given cost magnitude b_0. Furthermore we have drawn in a number of isoquants.

The problem is now to find the point situated on the most north-eastern of the isoquants which it is possible to reach if we are forced to remain on the given cost line. In the same way as in Section 10b we shall discover that we can do this by adjusting ourselves in the factor point where the given cost line *is tangential to* an isoquant. In the Figure this point will be *P*.

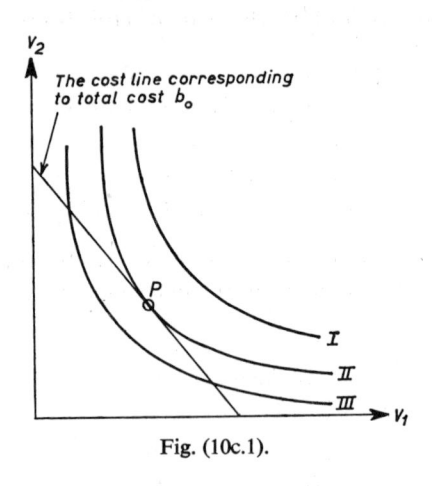

Fig. (10c.1).

In the tangential point between the cost line and the isoquant we must have

(10c.2) $\dfrac{dv_2}{dv_1}$ along the cost line = $\dfrac{dv_2}{dv_1}$ along the isoquant.

This, however, is the same as the condition (10b.5) we came across when the adjustment aim was cost minimisation with a given product quantity. As we saw, this condition can also be expressed in the form (10b.6) or (10b.7).

The side-condition, however, is different in the two cases. On the former occasion it was a given product quantity; now we are dealing with a given total cost. For this reason we shall not necessarily arrive at the same factor point in these two cases. It will all depend on the side-conditions envisaged.

We shall now undertake an analytical treatment of the general case involving *n* factors. The aim is now to find the factor combination which makes

(10c.3) $\qquad x(v_1, \ldots, v_n)$

as large as possible, with the side-condition

(10c.4) $\qquad \sum\limits_{i=1}^{n} q_i v_i = b_0 .$

This problem is also solved by Lagrange's method. First we form an auxiliary function

(10c.5) $$H(v_1, \ldots, v_n) = x(v_1, \ldots, v_n) - \mu(\Sigma\, q_i v_i - b_0),$$

where μ is a parameter which is kept constant during the process of maximisation. The necessary first order condition for maximum of (10c.3), with the side-condition (10c.4), can be found by putting all the partial derivatives of the auxiliary function (10c.5) equal to nought. This gives

(10c.6) $$\frac{\partial H}{\partial v_i} = x_i' - \mu q_i = 0 \qquad (i = 1, 2, \ldots, n).$$

The necessary first order conditions (10c.6), together with the side-condition (10c.4), give $n+1$ equations between $n+1$ quaesitum parameters, viz. the auxiliary parameter μ and the factor quantity $v_1, \ldots, v_n$ (since marginal productivities are functions of the factor quantities).

The system is consequently determined.

The system (10c.6) can be written in the form

(10c.7) $$\frac{x_1'}{q_1} = \frac{x_2'}{q_2} = \ldots = \frac{x_n'}{q_n} = \mu.$$

The first $(n-1)$ of these equations are precisely *the same* as in the first $(n-1)$ equations in (10b.12). They express the *tangential condition* as opposed to the side-condition. For cost minimisation x_0 was given, and for product maximisation b_0 was given.

The condition of the second order for a regular maximum of (10c.3), with the side-condition (10c.4), is

(10c.8) $$(-1)^k \begin{vmatrix} 0 & q_1 & \ldots & q_k \\ q_1 & H_{11}'' & \ldots & H_{1k}'' \\ \ldots & \ldots & \ldots & \ldots \\ \ldots & \ldots & \ldots & \ldots \\ q_k & H_{k1}'' & \ldots & H_{kk}'' \end{vmatrix} > 0 \qquad (k = 2, 3, \ldots, n),$$

where

(10c.9) $$H_{ij}'' = \frac{\partial^2 H(v_1, \ldots, v_n)}{\partial v_i \partial v_j} \qquad (i = 1, \ldots, n;\ j = 1, \ldots, n).$$

We can now proceed in the same way as in (10b.16) and (10b.17).

By differentiating (10c.6) with respect to v_j we get

(10c.10) $$H_{ij}'' = x_{ij}'' \qquad (i = 1, \ldots, n;\ j = 1, \ldots, n).$$

And if we insert (10c.10) in (10c.8) we get

$$(10c.11) \qquad (-1)^k \begin{vmatrix} 0 & q_1 & \cdots & q_k \\ q_1 & x_{11}'' & \cdots & x_{1k}'' \\ \cdots & \cdots & \cdots & \cdots \\ q_k & x_{11}'' & \cdots & x_{kk}'' \end{vmatrix} > 0 \qquad (k=2, 3, \ldots, n).$$

However, according to (10c.6) $q_i = x_i'/\mu$. If this is inserted in (10c.11), while at the same time we multiply the first line and the first column in the determinant by μ, we get

$$(-1)^k \frac{1}{\mu^2} \begin{vmatrix} 0 & x_1' & \cdots & x_k' \\ x_1' & x_{11}'' & \cdots & x_{1k}'' \\ \cdots & \cdots & \cdots & \cdots \\ x_k' & x_{k1}'' & \cdots & x_{kk}'' \end{vmatrix} > 0 \qquad (k=2, 3, \ldots, n).$$

At the adjustment point both x_1' and q_i will be positive and μ – on account of (10c.7) – will consequently be different from 0. The second order condition will therefore also be the same as (5i.11).

The fact that the isoquants are curved towards the origin in the neighbourhood of the adjustment point thus, both for cost minimisation and for cost maximisation, is sufficient to ensure that the second order condition is fulfilled.

10d. The in-every-respect economic substitution. The substitumal

Let us return to the graphic analysis of the case involving cost minimisation with two factors, cf. 10b. We shall now also carry out this cost minimisation for *other* given magnitudes of the product quantity than x_0.

The factor point which gives product quantity x_0 with a minimum of costs, will be tangential point F in the Figure (10d.1). In the same way we can find the tangential points when the given product quantities are respectively x_1, x_2, etc. See the Figure. We can deal with an infinite number of isoquants, and thus obtaining an infinite number of tangential points. If we join them all up in *a curve*, we shall get the curve $FGHJ$. At every point of this curve we shall have a minimum of costs for a given product quantity. Once the curve $FGHJ$ has been drawn, we can therefore find the adjustment point corresponding to a given product quantity, simply by constructing the isoquant concerned, and marking the point where it intersects the curve $FGHJ$.

Let us consider the problem we dealt with in Section 10c, product maximisation for a given total cost, still confining ourselves to two factors. Let us consider various magnitudes for total costs.

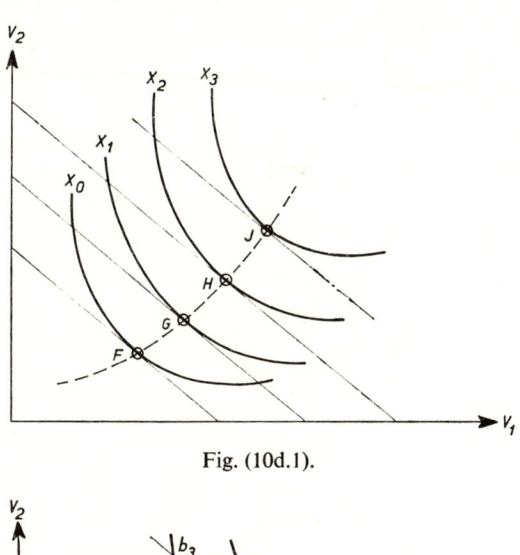

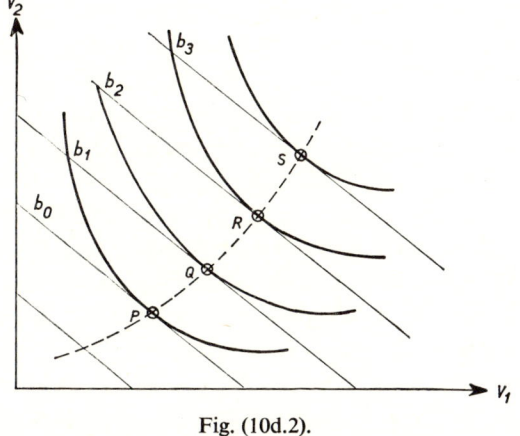

Fig. (10d.1).

Fig. (10d.2).

In Figure (10d.2) we shall get the tangential point P which determines product maximisation for total cost b_0. In the same way point Q will give us the tangential point corresponding to product maximisation for total costs equal to b_1, and R will give us the tangential point corresponding to product maximisation for total costs equal to b_2, etc. We can insert an infinite number of cost lines in the factor diagram, and in this way we shall get an infinite number of tangential points which can be joined up to the continuous curve *PQRS*. The curve *PQRS* has this quality, that at any point of this curve we have a maximum of product quantity for given total costs. Once the curve *PQRS* in Figure (10d.2) has been drawn, we can find the adjustment point corresponding to a given total cost, simply by constructing the total cost line concerned, and marking the point where it intersects the curve *PQRS*.

It is a fundamental fact that in both cases we arrive at *the same curve*. In other words *the curve PQRS in Figure (10d.2) is identical with the curve FGHJ* in Figure (10d.1). Indeed, the curve *PQRS*, by its definition, is the geometrical locus for all factor points possessing the property that they are tangential points for isoquants and cost lines. The curve *FGHJ*, however, has by its very definition precisely the same property. Or, to express it differently: both the curves mentioned are defined by one and the same equation, viz. (10b.7). See also the reasoning adduced in connection with (10c.2).

The curve *FGHJ* – which is the same as curve *PQRS* – thus solves *at one and the same time* the problem of cost minimisation and the problem of product maximisation. We have only to combine this curve with the side-condition applying in the problem concerned. For cost minimisation this side-condition is a given isoquant, and for product maximisation it is a given cost line.

But that is not all: the curve we are considering has *a still more general significance*. Let us consider a little more closely the concept 'substitution', which we touched on at the conclusion of Section 5b. This is a change in factor combination, but not just *any* change. We would, for example, not say that a proportional increase of all factors was 'substitution'. We should interpret it as an increase in the scale of production. If – on the same lines as was done in the text subsequent to Figure (8.2) – we also allow any movement *outwards* in the factor diagram (at any rate a movement which does not deviate too strongly from a proportional factor variation) to be designated as an increase in scale, then 'substitution' and 'change of scale' will in a way become contrary concepts. Roughly we can describe this graphically by saying that a change in scale is a movement *outwards* in the factor diagram, while a substitution is a movement *across* the factor diagram.

This must be explained in greater detail. The most obvious way of describing substitution, i.e. a movement 'across' would – as long as we are in the substitution area, – be to say that it is a movement along an isoquant, i.e. under a constant product quantity. Cost minimisation can then be described by saying that by means of a *substitution* we have reduced costs. This

ECONOMIC ADJUSTMENT TO FIXED PRICES 157

definition of substitution is in itself precise enough, but it limits the concept so much that in certain cases it appears artificial. When for example we replace one factor by another in such a way that the product quantity increases, while total costs are kept constant, then it would be quite natural to say that *in this case too* we have carried out a substitution. The factor which is expensive in relation to its marginal effect has been *substituted*, its place being taken by one that is cheap in relation to its marginal effect. By carrying out a *substitution* of this kind we have been able to raise the product quantity without increasing costs. The 'across' movement then becomes a movement along the cost line. Both definitions of substitution are plausible. Both can be contained within the following generalised concept of substitution:

DEFINITION (10d.3)
Any factor change which either decreases total costs without decreasing the product or increases the product without increasing total costs, we call *an in-every-respect economic substitution*.

We have here only used this definition in connection with the figures that apply for the case involving two factors. We have, moreover, assumed constant factor prices. In principle, however, we can apply the definition (10d.3) quite generally.

It is obvious that the kind of factor variation defined in (10d.3) must play a large role in economic adjustment processes. Practically speaking any reasonably defined adjustment process will, after all, be such that we are brought *a step in the right direction* if we carry out a factor variation of this kind. All processes dealt with in Chapter 10 are of this kind.

Between the substitution concept as formulated in Definition (10d.3) and the curve *FGHJ* in Figure (10d.1) – which is the same as the curve *PQRS* in Figure (10d.2) – there is a fundamental and precise connection, which is expressed in the following proposition.

PROPOSITION (10d.4)
The curve FGHJ – which is the same as the curve PQRS – represents the factor points where it is not *possible to carry out an in-every-respect economic substitution.*

In other words: if we are placed in any point in the factor diagram *outside* this curve, it is always possible, starting from this point, to undertake

158   MOMENTARY SINGLE PRODUCTION

an in-every-respect economic substitution. But if we are at a point *on* the curve, it is never possible to undertake an in-every-respect economic substitution. Any movement starting in a point on this curve must thus necessarily either increase costs or decrease the product quantity. We call this curve the *substitumal*. That is to say

DEFINITION (10d.5)

The *substitumal* is the locus of all points in the factor diagram from which it is *not* possible to undertake an in-every-respect economic substitution. Cf. Definition (10d.3). A point on the substitumal is called a substitumal point.

Definition (10d.5) can likewise be made to apply generally for n factors and for factor prices which are not necessarily constant.

It is easy to see graphically that the curve *FGHJ* – which is the same as *PQRS* – must be the substitumal in accordance with Definition (10d.5).

Let us, for instance, take point K in Figure (10d.6). Since this point lies outside the curve *FGHJ*, the isoquant and the cost line running through K will according to definition *form an angle* with one another. Consequently there must be a region, viz. the shaded portion – the crust –, which *at the same*

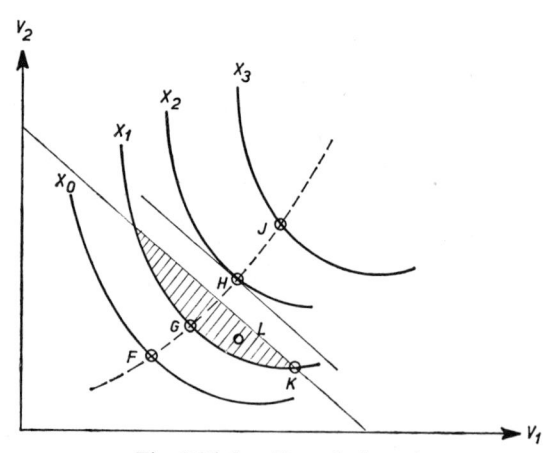

Fig. (10d.6). The substitumal.

time lies south-west of the cost line and north-east of the isoquant. Inside this region, therefore, costs will be lower and product quantity at the same time higher than in K. In other words, any movement leading from K to a point inside the crust, for example, to L, will be an in-every-respect economic substitution. A movement running from K to a point on the boundary of the crust will also be an in all respects economic substitution, as a movement of this kind will either increase the product, under constant cost (if it leads to a point on the north-east border of the crust), or decrease costs under constant product quantity (if it leads to a point on the south-west border of the crust). The shaded crust thus forms an *region of possibility* for an in-every-respect economic substitution running from *K*. Such would be the situation if we start from any point lying *outside* the curve *FGHJ*. But in any point lying *on* this curve, it will *not* be so; since the points on *FGHJ* are precisely defined as the points where the isoquant and the cost line do *not* form any angle with one another, but are *tangential* to one another. Taking a point of this kind, for example *H*, as our starting point, it is only on the north-east side of the common tangent that we find product quantities higher than in *H*, and only on the south-west side of the common tangent that we find costs lower than in *H*. Thus there is no point which, starting from *H*, can realise an in-every-respect an economic substitution. Thus any point on *FGHJ* possesses the property that here *substitution* is complete.

On the basis of the fundamental properties of the substitumal which we have discussed, it is easy to draw the following further conclusion: Any 'reasonable' adjustment, i.e. any adjustment whose object is such that it is an advantage to lower costs, if this can be done without detriment to the product quantity, or to increase the product quantity, if this can be done without increasing costs, must, if it is to be carried out, *finally lead to some point or other on the substitumal*. If we know nothing more about the aim of adjustment than that it is to be 'reasonable' in the sense we have mentioned above, we can thus say that adjustment *must* lead us to a point on the substitumal. A point *outside* it can never provide a solution. This movement in the direction of the substitumal can be conceived of as taking place in *successive* stages. In the first stage, for instance, we move from *K* to *L* in Figure (10d.6). *L* can be taken as the corner of a new and smaller crust-shaped region lying *inside* the large shaded portion. In other words, from *L* we get a new and smaller region of possibility. Making a new movement into it, we get a still smaller region of possibility, etc. In this way the movement *converges* towards a point on the substitumal.

For *which special point* of the substitumal, then, are we finally to look? *That* depends on *how in particular the aim or the side-condition of the adjustment is specified*. This specification provides the extra condition which determines the *point* on the substitumal. We have already seen two examples of this: with product maximisation under a given constant cost, the given cost line provided the necessary additional condition (intersection between this cost line and the curve *FGHJ*) and for cost minimisation, under a given constant product quantity, the given isoquant provided the additional condition (intersection between this isoquant and the curve *PQRS*). For other kinds of adjustment processes, the additional condition may be formulated in any number of other ways.

We thus get the best overall view of adjustment problems if in each case we divide the specifications of the solution into two sharply defined groups: in the first place *substitumal conditions* which characterise the form and position of the substitumal, and in the second place the *scale condition* (the volume condition, the scope condition) which expresses at what point in the substitumal we are to stop.

We might also put it in the following way: the first set of conditions expresses what can be achieved by a pure substitution – an interchange of one factor by another without changing the scale of production. The result is a certain *mutual relationship* between the factors, a relationship which is expressed by the form and position of the substitumal. The second set of condition defines a movement *outwards* in the factor diagram (cf. conclusion of section), expressing what can be achieved *in addition* by changing the scale. This last movement is a search along the substitumal, and it is here that the *special* aims or side conditions of adjustment count.

So far we have based our reasoning on a graphic presentation, and only used two factors. We shall now consider the general case with n factors. Our object is to pose the necessary and sufficient conditions for the points which are substitumal according to the general Definition (10d.5). For the time being we only consider fixed factor prices.

Let $v_1, v_2, \ldots, v_n$ be a given starting point in the n-dimensional factor diagram. We give the factors the infinitesimal but otherwise arbitrary increments $dv_1, dv_2, \ldots, dv_n$. In so doing the product quantity acquires the increment (5b.7), while total cost (10a.1) acquires the increment

(10d.7) $\quad db = q_1 dv_1 + q_2 dv_2 + \ldots + q_n dv_n \quad$ or, more briefly, $\quad db = \sum\limits_{i=1}^{n} q_i dv_i$.

The question whether the starting point $v_1, v_2, \ldots, v_n$ lies on the substitumal (10d.5) is the same as the question whether it is impossible to find a set of increments $dv_1, dv_2, \ldots, dv_n$ such that either db, that is to say (10d.7), is negative without dx, that is to say (5b.7), being negative, or dx is positive without db being positive. If it is *not* possible to find such a set of increments $dv_1, dv_2, \ldots, dv_n$ then and only then does the starting point for $v_1, v_2, \ldots, v_n$ lie on the substitumal.

ECONOMIC ADJUSTMENT TO FIXED PRICES

Both magnitudes (5b.7) and (10d.7) express a product sum in the increments $dv_1, dv_2, \ldots, dv_n$; the difference is merely that the *coefficients* by which $dv_1, dv_2, \ldots, dv_n$ are to be multiplied in (5d.7) are the marginal productivities $x_1', x_2', \ldots, x_n'$, and in (10d.7) the factor prices are $q_1, q_2, \ldots, q_n$. Both these sets of coefficients consist of non-negative figures (assuming that the factor prices are non-negative and that we are in the substitution region). The necessary and sufficient condition for the non-existence of a set of factor increments $dv_1, dv_2, \ldots, dv_n$ with the above-mentioned properties will then be that the two sets of coefficients are *proportional*, i.e. that we have

(10d.8)
$$\frac{x_1'}{q_1} = \frac{x_2'}{q_2} = \ldots = \frac{x_n'}{q_n}.$$

In the first place, it is obvious that this condition is sufficient. For, if (10d.8) is fulfilled, then – no matter how the increments $dv_1, dv_2, \ldots, dv_n$ are chosen – we must get

$$dx = \sum_{i=1}^{n} x_i' dv_i = \sum_{i=1}^{n} \mu q_i dv_i = \mu \sum_{i=1}^{n} q_i dv_i = \mu \cdot db,$$

where μ is the common magnitude of the proportionality figures (10d.8), that is to say a positive figure. No matter how $dv_1, dv_2, \ldots, dv_n$ is chosen, it is therefore impossible to have db made negative without dx being likewise, or having dx positive without db also being positive.

That this condition is also necessary, follows from the fact that, if we are at a factor point where *not all* conditions for proportionality (10d.8) are fulfilled, it will always be possible to choose increments in such a way that dx is positive and db negative. If, for example, we are at a point where $(x_1'/q_1') > (x_2'/q_2)$ we can choose $dv_3 = dv_4 = \ldots dv_n = 0$, dv_1 positive, dv_2 negative, and the numerical values of dv_1 and dv_2 such that

$$\frac{x_1'}{x_2'} > \frac{(-dv_2)}{dv_1} > \frac{q_1}{q_2}.$$

We shall then get

$$x_1' dv_1 > x_2'(-dv_2), \quad \text{that is to say} \quad dx = x_1' dv_1 + x_2' dv_2 > 0$$

and

$$q_1 dv_1 < q_2(-dv_2), \quad \text{that is to say} \quad db = q_1 dv_1 + q_2 dv_2 < 0$$

and correspondingly for other situations where (10d.8) is not fulfilled.

The $(n-1)$ equations (10d.8) thus express *the general substitumal condition* for n factors (under constant factor prices). It represents a one-dimensional curve running through the n-dimensional factor space.

If we compare the $(n-1)$ equations (10d.8) with the *first* $(n-1)$ equations in (10b.12) and (10c.7), we see that they are *identically the same equations*. Both a point where we have cost minimum under a given product quantity, as well as a point where we have product maximum under a given total cost, must satisfy (10d.8), and consequently *lie on the generally defined substitumal*. In other words: when the generally defined substitumal (10d.8) is determined, it is sufficient, for the fixing of the cost minimum point, to add the condition for a given product quantity, and, for the fixing of the product maximum point, sufficient to add the condition for the given total cost. Thus the argument previously set out with regard to the properties of the substitumal in two factors will apply with complete analogy in the case of n factors.

Using the same reasoning as that used in the case of two factors, cf. text subsequent to (10b.7), it will easily be seen from (10d.8) that if none of the factors is free, the generally defined substitumal must *run through the interior of the substitution region*.

The substitumal conditions (10d.8) give us, together with the product function (5a.2), n equations between the n factor quantities $v_1, \ldots, v_n$ and product quantity x. These equations implicitly define the factor quantities as *functions of the product quantity* along the substitumal. We can write them

(10d.9)
$$\begin{aligned} v_1 &= v_1(x) \\ v_2 &= v_2(x) \\ &\ldots \ldots \ldots \\ v_n &= v_n(x) \end{aligned}$$ along the substitumal.

This is *the parameter representation of the substitumal* with the product quantity as parameter. The functions on the right side of (10d.9) we call the *substitumal factor functions*. The substitumal factor function for factor No. i expresses how much of factor No. i must be used when the product quantity is given and the point is to be substitumal, i.e. satisfy any 'reasonable' formulation of an economic adjustment.

The factor functions are not only a 'reversal' of the technically given product function: they are based on a far more comprehensive set of information. In addition to the purely technical data contained in the product function, they are based on the economic data contained in the presupposition that the producer, under the given factor prices, has realised all the *substitution advantages* that he can achieve.

The derivatives of the substitumal factor functions we call the *substi-*

tumally marginal fabrication coefficients. In symbols they may be expressed

(10d.10) $$v_i' = \frac{dv_i(x)}{dx} \quad \text{along the substitumal} \quad (i=1, 2, ..., n).$$

The signs of the substitumally marginal fabrication coefficients indicate whether the substitumal rises or falls with respect to the factor quantities.

The explicit expressions for the substitumally marginal fabrication coefficients can be found by implicit differentiation of the equation system consisting of (5a.2) and (10d.8). We shall not undertake these calculations here, but shall limit ourselves to proving that the substitumally marginal fabrication coefficients satisfy the following *aggregation equation*:

(10d.11) $$\sum_{i=1}^{n} x_i' v_i' = 1.$$

The correctness of equation (10d.11) will immediately become apparent if we take as our point of departure the product function written in the following way: $x = x[(v_1(x), v_2(x), ..., v_n(x)]$. If we differentiate for x in this expression we get

$$1 = \frac{\partial x}{\partial v_1} \cdot \frac{dv_1(x)}{dx} + \frac{\partial x}{\partial v_2} \cdot \frac{dv_2(x)}{dx} + ... + \frac{\partial x}{\partial v_n} \cdot \frac{dv_n(x)}{dx}.$$

If we here substitute

$$\frac{\partial x}{\partial v_i} = x_i' \quad \text{and} \quad \frac{dv_i(x)}{dx} = v_i',$$

we get (10d.11).

If we compare the substitumal conditions (10d.8) with (5b.12), we shall see that in the case involving fixed factor prices, the substitumal is nothing more than *one specific isocline*, viz. the isocline along which the ratios between marginal productivities are equal to the ratios between the given factor prices. In Section 5b the isocline was defined purely technically, but we have now selected one specific isocline and given it a definitely *economic* significance, by introducing factor prices.

In Section 7b we found that under the pari-passu law the isoclines are straight lines running through the origin. In other words: *in the pari-passu law, and under given fixed factor prices, the substitumal is a straight line through the origin*. Thus in the factor diagram (7c.1) the substitumal must be a straight line through the inner part of the figure. The more expensive factor No. 1 is in relation to No. 2, the closer the substitumal lies to the upper boundary beam; and the cheaper No. 1 is in relation to No. 2, the closer it lies to the lower boundary beam. If No. 1 is a free good, and only in this case, the substitumal will coincide with the lower boundary.

In Figure (7d.1) the substitumal will be a beam in the interior of the dunce's cap. The more expensive a factor is in relation to the others, the closer will the substitumal lie to the *edge* where this factor is technically optimal, and the cheaper it is, the closer it will lie to the *wall* where the factor concerned is technically maximal. If, for example, factor No. 3 is almost gratis, the beam will lie close to the wall 3 max. *Where* along this wall the beam is to lie, will depend on the price ratio between the other factors. If No. 1 is expensive in relation to No. 2, it will lie well away to the right (near the edge 1 opt.); if the converse is true, it will lie well over to the left. In no circumstance, as we can see, can the beams (when No. 3 is cheap) come near the edge where No. 3 is technically optimal.

Under the ultra-passum law the isocline will not necessarily be a straight line running through origin. But *as a rule* it will point *outwards* into the factor diagram, i.e. in such a way that if we undertake a slight movement along the isocline, then all factor quantities will be changed in the *same* direction. As long as we are in the, with respect to scale, pre-maximal region, this will be tantamount to saying that all the substitumal marginal fabrication coefficients are positive (cf. (10d.10)). In the, with respect to scale, post-maximal region the substitution has no significance; since the substitumal must pass through the substitumal region – cf. text preceding (10d.9) – and a point lying in the, with respect to scale, post-maximal region cannot belong to the substitution region, but must have at least one of the marginal productivities negative. Cf. Proposition (8.8).

10e. Co-variation between costs and product quantity along the substitumal. The economic optimum law

In Section 10d. we noticed that any 'reasonable' adjustment was bound to lead to a point on the substitumal, and that any alteration in the scale of production to be undertaken, while fully exploiting the benefits of the substitution, must occur *along the substitumal*. It is therefore of interest to study the relationship between costs and product quantity along the substitumal.

Total costs (for the variable factors) are defined in (10a.1). Along the substitumal, however, there exists a well defined functional relationship between the quantity of each single factor and the product quantity, cf. (10d.9). If we insert the substitumal factor functions in (10a.1), we get

(10e.1) $$b = \sum_{i=1}^{n} q_i v_i(x) = b(x) \quad \text{(along the substitumal)}.$$

Function $b(x)$ is the *substitumal cost function* or, more briefly, the *cost function* (for the variable factors). It shows how total variable costs vary with product quantity when product quantity is achieved in the cheapest way, given the factor prices.

The *substitumal marginal cost* is defined as the derivative of the substitumal cost function (10e.1) with respect to product quantity x. Thus:

(10e.2) $\quad$ Substitumal marginal cost $= b' = \dfrac{\mathrm{d}b(x)}{\mathrm{d}x} = b'(x)$.

This gives us

$$b' = \frac{\mathrm{d}b(x)}{\mathrm{d}x} = \frac{\mathrm{d}\left[\sum_{i=1}^{n} q_i v_i(x)\right]}{\mathrm{d}x} = \sum_{i=1}^{n} q_i \cdot \frac{\mathrm{d}v_i(x)}{\mathrm{d}x},$$

viz.

(10e.3) $$b' = \sum_{i=1}^{n} q_i v_i',$$

where v_1' is the substitumal marginal fabrication coefficient according to Definition (10d.10).

Along the substitumal, we have according to (10b.12)

(10e.4) $\quad\quad\quad\quad q_i = \lambda x_i' \quad\quad\quad\quad (i=1,\ldots,n)$.

If we insert (10e.4) in (10e.3), we get

$$b' = \sum_{i=1}^{n} \lambda x_i' v_i' = \lambda \sum_{i=1}^{n} x_i' v_i'.$$

Thus, on account of (10d.11)

(10e.5) $\quad\quad\quad\quad b' = \lambda$.

The substitumal marginal cost is thus the same as the Lagrange multiplier λ in (10b.10) and (10b.12). The parameter μ in (10c.5) and (10c.7) is the reciprocal value of λ. By inserting the expression (10e.5) for λ in (10e.4), we get

(10e.6) $\quad\quad\quad\quad b' = \dfrac{q_i}{x_i'} \quad\quad\quad\quad (i=1, 2, \ldots, n)$.

Thus: *In the case involving fixed factor prices the substitumal marginal cost is equal to the ratio between the price of an arbitrary factor and the marginal productivity of this factor.*

The concept marginal cost can be generalised, by considering an arbitrary starting point $v_1, v_2, \ldots, v_n$ and arbitrary factor increments $dv_1, dv_2, \ldots, dv_n$, that is to say without constraining the factor change to take place partially or along the substitumal or in any other specified manner. The general marginal cost is the *ratio* between the change brought about by this arbitrary factor change in the total cost (cf. (10d.7)) and the corresponding change in product quantity (cf. 5b.7)), that is to say

$$(10e.7) \quad \text{General marginal cost} = \frac{\sum_{i=1}^{n} q_i dv_i}{\sum_{i=1}^{n} x_i' dv_i}$$

(at an arbitrary factor point and in an arbitrary factor direction).

The following general fundamental proposition applies to the general marginal cost thus defined:

PROPOSITION (10e.8)

Indifference proposition for the general marginal cost: Provided only the starting point $v_1, v_2, \ldots, v_n$ is substitumal, the general marginal cost (10e.7) will be the *same* – and equal to the substitumal marginal cost b' – *irrespective of* which (infinitesimal) factor changes it is calculated for, i.e. irrespective of what the factor increments $dv_1, dv_2, \ldots, dv_n$ may be.

Indeed, in any substitumal point (10e.6) applies, i.e. $q_i = b' x_i'$ for all i. If this is inserted in (10e.7), we immediately get

$$(10e.9) \quad \text{General marginal cost} = \frac{\sum_{i=1}^{n} b' x_i' dv_i}{\sum_{i=1}^{n} x_i' dv_i} = b'$$

(calculated from a substitumal point and in an arbitrary factor direction).

Average cost (piece cost) is at any factor point defined as the cost per product unit. For any point on the substitumal we can interpret this average cost as a function of the product quantity. Interpreted in this way we have

$$(10e.10) \quad \text{The substitumal average cost} = \bar{b} = \frac{b(x)}{x} = \bar{b}(x).$$

Substitumal cost flexibility is the elasticity of the cost function with respect to product quantity along the substitumal. That is to say:

$$\check{b} = \frac{db(x)}{dx} \cdot \frac{x}{b} = \frac{b'}{(b/x)},$$

i.e.

(10e.11) $\qquad$ Substitumal cost flexibility $= \check{b} = \dfrac{b'}{\check{b}}$.

Substitumal cost flexibility is thus equal to the ratio between the substitumal marginal cost and the substitumal average cost.

The substitumal cost concept can be associated with the *technical* nature of the production law, that is to say with that property of the law which is expressed in the *passus coefficient*. To see this let us take as our starting point the definition of total cost (10a.1). Along the substitumal we have (10e.4). By inserting (10e.4) in (10a.1) we get

(10e.12) $\qquad b = \sum_{i=1}^{n} q_i v_i = \sum_{i=1}^{n} \lambda x_i' v_i = \lambda \sum_{i=1}^{n} x_i' v_i.$

According to the passus equation (5h.3) this gives $b = \lambda \varepsilon x$. As according to (10e.5) $\lambda = b'$, we get

(10e.13) $\qquad\qquad b = \varepsilon b' x \qquad$ (in a substitumal point).

In other words: *In a substitumal point, given fixed factor prices, total cost (for the variable factors) is equal to the product of the passus coefficient, the substitumal marginal cost, and the product quantity.* This is *the passus proposition for total cost*.

By dividing by x on both sides of the equals sign in (10e.13) we get as per definition (10e.10) of the substitumal average cost

(10e.14) $\qquad\qquad \check{b} = \varepsilon b' \qquad$ (in a substitumal point)

In other words: in a substitumal point, given fixed factor prices, the substitumal average cost is equal to the product of the passus coefficient and the substitumal marginal cost.

If (10e.11) is combined with (10e.14), we get

(10e.15) $\qquad\qquad \check{b} = \dfrac{1}{\varepsilon} \qquad$ (in a substitumal point).

In other words: *In a substitumal point, given fixed factor prices, the substitumal cost flexibility is equal to the reciprocal value of the passus coefficient.*

This gives a new and interesting interpretation of the passus coefficient.

When we consider b as a function of x, cost is conceived of as a 'necessary evil', which we must accept with if we wish to increase product quantity. Occasionally, however, it may be practical to apply the opposite view, and to regard cost as a sort of abstract 'material' with a certain productive power. It is then natural to reverse the functional relationship between b and x, and to consider x as a function of b. We can then write (10e.15) in the form

(10e.16) $$\frac{dx}{db} \cdot \frac{b}{x} = \varepsilon \qquad \text{(in a substitumal point)}$$

In a substitumal point, given fixed factor prices, the passus coefficient in other words has precisely the same significance in relation to total costs (for the variable factors) as marginal elasticities have for every single factor.

Formula (10e.16) also tells us something else: the passus coefficient was originally defined purely technically at any factor point by a movement *along the factor beam* running through the factor point concerned. Instead of considering the factor beam running through the factor point, we can consider *the isocline* running through this factor point and the set of factor prices which are such that this isocline becomes the substitumal. If we take the elasticity of the product quantity with respect to total costs along this isocline, given these fixed factor prices, we get the passus coefficient ε.

With the help of Formula (10e.14) and (10e.15) we can also find expressions for a number of other concepts of elasticity.

For the elasticity of the substitumal average cost with respect to product quantity $\bar{b}$, by using the rule for elasticity of a fraction, we get:

(10e.17) $$\bar{b} = \text{El.} \frac{b}{x} = \text{El. } b - \text{El. } x = \bar{b} - 1 = \frac{1}{\varepsilon} - 1.$$

For the elasticity of the substitumal marginal cost with respect to product quantity $\bar{b}'$, using (10e.14) and (10e.17), we get:

(10e.18) $$\bar{b}' = \text{El.} \frac{\bar{b}}{\varepsilon} = \text{El. } \bar{b} - \text{El. } \varepsilon = \frac{1}{\varepsilon} - 1 - \breve{\varepsilon},$$

where $\breve{\varepsilon}$ is the elasticity of the passus coefficient with respect to x under a substitumal variation. Generally ε is a function of all factor quantities, and along the substitumal we can interpret every single factor quantity as a function of the product quantity.

On the basis of Formula (10e.13) and (10e.18), we can say something about the typical variations which the various *cost* concepts reveal when we

ECONOMIC ADJUSTMENT TO FIXED PRICES

undertake a movement along the substitumal. This is interesting because any 'reasonable' variation must take place along the substitumal. Cf. the comments after Figure (10d.6).

Let us first consider a production law which has a *pari-passu* character. In a pari-passu law the passus coefficient is equal to 1 in every factor combination (cf. Chapter 7). Therefore $\breve{\varepsilon}$ will be equal to nought in every factor point under the pari-passu law.

By inserting $\varepsilon=1$ and $\breve{\varepsilon}=0$ in (10e.14), (10e.15), (10e.17), and (10e.18), we get

(10e.14′) $\qquad b' = \bar{b}$

(10e.15′) $\qquad \bar{b} = \dfrac{1}{1} = 1$

(10e.17′) $\qquad \breve{b} = \dfrac{1}{1} - 1 = 0$

(10e.18′) $\qquad \breve{b}' = \dfrac{1}{1} - 1 - 0 = 0$

(Under the pari-passu law and given fixed factor prices).

Thus:

PROPOSITION (10e.19)

Under the pari-passu law, and given fixed factor prices, the substitumal marginal cost will be equal to the substitumal average cost, and both these magnitudes are constant. The substitumal total cost curve (with product quantity as abscissa) is a straight line running through origin and with an angular coefficient equal to the constant common magnitude of the substitumal marginal cost and the substitumal average cost.

Let us next consider the case where the production law is an *ultra*-passum law. We shall here assume the special case where we have a regular ultra-passum law (Cf. Definition 8.1). At the end of Chapter 8 we noticed that as a rule we shall get a regular ultra-passum law in the n specified and variable factors, if, in addition to these, one or more *fixed factors* are collaborating in the production process. In the analysis of the *economic* adjustment of a concern, given a fixed plant (short term adjustment) we shall therefore as a rule get a regular ultra-passum law in the variable (short-term variable) factors.

From Formula (10e.13) to (10e.18) we can see that the way in which cost and product quantity vary along that particular isocline which is the substitumal under given constant factor prices is essentially characterised by the way the *passus coefficient* varies along this particular isocline. The question is therefore: how does the passus coefficient vary if, in a regular ultra-passum law, we undertake a movement along an isocline? We can draw certain conclusions about this directly from the definition (8.1) of a regular ultra-passum law, and we can add a little more as a plausible assumption. We may collate this in the following rule:

RULE (10e.20)

In a regular ultra-passum law where each isocline is a rising curve in the factor diagram, the usual case, cf. end of 10d, the passus coefficient will always show the following typical course along any isocline: To start with the passus coefficient will be greater than 1, after which it will decrease monotonically, first passing 1 and finally reaching the value zero at the terminal of the isocline. Even though the isocline is strictly speaking not everywhere rising with respect to all factors, the typical course of ε along the isocline will in general be as described.

This is *the fundamental rule regarding the variation of the passus coefficient along the substitumal.*

With the help of the fundamental rule (10e.20) and the formulas (10e.14) to (10e.18), we can now study the course of total cost (for the variable factors), the substitumal average cost and the substitumal marginal cost along the substitumal. When in the sequel for brevity's sake we speak of 'average cost' and 'marginal cost', we are alluding throughout to substitumal concepts.

Let us first consider the substitumal average cost. According to (10e.20), the passus coefficient is, to start with, big (larger than 1). From (10e.17) we see that $\bar{b}$ is then negative. *The substitumal average cost curve will therefore, to start, with be a falling curve.* As we gradually move out along the substitumal, the passus coefficient will decrease and pass the value 1. In this point

$$\bar{b} = \frac{1}{1} - 1 = 0.$$

The substitumal average cost will therefore reach its minimum when $\varepsilon = 1$. In continued movement out along the substitumal the passus coeffcient will assume values less than 1. $\bar{b}$ will then be positive and the substitumal average cost will then be *rising*. The substitumal average cost curve will therefore be

U-shaped, as illustrated in Figure (10e.21). This typical shape, which is frequently taken for granted, we have here *derived* from the technical properties of the regular ultra-passum law.

Let us look at the substitumal marginal cost. According to (10e.14) the substitumal marginal cost is *less* than the substitumal average cost in the, with respect to the scale, technically pre-optimal region ($\varepsilon > 1$) and *greater* than average cost in the post-optimal region ($\varepsilon < 1$). In the technical optimum point ($\varepsilon = 1$) marginal cost will be equal to average cost. Since the piece-cost curve reaches its lowest value in the technical optimum point (where $\varepsilon = 1$), the marginal cost curve intersects the average cost curve in the point where the average cost curve reaches its lowest value.

Let us now use Formula (10e.18). In the technically post-optimal stage $\varepsilon < 1$ and consequently $1/\varepsilon > 1$, i.e. the term $1/\varepsilon - 1$ is positive. Furthermore, according to (10e.20) $\check{\varepsilon} < 0$, so that $(-\check{\varepsilon}) > 0$. That is to say: *in the, with respect to the scale, technically post-optimal stage $\check{b}' > 0$, and thus the marginal cost curve is constantly rising.*

This certainly applies provided merely that the fundamental rule of variation of the passus coefficient along the substitumal applies.

The same situation applies in the actual optimal point, since here the term $1/\varepsilon - 1$ is equal to nought and the term $(-\check{\varepsilon})$ is positive so that $\check{b}' > 0$). The marginal cost curve must therefore intersect the optimum point *as it rises*. Also for a little stretch just before the optimum point the curve is bound to rise, but further away the situation may be different.

In order to obtain more detailed information about the course of b' in the pre-optimal stage, we must know more about *how* the passus coefficient decreases along the substitumal than what is expressed in (10e.20). Most frequently – as suggested in Figure (10e.21) – marginal costs will diminish to start with, and then pass a minimum before once again rising. But it may also happen that marginal costs rise throughout the whole pre-optimal region, or that it shows *several* local minimum points.

In Figure (10e.21) we have not drawn in the *total cost curve*. This can be found either as the *area*, i.e. the integral curve of the marginal cost curve for any abscissae, or as the rectangle i.e. the product of the abscissae and the ordinate on the average cost curve.

As we move backwards along the substitumal towards the origin, that is to say as the product quantity x diminishes towards 0, it may happen that total costs diminish continuously towards 0, as they will, for example, do if all the substitumal factor functions (10d.9) diminish continuously towards 0 when x tends towards 0. But it may also happen that total costs tend towards a finite positive limit when x tends towards 0 (certain finite inputs may be required if production is even to start). In that case it will be a question of definition as to what we shall say the total costs are 'when x is equal to 0'. If we mean the limit towards which total costs tend when x tends towards 0 through positive values, we get a strictly positive figure,

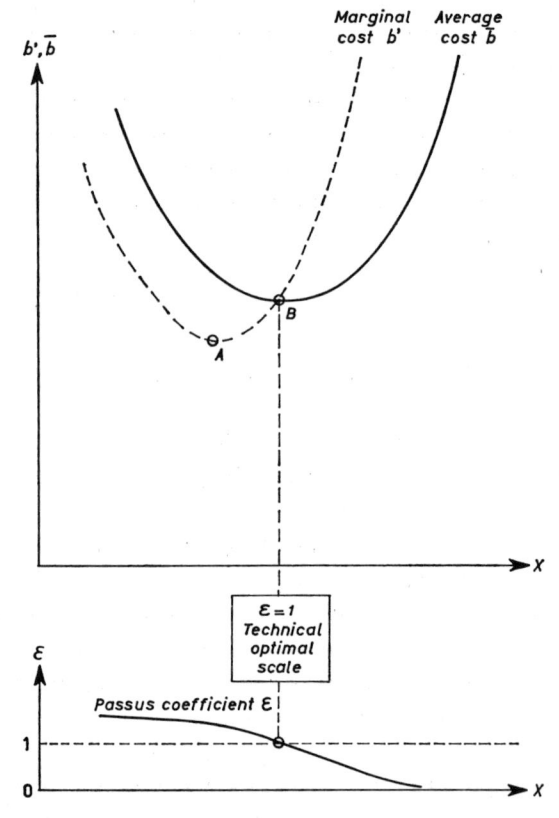

Fig. (10e.21). The optimum law along the substitumal.

but if we mean total (variable) costs when the concern as a whole has not started production, we get zero. If so, we must assume that total variable costs drop discontinuously at the point $x=0$, as x decreases. If we assume that the total (variable) costs vary in a continuous fashion towards zero when x tends towards zero, marginal cost and average cost must tend towards the same magnitude.[1]

Summing up, therefore, we can say:

[1] Details are given in my general lectures on economic theory (15.5).

PROPOSITION (10e.22)

The economic optimum law along the substitumal. If the fundamental, technical (as distinct from economic) rule (10e.20) for the variation of the passus coefficient along any isocline is fulfilled, we shall – if we undertake a variation along the substitumal which is economically defined through a set of constant factor prices – obtain an economic optimum law connecting product quantity and cost, and which, in its course, is entirely analogous to the technical optimal laws we got for each single factor (cf. Figure (6b.1)).

This state of affairs emerges with particular clarity if Formula (10e.16) – which shows that the elasticity of the product quantity with respect to total costs, under a substitumal variation, is *the same as* the passus coefficient –, is combined with the fundamental rule (10e.20) – which indicates that the passus coefficient varies in the same way along any isocline as a single marginal elasticity varies under a partial factor variation, when a technical optimum law exists for each factor.

Note that we get an optimum law along the substitumal only if the production law in the specified factors is an ultra-passum law. If the production law has a pari-passu character, we get no optimum law along the substitumal. In such cases – irrespective of what the factor prices are, provided merely they are constant, – marginal costs and piece costs will be constant, cf. (10e.17′) and (10e.18′). This point is not always brought out as consistently as it should.

Previously in this section we have mentioned that the presupposition of a regular ultra-passum law in the specified factors was particularly relevant for an analysis of a concern's short-term adjustment, given a certain plant, i.e. given *fixed* factors. Naturally the costs referring to fixed factors will be independent of the scale of production (within the limit given by the plant), and are therefore called *fixed costs*.

When speaking above of total costs, piece cost, etc., we have throughout assumed *variable* costs, i.e. costs for factors *included in the factor diagram* and for which *substitution adjustment has been carried out*. It is only when b is interpreted in this manner, that we have Formulae (10e.13) to (10c.18).

By adding the fixed costs B to the variable costs b, we get total costs in a strictly 'total' sense. We call this

(10e.23) $\qquad\qquad$ Global cost $= b + B$.

Global piece cost (global average cost) is equal to global cost per unit produced. In other words:

174   MOMENTARY SINGLE PRODUCTION

(10e.24) $$\text{Global piece cost} = \bar{\bar{b}} = \bar{b} + \frac{B}{x}.$$

The term B/x expresses the fixed costs per unit produced. This term will diminish like an equilateral hyperbole when x increases.

If in Figure (10e.21) the global piece cost is marked in, we get Figure (10e.25). The curve for $\bar{\bar{b}}$ will naturally throughout its length lie above the curve for $\bar{b}$ (provided fixed costs are strictly positive).

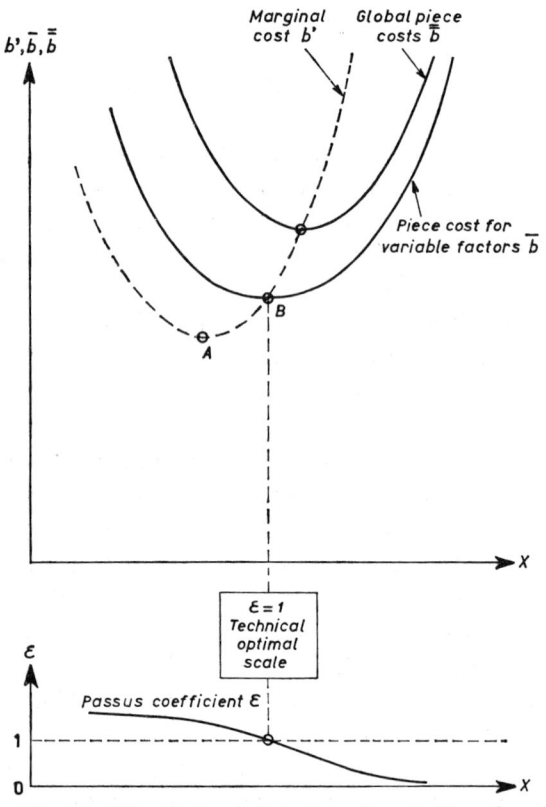

Fig. (10e.25). Optimum law along the substitumal.

The vertical distance between the curves $\bar{\bar{b}}$ and $\bar{b}$ tends towards 0 when x rises, as this distance is the same as the term B/x in (10e.24). The region between these two curves is called the region for *cut-throat competition*.

Marginal cost will naturally be the same whether we calculate them from total costs for variable factors or from global costs, since we have

(10e.26) $$\frac{d(b+B)}{dx} = \frac{db}{dx} + \frac{dB}{dx} = b'.$$

ECONOMIC ADJUSTMENT TO FIXED PRICES

Above we saw that the marginal cost curve cut the curve for variable piece cost b at the point where the variable piece cost has its lowest value. The same applies to global piece cost $\bar{b}$. The necessary condition for a minimum of $\bar{b}$ is, indeed, that

$$\frac{d\bar{b}}{dx} = \frac{d\left(\frac{B+b}{x}\right)}{dx} = \frac{x \cdot \frac{d(B+b)}{dx} - (B+b) \cdot 1}{x^2} = \frac{xb' - (B+b)}{x^2} = 0,$$

i.e.:

$$b' = \frac{B+b}{x} = \bar{b}.$$

10f. Profit maximisation

Let us first consider n variable factors with fixed given prices. In the pencil of isoclines a definite isocline is thereby selected, and acquires significance as *substitumal*. The adjustment point for any 'reasonable' or 'sensible' adjustment must, as we have seen, lie somewhere on this substitumal. The question is now: *where* on the substitumal will the concern stop, i.e. how will *volume* adjustment occur? That depends on the *object* pursued by the concern, and by its *strategic type* in the market for the product.

We shall first assume that the concern is an atomistic *quantity adjuster* in the product market, and that its adjustment purpose is to make *total profit as large as possible*.

We assume that we have a *regular ultrapassum law* in the variable factors. Under the conditions specified in (10e.20), we shall then have an economic optimum law along the substitumal, with a relationship between cost and product quantity as given in Figure (10e.21).

Total intake (total turnover) a is the value of the product quantity[1], that is to say:

(10f.1)   Total intake (total turnover) $= a = p \cdot x$,

where p is the given product price and x is the product quantity.

And the total profit r will be

(10f.2)   Total profit $= r = a - b = px - b(x) = r(x)$.

It may be termed total gross profit to indicate that no allowance has been made for fixed costs.

We must make a sharp distinction between the following two questions:

[1] Assuming sales to be equal to production.

(I) For what product quantity (at what point on the substitumal) will total profit be *greatest*? (II) How *large* will total profit be at this point? And especially: will it here be positive or negative?

In discussing what the concern will do in a certain situation, we must always bear clearly in mind the difference between these two questions. If we assume that the adjustment point is determined merely by the motive for the greatest possible profit, and the desire to keep the concern going, the adjustment may take place at a point with negative profit (in the short-term market). The greatest profit then simply means the smallest loss.

If total (variable) costs vary with a continuous derivative – possibly apart from a discontinuity in the point $x=0$ – the greatest profit must lie either at the *terminal point* $x=0$, or at one of the *local* maximum points, which profits may have. We shall get the best overall picture of the possibilities involved by distinguishing between the case where the product price lies *below* the minimum of average cost for the variable factors and the case where it is *equal to or greater than* this minimum. In the first case the point $x=0$ must obviously give the greatest profit, provided we allow the concept 'concern closed down' and there are no costs (for the variable factors) involved in 'concern closed down'. This follows simply from the fact that any positive x will give negative profit when the product price lies under the minimum of average costs. If, on the other hand, the product price is equal to or greater than this minimum (and total costs have the continuity properties mentioned), there will be points with non-negative profit, and then the greatest value of profits will be realised in one of the local maxima for gross profit. The necessary first order condition for a local maximum of this kind is that

(10f.3) $$r' = \frac{dr}{dx} = p - b' = 0,$$

that is to say the condition is that *marginal profit r'* is 0. This is the same as saying that

(10f.4) $$b' = p.$$

In other words: when the adjustment takes place under a given fixed product price, and the latter is equal to or greater than the minimum of average cost (for the variable factors), total profits are greatest at a point where the substitumal marginal cost is equal to the product price. (In the limiting case where the product price is exactly *equal to* the minimum of average costs, the terminal point $x=0$ will also give the maximal profit.)

Furthermore we get the following sufficient second order condition for a regular maximum of (10f.2):

(10f.5) $$r'' = \frac{d^2 r}{dx^2} = -b'' < 0,$$

where

$$b'' = \frac{d^2 b(x)}{dx^2} = \frac{d(b')}{dx}.$$

(10f.5) can be written

(10f.6) $$b'' > 0.$$

In other words: when the adjustment takes place, under a fixed given product price, and the latter is equal to or greater than the minimum of average cost, total profit has a maximum in a point where the substitumal marginal cost is equal to the product price and the substitumal marginal cost curve is rising.

We shall now investigate whether the two conditions (10f.4) and (10f.6) lead to a unique determination of the adjustment point.

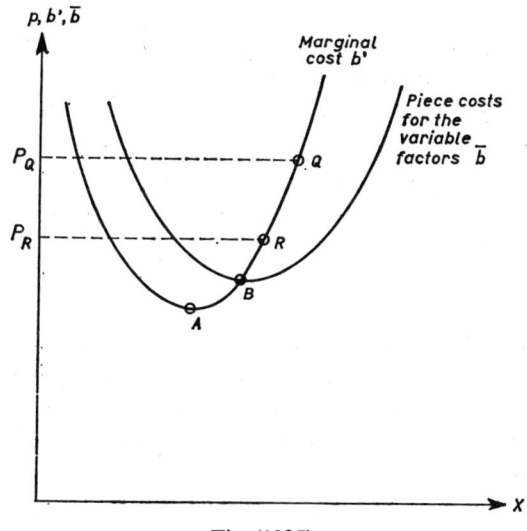

Fig. (10f.7).

To the right of point B (the optimum point) in Figure (10e.21), where *mean average* cost has its minimum, the marginal cost curve must be monotonically rising. But to the left of point B the marginal cost *may* have several rising and falling parts, in other words it is not altogether U-shaped. Cf. the argument relating to Figure (10e.21). Irrespective of whether the marginal cost curve possesses a course of this kind, it must to the left of point B lie below the average cost curve. Cf. the argument in connection with Figure (10e.21). Consequently a point which satisfies (10f.4) and lies to the left of point B, must give a negative profit[1], and therefore *cannot* give what is maximal profit when the product price is equal to or greater than the minimum of the marginal average costs, so that there exist points which provide a non-negative profit. It will thus only be the rising part of the cost curve to the right of point B which we need to take account of. We shall therefore have to consider only the unique point where *the horizontal price line (i.e., the horizontal line representing the given product price) intersects the monotonically rising part of the marginal cost curve lying to the right of point B*, that is to say, that part of the marginal cost curve which lies *in the*, *with respect to the scale, technically post-optimal region*. In Figure (10f.7) it will be point Q if the product price is P_Q and point R if the product price is P_R, etc. If we have

(10f.8) $$p < \bar{b}$$ (in the adjustment point),

if, in other words, the product price is less than the average cost in the adjustment point, the concern will not have all its costs covered and its activity will only be continued if *other considerations* are present, for example a desire *to retain customers* or to *maintain the production organisation* in the hope of better times, etc.

Let us now include the *fixed* costs in the analysis. If we take them into account, we get the following expression for *net* profit,

(10f.9) $$\text{Net profit} = \pi = px - b(x) - B,$$

where B – as before – represents fixed costs.

On account of (10e.26) the introduction of fixed costs has no influence on the adjustment conditions (10f.4) and (10f.6). The entire line of reasoning in connection with Figure (10f.7) remains unchanged, it being only remembered that point B for the variable factors is the minimum of average cost.

But the introduction of fixed costs will obviously be significant for the profit – the global, net profit – being positive. The condition for this is

(10f.10) $$p > \frac{b+B}{x} = \bar{b}$$ (in the adjustment point).

For the plant to be established and, if necessary, maintained (when only the economic considerations expressed in the global net profit are of importance),

[1] Because then $p < \bar{b}$.

the product price – or rather the expected value of the product price taken over a longer period – must be greater than global average cost.

Even though the price were to fall below $\bar{b}_{min}$, provided the plant is already *in situ*, it will in the short run be profitable to continue production as long as the price is higher than $\bar{b}_{min}$. By so doing the concern may not be able to cover all fixed costs, but if it is closed down, the loss will be even greater. It will therefore pay to maintain production until the plant has been worn out. The size of profit in the point of adjustment can be related to the magnitude of the passus coefficient. Along the substitumal in the factor diagram for the *variable* factors we have (10e.13). If (10e.13) is inserted in the expression for profit (10f.2), we get $r = px - b'\varepsilon x$. In the adjustment point $p = b'$. Thus $r = px - p\varepsilon x$, that is to say

(10f.11)   total gross profit $r = px(1-\varepsilon)$ (in the adjustment point).

The deviation of the passus coefficient from unity in the adjustment point is in other words a direct gauge of how large a portion of the production value px is made up of gross profit r.

From (10f.11) we see that the condition for positive gross profit (10f.8) can be written as $\varepsilon < 1$ in the adjustment point. If the producer is not influenced by outside considerations, production will therefore only be maintained if product price is so high that adjustment takes place in the, with respect to the scale, *technically post-optimal* region. This is merely another expression for the fact that the product price must be so high that adjustment takes place on the monotonically rising branch to the right of point B in Figure (10f.7). In the case involving two factors this means somewhere or other in the double-shaded region in Figure (8.6). Furthermore, from (10f.11) we can see that the further out in the, with respect to the scale, technically post-optimal region adjustment takes place (which depends on the level of product price), the greater is the gross surplus.

If fixed factors occur (and only economic considerations expressed in total net profits are of importance), the concern will not be maintained on a long-term basis, unless the product price is so great that adjustment can take place so far out in the, with respect to the scale, technically post-optimal region, that the fraction $(1-\varepsilon)$ of the total intake (total turnover) is sufficient to cover fixed costs. In this connection, ε must be conceived of as the passus coefficient in the *variable* factors, i.e. those that are substitution-adjusted. If the product price is so high that the fraction $(1-\varepsilon)$ covers *more* than the fixed costs, i.e. if $p > \bar{b}$, a *pure profit* arises.

Above we have discussed profit-maximisation adjustment in *two stages*.

First we discussed *substitution adjustment,* and found b as a function of x along the substitumal, we then discussed *volume adjustment* (scale adjustment) by finding the point on the substitumal where the difference between total income and variable costs was greatest.

Profit-maximisation adjustment can, however, also be discussed *directly in one stage,* that is to say, without going via the substitumal. This is done by determining the quantities of the variable factors $v_1, \ldots, v_n$, which make

$$(10\text{f}.12) \qquad r = p \cdot x(v_1, \ldots, v_n) - \sum_{i=1}^{n} q_i v_i$$

as large as possible. If we do not consider the possibility of maximum along the boundary of the region where the variables are allowed to move, adjustment must take place in a local maximum, cf. text following (10f.6). The necessary first order conditions for this are

$$(10\text{f}.13) \qquad \frac{\partial r}{\partial v_i} = p x_i'(v_1, \ldots, v_n) - q_i = 0 \qquad (i = 1, \ldots, n)$$

that is to say

$$(10\text{f}.14) \qquad p x_i' = q_i. \qquad (i = 1, \ldots, n).$$

These conditions correspond to those which we have previously worked with, but they do not show what part of the condition is connected with the special type of adjustment here considered – i.e. profit maximization – and what part is common to all 'sensible' types of adjustment. The term px_i' expresses factor No. i's marginal productivity calculated in money under constant product price. We can therefore say that in the case of fixed factor prices and a fixed product price (and disregarding the possibility of a terminal maximum), total profit is greatest at a point where, for each single factor, there is equality between its price and its marginal productivity calculated in money (cf. what has been said about the marginal distribution principle in Section 6a on Von Thünen).

The sufficient second order condition for a regular maximum of (10f.12) is

$$(10\text{f}.15) \quad (-1)^k \begin{vmatrix} \dfrac{\partial^2 r}{(\partial v_1)^2} & \dfrac{\partial^2 r}{\partial v_1 \partial v_2} & \cdots & \dfrac{\partial^2 r}{\partial v_1 \partial v_k} \\ \dfrac{\partial^2 r}{\partial v_2 \partial v_1} & \dfrac{\partial^2 r}{(\partial v_2)^2} & \cdots & \dfrac{\partial^2 r}{\partial v_2 \partial v_k} \\ \vdots & & & \vdots \\ \dfrac{\partial^2 r}{\partial v_k \partial v_1} & \dfrac{\partial^2 r}{\partial v_k \partial v_2} & \cdots & \dfrac{\partial^2 r}{(\partial v_k)^2} \end{vmatrix} > 0 \quad (\text{for all } k = 1, 2, \ldots, n).$$

By differentiating (10f.13) with respect to v_j, we get

(10f.16)
$$\frac{\partial^2 r}{\partial v_i v_j} = p \cdot x_{ij}''.$$

And by inserting (10f.16) in (10f.15) we get

(10f.17) $\quad (-1)^k \begin{vmatrix} px_{11}'' & \dots & px_{1k}'' \\ \dots & \dots & \dots \\ px_{k1}'' & \dots & px_{kk}'' \end{vmatrix} = (-1)^k p^k \begin{vmatrix} x_{11}'' & \dots & x_{1k}'' \\ \dots & \dots & \dots \\ x_{k1}'' & \dots & x_{kk}'' \end{vmatrix} > 0$

(for all $k=1, 2, \dots, n$).

Since p is positive, we get the second order condition for a regular profit maximum in the following form:

(10f.18) $\quad (-1)^k \begin{vmatrix} x_{11}'' & \dots & x_{1k}'' \\ \dots & \dots & \dots \\ x_{k1}'' & \dots & x_{kk}'' \end{vmatrix} > 0 \quad$ (for all $k=1, 2, \dots, n$).

This expresses a purely technical condition for the form of the product function. In order at least to suggest that (10f.18) leads to the same sort of conditions as those we have previously worked with, we shall first find an expression for the second order derivative b'' along the substitumal. We now consider the $(n+1)$ equations (10b.10) and (10b.12) as an implicit definition of λ, and $v_1, v_2, \dots, v_n$ as functions of x and $q_1, q_2, \dots, q_n$. By partial differentiation of these equations with respect to x and with $q_1, q_2, \dots, q_n$ as constants, we find

(10f.19)
$$\sum_{k=1}^{n} x_{ik}'' \frac{\partial v_k}{\partial x} + x_i' \left(\frac{\partial \lambda}{\lambda \partial x}\right) = 0 \quad (i=1, 2, \dots, n)$$
$$\sum_{k=1}^{n} x_k' \frac{\partial v_k}{\partial x} = 1.$$

We have here $(n+1)$ linear equations in the $(n+1)$ unknowns

$$\left(\frac{\partial \lambda}{\lambda \partial x}\right) \quad \text{and} \quad \frac{\partial v_1}{\partial x}, \frac{\partial v_2}{\partial x}, \dots, \frac{\partial v_n}{\partial x}.$$

From this we find, noting that $\lambda = b'$, cf. (10e.5), and consequently $\partial \lambda/\partial x = b''$,

(10f.20)
$$\frac{b''}{b'} = \frac{\begin{vmatrix} x_{11}'' & x_{12}'' & \cdots & x_{1n}'' \\ x_{21}'' & x_{22}'' & \cdots & x_{2n}'' \\ \cdots & \cdots & \cdots & \cdots \\ x_{n1}'' & x_{n2}'' & \cdots & x_{nn}'' \end{vmatrix}}{\begin{vmatrix} 0 & x_1' & x_2' & \cdots & x_n' \\ x_1' & x_{11}'' & x_{12}'' & \cdots & x_{1n}'' \\ \cdots & \cdots & \cdots & \cdots & \cdots \\ x_n' & x_{n1}'' & x_{n2}'' & \cdots & x_{nn}'' \end{vmatrix}}.$$

When we are in a point with positive and rising marginal costs, cf. (10f.6), that is to say $b' > 0$ and $b'' > 0$, then consequently numerator and denominator in (10f.20) must have the same sign. That is to say that the last of the conditions in (5i.11) is the same as the last of the conditions in (10f.18). Furthermore, we note that since adjustment takes place in the, with respect to the scale, technically post-optimal region (which corresponds to the branch of the curve in Figure (10f.7) rising from B), the first of the conditions in (10f.18) follows from (8.9). In a more detailed discussion of the various sets of presuppositions, the other conditions in (10f.18) can also be connected with our reasons in the two-stage analysis, when the assumption in the various cases is accurately specified.

The conclusions the *opposite* way – that is to say, from (10f.18) to (5i.11) – can be carried out for all k without any difficulty, if one uses a number of classical propositions on positive definite matrices and positive definite quadratic forms. This is done as follows.

We shall consider first a general rule of development for a bordered determinant. Let $r_1, r_2, \ldots, r_n$ and $s_1, s_2, \ldots, s_n$ be two sets of n figures, and let A_{ij} ($i = 1, 2, \ldots, n$, $j = 1, 2, \ldots, n$) be a matrix chosen arbitrarily, and $\hat{A}_{ji}$ its adjoint, i.e. the matrix which arises from A_{ij} when the element No. (ij) is replaced by $(-1)^{i+j}$ times the corresponding subdeterminant, and one finally changes lines and columns. For example, in the case $n = 2$.

(10f.21)
$$\begin{pmatrix} \hat{A}_{11} & \hat{A}_{12} \\ \hat{A}_{21} & \hat{A}_{22} \end{pmatrix} = \begin{pmatrix} A_{22} & (-A_{12}) \\ (-A_{21}) & A_{11} \end{pmatrix}.$$

In the case of the elements in the adjoint, we have the following development of a bordered determinant:

ECONOMIC ADJUSTMENT TO FIXED PRICE 183

(10f.22)
$$-\begin{vmatrix} 0 & s_1 & s_2 & \ldots & s_n \\ r_1 & A_{11} & A_{12} & \ldots & A_{1n} \\ r_2 & A_{21} & A_{22} & \ldots & A_{2n} \\ \ldots & \ldots & \ldots & \ldots & \ldots \\ r_n & A_{n1} & A_{n2} & \ldots & A_{nn} \end{vmatrix} = \sum_{j=1}^{n} \sum_{i=1}^{n} s_j \hat{A}_{ji} r_i.$$

The expression to the right in (10f.22) is a *bilinear form* in the two sets of numbers $r_1, r_2, \ldots, r_n$ and $s_1, s_2, \ldots, s_n$.

In the case $n=2$ we have for example

(10f.23)
$$-\begin{vmatrix} 0 & s_1 & s_2 \\ r_1 & A_{11} & A_{12} \\ r_2 & A_{21} & A_{22} \end{vmatrix} = \sum_{j=1}^{2} \sum_{i=1}^{2} s_j \hat{A}_{ji} r_i,$$

thus by (10f.21)

(10f.24)
$$-\begin{vmatrix} 0 & s_1 & s_2 \\ r_1 & A_{11} & A_{12} \\ r_2 & A_{21} & A_{22} \end{vmatrix} = s_1 A_{22} r_1 - s_1 A_{12} r_2 - r_2 A_{21} r_1 + s_2 A_{11} r_2.$$

In the case where the r-set and the s-set are *one and the same* set, that is to say $r_i = s_i$ ($i=1, 2, \ldots, n$) and the matrix A_{ij} is symmetric, that is to say $A_{ij} = A_{ji}$, we have a *quadratic form* as a special case of the bilinear form. The equality of the right side in (5i.8) and in (5i.9) will then follow from (10f.24).

A matrix A_{ij} is called *positive definite*, when, and only when, it is symmetrical and we have

(10f.25)
$$\begin{vmatrix} A_{11} & A_{12} & \ldots & A_{1k} \\ A_{21} & A_{22} & \ldots & A_{2k} \\ \ldots & \ldots & \ldots & \ldots \\ A_{k1} & A_{k2} & \ldots & A_{kk} \end{vmatrix} > 0 \qquad (k=1, 2, \ldots, n).$$

In this case the quadratic form built on this matrix will *always be positive* expect when all the variables are 0. That is to say, if the matrix A_{ij} is positive definite we shall have

(10f.26) $\quad \sum_{i=1}^{n} \sum_{j=1}^{n} r_i A_{ij} r_j > 0$, for all real values of $\quad r_1, r_2, \ldots, r_n,$ except
$$r_1 = r_2 = \ldots = r_n = 0.$$

As an example, let us take the case $n=2$. When (10f.25) is fulfilled, we have $A_{11} > 0$ and $A_{11} A_{22} - A_{12}^2 > 0$. From the last-mentioned inequality it follows that $A_{11} A_{22}$ is positive, i.e. also that $A_{22} > 0$. We wish to show that when these conditions for the A's are fulfilled, the quadratic form

$A_{22}r_1^2 - 2A_{12}r_1r_2 + A_{11}r_2^2$ will be positive, *no matter* what (real) values r_1 and r_2 assume. This follows from the fact that we can write the quadratic form in question as a sum of two squares, with positive coefficients. One way of doing this is, for example, to write the quadratic form in this way

(10f.27)
$$A_{22}r_1^2 - 2A_{12}r_1r_2 + A_{11}r_2^2 = \frac{1}{A_{22}}[A_{22}r_1 - A_{12}r_2]^2 + \frac{A_{11}A_{22} - A_{12}^2}{A_{22}} r_2^2.$$

By multiplying out the expression on the right in (10f.27), it is easy to see that this expression is equal to the left side in (10f.27) identically in r_1 and r_2, that is to say irrespective of the values we allow r_1 and r_2. But the right side of (10f.27) is positive for all values of r_1 and r_2, except for $r_1 = r_2 = 0$; since the coefficient $1/A_{22}$ is positive, and the same applies to the coefficient $(A_{11}A_{22} - A_{12}^2)/A_{22}$. Thus the expression cannot be equal to 0 unless both the bracket in (10f.27) and r_2 are 0. But this is the same as $r_1 = r_2 = 0$. This shows that (10f.26) is fulfilled in the case $n = 2$.

In the theory of positive definite matrices, it is shown that if a matrix is positive definite, then its adjoint, too, is positive definite. This is all we need to use in the sequel.

Condition (10f.18) can be written

(10f.28)
$$\begin{vmatrix} (-x_{11}'') & (-x_{12}'') & \ldots & (-x_{1k}'') \\ (-x_{21}'') & (-x_{22}'') & \ldots & (-x_{2k}'') \\ \vdots & & & \vdots \\ (-x_{k1}'') & (-x_{k2}'') & \ldots & (-x_{kk}'') \end{vmatrix} > 0 \quad (k = 1, 2, \ldots, n).$$

If we now consider a specific value of k, for example K, then according to (10f.28) the K-rowed matrix of the type $(-x_{ij}'')$ will be positive definite and consequently its adjoint will also be positive definite. Since

(10f.29)
$$-\begin{vmatrix} 0 & r_1 & r_2 & \ldots & r_K \\ r_1 & (-x_{11}'') & (-x_{12}'') & \ldots & (-x_{1K}'') \\ r_2 & (-x_{21}'') & (-x_{22}'') & \ldots & (-x_{2K}'') \\ \vdots & & & & \vdots \\ r_K & (-x_{K1}'') & (-x_{K2}'') & \ldots & (-x_{KK}'') \end{vmatrix}$$

by (10f.22) can be written as a quadratic form, whose matrix is the adjoint of the K-rowed $(-x_{ij}'')$ and this matrix is positive definite, then (10f.29) must be positive, irrespective of what $r_1, r_2, \ldots, r_K$ are. In other words, if (10f.18) is fulfilled, (10f.29) must be positive irrespective of what $r_1, r_2, \ldots, r_K$ are (provided only these figures are real and at least one of them is $\neq 0$).

If we now, in (10f.29), extract (-1) from the line beginning with r_1, and likewise (-1) from the line beginning with r_2, etc., we shall get as a factor outside the determinant $(-1)^K$. We next extract (-1) out of the first column, in order to get back from the first column $(-r_1), (-r_2), \ldots, (-r_K)$ to the first column $r_1, r_2, \ldots, r_K$. Altogether, the sign will therefore – taking account of the minus sign in (10f.29) – be $(-1)^K$. If we now insert $r_1 = x_1', r_2 = x_2'$, etc., and write k instead of K, we get condition (5i.11), which was the same condition we found in the text subsequent to (10b.17). For $k=1$, condition (5i.11) is only trivial, as it only shows $(x_1')^2 > 0$.

From the above argument it follows in particular that if (10f.18) applies, then the numerator and denominator in (10f.20) must have the same sign and consequently – provided the substitumal marginal cost b' is positive – profit maximisation adjustment must take place on a *rising* part of the marginal cost curve, i.e. where b'' is positive.

So far in this Section we have assumed that production follows a regular ultra-passum law in the specified variable factors. We shall now consider the case of a *pari-passu law* in the variable factors. In such a case the cost structure of the concern, by variation along the substitumal, will be as given in proposition (10e.19). That is to say the substitumal marginal cost is constant.

If the product price is *higher* than the constant size of the substitumal marginal cost, the profit will constantly become greater during an expansion of the production volume (since then $dr/dx = p - b' > 0$ at every point). The equilibrium condition $p = b'$ is then not fulfilled in any point on the substitumal.

If the product price is *lower* than the constant size of the substitumal marginal cost, the profit will constantly become greater (or in other words the loss will constantly become smaller) during a *contraction* of the production volume (since then $dr/dx = p - b' < 0$ at every point). Nor in this case is the equilibrium condition $p = b'$ fulfilled in any point of the substitumal.

Finally we have the case where the product price is exactly equal to the constant size of the substitumal marginal cost. The equilibrium condition $p = b'$ will then be fulfilled in every point on the substitumal and the localisation of the adjustment point will consequently be indeterminate. In other words, under the pari-passu law there is either *no* point or an *infinite number* of points satisfying the condition for profit maximisation. This too is a fact that is usually not brought out with sufficient clearness in discussions on production theory.

In the pari-passu law, given fixed factor prices and a fixed product price, volume adjustment can therefore *not* be determined by profit maximisation, but must be replaced by other criteria, for example the presupposition of a given product quantity or a given total cost.

10g. Profit optimisation

Profit optimisation means making the profit rate r/b (or in some cases $r/(b+B)$) as large as possible. We shall only consider

$$(10\text{g}.1) \qquad \frac{r}{b} = \frac{px - b(x)}{b(x)}.$$

The necessary first order condition for the maximum of (10g.1) is

$$(10\text{g}.2) \qquad \frac{\mathrm{d}(r/b)}{\mathrm{d}x} = \frac{b \cdot p - px \cdot b'}{b^2} = \frac{px}{b^2}\left(\frac{b}{x} - b'\right) = 0.$$

px/b^2 is always positive. Consequently the equilibrium condition will be

$$(10\text{g}.3) \qquad \frac{b}{x} = b'.$$

The profit rate is therefore greatest at a point where the substitumal marginal cost is equal to the substitumal average cost. With fixed factor prices this point is characterised by $\varepsilon = 1$, cf. (10e.14), that is to say adjustment occurs in the substitumal point where the scale is technically optimal.

The point where the rate of profit is greatest is thus *independent of the price of the product*.

We have here assumed that the regular ultra-passum law applies. If the production law has a pari-passu character, volume adjustment will be indeterminate also under profit optimisation. With the pari-passu law, marginal cost is, indeed, equal to average cost at every point on the substitumal.

10h. The general demand functions for the factors and the general supply function for the product

Let us return to the case where the adjustment aim of the concern was *profit maximisation* (cf. 11f) and the concern was a quantity adjuster both in the factor markets and in the product market.

Then if the product price and factor prices are such that the product price is equal to or greater than the minimum of average cost (point B in Figure (10f.7)), the adjustment conditions will be (10f.14). These give n equations between the n factor quantities $v_1, v_2, \ldots, v_n$, the product price p and the n

factor prices $q_1, q_2, \ldots, q_n$. Each marginal productivity x_i' is then interpreted as a technically given function of the factor quantities $v_1, v_2, \ldots, v_n$.

Consequently the system is in principle determinate in the sense that for every given set of values of the prices $p, q_1, \ldots, q_n$ all the factor quantities $v_1, v_2, \ldots, v_n$ are defined. Thus each of the factor quantities can be expressed as a function of the prices. We write these functions

(10h.1)
$$v_1 = g_1(p, q_1, \ldots, q_n)$$
$$v_2 = g_2(p, q_1, \ldots, q_n)$$
$$\ldots\ldots\ldots\ldots\ldots\ldots$$
$$v_n = g_n(p, q_1, \ldots, q_n).$$

The functions g_i in (10h.1) tell us something about how much is demanded of each individual factor in various price situations. (10h.1) is therefore called *the general demand functions for the factors*.

When the factor quantities are given, however, the product quantity is known by the product function. In other words, the product quantity can be regarded as a function of the prices $p, q_1, q_2, \ldots, q_n$. We write this function

(10h.2)
$$x = x(v_1, \ldots, v_n)$$
$$= x[g_1(p, q_1, \ldots, q_n), \ldots, g_n(p, q_1, \ldots, q_n)] = h(p, q_1, \ldots, q_n).$$

The function $h(p, q_1, \ldots, q_n)$ tells us how much is offered of the product in given price situations. For this reason (10h.2) is called *the general supply function of the product*.

We are interested in studying the form of the general demand functions for the factors, and the general supply function for the product. This is the same as studying the producer's reactions to changes in prices.

We shall first consider briefly the effects of an alteration merely in the product price. Next we shall consider the case where an alteration takes place merely in one of the factor prices.

10i. The effect of a change in the product price

When the product price is changed, though at all times in such a way that it is equal to or greater than the minimum of average costs, we are first and foremost interested in the following question: If the product price increases slightly, will the quantity offered of the product then increase or diminish, and how *great* will the change be? This leads to the introduction of the concept of *the direct (ordinary) supply elasticity for the product*. This is defined as the partial elasticity of the general supply function for the product (10h.2) with respect to product price. That is to say

MOMENTARY SINGLE PRODUCTION

(10i.1) $$\check{x}_p = \frac{\partial h(p, q_1, \ldots, q_n)}{\partial p} \frac{p}{h(p, q_1, \ldots, q_n)}.$$

This elasticity can be found by implicit elasticisation of the system of equations consisting of (10f.14) and the product function, with $q_1, q_2, \ldots, q_n$ considered as constants. When $q_1, q_2, \ldots, q_n$ are constants, the substitumal will remain unchanged. We can therefore also find $\check{x}_p$ by an elasticisation for p along the substitumal. For this purpose (10f.4) can be used, with b' regarded as a function of x. By using the rule for elasticisation of a function-function we get $\check{b}' \cdot \check{x}_p = 1$, that is to say

(10i.2) $$\check{x}_p = \frac{1}{\check{b}'}.$$

In a regular profit maximisation point b'' must be greater than 0, cf. (10f.6). When $b'' > 0$, then $(\check{b}') = b'' x/b'$ must also be positive since both x and b' are positive. Thus we have

(10i.3) $$\check{x}_p > 0$$

(for all values of p which are equal to or greater than the minimum of the average cost.)

That is to say: the direct supply curve for the product is *rising* for all p which satisfy the specified condition.

This can also be shown by taking a starting point in Figure (10f.7). A change of the product price is equivalent to a parallel displacement of the horizontal price line in Figure (10f.7). When a parallel displacement of this kind is made, the adjustment point will move along the rising main branch of the marginal cost curve, since at any given horizontal product price line the adjustment will take place at the point where this line intersects the rising main branch of the marginal cost curve. If the product price has a height such as that mentioned, then consequently *the direct supply curve for the product will simply be the same as the rising main portion of the marginal cost curve.*

If the producer carries out profit maximisation to a given product price, and does not allow himself to be influenced by extraneous non-economic considerations, *the short-term supply curve* – that is to say, the supply curve when the fixed plant is already present – will be as indicated by the two heavily drawn segments of curves in Figure (10i.4), and *the long-term supply curve* by the two heavily drawn portions of the curve in Figure (10i.5).

Some authors depict the direct supply curve as consisting of the marginal

ECONOMIC ADJUSTMENT TO FIXED PRICE 189

cost curve over the interval where both this curve and the piece cost curve are rising, but as consisting of the *piece* cost curve, where this is falling. In other words, of the two curves the one whose ordinate is the largest

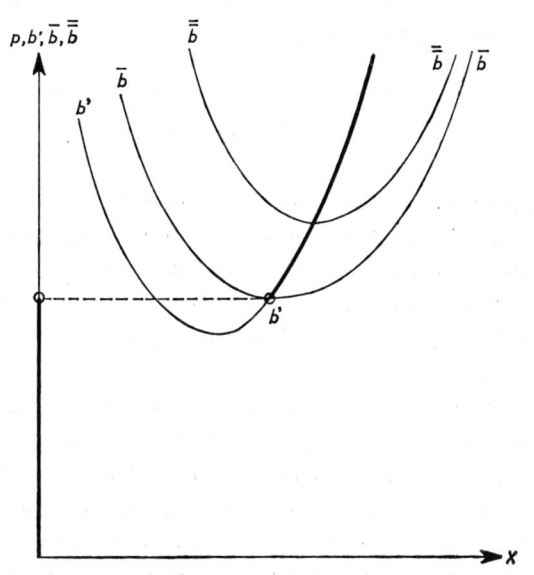

Fig. (10i.4). Short-term supply curve.

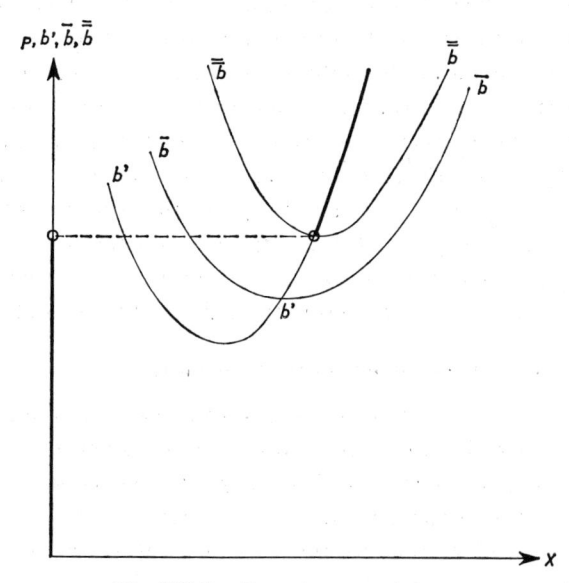

Fig. (10i.5). Long-term supply curve.

is taken. This, however is a confusion of two strategic types. In the case of profit maximisation and quantity adjustment the piece cost curve will not become a supply curve in any part of its course.

If we insert the expression for $\check{b}'$ from (10e.18) in the formula for the direct supply elasticity (10i.2), we get

$$(10\text{i}.6) \qquad \check{x}_p = \frac{1}{\dfrac{1}{\varepsilon} - 1 - \check{\varepsilon}}.$$

This formula provides an interesting link between the passus character of the production law and the producer's supply structure. If we have information about the passus character of the production law in the vicinity of the actual market point, we can deduce the supply elasticity.

We shall now turn to an investigation of *how a change in the product price affects the demand for production factors*.

We have previously seen that when the product price increases, more will be produced (provided the concern is actually operating). In the case of unchanged factor prices an increase of product quantity will involve a movement (in a positive direction) along the substitumal corresponding to the given factor prices. If the substitumal is rising with respect to a particular factor in the vicinity of the equilibrium point, a slight increase in the product price will lead to an increase in the use of the factor concerned, but if the substitumal should be declining with respect to the factor concerned, an increase in the product price will cause a reduction in the producer's demand for the factor concerned. As a rule, however, – as mentioned above – the substitumal will be rising everywhere for all factors, and *as a rule a higher product price will therefore mean increased demand for all factors*.

Furthermore, it is clear that the change in the demand for a definite factor becomes *stronger*, the stronger the substitumal rises with respect to the factor concerned, that is to say the greater the substitumally marginal manufacturing coefficient (10d.10) is in the vicinity of the equilibrium point.

10j. The effect of a change in one of the factor prices

We shall now turn to a study of the effects of a change in the price of one of the factors when the other factor prices are constant and likewise the product price remains constant. This leads to the concept producer's *demand elasticity* for a specific factor with respect to a change in the price of one of the factors (the demand for the same factor whose price has changed or the demand for one of the others):

(10j.1) $$\check{v}_{(ij)} = \frac{\partial g_i(p, q_1, \ldots, q_n)}{\partial q_j} \cdot \frac{q_j}{g_i(p, q_1, \ldots, q_n)} \qquad \begin{matrix}(i=1,\ldots,n);\\(j=1,\ldots,n).\end{matrix}$$

As a special case of (10j.1) we have

(10j.2) $$\check{v}_{(ii)} = \frac{\partial g_i(p, q_1, \ldots, q_n)}{\partial q_j} \cdot \frac{q_j}{g_i(p, q_1, \ldots, q_n)} \qquad (i=1,\ldots,n).$$

(10j.2) is *the direct demand elasticity* for factor No. i, while (10j.1) for $i \neq j$ expresses *cross-demand elasticities* between the factors. If we are only interested in studying the *signs* of the demand elasticities, we can equally well work with *derivatives* as with elasticities. We shall do so below, and will therefore differentiate (10f.14) implicitly with respect to q_j.

Let us first consider the case involving two factors ($n=2$). Then (10f.14) has the form

(10j.3) $$\begin{aligned}px_1'(v_1, v_2) &= q_1, \\ px_2'(v_1, v_2) &= q_2.\end{aligned}$$

By differentiating these two equations implicitly with respect to q_1 we get (while considering v_1 and v_2 as functions of the three prices, cf. (10h.1)):

$$p \cdot x_{11}'' \frac{\partial v_1}{\partial q_1} + p \cdot x_{12}'' \frac{\partial v_2}{\partial q_1} = 1,$$

$$p \cdot x_{21}'' \frac{\partial v_1}{\partial q_1} + p \cdot x_{22}'' \frac{\partial v_2}{\partial q_1} = 0.$$

This is a linear equation with two unknowns $\partial v_1/\partial q_1$ and $\partial v_2/\partial q_1$.

With the help of Cramer's rule for solution of linear equation systems we get[1]:

(10j.4) $$\frac{\partial v_1}{\partial q_1} = \frac{1}{p} \cdot \frac{x_{22}''}{\begin{vmatrix} x_{11}'' & x_{12}'' \\ x_{21}'' & x_{22}'' \end{vmatrix}}$$

(10j.5) $$\frac{\partial v_2}{\partial q_1} = -\frac{1}{p} \cdot \frac{x_{21}''}{\begin{vmatrix} x_{11}'' & x_{12}'' \\ x_{21}'' & x_{22}'' \end{vmatrix}}.$$

By changing round the subscript 1 and 2 in (10j.5) we shall see that the expression remains unchanged. That is to say, we have

(10j.6) $$\frac{\partial v_1}{\partial q_2} = \frac{\partial v_2}{\partial q_1}.$$

---

[1] If we also wish to find the explicit expressions for the corresponding *elasticities*, these can be found with the aid of suitable normalisations.

In the case involving two factors (10f.18) – the condition for a regular profit maximum – gives the following conditions

(10j.7) $$\begin{cases} x_{11}'' < 0 \\ x_{22}'' < 0 \\ \begin{vmatrix} x_{11}'' & x_{12}'' \\ x_{21}'' & x_{22}'' \end{vmatrix} > 0. \end{cases}$$ (p is positive).

Formula (10j.7) shows that in the vicinity of a regular maximum point for profit, (10f.18), the common denominator of (10j.4) and (10j.5) must be positive, and the numerator in (10j.4) must be negative. In other words

(10j.8) $$\frac{\partial v_1}{\partial q_1} < 0,$$

(10j.9) $$\frac{\partial v_2}{\partial q_1} \lessgtr 0 \quad \text{accordingly as } x_{21}'' = x_{12}'' \lessgtr 0.$$

By differentiating (10j.3) implicitly with respect to q_2, we get correspondingly

(10j.10) $$\frac{\partial v_2}{\partial q_2} < 0,$$

(10j.11) $$\frac{\partial v_1}{\partial q_2} \lessgtr 0 \quad \text{accordingly as } x_{12}'' = x_{21}'' \lessgtr 0.$$

From (10j.8) and (10j.10) we get the following proposition:

PROPOSITION (10j.12)

In the case involving two factors a profit maximating quantity adjuster will always demand *less* of a factor when the price of this factor rises (while the other factor prices and the product price are constant) or in other words for both factors *the direct* demand curve will be declining. (Assuming that we have a regular maximum point for the profit and that we do not have profit maximum at a terminal point.)

And from (10j.9) and (10j.11) we get the following proposition:

PROPOSITION (10j.13)

In the case involving only two factors a profit maximum quantity adjuster will demand more of one factor when the price of the other factor goes up if the two factors are *technically alternative* in the vicinity of the equilibrium point, and less of the one factor if the two factors are *technically complementary* in the vicinity of the equilibrium point, or in other words: complementarity in the technical sense involves complementarity in demand and alternativity in the technical sense involves alternativity in demand, (assuming that we have a regular maximum point for the profit and that we do not have profit maximum at a terminal point.)

We shall now investigate whether these results may be generalised to apply to the case of n factors. We shall therefore differentiate (10f.14) implicitly with respect to q_j. We then get

$$(10\text{j}.14) \qquad \sum_{k=1}^{n} p x_{ik}'' \frac{\partial v_k}{\partial q_j} = e_{ij} \qquad (\text{for all } i=1, 2, \ldots, n),$$

where

$$e_{ij} = \begin{cases} 1 & \text{when } i=j \\ 0 & \text{when } i \neq j \end{cases} \text{ are the unit numbers.}$$

(10j.14) gives n linear equations between the n unknowns

$$\frac{\partial v_1}{\partial q_j}, \frac{\partial v_2}{\partial q_j}, \ldots, \frac{\partial v_n}{\partial q_j}.$$

This gives

$$(10\text{j}.15) \qquad \frac{\partial v_k}{\partial q_j} = \frac{(-1)^{k+j} D_{jk}}{p \cdot D} \qquad \begin{pmatrix} k=1, \ldots, n \\ j=1, \ldots, n \end{pmatrix}$$

where

$$(10\text{j}.16) \qquad D = \begin{vmatrix} x_{11}'' & \ldots & x_{1n}'' \\ x_{21}'' & \ldots & x_{2n}'' \\ \vdots & & \vdots \\ x_{n1}'' & \ldots & x_{nn}'' \end{vmatrix}$$

and where D_{jk} is the subdeterminant which occurs when we erase line No. j and column No. k in (10j.16).

By interchanging k and j in (10j.15) we see that the expression remains unchanged, as D is a symmetrical determinant. We consequently get

$$(10\text{j}.17) \qquad \frac{\partial v_k}{\partial q_j} = \frac{\partial v_j}{\partial q_k}.$$

This is a generalisation of (10j.6).

As a special case of (10j.14) we have

$$\frac{\partial v_i}{\partial q_i} = \frac{(-1)^{i+i} D_{ii}}{p \cdot D} \qquad (i=1, 2, \ldots, n).$$

In other words

(10j.18) $$\frac{\partial v_i}{\partial q_i} = \frac{D_{ii}}{p \cdot D} \qquad (i=1, 2, ..., n).$$

On account of our presupposition that the technical condition (10f.18) is fulfilled, D_{ii} and D must always have opposite signs in the vicinity of a regular profit maximisation point. Consequently (10j.18) – since p is assumed to be positive – is always negative. This shows that proposition (10j.12) may be generalised as follows:

PROPOSITION (10j.19)

The profit maximating quantity adjuster will always demand *less* of a factor when the price of this factor rises, or in other words for all factors *the direct demand curve will be declining* (under the proposition that we have a regular maximum point for the profit and that we do not have the profit maximum in a terminal point).

Proposition (10j.13) does *not* permit of any simple generalisation. From formula (10j.15) we see that the cross-derivatives depend in a very complicated way on all product accelerations.

When a change occurs in one of the factor prices (the other factor prices and the product price remaining constant) the quantity of the product will also change (cf. (10h.2)). This leads to the introduction of the *concept of elasticity of supply for the product with respect to the price of factor No. j*:

(10j.20) $$\check{x}_j = \frac{\partial h(p, q_1, ..., q_n)}{\partial q_j} \frac{q_j}{h(p, q_1, ..., q_n)}.$$

Since $h(p, q_1, ..., q_n)$ is defined implicitly by (10f.14) and the product function, the expression for $\check{x}_j$ can be found by implicit elasticisation of (10f.14) and the product function for q_j. We shall not carry out the computation here, but merely content ourselves by noting that $\check{x}_j$ is as a rule negative.

10k. Capacity adjustment

In Section 2b we gave a provisional definition of the concept of capacity. We now have the means of elaborating this definition. The capacity of a permanent plant can be regarded either as a *maximum capacity* or as an *optimum capacity*. The first of these is the greatest product quantity the plant can produce (per time unit) when the plant is running at its greatest level of performance, that is to say when the other factors are added until their marginal productivities are nil. The latter is the product quantity which is produced when the plant is exploited in 'the technically most advantageous manner'. By this we mean that the factor point for the variable factors have to lie on the surface of the technically optimal scale ($\varepsilon=1$). Technical conditions may be such that this determines the product quantity practically speaking uniquely (a narrow substitution region or isoquants running almost parallel to the surface of the technically optimal scale). In a contrary case optimal capacity must be *calculated on an index basis*. One then calculates with what *probability* the various combinations of factor prices will occur during the life of the plant, and then one takes the average of product quantities at *those* points in the surface of the technically optimal scale which will become the adjustment points if these price combinations apply, each product quantity being assessed with the corresponding probability.

An average assessment of this kind – carried out more or less roughly – is required *inter alia* in deciding on the profitability of various capacity alternatives which are taken into consideration when the plant is erected. Two considerations will have to be balanced against one another: in the case of a large plant it will nearly always be possible to make considerable reductions in the variable piece-costs, *for a product quantity lying in the vicinity of the technical optimum* ($\varepsilon=1$), cf. Figure (10e.25). But the piece costs can be big for other product quantities. On the other hand a plant of this kind will demand a large outlay; once this outlay has been undertaken, reimbursement will come in the form of a *quasi-rent*. There will be no guarantee that the product quantity can be kept near the optimal (or post-optimal) region. In weighing up these two considerations, the anticipated *optimal capacity* is determined.

CHAPTER 11

ECONOMIC ADJUSTMENT UNDER ELASTICITY INFLUENCED PRICE-QUANTITY ADJUSTMENT

11a. Introduction

We shall continue to base ourselves on the presuppositions about the technical character of production as mentioned in the introduction to Part II (momentary single production with only continuity factors, whose quantities – and likewise product quantities – can be measured in technical units).

Furthermore, in this chapter we shall presuppose that the concern is functioning as an *elasticity-influenced price-quantity adjuster* (cf. Section 9d) both in the market for the product and in the market for the n production factors used in the manufacture of this product. If – as previously – we let p represent the product price and $q_1, \ldots, q_n$ the factor prices, we are assuming that the concern, as far as the product is involved, is faced with a *demand function* and, as far as the factors are concerned, is faced with *supply* functions. In what follows we shall assume that the demand function for the product only depends on the product price, in other words is of the form

(11a.1) $\qquad p = p(x)$.

The supply functions for the factors are assumed to be of the forms

(11a.2)
$$q_1 = q_1(v_1)$$
$$q_2 = q_2(v_2)$$
$$\cdots\cdots$$
$$\cdots\cdots$$
$$q_n = q_n(v_n).$$

Thus we presuppose that the supply of the factors are *independent* in the sense that the price the concern has to pay for a certain factor may possibly depend on the quantity the concern uses of *this* factor (as expressed in (11a.2)), but is independent of the quantities that the concern uses of *other* factors. Furthermore we presuppose in the same sense independence between the product and the factors. A more general case is naturally the one where one is operating with various forms of *supply connection* between the factors and, possibly, a connection between the demand for the product and the supply of the factors. This, however, leads to more complicated formulas which we are not going to discuss here. They can however be worked out if need be. Even though we presuppose independence, we shall include a great many points of interest, and our treatment will be considerably more general than it would be if we merely based ourselves on price-fixed quantity adjustment, as we did in Chapter 10.

The product demand function (11a.1) and the factor supply functions (11a.2) which we consider, are those which the concern believes will apply for *this* concern. This does not necessarily mean that the concern is monopolist in both directions. It could, for example, mean that a total demand curve is valid for the product, and that the concern believes that the *other producers* do not allow themselves to be notably influenced in their production policy because our concern produces a little more or a little less. If this is the case, and our concern produces a quantity which is not of infinitesimal size in relation to the whole production in the market, the concern must reckon with the price being influenced somewhat by its production and sales policy, though not to the extent that the price would have been influenced if the concern had been the sole producer. This is only one example of a situation which results in our concern having to calculate with a certain given connection between product price and the quantity *it* produces. Many other situations, however, may also lead to a connection of the kind described above. What has created this connection is, in the present context, of no consequence. The only thing that interests us here is that the concern believes it must take into account a given connection of the type (11a.1). The same applies to the functions (11a.2) which express the connection between factor prices and the factor quantities used by our concern.

In principle it is of little consequence whether we regard the quantity as a function of the price or conversely (cf. Section 9d). In what follows we have chosen to consider the demand function for the product and the supply functions for the factors in the form defined by the formulae (11a.1) and (11a.2).

For the sake of simplicity we shall assume that the demand function (11a.1) and the supply functions (11a.2) are continuous with continuous derivatives of the first and second order. To characterise these functions we shall introduce *demand flexibility*

$$(11a.3) \qquad \check{p} = \frac{dp}{dx} \cdot \frac{x}{p},$$

and *supply flexibilities*

(11a.4) $$\check{q}_i = \frac{dq_i}{dv_i} \cdot \frac{v_i}{q_i}. \qquad (i=1, 2, ..., n)$$

Most frequently $\check{p}$ will be negative – this means that the demand curve which the concern believes is directed towards the product of the concern is declining – and $\check{q}_i$ is positive for all $i=1, 2, ..., n$ – this means that the supply curves which the concern believes it will have to face in the factor market are rising.

If the concern is a price-fixed quantity adjuster in the market for factor No. k, $\check{q}_k=0$, and correspondingly $\check{p}=0$ if the concern is a price-fixed quantity adjuster in the product market.

Also when the concern is an elasticity-influenced price-quantity adjuster, the total costs are defined by (10a.1), but in this case the factor prices are *not* given constants as in Chapter 10. Thus, total costs are no longer a linear function of the factor quantities, but we have

(11a.5) $$b = \sum_{i=1}^{n} q_i(v_i) \cdot v_i = \phi(v_1, ..., v_n).$$

The *marginal outlay* for a specific factor is now defined as

(11a.6) Marginal outlay for factor No. $k = \dfrac{\partial b}{\partial v_k} = \dfrac{\partial \phi(v, ..., v_n)}{\partial v_k}.$

By differentiating we get

$$\frac{\partial b}{\partial v_k} = \frac{\partial \left[\sum_{i=1}^{n} q_i(v_i) \cdot v_i\right]}{\partial v_k} = \frac{d[q_k(v_k) \cdot v_k]}{dv_k} = \frac{dq_k}{dv_k} \cdot v_k + q_k =$$
$$= q_k\left(1 + \frac{dq_k}{dv_k} \cdot \frac{v_k}{q_k}\right),$$

Hence, according to (11a.4):

(11a.7) Marginal outlay with respect to factor No. $k = q_k(1+\check{q}_k)$.

As we presuppose that the factor prices are positive and that the factor price functions are rising, marginal outlay will be positive and *greater* than the appurtenant factor prices. In the limiting case of fixed factor prices we have $\check{q}_k=0$, and the marginal outlay is equal to the factor price.

The expression to the right in (11a.7) shows that marginal outlay can also be conceived of as a *corrected factor price*. The factor price is corrected by a multiplicator which is equal to one plus the supply flexibility of the factor. This correction is an expression of the fact that, if more of a specific

ELASTICITY-INFLUENCED PRICE-QUANTITY ADJUSTMENT 199

factor is used, total outlay increases, not only because we get more units of this factor to pay for, but also because *all* units now have to be paid for at a higher price (if $\check{q}_k$ is positive).

In the case involving two factors, the cost equation (11a.5) has the following form:

(11a.8) $$b = q_1(v_1) \cdot v_1 + q_2(v_2) \cdot v_2 = \phi(v_1, v_2).$$

When the cost sum b and the supply functions (11a.2) are given, this is an equation between the two variables v_1 and v_2. (11a.8) consequently implicitly defines v_2 as a function of v_1. The graphic picture of this function is *the cost line*, corresponding to the given cost amount b. By using an argument similar to that which resulted in (5i.6), we get the following formula for the tangential steepness along a cost line

(11a.9) $$\frac{dv_2}{dv_1} \text{ (along a cost line)} = -\frac{\dfrac{\partial \phi(v_1, v_2)}{\partial v_1}}{\dfrac{\partial \phi(v_1, v_2)}{\partial v_2}}.$$

By inserting (11a.7) in (11a.9), we get

(11a.10) $$\frac{dv_2}{dv_1} \text{ (along a cost line)} = -\frac{q_1(1+\check{q}_1)}{q_2(1+\check{q}_2)}.$$

Since marginal outlays are positive, dv_2/dv_1 (along a cost line) <0 and *the cost lines are consequently falling*. Since (11a.10) in the general case is dependent on the factor point where we happen to be, the cost lines will not be straight lines as in Figure (10a.5), but *curved* lines as suggested in Figure (11a.11).

As a rule the curvature will be as given in Figure (11a.11). This follows from the following reasoning.

If we wish to investigate how cost lines are curved, we must consider the second derivative along a cost line. This can be done on the lines of an argument similar to that which resulted in (5i.8). Thus:

(11a.12)
$$\frac{d^2 v_2}{dv_1^2} = -\frac{1}{\left(\dfrac{\partial b}{\partial v_2}\right)^3} \left[\left(\frac{\partial b}{\partial v_2}\right)^2 \frac{\partial^2 b}{\partial v_1^2} - 2 \cdot \frac{\partial b}{\partial v_1} \cdot \frac{\partial b}{\partial v_2} \cdot \frac{\partial^2 b}{\partial v_1 \partial v_2} + \left(\frac{\partial b}{\partial v_1}\right)^2 \cdot \frac{\partial^2 b}{\partial v_2^2} \right].$$

As in the above cases we have assumed independence between the various factor quantities, cf. the comments to (11a.2), we shall get

$$\frac{\partial^2 b}{\partial v_1 \partial v_2} = \frac{\partial [\partial b/\partial v_1]}{\partial v_2} = \frac{\partial [q_1(1+\check{q}_1)]}{\partial v_2} = 0,$$

and

(11a.13) $$\frac{d^2 v_2}{d v_1^2} = - \frac{1}{\left(\frac{\partial b}{\partial v_2}\right)^3} \left[\left(\frac{\partial b}{\partial v_2}\right)^2 \frac{\partial^2 b}{\partial v_1^2} + \left(\frac{\partial b}{\partial v_1}\right)^2 \frac{\partial^2 b}{\partial v_2^2} \right]$$

along a cost line.

The criterion for a cost line being curved away *from* the origin – that is to say, turns its hollow side towards the origin, as in Figure (11a.11) – is that $d^2 v_2/d v_1^2$ along a cost line is negative. Let us consider some sufficient conditions for the fulfilment of this.

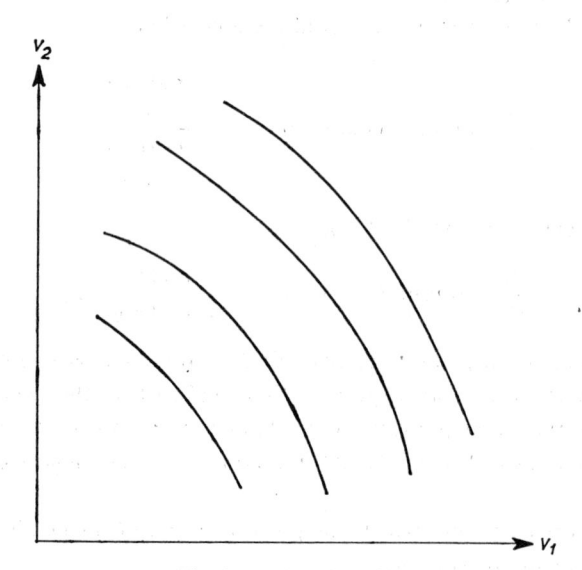

Fig. (11a.11). Cost lines.

When both $\partial^2 b/\partial v_1^2$ and $\partial^2 b/\partial v_2^2$ are positive, the term in the square bracket in (11a.13) will be positive and $d^2 v_2/d v_1^2$ negative, as we assume that the marginal outlays are positive, cf. comments to (11a.7).

In order to investigate the positivity of $\partial^2 b/\partial v_1^2$ and $\partial^2 b/\partial v_2^2$, we shall rewrite the expression $\partial^2 b/\partial v_i^2$ thus

$$\frac{\partial^2 b}{\partial v_i^2} = \frac{d[q_i(1+\check{q}_i)]}{dv_i} = \frac{dq_i}{dv_i} + \frac{d(q_i \check{q}_i)}{dq_i} \cdot \frac{dq_i}{dv_i} = \frac{dq_i}{dv_i}\left[1 + \check{q}_i + q_i \frac{d\check{q}_i}{dq_i}\right].$$

The last term in this square bracket is

ELASTICITY-INFLUENCED PRICE-QUANTITY ADJUSTMENT 201

$$q_i \frac{d\check{q}_i}{dq_i} = q_i \frac{d\check{q}_i}{dv_i} \frac{dv_i}{dq_i} = v_i \frac{d\check{q}_i}{dv_i} \cdot \frac{1}{\frac{dq_i}{dv_i} \frac{v_i}{q_i}} = \frac{d\check{q}_i}{dv_i} \cdot \frac{v_i}{\check{q}_i} = \tilde{q}_i$$

as we define

(11a.14) price flexibility-flexibility for factor No. $i = \tilde{q}_i = \frac{d\check{q}_i}{dv_i} \frac{v_i}{\check{q}_i}$,

we get

(11a.15) $$\frac{\partial^2 b}{\partial v_i{}^2} = \frac{dq_i}{dv_i}(1+\check{q}_i+\tilde{q}_i).$$

The coefficient preceding the parenthesis in (11a.15) is positive, and inside the parenthesis $1+\check{q}_i$ is positive since $\check{q}_i$ is positive. Only if the price flexibility-flexibility $\tilde{q}_i$ is negative and numerically so great that it dominates $1+\check{q}_i$, will (11a.15) be negative. We must assume that this is an unusual case. We can therefore expect that the cost line generally will be curved as in Figure (11a.11).

11b. Cost minimisation under a given product quantity and variable factor prices

Using an argument analogous to the one used in the case involving fixed factor prices, cf. Section 10b, we recognise that in the case involving two factors the problem of finding the factor point that produces a given product quantity x_0 with the lowest total costs, is solved by finding the factor point where the isoquant corresponding to the given product quantity x_0 *is tangential to* a cost line. Thus in Figure (11b.1) point Z gives the cost minimum for product quantity x_0.

We shall now express this analytically. In the tangent point the tangent steepness of the isoquant is equal to the tangent steepness of the cost line.

Bearing in mind (5i.6) and (11a.10), we therefore get the following equilibrium condition:

(11b.2) $$\frac{q_1(1+\check{q}_1)}{q_2(1+\check{q}_2)} = \frac{x_1'}{x_2'},$$

that is to say

(11b.3) $$\frac{x_1'}{q_1(1+\check{q}_1)} = \frac{x_2'}{q_2(1+\check{q}_2)}.$$

We can thus express the condition by saying that at the adjustment point *marginal productivities are proportional to the corrected factor prices.*

For $\check{q}_1 = \check{q}_2 = 0$, (11b.3) reduces to (10b.7).

Let us now consider the general case involving n factors. Our task is to determine the factor quantities $v_1, \ldots, v_n$ in such a way that (11a.5) is as small as possible, given the condition

(11b.4) $$x(v_1, \ldots, v_n) = x_0,$$

where x_0 is the given product quantity. Using Lagrange multipliers, we find that the necessary first order condition for the minimum of (11a.5), with (11b.4) as a supplementary condition, is

(11b.5) $$\frac{\partial b}{\partial v_i} - \lambda x_i' = 0 \qquad (i = 1, 2, \ldots, n),$$

where λ is a Lagrange multiplier, that is to say a magnitude which is assumed to be kept constant during the process of minimisation.

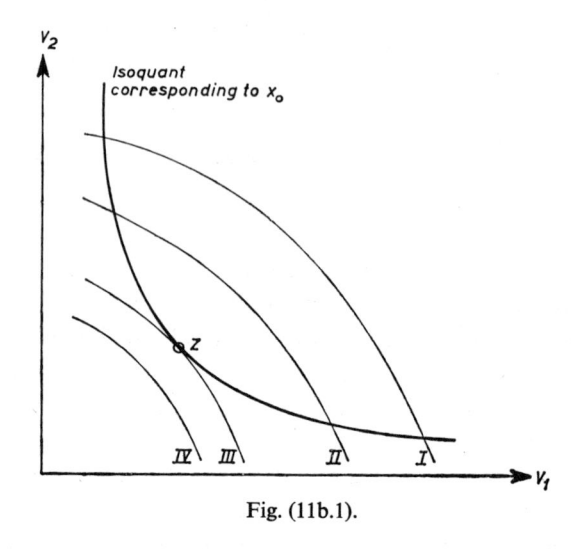

Fig. (11b.1).

By substituting for $\partial b / \partial v_i$ from (11a.7), (11b.5) can be written as

(11b.6) $$q_i(1 + \check{q}_i) - \lambda x_i' = 0 \qquad (i = 1, 2, \ldots, n).$$

This gives n conditions. Furthermore we have the condition (11b.4) regarding constant product quantity, that is to say a total of $n+1$ equations. At the same time we have $n+1$ quaesitum-parameters, viz. the Lagrange parameter λ and the n factor quantities $v_1, \ldots, v_n$ (marginal productivities are functions of all factor quantities, and each single one of the factor prices and factor price flexibilities is a function of the appurtenant factor quantity). Thus in principle the system is determined.

The equation system (11b.6) can be written in the form:

(11b.7) $$\frac{x_1'}{q_1(1+\check{q}_1)} = \frac{x_2'}{q_2(1+\check{q}_2)} = \ldots = \frac{x_n'}{q_n(1+\check{q}_n)} = \frac{1}{\lambda}.$$

If we so desire, we need only consider the first $n-1$ of these equations. This is tantamount to eliminating λ.

In the general case involving n factors the tangent condition can thus be expressed by saying that at the adjustment point marginal productivities are proportional to the corrected factor prices.

For $\check{q}_1 = \check{q}_2 = \ldots = \check{q}_n = 0$ (11b.7) reduces to (10b.12).

As in the case involving fixed factor prices the individual proportionality figures in (11b.7) can be given a concrete interpretation through the concept partial marginal cost. In the case under consideration we get:

(11b.8)

The partial marginal cost for factor No. k
$$= \frac{\partial \left(\sum_{i=1}^{n} q_i(v_i) v_i\right)}{\partial v_k} \bigg/ \frac{\partial x(v_1, \ldots, v_n)}{\partial v_k} = \frac{q_k(1+\check{q}_k)}{x_k'}.$$

The tangent condition (11b.7) can therefore be expressed by saying that *all the partial marginal costs must be equal* and equal to the Lagrange parameter λ. Cf. the text following (10b.13).

In addition to the above-mentioned necessary first-order conditions we have conditions of the second order. However, we shall not deal with these in detail in the case involving variable factor prices, but merely note that from Figure (11b.1) it is easy to see that in the vicinity of the equilibrium point the isoquant must lie to the north-east of the cost line and with a curvature that assures a stable equilibrium.

11c. Product maximisation under a given total cost and variable factor prices

Using an argument analogous to that in Section 10c, we shall find that in the case involving two factors the problem of finding the factor point which, at a given total cost b_0, gives the highest product quantity, is solved by finding the factor point where the cost line corresponding to the given cost quantity b_0 *is tangential to* an isoquant. Thus in Figure (11c.1) point Y gives the maximum product for total cost b_0.

At a tangential point between cost line and isoquant

(11c.2) $\quad \dfrac{dv_2}{dv_1}$ (along the cost line) $= \dfrac{dv_2}{dv_1}$ (along the isoquant).

By inserting from (5i.6) and (11a.10), this gives (11b.2). Thus in the case involving elasticity-influenced price-quantity adjustment in the factor markets we get the *same* tangent condition in the case of product maximisation as for cost minimisation. The side-condition, however, is different in the two cases. In Section 11b it was a given product quantity, now it is a given total cost.

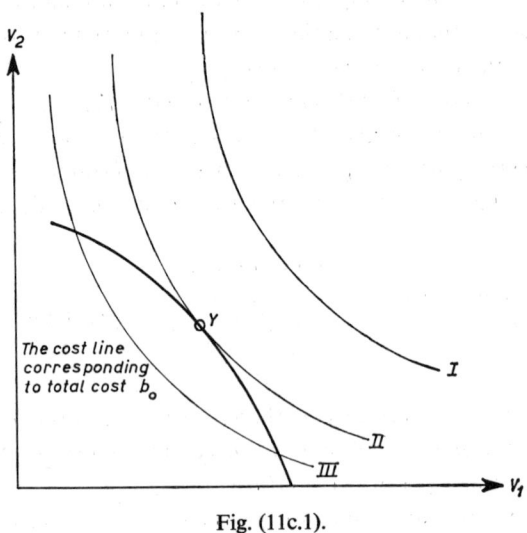

Fig. (11c.1).

In the general case involving n factors, the problem of product maximisation under given total costs involves determining the factor quantities $v_1, \ldots, v_n$ in such a way that (5a.2) is as big as possible under the side-condition

(11c.3) $$\sum_{i=1}^{n} q_i(v_i) \cdot v_i = b_0,$$

where b_0 is a given total cost. By Lagrange's method we find that the first order necessary condition for a maximum of (5a.2), under the side-condition (11c.3) is

(11c.4) $$x_i' - \mu \frac{\partial b_i}{\partial v_i} = 0 \qquad (i=1, 2, \ldots, n),$$

where μ is a Lagrange multiplier which is assumed constant during the maximisation process. By inserting in (11c.4) the expressions for marginal outlays $\partial b / \partial v_i$ taken from (11a.7), we get

(11c.5) $$x_i' - \mu \cdot q_i(1 + \check{q}_i) = 0 \qquad (i=1, 2, \ldots, n).$$

ELASTICITY-INFLUENCED PRICE-QUANTITY ADJUSTMENT 205

The necessary first order conditions (11c.5) together with the side-condition (11c.3), give $n+1$ equations among $n+1$ quaesitum parameters, viz. the Lagrange parameter μ and the factor quantities $v_1, \ldots, v_n$ since the marginal productivities are given functions of the factor quantities and the factor prices and the factor price flexibilities are given functions of the appurtenant factor quantities). Consequently the system is determined in principle.

The equation system (11c.5) can be written in the form

(11c.6) $$\frac{x_1'}{q_1(1+\check{q}_1)} = \frac{x_2'}{q_2(1+\check{q}_2)} = \ldots = \frac{x_n'}{q_n(1+\check{q}_n)} = \mu.$$

For $\check{q}_1 = \check{q}_2 = \ldots = \check{q}_n = 0$ (11c.6) reduces to (10c.7).

The first $n-1$ of the equations (11c.6) are precisely *the same* as in (11b.7). They express the tangent condition as distinct from the side-condition, which for cost minimisation was a given x_0 and for product maximisation a given b_0.

11d. The in-every-respect economic substitution under variable factor prices. The substitumal under variable factor prices

With the help of a line of reasoning analogous to that at the beginning of Section 10d, we shall find that in the case involving two factors the curve that arises when we link up all tangential points between the isoquants and the cost lines, that is to say curve *WYZ* in Figure (11d.1), at the same time solves both the problem of cost minimisation and that of product maximisation. In the same way as in the case involving fixed factor prices, we have only to combine this curve with the particular side-condition which applies to the problem concerned.

Furthermore, in the same way as in the line of argument used in connection with Figure (10d.6), it can be shown that any point on the curve *WYZ* is a factor point where it is *not* possible to undertake an in-every-respect economic substitution, that is to say a factor variation of the type (10d.3). And any point outside the curve *WYZ* does not have this property. Thus this curve is the *substitumal* corresponding to the given factor supply *functions*; cf. the general definition (10d.5).

In the general case of n factors, the first $(n-1)$ equations in (11b.7) – which are identical with the first $(n-1)$ equations in (11c.6) – that is to say

(11d.2) $$\frac{x_1'}{q_1(1+\check{q}_1)} = \frac{x_2'}{q_2(1+\check{q}_2)} = \ldots = \frac{x_n'}{q_n(1+\check{q}_n)},$$

will define a one-dimensional curve through the n-dimensional factor diagram. This curve possesses the property that it not only solves the problem of cost minimisation and the problem of product maximisation for variable factor prices, but it is quite generally the geometrical locus of factor points where it is *not* possible to undertake an in-every-respect economic substitution, that is to say it is the *substitumal* corresponding to the given factor supply *functions*. This is seen as follows:

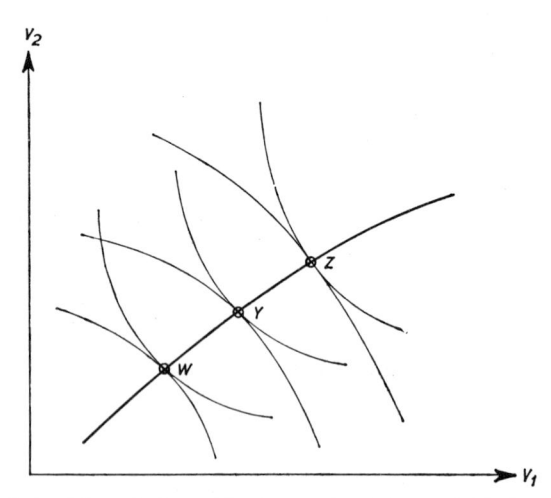

Fig. (11d.1). The substitumal in the case involving variable factor prices.

In the first place it is clear that, by starting from a point lying on the curve (11d.2), it is *impossible* to undertake an in-every-respect economic substitution. For let us, starting from a point on this curve, give the factor quantity the arbitrary infinitesimal increments $dv_1, dv_2, \ldots, dv_n$. The corresponding increment in total cost will then be

$$db = \sum_{i=1}^{n} \frac{\partial b}{\partial v_i} \cdot dv_i = \sum_{i=1}^{n} q_i(1+\breve{q}_i)dv_i.$$

And the increment in the product quantity will be

$$dx = \sum_{i=1}^{n} x_i' dv_i.$$

If the starting point lies on the curve under consideration, then according to (11d.2) $x_i' = \mu \cdot q_i(1+\breve{q}_i)$, that is to say $dx = \mu \cdot db$, where μ is the common magnitude of all proportion figures (11d.2), and consequently a positive figure. No matter how $dv_i, \ldots, dv_n$ are chosen, it will therefore be impossible to undertake a factor variation of the type (10d.3) starting from a point on

ELASTICITY-INFLUENCED PRICE-QUANTITY ADJUSTMENT

this curve. All points on the curve under consideration are in fact substitumals according to the general definition (10d.5).

That no other factor points can be substitumal may be seen as follows: If we are situated at a point outside this curve, for example at a point where we have

$$\frac{x_1'}{q_1(1+\check{q}_1)} > \frac{x_2'}{q_2(1+\check{q}_2)},$$

we may choose $dv_3 = dv_4 = \ldots dv_n = 0$ and dv_1 positive and dv_2 negative and the absolute values for dv_1 and dv_2 in such way that

$$\frac{x_1'}{x_2'} > \frac{(-dv_2)}{dv_1} > \frac{q_1(1+\check{q}_1)}{q_2(1+\check{q}_2)}.$$

We shall then get $x_1' dv_1 > x_2'(-dv_2)$, that is to say

$$dx = x_1' dv_1 + x_2' dv_2 > 0 \quad \text{and} \quad \frac{\partial b}{\partial v_1} dv_1 < \frac{\partial b}{\partial v_2}(-dv_2),$$

that is to say

$$db = \frac{\partial b}{\partial v_1} dv_1 + \frac{\partial b}{\partial v_2} dv_2 < 0,$$

i.e., we have a factor variation of the type (10d.3).

Similarly for other situations where (11d.2) is not fulfilled.

In the same way as in the case involving fixed factor prices, we can also, in the case involving variable factor prices, express the factor quantities as functions of the product quantity along the substitumal. We designate these functions

(11d.3) $\quad\quad\quad v_i = v_i(x) \quad$ along the substitumal $\quad (i=1, 2, \ldots, n)$.

Furthermore, we define the substitumally marginal fabrication coefficients as the derivatives of (11d.3). In symbols

(11d.4) The substitumally marginal fabrication coefficient for factor No. i:

$$v_i' = \frac{dv_i(x)}{dx} \quad \text{along the substitumal} \quad (i=1, \ldots, n).$$

By comparing the substitumal conditions (11d.2) with (5b.12), we see that in the case now considered the substitumal is *not* necessarily one of the isoclines. In the pari-passu law, in the case of variable factor prices, the substitumal will thus not necessarily be a straight line running through the origin. But as a rule it will be directed *outwards* into the factor diagram, both in the case of an ultra-passum law and a pari-passu law.

11e. The covariation between costs and product quantity along the substitumal corresponding to the given factor supply functions. The economic optimum law under variable factor prices

On account of the properties of the substitumal – for fixed as well as variable prices – any 'reasonable' adjustment will lead to a point on the substitumal, and any change in the scale of production will take place *along the substitumal*. It is therefore of interest to study the connection between costs and product quantity along the substitumal.

Along the substitumal there will also exist in the case involving variable factor prices a functional relationship between every single factor quantity and the product quantity, cf. (11d.3). If we insert these expressions in (11a.5) we get

$$\text{(11e.1)} \qquad b = \sum_{i=1}^{n} q_i[v_i(x)] \cdot v_i(x) = b(x).$$

The function $b(x)$ is *the substitumal cost function* under variable factor prices, or, more briefly, the cost function. It shows how total costs vary with the product quantity when the product quantity is produced in the cheapest possible manner under the given factor supply functions.

In the same way as in the case involving fixed factor prices, this function can be characterised with the help of the substitumal *marginal cost*, the substitumal *average cost (piece cost)*, and the substitumal *cost flexibility*.

In the general case under consideration, too, it will be seen that the substitumal marginal cost $b' = \mathrm{d}b(x)/\mathrm{d}x$ will be equal to the Lagrange multiplier λ, since we have

$$\text{(11e.2)} \qquad b' = \frac{\mathrm{d}b}{\mathrm{d}x} = \sum_{i=1}^{n} \frac{\partial b}{\partial v_i} \cdot \frac{\mathrm{d}v_i}{\mathrm{d}x} = \sum_{i=1}^{n} q_i(1+\breve{q}_i) \frac{\mathrm{d}v_i}{\mathrm{d}x}.$$

However, along the substitumal, according to (11b.7) $q_i(1+\breve{q}_i) = \lambda x_i'$. If this is inserted in (11e.2), we get $b' = \lambda \sum x_i' v_i'$. In the case involving variable factor prices, too, the aggregating equation $\sum x_i' v_i' = 1$ applies. Cf. (10d.11). Thus

$$\text{(11e.3)} \qquad\qquad\qquad b' = \lambda.$$

By inserting this in (11b.7), we get

(11e.4) $$b' = \frac{q_i(1+\check{q}_i)}{x_i'}$$

for any i (at a substitumal point).

That is to say: In the case involving variable factor prices, the substitumal marginal cost is equal to the ratio between the corrected price for an arbitrary factor and the marginal productivity of this factor.

If $\check{q}_1 = \check{q}_2 = \ldots = \check{q}_n = 0$, then (11e.4) reduces to (10e.6).

With the help of (11e.4) it can be shown that the indifference proposition for marginal cost – (10e.8) – also applies in the general case with variable factor prices. Indeed at any point on the substitumal (11e.4) applies, that is to say $\partial b/\partial v_i = q_i(1+\check{q}_i) = b'x_i' = b'x_i'$ for all $i=1, 2, \ldots, n$. If this is inserted in the formula for general marginal cost, which in this case will be

$$\frac{\sum_{i=1}^{n} \frac{\partial b}{\partial v_i} \cdot dv_i}{\sum_{i=1}^{n} x_i' dv_i},$$

we get:

(11e.5) General marginal cost (determined by starting from a substitumal point given variable factor prices)

$$= \frac{\sum_{i=1}^{n} b' x_i' dv_i}{\sum_{i=1}^{n} x_i' dv_i} = b'.$$

In the case involving variable factor prices, too, the various substitumal cost concepts can be related to the *passus coefficient*.

Let us take our starting point in (11b.7), which can be written $\lambda x_i' = q_i(1+\check{q}_i)$ $(i=1, 2, \ldots, n)$. Multiplying by v_i on both sides of the equals sign, and adding up for all i's, we get

$$\sum_{i=1}^{n} \lambda x_i' v_i = \sum_{i=1}^{n} q_i v_i \cdot (1+\check{q}_i).$$

According to the passus equation (5h.3), $\Sigma x_i' v_i = \varepsilon x$, that is to say

$$\lambda \varepsilon x = \sum_{i=1}^{n} q_i v_i \cdot (1+\check{q}_i) = \sum_{i=1}^{n} q_i v_i + \sum_{i=1}^{n} q_i v_i \check{q}_i.$$

If we introduce the average $\check{q}_0$ of the factor price flexibilities weighted by the factor outlays $(q_i v_i)$, that is to say

(11e.6) $$\check{q}_0 = \frac{\sum_{i=1}^{n}(q_i v_i) \cdot \check{q}_i}{\sum_{i=1}^{n} q_i v_i}.$$

we get

$$\lambda \varepsilon x = \sum_{i=1}^{n} q_i v_i + \check{q}_0 \sum_{i=1}^{n} q_i v_i = b + \check{q}_0 b.$$

that is to say $\lambda \varepsilon x = b(1+\check{q}_0)$.

If $\lambda = b'$ is inserted here, cf. (11e.3), we get

(11e.7) $$b = \frac{\varepsilon b' x}{1+\check{q}_0}.$$

This can also be written as

(11e.8) $$\bar{b} = \frac{\varepsilon b'}{1+\check{q}_0}.$$

If we compare these formulae with (10e.13) and (10e.14), we see that there is complete agreement, except for the fact that

(11e.9) $\qquad \varepsilon$ is replaced by $\dfrac{\varepsilon}{1+\check{q}_0}$.

The proportionality figure $\varepsilon/1+\check{q}_0$ we shall call the flexibility-corrected passus coefficient.

It will be seen, too, that in the remainder of our argument we get a high degree of agreement on the basis of the principle of correspondence (11e.9).

For $\check{q}_0=0$, (11e.7) and (11e.8) reduce to (10e.13) and (10e.14).

By a simple transformation of (11e.8), we get for the substitumal cost flexibility, $\breve{b}$,

(11e.10) $$\breve{b} = \frac{1+\check{q}_0}{\varepsilon} \qquad \text{Cf. (10e.15)}.$$

For the elasticity of the substitumal average cost with respect to the product quantity, $\tilde{b}$, we get in the case involving variable factor prices

(11e.11) $\quad \tilde{b} = \text{El.} \dfrac{b}{x} = \text{El. } b - \text{El. } x = \breve{b}-1 = \dfrac{1+\check{q}_0}{\varepsilon} - 1 \quad$ Cf. (10e.17).

From (11e.8) we get

$$b' = \frac{\bar{b}(1+\check{q}_0)}{\varepsilon}.$$

For the elasticity of the substitumal average cost with respect to the product quantity along the substitumal we therefore get by the help of (10e.10):

$$\check{b}' = \text{El.}\left(\frac{\bar{b}(1+\check{q}_0)}{\varepsilon}\right) = \text{El.}\,\bar{b} + \text{El.}\left(\frac{1+\check{q}_0}{\varepsilon}\right) = \text{El.}\,\bar{b} - \text{El.}\left(\frac{\varepsilon}{1+\check{q}_0}\right),$$

thus

(11e.12) $$\check{b}' = \frac{1+\check{q}_0}{\varepsilon} - 1 - \text{El.}\left(\frac{\varepsilon}{1+\check{q}_0}\right). \qquad \text{Cf. (10e.18)}.$$

Here El. $[\varepsilon/(1+\check{q}_0)]$ is the elasticity of $\varepsilon/(1+\check{q}_0)$ with respect to x under a substitumal variation. Also in the case involving variable factor prices, ε can be interpreted as a function of x along the substitumal, and the same applies to $(1+\check{q}_0)$, as each of the factor prices $q_1, q_2, \ldots, q_n$ and factor price flexibilities $\check{q}_1, \check{q}_2, \ldots, \check{q}_n$ is a function of the appurtenant factor quantity, so that $\check{q}_0$ is a function of the factor quantities and each of the factor quantities can along the substitumal be interpreted as a function of x, cf. (11d.3).

On the basis of the Formulae (11e.7)–(11e.12), we can say something about the typical variations the various cost concepts show under a movement along the substitumal in a regular ultra-passum law.

From the formulae we can see that these variations are essentially characterised by the manner in which the flexibility-corrected passus-coefficient $\varepsilon/(1+\check{q}_0)$ varies along the substitumal.

The simplest case is the one where ε varies relatively stronger than $(1+\check{q}_0)$ along the substitumal. In this case the proportionality figure $\varepsilon/(1+\check{q}_0)$ will in its essential features follow the variation of ε. As the substitumal, too, in the present case involving variable factor prices is, as a rule, a rising curve in the factor diagram, cf. the end of Section 11d, the *fundamental rule* (10e.20) about the variation of the passus coefficient along the substitumal will most frequently apply also in the present case, and we thus get the following rule:

RULE (11e.13)

In a regular ultra-passum law, with variable factor prices, if the variation in ε is relatively stronger than the variation in $(1+\check{q}_0)$, $\varepsilon/(1+\check{q}_0)$ will have the following course during a movement along the substitumal: to start with this proportionality figure – the flexibility-corrected passus coefficient – will be greater than 1, after which it will steadily decrease, passing 1 and finally assuming values less than 1.

On the basis of this rule let us first consider the course of the substitumal *average cost* during a movement along the substitumal corresponding to the given price functions. According to rule (11e.13) $\varepsilon/(1+\check{q}_0)$ is to start with greater than 1. From (11e.11) we see that $\bar{b}$ is then negative, and consequently the substitumal average cost curve is declining. After a while, according to (11e.13), $\varepsilon/(1+\check{q}_0)$ will pass the value 1. Here according to (11e.11), $\bar{b}=0$. Thus the substitumal average cost curve in the case involving variable factor prices reaches its minimum at a point where $\varepsilon/(1+\check{q}_0)=1$. As $\check{q}_0$ is positive, this point must lie in the with respect to the scale technically *pre-optimal* region ($\varepsilon>1$). To the right of this point (i.e., for a greater x) according to (11e.13) $\varepsilon/(1+\check{q}_0)$ will be less than 1, and $\bar{b}$ will thus according to (11e.11) be positive and the substitumal average cost curve will in this region consequently be rising.

If (11e.13) is fulfilled, we shall thus get in the case involving variable factor prices, too, a U-shaped average cost curve. Cf. Figure (10e.21).

Let us now consider the substitumal *marginal cost curve*. According to (11e.8) b' is less than $\bar{b}$, when $\varepsilon/(1+\check{q}_0)>1$, that is to say, to the left of $\bar{b}_{min}$, and greater than $\bar{b}$ when $\varepsilon/(1+\check{q}_0)<1$, that is to say, to the right of $\bar{b}_{min}$. Furthermore we see from (11e.8) that $b'=\bar{b}$ when $\varepsilon/(1+\check{q}_0)=1$, in other words, in the case involving variable factor prices, too, the marginal cost curve cuts the average cost curve from below at a point where the average cost curve has its lowest value. Incidentally the last-mentioned fact is also a direct consequence of the definitional relation, between marginal cost and average cost.

With the help of formula (11e.12) we can say a little more about the course of b' along the substitumal. To the right of the minimum point on the $\bar{b}$-curve, $\varepsilon/(1+\check{q}_0)<1$ and the term $(1+\check{q}_0)/\varepsilon-1$ is therefore positive. Furthermore, according to (11e.13) $\varepsilon/(1+\check{q}_0)$ is constantly declining, so that El. $[\varepsilon/(1+\check{q}_0)]<0$. To the right of the minimum point on the *average* cost curve, $\bar{b}'$ is thus positive, and the marginal cost curve constantly rising. The same applies in the actual minimum point on the average cost curve (where of course the term $(1+\check{q}_0)/\varepsilon-1$ is equal to nought and the term El. $[\varepsilon/(1+\check{q}_0)]$ is negative, so that $\bar{b}'>0$).

To the *left* of $\bar{b}_{min}$ it is not quite as simple to say something about the course of b'. As a rule, however, its course will be U-shaped, as in Figure (10e.21).

ELASTICITY-INFLUENCED PRICE-QUANTITY ADJUSTMENT 213

Above we have presupposed that $(1+\check{q}_0)$ changes relatively less markedly than ε under a variation along the substitumal. If $(1+\check{q}_0)$ varies considerably, and is constantly rising under a variation along the substitumal, the main gist of the conclusions above is the same, and we shall then still first have a region where $\varepsilon/(1+\check{q}_0) > 1$, then have a point where $\varepsilon/(1+\check{q}_0) = 1$, and finally a region where $\varepsilon/(1+\check{q}_0) < 1$.

If, however, $1+\check{q}_0$ is strongly and persistently sinking, or if it alternately rises and falls, it may happen that the cost curves show a different course.

To sum up, we can say that in the case involving elasticity-influenced adjustment to factor markets, too, the substitumal cost curves will in a regular ultra-passum law as a rule have a similarly typical optimum course as in the case involving fixed factor prices.

If we wish to *compare* the course of cost curves in the case involving variable factor prices with the course of the cost curves in the case involving fixed factor prices, we must specify *what levels* these fixed factor prices are to have during our comparison. A few examples will show how the reasoning will then have to be carried out.

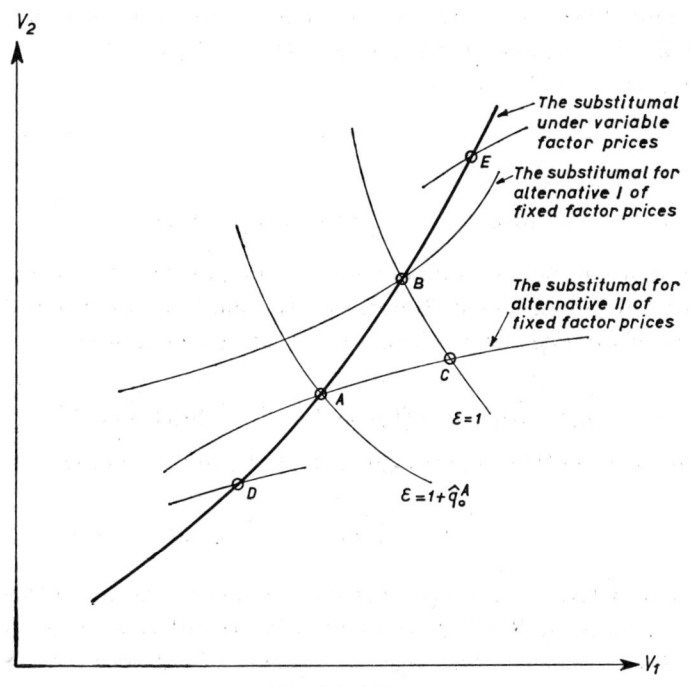

Fig. (11e.14).

Let us assume that we first have given a set of factor supply functions and have constructed the substitumal appertaining to it, and determined the minimum point on the average cost curve along this substitumal. Figure (11e.14) illustrates the situation in two factors. The heavily drawn curve *DABE* in this figure is the substitumal under variable factor prices and A is the point where $\varepsilon = 1 + \check{q}_0$, and where we therefore have a minimum of average cost along the substitumal under consideration.

Along the substitumal $\check{q}_0$ varies. Let $\check{q}_0{}^A$ be the value of $\check{q}_0$ in the point A. We construct the $(n-1)$ dimensional contour surface for $\varepsilon = 1 + \check{q}_0{}^A$. This surface must obviously run through point A. (In Figure (11e.14) where $n=2$, this 'surface' will be a one-dimensional curve.) We also construct the $(n-1)$ dimensional surface for $\varepsilon = 1$, and mark its point of intersection with the substitumal which applies under variable factor prices. In Figure (11e.14) this point is B. As we assume that the substitumal is rising and that ε in a regular ultra-passum law, as per definition, declines under a movement outwards along an arbitrary rising curve, point B must lie further out on the substitumal concerned[1] than point A, and consequently give a *larger product quantity* than point A.

In point B the corrected factor prices are determined when we know the factor supply functions. Let them be $[q_i(1+\check{q}_i)]^B$ $(i=1, 2, \ldots, n)$. We now define a set of *fixed* factor prices

$$q_i{}^{\text{fix.I}} \qquad (i=1, 2, \ldots, n)$$

by

(11e.15)   Alternative I: $q_i{}^{\text{fix.I}} = [q_i(1+\check{q}_i)]^B$.

There is a fixed-price-substitumal corresponding to the factor prices (11e.15). It must run through point B. For, as this point lies on the substitumal in the case of variable factor prices, we must at this point have

$$\frac{x_1'}{[q_1(1+\check{q}_1)]^B} = \frac{x_2'}{[q_2(1+\check{q}_2)]^B} = \cdots = \frac{x_n'}{[q_n(1+\check{q}_n)]^B}.$$

If we insert from (11e.15), we shall see that at point B we have

$$\frac{x_1'}{q_1{}^{\text{fix.I}}} = \frac{x_2'}{q_2{}^{\text{fix.I}}} = \cdots = \frac{x_n'}{q_n{}^{\text{fix.I}}}.$$

That is to say, point B must lie on the fixed-price-substitumal under consideration. As point B simultaneously lies in the surface $\varepsilon = 1$, we know that point B is a minimum of average cost along this fixed price substitumal. As

[1] ε^A is $>$ since $\check{q}_i$ and hence $\check{q}_0$ are positive (or zero). Cf. (11a.4) and (11e.6).

ELASTICITY-INFLUENCED PRICE-QUANTITY ADJUSTMENT   215

point B gives a larger product quantity x than point A, we can conclude that the minimum point for average cost $\bar{b}$ along the considered fixed-price-substitumal in an $(x, \bar{b})$ diagram must lie *to the right* of the point which is the minimum point for average cost along the substitumal for variable factor prices. Furthermore, as we assume that along the substitumal under variable factor prices all $\check{q}_i$ will be positive, then $q_i(1+\check{q}_i) > q_i$ everywhere. This applies in particular at point B, thus $[q_i(1+\check{q}_i)]^B > q_i^B$, where q_i^B are the factor prices in point B under variable factor prices, that is to say

(11e.16) $\qquad\qquad q_i^B < q_i^{\text{fix.I}} \qquad\qquad (i=1, 2, ..., n)$.

Consequently, at point B – that is to say, for the abscissa x^B in the $(x, \bar{b})$ diagram in Figure (11e.17) – the average cost under Alternative I of the fixed

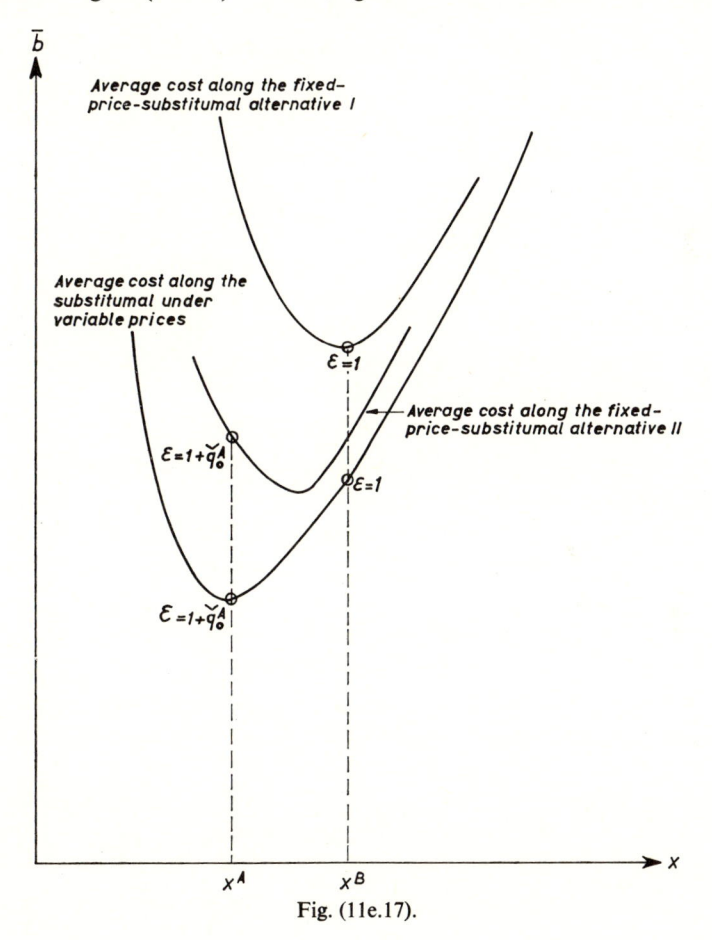

Fig. (11e.17).

factor prices will be *greater* than the average costs at x^B under variable factor prices, and therefore still larger than the *minimum* of average cost under variable factor prices (which occur at point A in the factor diagram – that is to say, for the abscissa x^A in the $(x, \bar{b})$ diagram). The minimum of average cost under Alternative I of fixed factor prices consequently lies in the $(x, \bar{b})$ diagram *to the right of* and is *higher than* the minimum for average cost under variable factor prices. Thus we have a situation as in Figure (11e.17).

Next let us consider the fixed-price substitumal defined by the fixed factor prices:

(11e.18) Alternative II: $\quad q_i^{\text{fix.II}} = [q_i(1+\check{q}_i)]^A$.

It must run through point A. Let C be its point of intersection with the surface $\varepsilon = 1$. At this point the average cost along the fixed-price-substitumal Alternative II has its minimum. Using the same argument as in the comparison between points A and B in Alternative I of fixed factor prices, we shall see that $x^C > x^A$. At point A, in other words, the average cost along the fixed-price-substitumal Alternative II must not yet have reached its minimum, i.e. in the $(x, \bar{b})$ diagram in Figure (11e.17) it is *declining* at the abscissa x^A. That is to say, the minimum point on the average cost curve under Alternative II of fixed factor prices lies in the $(x, \bar{b})$ diagram *to the right* of the minimum point on the average cost under variable prices. In the case under consideration we cannot state whether one minimum is higher or lower than the other, but we can say that at the abscissa x^A the average cost under fixed factor prices is *greater* than the average cost along the substitumal under variable prices, since $\check{q}_i$ in (11e.16) is positive. How in other respects the fixed price average cost curve in Alternative II runs in comparison to the average cost curve under variable prices, cannot be deduced from the presuppositions we have used so far.

If we define a fixed-price-substitumal by choosing a set of fixed factor prices q_i^{fix}, equal to the corrected factor prices $[q_i(1+q_i)]^D$ at any other point D on the substitumal for variable factor prices, we shall, when point D lies in the technically pre-optimal region (thus in Figure (11e.14) to the southwest of B), have a fixed price average cost curve which *at this point D* is declining and at this point lies higher than the average cost curve under variable factor prices. If we choose the fixed factor prices in such a way that we get an intersection at point E in the technically post-optimal region (thus in Figure (11e.14) northeast of B), then at this point the fixed price average cost will be *rising*, and at this point it will still be higher than average cost under variable prices. Under our general presuppositions we cannot say more in these two cases.

For all alternatives of fixed prices in the examples above, the fixed prices are presupposed to be *greater than* the factor prices which, in the case of elasticity-influenced adjustment are realised in the reference situation. This is a plausible presupposition. Indeed, the fact that the producer is an elasticity-influenced adjuster in the factor markets gives him to some extent a strengthened bargaining power which enables him to exert pressure on factor prices (by limiting the use of the factors). And the strength of this power is indicated by the magnitude of $(1+\dot{q}_0)$.

Intuitively: If there is only a single factor of production and the concern is a *quantity adapter* (under prices which the concern believes will not be affected by its own action) both in the product market and in the factor market, and it tries to maximise its profit, the equilibrium point will be determined by the intersection of the rising supply curve for the factor and the declining curve which depicts the marginal productivity multiplied by the product price. On the contrary if the concern *takes account of the fact* that the factor price will increase if the concern uses more of the factor, then it will *reduce* production and thereby contribute to reducing the factor price.

11f. Profit maximisation under variable product price

Let us assume that the concern is an elasticity-influenced price quantity adjuster in the product market – for example, a monopolist, cf. Section 9d – and that its adjustment purpose is to make total profits as large as possible. We shall here only discuss the main features of the situation which then arises.[1]

When the concern operates as an elasticity-influenced price quantity adjuster in the product market, the total intake (total sales or turnover), a, is defined by (10f.1), but now the product price is not a given constant as in Section 10f, but a function of the product quantity, cf. (11a.1). That is to say

(11f.1) $\qquad a = p(x) \cdot x = a(x)$,

where x is the product quantity and where $p(x)$ is the given demand function directed at the concern (Cf. (11a.1) and Section 9d).

Marginal intake (marginal sales) are equal to the derivative of the total

---

[1] A more detailed treatment of this subject is provided in my general lectures on economic theory.

intake with respect to the product quantity. That is to say:

(11f.2) Marginal intake (marginal sales) $= a' = \dfrac{da(x)}{dx}$.

By differentiation, we get (cf. the differentiation of marginal outlay (11a.7)):

(11f.3) $\qquad\qquad a' = p(1+\check{p})$,

where $\check{p}$ is the flexibility of the product price (cf. (11a.3)), that is to say the flexibility which the concern in question is calculating on.

The expression to the right in (11f.3) shows that marginal intake can be interpreted as a *corrected product price*. The product price is corrected by the demand flexibility of the product. This correction expresses the fact that, if the product quantity rises, there will be more units for which the concern will receive payment, but at the same time each single unit will bring a lower price.

In the quantity adjustment case $\check{p}=0$ and marginal intake is consequently equal to the product price, otherwise it will as a rule be somewhat less, as the flexibility $\check{p}$ is generally negative.

It is probable that not only the demand price p but also the marginal intake $p(1+\check{p})$ will fall when x rises. Indeed we have

$$\text{El. } p(1+\check{p}) = \check{p} + \text{El. } (1+\check{p}) = \check{p} + \frac{\check{p}\widetilde{\check{p}}}{1+\check{p}},$$

that is to say

(11f.4) $\qquad\qquad \text{El. } p(1+\check{p}) = \check{p}\left(1 + \dfrac{\widetilde{\check{p}}}{1+\check{p}}\right)$,

where

(11f.5) The product price flexibility-flexibility $= \widetilde{\check{p}} = \text{El. } \check{p} = \dfrac{d\check{p}}{dx} \cdot \dfrac{x}{\check{p}}$.

The flexibility-flexibility $\widetilde{\check{p}}$ is not changed if $\check{p}$ is multiplied by a constant, and therefore $\widetilde{\check{p}}$ can equally well be regarded as the flexibility of the *numerical value* of $\check{p}$.

It is probable that the elasticity of demand for the product *decreases* as one approaches the saturation point of demand. This is the same as saying that it is probable that the numerical value of the flexibility $\check{p}$ will *increase* when x is augmented. Thus we can calculate on $\widetilde{\check{p}}$ being positive or at any rate not markedly negative. At the same time we can assume that $1+\check{p}$ is positive in the region which interests us, cf. the observations after Figure (11f.10). It is therefore probable that the parenthesis to the right in

ELASTICITY-INFLUENCED PRICE-QUANTITY ADJUSTMENT 219

(11f.4) is positive, and thus El.$p(1+\breve{p})$ *negative*, i.e. the marginal intake curve is falling as suggested in Figure (11f.10).

In the case now under consideration, too, the total profit, r, is defined by (10f.2), and in the same way we must now likewise distinguish between the two questions I and II from Section 10f. cf. the text following (10f.2).

Let us first consider question I. We shall fix x in such a way that (10f.2) becomes as large as possible, assuming a given relation between p and x, viz. (11a.1). If we ignore any terminal maximum points, cf. Section 10f, the necessary first order condition can be written

$$(11\text{f.6}) \qquad r' = \frac{dr}{dx} = \frac{da}{dx} - \frac{db}{dx} = p(1+\breve{p}) - b' = 0,$$

that is to say

$$(11\text{f.7}) \qquad b' = p(1+\breve{p}),$$

that is to say the substitumal marginal cost has to be equal to the corrected product price. Or, to put it in another way: marginal cost is to be equal to marginal intake (marginal sales).

In the limiting case $\breve{p}=0$ this formulation is reduced to (10f.4).

Furthermore, we get the following sufficient second order condition for a regular maximum of (10f.2):

$$(11\text{f.8}) \qquad r'' = \frac{d^2 r}{dx} = a'' - b'' < 0,$$

where

$$b'' = \frac{d^2 b(x)}{dx^2} \quad \text{and} \quad a'' = \frac{d^2 a(x)}{dx^2}.$$

(11f.8) is synonymous with

$$(11\text{f.9}) \qquad a'' < b''.$$

In other words, the substitumal marginal cost curve should rise more steeply than the marginal intake curve in order to produce a regular profit maximum.

To conclude: apart from possible terminal maximum points, profit maximation adjustment will occur at a point on the substitumal corresponding to the given factor price functions where *the substitumal marginal cost curve intersects the marginal intake curve from its lower side*. This will most frequently occur on the rising portion of the marginal cost curve, but it can also occur on its falling portion, provided that the marginal intake curve in the point of intersection falls more steeply than the marginal cost curve.

The entire line of argument in connection with Figure (10f.7) can thus be repeated now, if, instead of the horizontal line which expresses the given product price, we draw a curved line showing how the marginal intake, that is to say, the corrected product price, depends on x. Cf. Figure (11f.10).

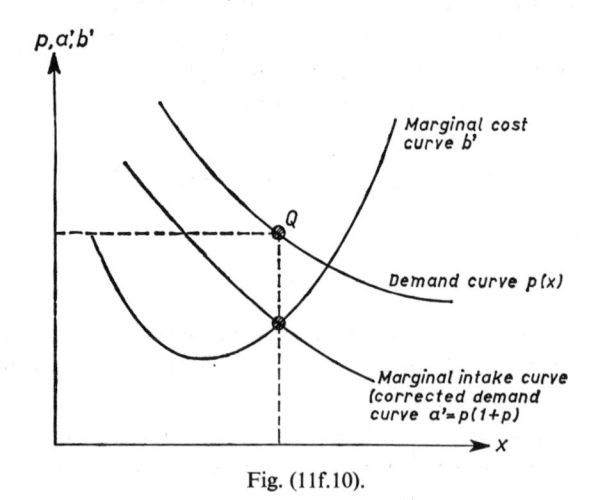

Fig. (11f.10).

In this way the *quantity* of the product which the concern brings to market is determined. The appurtenant *price* is found by inserting the value which we have found for x, in the demand function (11a.1). In this way the (x, p) point Q in Figure (11f.10) is determined.

Question II is answered as in the quantity adjustment case, cf. Section 10f.

From (11f.7) we see that a point (that is to say, a product quantity) which is to be a maximum point for total profits (that is to say where total profits are greater than at other points in the neighbourhood) must, if the marginal cost and price are positive, lie in the super-elastic region of the demand curve, i.e. the numerical value of the *demand-elasticity must be greater than 1*, that is to say $-\check{x}>1$ and consequently $-\check{p}<1$. For, in the opposite case, $p(1+\check{p})$ is negative, and therefore certainly less than marginal cost b' (when this is positive). Or to put it in another way: if demand elasticity in numerical value is less than 1 and marginal cost positive, then with reduction of production the product value will increase and production costs decrease, consequently net profits will certainly rise. A monopolist will thus always – under the presupposition that the circumstances mentioned in question II in Section 10f make it profitable to keep the concern going, and

ELASTICITY-INFLUENCED PRICE-QUANTITY ADJUSTMENT

no political or other motives prevent him from exploiting his monopolist position to the full, *contract production until he has reached a point on the demand curve where demand elasticity is greater than 1*. Since the demand curve – at any rate for an ordinary consumer article – will as a rule be more elastic in its first part and less in its later part, where the market is beginning to approach saturation, the procedure of moving into a region with great elasticity will as a rule mean *reducing* sales. The reduction will be the greater, the longer the super-elastic region of the demand curve is, and the higher the marginal cost curve lies in the region where final adjustment takes place.

The rule for quantity adjustment[1] to the effect that in the profit maximisation point (apart from any possible terminal maximum point) there must for every factor be equality between its price and its marginal productivity reckoned in money – cf. the text following after (10f.14) – will *no longer* apply under price-variable adjustment.

For, by inserting (11e.4) in (11f.7), we get

(11f.11) $\qquad p(1+\check{p}) \cdot x_i' = q_i(1+\check{q}_i) \qquad (i=1, 2, \ldots, n).$

Since $\check{p}$ is generally negative, $p(1+\check{p})$ will be less than p. In other words

(11f.12) $\qquad p(1+\check{p}) \cdot x_1' < p x_i'.$

Since $\check{q}_i$ is generally positive, we have furthermore

(11f.13) $\qquad q_i < q_i(1+\check{q}_i).$

By combining (11f.11), (11f.12) and (11f.13), we get

(11f.14) $\qquad p x_i' > p(1+\check{p})x_i' = q_i(1+\check{q}_i) > q_i,$

that is to say

(11f.15) $\qquad p x_i' > q_i.$

In other words: When the concern operates as an elasticity influenced price quantity adjuster in the factor markets as well as in the product market, the concern achieves greatest profits (apart from possible terminal maximum points) by operating in such a way that every factor acquires a price which is *less* than its marginal productivity calculated in terms of money. This applies even when all factor prices are constant (all $q_i = 0$). For the fact that the factor prices are constant means that the inequality sign on the extreme right of (11f.14) is replaced by an equality sign, while

[1] Under constant prices.

the first inequality sign in (11f.14) still applies; hence (11f.15) will still hold good. Similarly it is easy to show that (11f.15) applies even though the product price is constant and only the factor prices are variable.

The magnitude of the profit at the equilibrium point can also, in the case involving price-variable adjustment, be related to the magnitude of the passus coefficient in this point. For along the substitumal we have (11e.7), and if (11e.7) is inserted in the expression for total profits (10f.2), we get

$$r = px - \frac{\varepsilon b' x}{1+\check{q}_0}.$$

In the equilibrium point $b' = p(1+\check{p})$. That is to say:

$$r = px - \frac{\varepsilon \cdot p(1+\check{p}) \cdot x}{1+\check{q}_0}$$

i.e.

(11f.16) $$r = px\left(1 - \frac{1+\check{p}}{1+\check{q}_0}\varepsilon\right).$$

Here, $\check{q}_0 > 0$ and $\check{p} < 0$, hence $(1+\check{p})/(1+\check{q}_0)$ is less than 1. Thus the profit can in the case involving variable prices be positive, even though $\varepsilon > 1$ in the equilibrium point; that is to say, the adjustment may take place in the with respect to scale technically *pre*-optimal region.

This may happen even though the concern is a quantity adjuster in the product market, as $(1+\check{p})/(1+\check{q}_0)$ is then less than 1, provided at least one of the factor prices is variable. And it may also happen if the concern is a price-fixed quantity adjuster, in all factor markets, provided it is an elasticity-influenced adjuster in the product market.

By adjustment (11f.7) we get *no supply curve for the product*. And especially, the monopolist supply curve does not exist. For there is no meaning in asking what quantity the monopolist wants to sell if the price is so and so high.

But there is significance in the statement: if the *form* of the demand curve is such and such (and thus the form of the *corrected* demand curve is given), the quantity sold will be so and so large. Thus the monopolist supply pattern is not so simple that it can be represented by a curve. It does not express how one magnitude depends on another, but how one magnitude (the quantity produced) depends on the shape of a curve (the demand curve).

PART THREE

MOMENTARY SINGLE PRODUCTION WITH LIMITATION FACTORS

CHAPTER 12

TECHNICAL ANALYSIS OF LIMITATION LAWS

12a. The simple minimum law

Let us consider a production where for every *product unit* we need a certain *technically given* and *constant* amount of each factor, e.g. 2 kilos of factor No. 1 and 1 litre of factor No. 2, for every gramme of the product under all circumstances. The fabrication coefficients in the technical sense mentioned are then constant; no substitution possibilities exist between the factors. The straight line in Figure (12a.1) represents this technically given

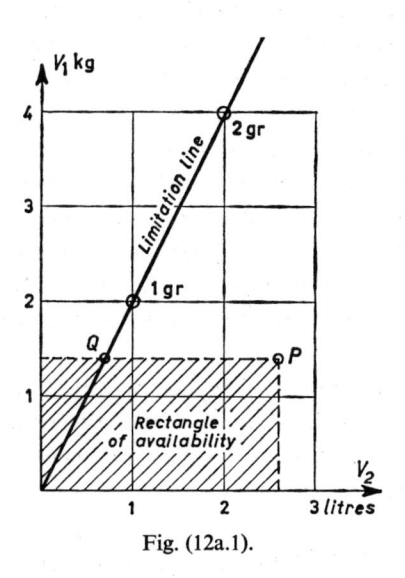

Fig. (12a.1).

relationship. The product quantities are indicated along this straight line. If we only consider the relationship between the factors expressed by the line, then this will be a *confluence line* (amongst factor quantities). In considering the relationship between the factors and the product, we shall call it a *limitation* line in conformity with the terminology used below.

Along the axes v_1 and v_2 in Figure (12a.1) we measure the *available* factor quantities, for the time being without considering whether these quantities actually enter into the product. It is assumed that none of the quantities can exercise a detrimental effect merely by being available. If for example we have 1.5 kilos and 2.5 litres, we shall then be able to make 0.75 grammes of the product. In this case all of factor No. 1 will be used, but of factor No. 2 $2.5-0.75=1.75$ litres will remain unused. In this case we say that 1 is a minimum factor, or a *minimal* factor. It is *this* factor which in this case limits the product quantity. This can be graphically illustrated by plotting the point of availability $P=(1.5, 2.5)$, then drawing the shaded rectangle – *the rectangle of availability* – and marking off the point Q where the limitation line *erupts from* this rectangle. The point of eruption lies on the side of the rectangle along which $v_1 =$ constant, when No. 1 is the minimum factor.

To the north-west of the line of limitation No. 2 is the minimum factor; to the south-east of the line No. 1 is the minimum factor. Along the line itself both factors are simultaneously minimum factors. The figures $v_1^* = 2$ kg per gramme of the product and $v_2^* = 1$ litre per gramme of the product we call *limitation-fabrication coefficients* or constant input-coefficients. The production law will be called a minimum law or more precisely a proportional minimum law.

An entirely analogous reasoning can be applied in the case of several factors. With three factors we can construct an *availability box*. The one of the three outer walls of the box through which the limitation line erupts, defines the minimum factor. If the limitation line erupts through an *edge*, then the two factors are simultaneously minimum factors, and if it erupts through the *external corner* of the box, then all three are simultaneously minimum factors.

Quite generally, in the case of N factors, the relationship can be represented analytically. Let $v_1^*, v_2^*, ..., v_N^*$ be the technically given limitation-fabrication coefficients. If $v_1, ..., v_N$ are the available factor quantities, the product quantity will be

$$12a.2) \qquad x = \text{Min}\left[\frac{v_1}{v_1^*}, \frac{v_2}{v_2^*}, ..., \frac{v_N}{v_N^*}\right],$$

where Min [ ] is a symbol (a 'minimal' form) indicating *the smallest* of the figures shown in square brackets, or *the smallest ones*, if two or more of them are equal. In the example (12a.1), $N=2$, $v_1^*=2$, $v_2^*=1$, $v_1=1.5$, $v_2=2.5$, viz. $x = \text{Min}[0.75, 2.5] = 0.75$.

A minimum factor, that is to say a factor which is *effective* in its influence on x, will now be characterised by the fact that for this factor, e.g. No. k, the fraction v_k/v_k^* will be *not greater* than any of the other fractions in (12a.2), so that we get exactly $x = (v_k/v_k^*)$.

The minimal form (12a.2) can be illustrated by a *water barrel* made of staves of different heights. The level of the water will be exactly as high as the lowest stave (staves). This (these) lowest stave(s) will indicate the minimum factor(s).

In a factor point where one *and only one* factor No. k is minimal, the marginal productivity of this factor will be equal to $1/v_k^*$ (irrespective of whether we consider the marginal productivity for increase or decrease) and the marginal productivities of all other factors are zero. At a point where more than one factor is minimal, the marginal productivity of a minimum factor No. k will be zero for increase and $1/v_k^*$ for decrease. For the other factors, marginal productivity will still be zero both for increase and decrease.

Let us plot total and marginal productivity curves for the example (12a.1), with $v_2 = $ constant $= 2.5$, and varying v_1, cf. (6b.1). This will bring out the fact that in the case of the minimum law (the proportional one) *there is no factor point where two or more of the factors stand in a substitution relationship to one another*. In other words, there is no point where conditions are such that the same product quantity can be obtained by giving one factor a certain increase and another a certain decrease, except in the trivial case where *both* factors are ineffective in the points concerned (and hence have marginal productivities zero), which is not a 'substitution relationship'. The two factors are then not substitution factors according to the definition given in the remarks subsequent to (5b.8).

A production law of the kind we have here dealt with we shall also call a *simple minimum law*. The general expression of the *product function* in this case is as stated in (12a.2). This law is an example of a *limitation law*, but only a very *simple* example. The general definition of a limitation law and limitation factors will subsequently be formulated in a much more elaborate way.

12b. Marginal definition of minimum, maximum, and limitation factors. General definition of the limitation law

In Section 12a a minimum factor has been defined on the basis of a *total* consideration extended over the whole of the factor diagram, that is to say, by basing ourselves on a knowledge of the production law over an unrestricted area. We shall now provide a definition which is *marginal*. This approach is more general. It is based on the same principle as the definition of the continuity factor (continuous marginal productivity, cf. (5b.8) and of a substitution factor (continuous and positive, not zero, marginal productivity, cf. remarks subsequent to (5b.8)).

We shall proceed from any given factor point in a so far arbitrary production law with N factors. If from this point it is impossible to increase the product quantity without increasing factor No. k, then we say that the latter is an (effective) *minimum factor* at this point. A minimum factor which is further such that the product quantity does not increase when this factor *alone* is increased, is said to be an (effective) *limitation factor* or *limitational* at this point. At a point in a continuity law where all marginal productivities are zero, except that for factor No. k, which is positive, No. k will be a minimum factor, but not limitational. At a factor point in (12a.2) where v_k/v_k^* is less than all the other fractions in the bracket, No. k is also a minimum factor, but not limitational. If on the other hand two quantities v_k/v_k^* and v_h/v_h^* in (12a.2) are equal and less than the others, then No. k and No. h are both not only minimum factors, but both are limitational at this point. For a factor to be limitational at a given point, we must in fact be able to say that not only 'at least as much is required' (its minimum quality) but also 'no more, however, is required'. In other words, in a certain sense the factor quantity has 'come right'. At any point on the limitation line in (12a.1) factor No. 1 is limitational. And this is also true of No. 2. At a point where a factor is limitational, its marginal productivity must differ on increase and on decrease (apart from the absolute top-point, if such a point exists, see below).

When we talk of a limitation factor without any further specification – that is to say, when we make a statement about a factor generally without specifying the point – we mean a factor which *can be* limitational if the factor combination is chosen in a suitable manner. Thus a limitation factor – in this general sense – is a factor which 'should' be adapted to 'something else' in a definite way. And a criterion for this property can be given purely *technically*, without prices or other value judgment coefficients being introduced. *Herein lies a decisive difference from the substitution factors*, where adaptation to the other factors (substitution adaptation) is not determined before the prices of the factors (or the supply functions) are given.

A limitation factor is a special case of *discontinuity factors*, cf. (5b.8). Other cases of discontinuity factors are of minor interest from the point of view of economics.

If at a given factor point the product quantity remains unchanged, even though the quantity of a certain factor is slightly reduced while the other factors are unchanged, we say that the factor concerned is an (effective) maximum factor at this point.

Basing ourselves on the above-mentioned marginal criterion with regard to the factors, we can now classify various types of production laws taken as a whole. We can consider a certain region of the factor diagram, and within it we distinguish between the following cases:

I. A complete substitution law: Everywhere within the delimited factor region all factors are continuity factors. Furthermore points exist where all factors are *effective* substitution factors, i.e. with marginal productivities that are positive, not zero.

II. A limitation law in the wide sense: Within the delimited factor region no point exists where all factors simultaneously are effective substitution factors (i.e., have marginal productivities which are continuous and positive, not zero). Thus at any point there is at least one factor which is not an effective substitution factor. But it may happen that in some places there are two or more factors that are in a substitution relationship to one another.

III. A complete limitation law: Within the delimited factor region there is no point where *two or more factors* are in substitution relation to one another (i.e., have marginal productivities which are continuous and positive, not zero). Thus the law is entirely devoid of each and every substitution possibility.

This subdivision is not entirely exhaustive, but it does cover the most important cases in practice. (12a.2) is an example of a complete limitation law. At a factor point – an availability point – where one of the fractions v_k/v_k^* is effectively less than all the others, all marginal productivities will no doubt be continuous, but only one of them will be different from zero. And at a point where two (or more) of the fractions are equal and less than the others, the marginal productivities for these two (or more) factors will be discontinuous and the marginal productivities for the others zero. Thus, in no case will there exist two or more factors which both have continuous and positive, not zero, marginal productivities. So far we have given no example of II, but this is done in Section 12d.

One of the most important objections raised against marginal productivity analysis has been that in many cases the fabrication coefficients are practically speaking fixed, so that the customary marginal considerations cannot be carried out. This is correct in a certain limited sense: the simple marginal productivity analysis which is only based on continuity factors is not sufficient. But by means of the extension of the analytical apparatus here considered, not only the case involving factors with fixed fabrication coefficients, but far more general limitation laws can be dealt with in a fully satisfactory manner. And in this process the marginal productivity concept is of very great help, I would even say indispensable. Cf. e.g. the precision with which the concept limitation factor can be defined when this is done marginally, as mentioned above.

12c. The production law in the case of technically given but not constant limitation-fabrication coefficients. Independent limitation factors

In the case of variable fabrication coefficients, too, provided only the fabrication coefficients are technically given as functions of the product quantity, a limitationally determined confluence line will exist. This will be a *straight* line running through origo, not only in the special case involving fixed fabrication coefficients, but also when the fabrication coefficients vary in the *same* ratio for expansion or contraction of the production.

The manner in which the factor quantities vary with the product quantity along the confluence line can be expressed by a set of *factor functions*:

(12c.1) $\quad\quad v_1 = v_1(x), \quad v_2 = v_2(x), \ldots, v_N = v_N(x)$.

If all these functions are constantly increasing, i.e. v_1 is an increasing function of x, v_2 an increasing function of x, etc., then the functions can be *inverted* in a unique way. That is to say, we shall be able to determine the product quantity x that can be produced when we have a given quantity v_1 of No. 1, and *sufficient* (or more than sufficient) quantities of all the other factors. We can do the same for v_2, etc. We then get N functions, one of v_1, one of v_2, etc., all expressing, the *product quantity* but in each case on the assumption that the *other* factors are present in sufficient (or more than sufficient) quantities. We call these functions the *limitation functions*, and designate them

(12c.2) $\quad\quad x = x_1(v_1), \quad x = x_2(v_2), \ldots, x = x_N(v_N)$.

In arbitrary quantities $v_1, v_2, \ldots, v_N$ are given, that is to say, if an arbitrary factor point is given, the actual product quantity realised will be

(12c.3) $\quad\quad x = \mathrm{Min}\ [x_1(v_1), x_2(v_2), \ldots, x_N(v_N)]$.

If $x_1, x_2, \ldots, x_N$ in (12c.2) are increasing functions of the argument (the regular case) we say that (12c.3) represents a direct, but not necessarily a proportional minimum law. (12c.3) is the general expression of the *prod-*

uct function in this case, each factor quantity v_k in (12c.3) designating an available (but not necessarily actually utilised) quantity. If each of the limitation functions in (12c.2) is simply a constant times the factor quantity concerned, we get the special case (12a.2).

If the product function is of the form (12c.3), we say that all the factors $v_1, v_2, ..., v_N$ are *directly limiting*. (12c.3) is obviously a complete limitation law in accordance with the general definition in (12b.III). This will be apparent if we use the same kind of reasoning as is given in connection with (12b.III). At a factor point where there are no functions in the right member of (12c.3) whose value is less than $x_k(v_k)$, we say that No. k is a minimum factor in this point.

The confluence line in the case (12c.3) is defined by putting all limitation functions equal, viz.:

(12c.4) $$x_1(v_1) = x_2(v_2) = ... = x_N(v_N).$$

As this constitutes $(N-1)$ equations between the N variables $v_1, v_2, ..., v_N$, it defines a one-dimensional curve running through the factor diagram.

12d. Separate factor rings

Let us take a product composed of two or more parts (1), (2), ..., (ν) (e.g., (1) = blade and (2) = handle of a knife), in such a way that the factors fall into separate groups, serving each to produce its own particular part according to a certain product function (which may be different from one group to another). Let us assume that the quantity of each part is well defined (e.g., the *number* of blades) and that well defined product functions apply for each part:

(12d.1) $x_{(1)}(v_1, v_2, ..., v_\alpha), x_{(2)}(v_{\alpha+1}, v_{\alpha+2}, ..., v_\beta) ... x_{(\nu)}(v_{\gamma+1}, v_{\gamma+2}, ..., v_N)$.

As a special (and not infrequent) case a factor quantity, say $v_{\alpha+2}$ appearing in one of the functions in (12d.1), may refer to the same *kind* of factor as the factor quantity, say $v_{\gamma+1}$, appearing in one of the other functions. Let us assume that each of the ordinates $x_{(1)}, x_{(2)}, ..., x_{(\nu)}$, taken by itself acts as a limitation factor in the same way as the factors in (12a.2). In this case the total production function will be:

(12d.2) $\quad x = \text{Min}\,[x_{(1)}(v_1, ..., v_\alpha), x_{(2)}(v_{\alpha+1}, ..., v_\beta), ..., x_{(\nu)}(v_{\gamma+1}, .., v_N)]$.

We call the factor groups concerned *factor rings*: In other words, the individual factors Nos. $1, 2, ..., \alpha$ form the first ring, the individual factors Nos. $\alpha+1, ..., \beta$ form the second ring, etc. We call the individual product functions (12d.1) *ring functions*. If need be, for precision we may call them separate rings, and separate ring functions. We say that the total product function is *ring-built*, or more precisely, built up of separate rings. This definition applies irrespective of the nature of the single ring functions.

A confluence region is now defined by making all ring functions equal, viz.

(12d.3)
$$x_{(1)}(v_1, v_2, \ldots, v_\alpha) = x_{(2)}(v_{\alpha+1}, v_{\alpha+2}, \ldots, v_\beta) = \ldots = x_{(\nu)}(v_{\gamma+1}, v_{\gamma+2}, \ldots, v_N).$$

The confluence region has a dimension (number of degrees of freedom) equal to $N - \nu + 1$, where N is necessarily equal to or greater than ν. For $N = \nu$, (12d.2) reduces to (12c.3).

If each of the ring functions has continuous derivatives, then each of the partial productions (sub-productions) can be studied separately, according to the principles developed in Part II. And their composition can be studied according to principle (12c.3). No essential difficulties of principle are, in fact, involved in this analysis. If (12d.2) consists of more than one ring and all the partial derivatives of $x_{(1)} \ldots, x_{(\nu)}$ are positive, we can say that (12d.2) represents an indirect minimum law. This is an example of (12b.II).

Nor is any essential difficulty involved if one or more of the ring functions themselves are built up from separate sub-rings, but the situation is essentially more complicated if one and the same factor occurs in more than one ring function.

12e. Mixed factor rings

If one and the same individual factor occurs in more than one ring function, we say that the rings are mixed, i.e. not separate. In many cases that are of practical importance we must take this into account.

As a simplified example let us take a sawmill which gets its timber from two separate forests A and B, situated respectively at a distance from the sawmill of a and b kilometres, where $b > a$. See Figure (12e.1). Let us assume that the extent of each forest area is small in relation to its distance to the sawmill, so that we need not make any allowance for transport *within* each forest area. The product quantity we shall consider is $x =$ the number of cubic metres of timber delivered at the sawmill (this 'product quantity' will subsequently reappear as a factor quantity in the sawmilling process, but this is of no interest in this connection). The individual factor quantities we are considering are $v_1 =$ the number of cubic metres of timber marked for felling in A, $v_2 =$ the number of cubic metres of timber marked for felling in B, $v_3 =$ the work of felling and barking, $v_4 =$ timber transport measured in cubic metre/kilometres. We shall assume that a constant amount γ of felling and barking work per cubic metre is required. If there had been only one forest B, the individual factors Nos 2, 3, and 4 would have been three direct limitation factors and we can use (12c.3). We should

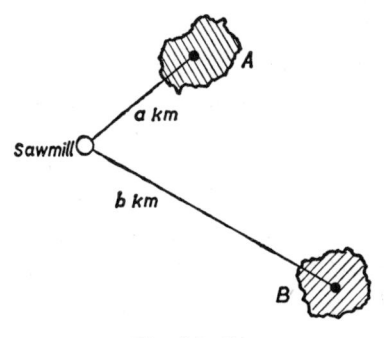

Fig. (12e.1).

have a similar reduction if $a=b$, i.e., if both areas of forest are situated at the same distance from the sawmill (and transport costs per kilometre are the same along both the roads). In the hypothetical case as set up above, felling and barking work will have the same effect as the direct limitation factors in previous examples, viz. we must have $x \leqslant v_3/\gamma$. Neither v_1 nor v_2 taken separately will possess this quality, but their sum will, viz. $x \leqslant v_1 + v_2$. The work of transporting the logs, v_4, holds a special position. In the first case it limits the product absolutely: even if we fetch all the logs from the nearest forest $x \leqslant v_4/a$. But it also limits the product in another way: if v_1 is *given*, only a limited amount can be fetched from A, and the rest will have to be fetched from the remoter area at B. In order to fetch v_1 we shall require a transport amount av_1, and with the rest of the transport at our disposal, viz. $v_4 - av_1$, we can fetch from B a quantity $(v_4 - av_1)/b$, viz.

$$(12\text{e}.2) \qquad x \leqslant v_1 + \frac{v_4 - av_1}{b} = \frac{v_4 + (b-a)v_1}{b}.$$

This gives a total of four upper bounds for x. Each of them can be effective. For example if $v_1 + v_2$ is the least of the bounds, then $v_3 \geqslant \gamma(v_1 + v_2)$, that is to say, the felling and barking work is sufficient for the entire quantity $(v_1 + v_2)$. And

$$v_4 + (b-a)v_1 \geqslant b(v_1 + v_2), \quad \text{i.e.} \quad v_4 \geqslant av_1 + bv_2,$$

that is to say, there is sufficient transport, too, so that x can effectively become equal to v_1+v_2. In the same way it can be seen that any of the other bounds can become effective. The product function in this case will therefore be

$$(12\text{e}.3) \qquad x = \text{Min}\left[v_1+v_2, \frac{v_3}{\gamma}, \frac{v_4}{a}, \frac{v_4+(b-a)v_1}{b}\right] \quad (b>a).$$

Each of the factor groups 1 plus 2, 3 alone, 4 alone, 4 plus 1, here forms a *factor ring*. The corresponding ring function can be read off from (12e.3). As will be seen, they are *not separate*. There are four ring functions and four individual factors. And, as we have seen, the factors act in such a way that any one of the ring functions *can* be effective, i.e., we can get a combination of (v_1, v_2, v_3, v_4) such that the value of the first ring function is not larger than any of the values of the others, and we can get a combination of individual factors such that for any of the other ring functions the value is not larger than that of all the others.

Each of these cases has a definite concrete significance. If, for example, the value of the first ring function is smaller than that of any of the others then a comparison between the first and the second, which now means $v_1+v_2 < v_3/\gamma$, will tell us *that sufficient felling and barking work has been provided for*. And the comparison between the first and the last shows us that *sufficient transport work* has also been provided for. In this special case (but not in all other cases) the condition expressed by the *third* ring function will be automatically fulfilled.

This example suggests that the general case of a ring-constructed product function of N individual – or elementary – factors $v_1, ..., v_N$, is the one where we consider a product function of the following kind

$$(12\text{e}.4) \quad x = \text{Min}\,[x_{(1)}(v_1, ..., v_N), x_{(2)}(v_1, ..., v_N) ... x_{(\nu)}(v_1, ..., v_N)],$$

where $x_{(1)}, x_{(2)}, ..., x_{(\nu)}$ will constitute a certain number of ring functions, some or all of which may contain any of the elementary factors.

The fact that we have indicated *all* factor quantities as variables for each ring function in (12e.4), does not, of course, mean that we assume that all the factor quantities occur *effectively* everywhere. In special cases certain elementary factor quantities may be lacking as effective factors in some of the rings.

We stipulate no conditions for the numbers ν and N; the number of rings may be less than, equal to, or greater than the number of elementary factors. In the example (12e.3) $\nu = N = 4$.

In the general case (12e.4) we can without further ado define a confluence region by making the ring functions equal to one another.

12f. Confluence analysis, all-region analysis and delimitation analysis. Basis variables

Let us for a moment turn back to the simple example of (12a.1). In this case the investigation of the production law can be approached in two ways: we can either limit ourselves to considering what happens along the *confluence line* (the limitation-determined confluence line), viz. only study the factor variations where we shall all the time be using 2 kilos for factor No. 1 for each litre of factor No. 2; or we can raise the further question: *why* are these special factor combinations of such great interest? To answer this we must naturally also describe what the product quantity will be if we stand at a point *outside* the confluence line. In other words, we must study the production law for a free variation of the factors in the entire factor diagram. Only in this way can we reach a logical conclusion to explain why it seems reasonable to study more particularly the confluence line and to show what special features are possessed by the factor points along it, as compared to points in other parts of the diagram. We call the first kind of analysis a *confluence analysis*, and the second kind an *all-region analysis*. An important part of the all-region analysis is the *delimitation analysis*, that is to say, the demonstration of the special form possessed by the confluence line, viz. its structure.

Example (12a.1) is so simple that in this case the answer is a matter of course. But this same kind of question arises in the more general cases (12c.3), (12d.2), and (12e.4). Here the purpose of the all-region analysis is first and foremost to arrive at the minimal form defining the product quantity. The structure of this minimal form will be determined when the number and kind of the ring functions is determined. From the shape of the product function as thus defined we can then deduce the marginal productivities and other production concepts analogous to those with which we are already familiar. And finally, the variations within the confluence region must be studied. This will generally be a whole region, and not necessarily a line, as in the example of (12a.1). As a rule we shall find that the all-region analysis is the most difficult. And especially that part of the all-region analysis which we have termed the delimitation analysis will contain a great many fundamental questions. But once the confluence region is determined, then the remainder of the analysis will be quite simple. It can essentially be carried out by the same methods known from the study of production laws with only continuity factors.

The construction of the minimal form expressing the product function is done by systematically going through the list of elementary production factors. In the case of factor No. 1 we ask: How big could the product be if v_1 is given, and we have as much as we want of all the other factors? The answer is a certain function $f_1(v_1)$, possibly the figure ∞, if the fact that factor No. 1 is given does not result in any limiting of the product. The same question for factor No. 2 leads to a certain function $f_2(v_2)$, etc. We then take the factors *two and two*, and put similar questions. For the pair of factors 1 and 2 we ask: How big could the product be if both v_1 and v_2 are given and we have as much as we want of all the other factors? The answer is a certain function $f_{12}(v_1, v_2)$. For the factor set 13 we get a certain function $f_{13}(v_1, v_3)$, for set 23 a certain function $f_{23}(v_2, v_3)$, etc. We then take the factors *three and three*. This leads to a certain function $f_{123}(v_1, v_2, v_3)$, and so on. Out of these functions we may, if we want to simplify the analysis, omit as *redundant* some of the functions which have the property that they can never become smaller than the others. It may happen, for example, that $f_{12}(v_1, v_2)$ can never be less than the least of the functions $f_1(v_1)$ and $f_2(v_2)$, in which case $f_{12}(v_1, v_2)$ can be left out, as it introduces no new information, i.e. no fresh limit to the product quantity. In this way the analysis can proceed in a systematic way. For every new step we shall have to discuss carefully the nature of the functions already introduced. This discussion will reveal whether the new factor rings we are considering introduce any new limits in addition to the ones we already dealt with. *The functions which then finally remain are the ring functions* we need to consider. The product function can then be expressed as a minimal form in these functions. In the first place, it is indeed clear that the product can never be greater than any of these functions. But on the other hand there cannot be any other circumstances that put a limit to the product quantity, as in the procedure mentioned we have already dealt with all the possibilities. For example, thanks to a systematic approach of this kind, we shall see that the minimal form (12e.3) correctly expresses the smallest number of conditions in the example. We call this the minimal *construction principle* for the minimal form. The omission of redundant limits as explained above is not *necessary* in principle. It only constitutes a computational simplification. But from this viewpoint it is very valuable.

A minimal form constructed in the way discussed above provides the basis for the most general all-region analysis. It provides the answer to the question as to what the product will be if the factor quantities have arbitrarily given values.

A more restricted analysis – but one which nevertheless in certain cases is useful – can be obtained by approaching it as a confluence analysis already from the beginning. We then formulate certain *factor relations*, which will retain the factor point within the area which is of special interest. The whole analysis will then proceed with a smaller number of degrees of freedom. In the timber example in Section 12e we could, for example, already at the formulation stage of the problem, have insisted that both the quantity of felling and barking work, as well as the quantity of transport, should be precisely as much as required for *given* timber quantities v_1 and v_2. Setting out the production problem could then have been done simply with the help of the three equations

(12f.1)
$$x = v_1 + v_2,$$
$$v_3 = \gamma(v_1 + v_2),$$
$$v_4 = av_1 + bv_2.$$

These are three equations with five variables. When formulated in this way the problem has only two degrees of freedom instead of the four degrees represented by v_1, v_2, v_3, v_4 in the all-region formulation in (12e.3). (12f.1) is a simpler starting point, but less illuminating.

In this simpler approach the confluence equations in (12f.1) (the definition of confluence region) are formulated by choosing two variables as *basic variables* (here v_1 and v_2). That is to say, we have considered them as *independent* variables, and we have then expressed both the product quantity and each of the other factor quantities as *given functions* of these two independent variables. This may often prove practical, but it is not the only way in which a confluence region may be defined. Generally speaking we can say that in this simple approach we establish *some system or other* of equations between the factor quantities, or between these and the product, *beyond* the one equation defining the product function through a minimal form as (12e.4). We have then organised our investigation as a confluence analysis already from the beginning.

12g. The marginal productivity concept when the production law contains limitation factors

As a basis for our further discussion we can now define the marginal productivity concept for the case involving limitation factors. (12e.4) is the product function in the general case with mixed factor rings. In the usual way we imagine all factors constant except for one. We give this one factor a slight increase, and then note what the corresponding increase of the product will be. The ratio between product increase and factor increase is the marginal productivity. Whenever this line of argument is to be applied to (12e.4), we must make a sharp distinction between the marginal productivity occurring *on increase* and *on decrease*, and we must distinguish between the various cases according to *which* of the ring functions is the minimum function in the factor point concerned. The variation in *those* ring functions which are *not* minimum functions at the factor point considered need not concern us. It makes no difference one way or the other whether they rise or fall slightly. If we assume that at the starting point they were at a *finite distance* from being minimum functions (and are continuous), and at the same time we operate with a partial increment $d^{pa}v_h$, which we may imagine to be *as small as we like*, these functions – after the increase $d^{pa}v_h$ has been given, – must still be non-minimum functions, and therefore still be without effective influence on the size of the product. On the other hand we must consider the variations in the ring functions which *are* minimum functions at the factor point from which we start.

Let Nos. (i), (j), ..., (k) be minimum rings at the factor point $(v_1, v_2, ..., v_N)$ from which we start. Thus at this point the functions to begin with are *equally great*, viz.

(12g.1) $\quad x_{(i)}(v_1, ..., v_N) = x_{(j)}(v_1, ..., v_N) = ... = x_{(k)}(v_1, ..., v_N)$.

Furthermore, at this factor point, they are *smaller* than all the other ring functions. At any factor point there must obviously be *at least one* ring function which possesses this minimum property. And there may be more. Possibly all ring functions have this property, that is to say, all ring functions are equally great at the factor point concerned.

We assume that all the ring functions at the factor point involved have a unique first-order derivative calculated on increase and a unique first-order derivative calculated on decrease (the two are equal if the derivative is continuous in the point). The way in which the total minimal form then varies is illustrated in Figures (12g.2) and (12g.3). In both figures three minimum rings Nos. (1), (2), (3) are assumed in the factor point concerned, factor No. h being the variable whose marginal productivity we are studying (while all the other factors are constant). The variations of the values of the three ring functions are illustrated by the three straight lines. They are drawn as *straight* lines as we are considering only *small* variations (tangential variations). In Figure (12g.2) the tangent directions of the individual ring functions are assumed to be *the same* forwards and backwards (continuous

TECHNICAL ANALYSIS OF LIMITATION LAWS 239

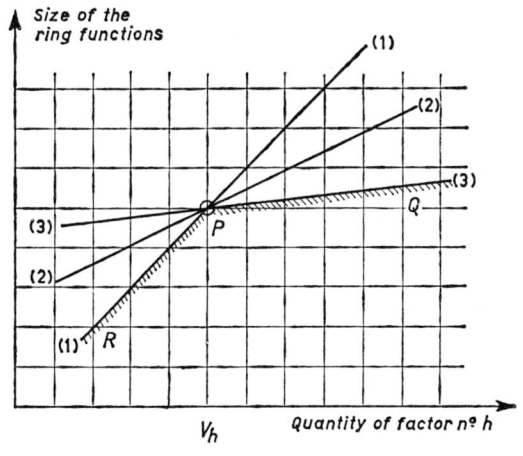

Fig. (12g.2).

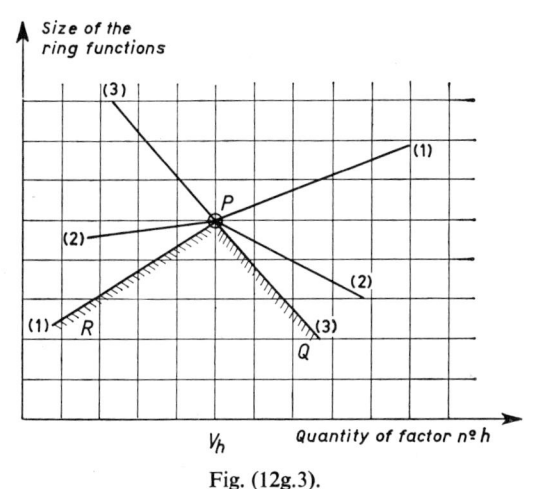

Fig. (12g.3).

tangents at point P). In Figure (12g.3), on the other hand, it is assumed that the tangent direction for rings (1) and (2) has a kink at P, while ring function (3) has the same tangential direction forwards and backwards. As the total product quantity has to be throughout equal to the ordinate on that one of the lines where it is *lowest*, the total product quantity in the vicinity of the point considered will vary *as the shaded curve RPQ*.

We shall express this variation *RPQ* with the aid of the *steepnesses* of the individual lines. Take Figure (12g.2) first: here all the three lines are (positively) *rising* through *P*. (1) rises most sharply, and (3) least sharply. It is the *least sharply* rising curve, viz. (3), that determines the forward variation of the total product, but the *most sharply* rising, viz. (1), which determines its backward variation. If one of the lines had been on the *decline* through *P*, viz. with a negative angular coefficient, then *that* one would have been decisive in determining the forward variation of the total product. And if several of the single lines had been falling through *P*, the *most strongly declining* would have been decisive in determining the forward variation of the total product. For the *backward* variation of the total product we would have had the converse rule, i.e. if all the lines had been declining through *P* (that is to say, with a negative angular coefficient), the *most slackly declining* would have been decisive in determining the backward variation of the total product.

These rules apply in a similar way to Figure (12g.3). If we investigate the forward variation of the total product, then we have only to compare in Figure (12g.3) the steepness of the lines *to the right* of *P* without concerning ourselves with the steepness of those to the left of *P*. And if we investigate the backward variation of the total product, then in Figure (12g.3) we have only to compare the steepnesses of the lines *to the left* of *P*, without concerning ourselves with the steepness that they might have to the right of *P*.

When we recall that a negative number is less than a positive, and that of two negative numbers the one which has the largest numerical value is least, these rules can be summarised as follows:

(12g.4) *On a positive increase in the quantity of the variable factor the (positive, negative or zero) rate of increase of the total product is equal to the rate of increase for the minimum function which has the least forward rate of increase. On a negative increase of the quantity of the variable factor the (positive, negative or zero) rate of increase of the total product is equal to the rate of increase of the minimum function which has the greatest backward rate of increase.*

Expressed in symbols this shows the general definition of the marginal productivity with respect to factor No. *h* and can be written as follows:

(12g.5) $\quad x'_{h, \text{ forward}} = \text{Min}\,[x'_{(i)h},\, x'_{(j)h},\, \ldots,\, x'_{(k)h}]_{\text{forward}}$

(when $(i), (j), \ldots, (k)$ are minimum rings).

(12g.6) $x'_h.\text{ backward} = \text{Max}\,[x'_{(i)h},\, x'_{(j)},\, \ldots,\, x'_{(k)h}]_{\text{backward}}$
(when $(i), (j), \ldots, (k)$ are minimum rings).

Here x'_h indicates the marginal productivity of the total product function (minimal form), while $x'_{(i)h}$, etc., indicate the marginal productivities of the single ring functions. 'Min' indicates the smallest of the figures in the square bracket, and 'Max' indicates the largest of the figures in the square bracket.

In (12g.5) and (12g.6) the marginal productivity of any factor is defined quite generally in any factor point whatever in a production law of a very general type. As a special case it gives e.g. the marginal productivities in the simple minimum law described in Section 12a, and as an other special case it gives the marginal productivity for continuity factors, viz. (5b.1). In the latter case the number of rings is only 1. Even though the single ring functions have the same tangential direction backwards and forwards for a partial variation of factor No. h, the tangential direction for the total product – determined by (12g.5) and (12g.6) – will as a rule show a kink. Cf. Figure (12g.2). If one or more of the ring functions are *themselves* product functions expressed by minimal forms, the corresponding marginal productivities which are indicated inside the square brackets in (12g 5) and (12g.6) will therefore as a rule have a tangential kink. This, however, is of no importance, since formulas (12g.5) and (12g.6), as we have seen, also apply to this case. We have therefore defined the concept of marginal productivity even in the very general case when the total product function is *pyramidised*, i.e. is a minimal form in certain ring functions which themselves are minimal forms which may or may not contain sub-functions which *again* are minimal forms, and so on.

That we have been able to provide such a complete generalisation of the concept of marginal productivity does *not* mean that we can also generalise the marginal increment formula (5b.7), since *this* formula as a general rule only applies when the marginal productivities vary *continuously* with the factor point. And in (12g.5) and (12g.6) the marginal productivities defined may *not* do so.

With the aid of the *generally defined* concept of marginal productivity here given we can now tackle the problem of delimitation in the general limitation law.

12h. The delimitation definition of the confluence region. The relationship with substitution region. The limitation law as an extreme case of the optimum law

The confluence region represents the factor points which are of 'special interest'. This is brought out by the following definition:

DEFINITION (12h.1)

Outside the confluence region there is everywhere at least one factor which is such that its quantity can be decreased (while the others are constant), without the product quantity being decreased. But in the confluence region no factor will be of this kind.

By using the marginal productivity concept from (12g.6) the definition (12h.1) can also be stated as follows:

DEFINITION (12h.2)

The confluence region consists of those and only those factor points where all the generally defined backward marginal productivities are positive, not zero.

A generally defined marginal productivity is, indeed, positive, not zero, on decrease, when and only when a decrease of the factor concerned (while the others are constant) effectively leads to a decrease of the product quantity. And (12h.1) says precisely that if an effective product decrease of this kind is produced, no matter which factor we decrease, then we have a point in the confluence region. The two formulations of the definition are therefore equivalent.

These general definitions can of course also be used in the special case when the entire production law merely contains continuity factors. In such cases we simply get what we previously called the substitution region, or more correctly: the *interior* of the substitution region. The *boundary* of the substitution region, viz. the points where one or several marginal productivities are exactly zero, is omitted according to definition (12h.2). This provides the most useful formulation for the discussion of the very general cases involving mixed substitution and limitation effects.

(12h.1) and (12h.2) are *technical* definitions, as they do not contain the price concept. Nevertheless it is clear that the region thus defined is of 'particular interest', when the 'interest' is defined in an economic sense. For outside the region the situation will *certainly* be such that costs can be reduced without the product quantity being decreased (provided merely that the factor costs have the property that larger factor quantities mean larger factor costs.

This circumstance shows that there must be a connection between the concept of confluence region and the *substitumal*, which was defined as the set of points where the in-every-respect economical substitution has been carried out. But there is also a difference. The substitution was defined by introducing the price concept and by considering arbitrary factor variations. The confluence region (12h.2) on the contrary is defined without introducing the price concept, and by considering partial factor variations. Only by considering the effect of each factor taken separately shall we avoid such comparisons between factors which presuppose the price concept. The latter procedure, i.e. the method of partial variation, based on technical considerations only, can result in a *sufficient* condition regarding the possibility of undertaking a substitution, but it cannot lead to a *necessary* condition. We can say definitely that in a point *outside* the confluence region (12h.2) it will *certainly* be possible to undertake an in-every-respect economic substitution (provided the factor costs are of such a kind that larger factor quantities involve greater total costs), but merely on the basis of the technical definition (12h.2) – or, if we like, (12h.1) – we cannot make any definite statement with regard to the situation *within* the confluence region. Inside this region there may exist points where it is possible to undertake an in-every-respect economic substitution. Whether – and, if so, where – this is to be possible, depends in general on the factor prices, or on the factor price functions. The confluence region (12h.2) is thus a certain region of the factor diagram which can be fixed technically, and *within which* we can be sure that the substitumal points *must* be situated. But not all points in the confluence region need be substitumal. It may be that the substitumal points only constitute a *narrower* region which in turn lies in the interior of the confluence region. In the simple case involving only continuity factors, each of which conforms to an optimum law, we *know* already that as a rule this is so: the substitumal is here a one-dimensional curve within the substitution region. The substitution region is here of the same dimensionality as the factor diagram, but it is a *delimited part* of it. Cf. *inter alia* Figure (7c.1). We shall get something similar when the production law exhibits a mixed limitation- and substitution-effect, e.g. when one of the ring functions itself is a product function with a continuity- and optimum-character in some of its factors. But in the general limitation case it *may* happen, too, that the substitumal fills the entire confluence region, in such a way that these two concepts – that of confluence region and that of substitumal – *coincide*.

This is, for example, the case in the simplified example (12a.1).

It is illuminating to see how a pure limitation law of the type (12a.1) may be thought of as emerging as an *extreme case* of a substitution- and optimum-law. As an example let us take the substitution law set out in (6b.1) and (7c.1). Let us imagine that the technical character of this production law is gradually modified in such a way that there is a smaller and smaller distance between the optimum and the maximum in (6b.1). This means in (7c.1) that the angle between the two beams forming the boundary of the substitution region becomes smaller and smaller. Finally the region collapses completely, and is reduced to a technically determined confluence line as in (12a.1). This line now also becomes the *substitumal*, no matter what the factor prices are. For throughout the transformation process considered the substitumal – interpreted as the result of an in-every-respect economic substitution involving continuity factors – has been situated inside the substitution region, that is to say in the region which has now thinned down and become a line. In other words along this line each one of the factors can now be said to be *simultaneously* optimal and maximal.

A situation of this kind *cannot* occur as long as the law possesses a continuity and optimum character.

This is easily seen by noticing that provided all factors are used *optimally*, the passus coefficient (which is the sum of the individual optimality coefficients, cf. (5h.11)) must be equal to $N=$ the number of factors, but if all factors are added *maximally*, the passus coefficient must be nought.

12i. The delimitation problem. A method of constructing the confluence region

When the product quantity is given by a minimal form of the type (12c.3) or (12d.2) with *separate* factor rings, and the individual ring functions have backward partial derivatives (marginal productivities) which are positive, not zero, it is clear that the factor region where (12h.2) is fulfilled, is bound to be precisely where all the ring functions are equal. Should any of the derivatives of the ring functions change their sign anywhere, the argument will nevertheless apply within that region in the large factor diagram where all the individual backward derivatives of the ring functions are positive, not zero (if a region of this kind exists). We shall now see how the confluence region can be determined in the general case where some of the rings may be *mixed*.

We must find the factor points where a given product function of the general form (12e.4) has *all* the marginal productivities for decrease positive, not zero. In order to do this we must systematically investigate all possible cases. This can best be done according to the following procedure: first the case must be considered when only one of the rings is a minimum ring; there will be a total of ν cases of this kind (if ν is the number of rings), that is to say the case where ring (1) is a minimum ring, the case where ring (2) is a minimum ring, etc. Next we must consider the cases where two of the rings simultaneously are minimum rings; there will be a total of $\binom{\nu}{2}$ cases of this kind, namely the case where rings (1) and (2) are simultaneously minimum rings, the case where rings (1) and (3) are minimum rings, the case where (2) and (3) are minimum rings, etc. Next we consider the cases where three of the rings are minimum rings; there will be a total of $\binom{\nu}{3}$ cases of this kind, etc. From all these we must pick out the cases in which all the N backward marginal productivities x_1', x_2', ..., x_N' – as defined in (12g.6) – are positive, not zero. And for these cases we set up the equations that express the relevant ring functions as equal. Indeed, by the procedure described a point where these ring functions are equal is then precisely a point with the property which the points in the confluence region are to have. Since the ring functions are dependent on the factor quantities, certain factor bands (cf. Section 2e) are thereby defined. They are the analytical expression of the confluence region. We may have to exclude parts of this region owing to certain *accessory* conditions, such as e.g. the condition that all factor quantities must be nonnegative, or the like.

As an illustration we shall make a complete analysis of the example given in (12e.3). The derivatives of the four ring functions with regard to the four factors are here:

(12i.1)
$$\frac{\partial x_{(1)}}{\partial v_1} = 1 \qquad \frac{\partial x_{(1)}}{\partial v_2} = 1 \qquad \frac{\partial x_{(1)}}{\partial v_3} = 0 \qquad \frac{\partial x_{(1)}}{\partial v_4} = 0$$
$$\frac{\partial x_{(2)}}{\partial v_1} = 0 \qquad \frac{\partial x_{(2)}}{\partial v_2} = 0 \qquad \frac{\partial x_{(2)}}{\partial v_3} = \frac{1}{\gamma} \qquad \frac{\partial x_{(2)}}{\partial v_4} = 0$$
$$\frac{\partial x_{(3)}}{\partial v_1} = 0 \qquad \frac{\partial x_{(3)}}{\partial v_2} = 0 \qquad \frac{\partial x_{(3)}}{\partial v_3} = 0 \qquad \frac{\partial x_{(3)}}{\partial v_4} = \frac{1}{a}$$
$$\frac{\partial x_{(4)}}{\partial v_1} = \frac{b-a}{b} \qquad \frac{\partial x_{(4)}}{\partial v_2} = 0 \qquad \frac{\partial x_{(4)}}{\partial v_3} = 0 \qquad \frac{\partial x_{(4)}}{\partial v_4} = \frac{1}{b}.$$

All the derivatives here which are not zero, are *positive*. For we assume a, b, and γ to be positive, and $b > a$. As we are here only interested in the positiveness of the derivatives, we can reproduce (12i.1) in the condensed form used in the upper portion of the *delimitation table* (12i.2). The positivity structure which this table gives applies in our example to the whole factor diagram, so that we do not need to specify any definite area of the diagram to which we shall confine the analysis. In other cases it may of course happen that the derivative of the ring functions have different signs in different regions of the factor diagram, and we must then make suitable reservations as to which part of the factor diagram we are concerned with.

A systematic, complete and precise discussion of the various possibilities in our example can be carried out quickly and quite mechanically with the aid of Table (12i.2). In line (12), for example – that is to say, the first line below the section in (12i.2) where the contents of (12i.1) are summed up – we take down what the signs will be for the four marginal productivities of the total product function at a point such that rings (1) and (2), but no others, are minimum rings. The first sign on this line is $+$. This is determined by applying (12g.6) for $h=1$, when there are two minimum rings, viz. $(i)=(1)$ and $(j)=(2)$. The marginal productivity x_1' at a point of this kind will thus be equal to the greatest of the figures $x'_{(1)1}$ and $x'_{(2)1}$. These two figures – or more precisely their signs – are to be found already entered in the first column of Table (12i.2), respectively on lines (1) and (2). Here the signs are $+$ and 0. Let us take the largest of them. It shows that x_1' is positive at every point where rings (1) and (2), but no others, are minimum rings. We can condense this into the following mechanical rule: for the time being only consider the figures in the first column. *At least one* of lines (1) and (2) have $+$ in the first column. For this reason we also put $+$ in line (12) of the first column. The same rule applies for the second column: at least one of lines (1) and (2) have $+$ in the second column. For this reason we also put $+$ in line (12) of the second column. In the fourth column *none* of lines (1) and (2) has $+$. The largest sign in lines (1) and (2) is here 0, and so we enter a 0 in line (12) of the fourth column. The same rule applies to line (13), line (23), etc.

If we apply (12g.6) at points which are such that three of the rings, but not more, are simultaneously minimum rings, we shall find that we get the following rule: In the first column there is a $+$ in *at least one* of lines (1), (2), and (3). For this reason we also enter a $+$ in line (123) in the first column. In the third column there is no $+$ in any of the three lines (1), (3), and (4). The largest sign we find here is 0. And so we also put a 0 in line (134) in the third column. A corresponding rule applies to line (1234). By *covering over* one or more of the lines in the upper part of the table (the single lines (1), (2), (3), (4)) one after the other with a movable pencil

TABLE (12i.2). Delimitation Table

	In minimum ring	Marginal productivity with respect to factor No.			
		1	2	3	4
The marginal productivities of the individual ring functions. This is the same as the marginal productivity of the total product function when there is only one minimum ring.	(1)	+	+	0	0
	(2)	0	0	+	0
	(3)	0	0	0	+
	(4)	+	0	0	+
The marginal productivity calculated backward for total product function when there are two minimum rings.	(12)	+	+	+	0
	(13)	+	+	0	+
	(23)	0	0	+	+
	(14)	+	+	0	+
	(24)	+	0	+	+
	(34)	+	0	0	+
Ditto when there are three minimum rings	(123)	+	+	+	+*
	(124)	+	+	+	+*
	(134)	+	+	0	+
	(234)	+	0	+	+
Ditto when there are four minimum rings (viz., all rings are minimum signs in the factor point considered).	(1234)	+	+	+	+*

stub or the like, and copying the highest sign in what is left, the whole table can be filled in quite automatically and in a very short time.

When the whole table has been filled out, a survey should be undertaken and *those lines* which contain only + should be noted. There are three lines of this kind in the table, viz. (123), (124), and (1234). These are marked in the righthand margin with an asterisk.

Let us consider these three lines a little more closely. (123) indicates a situation where rings (1), (2), and (3) are simultaneously minimum rings. Since the four marginal productivities calculated on decrease are here positive, not zero, we must now be in a point in the confluence region. Any point where the ring functions (1), (2), and (3) are equal while (4) is *larger* is thus a point in the confluence region. Correspondingly for the two other cases marked, viz. (124) and (1234). This gives us the following three sets of equations

(12i.3)
$$\text{(I)} \quad v_1+v_2 = \frac{v_3}{\gamma} = \frac{v_4}{a} \,;$$
$$\text{(II)} \quad v_1+v_2 = \frac{v_3}{\gamma} = \frac{v_4+(b-a)v_1}{b} \,;$$
$$\text{(III)} \quad v_1+v_2 = \frac{v_3}{\gamma} = \frac{v_4}{a} = \frac{v_4+(b-a)v_1}{b} \quad (b>a).$$

These three alternatives represent points where the criterion (12h.2) has been fulfilled. And they contain *all* these points, since the cases we have discussed exhaust all possibilities. Owing to certain *accessory* conditions the alternatives can be further reduced somewhat. It is true that (I) represents a situation where the criterion (12h.2) is fulfilled, but it is only a formal solution because in this case v_2 would then have to be negative. For if (I) is fulfilled and the fourth ring function is *greater* than the common magnitude (I), then we get

$$\frac{v_4+(b-a)v_1}{b} > v_1+v_2 \,.$$

If we here introduce for v_4 its expression in terms of v_1+v_2, taken from (I), we get

$$\frac{av_2+bv_1}{b} > v_1+v_2 \,,$$

that is to say, as b is positive, $av_2+bv_1 > b(v_1+v_2)$ and consequently $(b-a)v_2 < 0$. Since $(b-a)$ is positive, v_2 must be negative. We can therefore ignore alternative (I).

We shall write the two equations in alternative (II) in the form

(12i.4)
$$v_3 = \gamma(v_1+v_2) \,,$$
$$v_4 = av_1+bv_2 \,.$$

This is the result if (II) is solved with respect to v_3 and v_4. Alternative (III) is only the special case $v_2=0$ of (12i.4). As v_1 and v_2 in (12i.4) are two independent variables, which we can allow to assume any non-negative magnitudes we like, (12i.4) contains *the complete description of the confluence region*. As will be seen it is a two-dimensional region in the four-dimensional space (v_1, v_2, v_3, v_4).

The two equations in (12i.4) are the same as the two factor bands (the two last equations) in (12f.1). But the nature of the analysis is very different in the two cases. In order to reach (12f.1) we assumed that v_1 and v_2 kept such a *special position* in the problem that they could be taken as given. (12i.4) then becomes, so to speak, our *datum*, and not our desideratum. Now, on the other hand, we have not made any assumption about one or more of the factors standing in a special position. The only thing we have assumed is that the datum of the problem is the minimal form (12e.3). We have not taken the confluence formulation (12f.1) as a datum. The object of the analysis was now precisely to show how it is possible to derive the confluence region from a given minimal form.

12j. Basis factors and shadow factors. Product shadows and factor shadows

We assume that a confluence region has been delimited and that the *remainder* of the analysis is to consist in studying variations within this region. We assume that the equations defining the confluence region are such that they can be brought over into a *basis form*. The object of this is as follows: Let N indicate the total number of production factors, and let us assume that from among them it is possible to choose n ($\leq N$), so that the confluence equations can be solved *single valuedly* with respect to the other factors and with respect to the product, and such that the chosen factors can vary freely (they have n degrees of freedom). If we allow the chosen factors to be numbered as the *first* ones – i.e., their quantities indicated by $v_1, v_2, \ldots, v_n$ – then it ought to be possible for the confluence equations to be written in the following form

(12j.1)
$$\begin{aligned} x &= x(v_1, \ldots, v_n), \\ v_{n+1} &= v_{n+1}(v_1, \ldots, v_n), \\ v_{n+2} &= v_{n+2}(v_1, \ldots, v_n), \\ &\cdots \\ v_N &= v_N(v_1, \ldots, v_n), \end{aligned}$$

where $x, v_{n+1}, \ldots, v_N$ are $N-n+1$ *single valued* functions of the n variable $v_1, \ldots, v_n$. These last-mentioned are called the *basis factors*; the $N-n$ others are called *shadow factors*. Cf. 2e. The factor diagram in the N factors $v_1, v_2, \ldots, v_N$ we shall call the *large* factor diagram and the diagram in $v_1, v_2, \ldots, v_n$ the *little* factor diagram. The first line in (12j.1) expresses how the product quantity varies within the confluence region. We can interpret it as a variation in the small factor diagram, and the function $x(v_1, \ldots, v_n)$ *can simply be studied as a product function in this diagram*, provided only that we remember that the factors $v_{n+1}, \ldots, v_N$ (those that are not specified in the little diagram) now follow 'as shadows' whenever the basis factors vary.

For this *reduced* product function $x(v_1, \ldots, v_n)$ we can in the usual way introduce the concept of marginal productivity with respect to a given basis factor, which will give

(12j.2) $$x_h' = \frac{\partial x}{\partial v_h}$$

with $v_1, v_2, \ldots)v_h(\ldots v_n$ constant and $v_{n+1}, v_{n+2}, \ldots, v_N$ accompanying v_h as shadow factors. (12j.2) indicates the *reduced* (or basis form) marginal productivity with respect to factor No. *h*. If it is necessary symbolically to distinguish this concept from (12g.5) and (12g.6) the latter may be denoted $x_h'[\ ]$. The other usual technical productivity concepts can also be constructed for the reduced product function. As long as we merely consider the *technical* sides of the production law, we can to a large extent *ignore* the shadow factors, and confine ourselves to examining how the product quantity changes within the little factor diagram. In the various forms of cost analysis, on the other hand, we must take the shadow factors into account. It is the study of the *cost addition* which the shadow factors cause that is the new feature of the problem.

The last $N-n$ functions in (12j.1) we call the shadow functions. We call their partial derivatives *shadow coefficients*. They are defined by

(12j.3) The shadow coefficient for factor No. *i* with respect to factor No. $k = v_{ik}' = \dfrac{\partial v_i}{\partial v_k}$

with $v_1, v_2, \ldots)v_k(\ldots, v_n$ constant and $v_{n+1}, v_{n+2}, \ldots, v_N$ accompanying v_k as shadow factors. Conventionally we put $v_{kk}' = 1$ and $v_{ik}' = 0$ for $i \leq n$ and $i \neq k$.

We assume that all the partial derivatives of the functions (12j.1), that is to say, the reduced marginal productivities and the shadow coefficients, are *continuous* functions of the basis variables. This certainly does not cover absolutely all cases, but at any rate most of what is required, as such tangent kinks as occur through the product quantity, being a minimal form in certain ring functions, *will be eliminated* through the formulation in 12i, except for exceptional cases. If, for example, x in (12j.1) should still be a minimal form in basis factors, for instance depending on two ring functions f and g, i.e.

(12j.4) $$x = \text{Min}\,[f(v_1, \ldots, v_n),\ g(v_1, \ldots, v_n)]$$

and if at least one of the variables is missing in f, and at least one of the others is missing in g, then we see, using the delimination method in Section 12i, that we would have $f(v_1, ..., v_n) = g(v_1, ..., v_n)$. This shows that $v_1, ..., v_n$ are in fact not *free* basis variables, but functionally connected. In other words we have not carried out the limitation analysis completely; we must go further, and construct a *narrower* confluence region. Within this narrower region the discontinuity in marginal productivities will then be eliminated in all 'non-pathological' cases.

As a special case we shall consider the one in which the shadow functions can be written in the following form

(12j.5)
$$v_{n+1} = v_{n+1}(x),$$
$$v_{n+2} = v_{n+2}(x),$$
$$\dots\dots\dots\dots$$
$$v_N = v_N(x).$$

That is to say, we here assume that *for every given product quantity a technically determined quantity of each shadow factor is required*. In this case the fabrication coefficients are well defined single-value functions of the product quantity. It is clear that this is a special case of (12j.1), as can be seen by expressing in (12j.5) the product quantity in terms of the basic factors. A shadow factor which has the property that its amount can be expressed as a function of the product quantity alone is said to be a *product shadow*. If, on the contrary, its quantity can only be expressed in terms of basis factors, it is said to be *factor shadow*. In (12f.1), v_3 is a product shadow, but v_4 is a factor shadow.

In the case where factor No. i is a product shadow, we can give a very simple expression of the shadow coefficient (12j.3). Indeed, the derivative of v_i with respect to v_k is in this case equal to the derivative of v_i with respect to x times the derivative of x with respect to v_k. The former is

(12j.6)   The marginal fabrication coefficient for the product shadow factor No. $i = v_i' = \dfrac{dv_i}{dx}$

and the latter is the marginal productivity x_k' defined in (12j.2). In other words

(12j.7) $$v_{ik}' = v_i' \cdot x_k'$$

(when i is a product shadow).

CHAPTER 13

ECONOMIC ANALYSIS OF LIMITATION LAWS

13a. The economic production concepts within the confluence region

Let us consider a variation within the reduced factor diagram $(v_1, \ldots, v_n)$ with $v_{n+1}, \ldots, v_N$ as shadow factors. When we speak of a *partial* variation we mean – as in the case of (12j.2) and (12j.3) – a partial variation within the *reduced factor diagram*, with the shadow factors always following. Let $q_1, \ldots, q_n, q_{n+1}, \ldots, q_N$ be the factor prices. We shall call the cost of the basis factors, that is to say, those on which the reduced product function depends:

(13a.1)   The *reduced* cost $= q_1 v_1 + \ldots + q_n v_n = \sum_{i=1}^{n} q_i v_i$ [cf. (10a.1)],

By contrast we have

(13a.2) The *unreduced* cost $= b = q_1 v_1 + \ldots + q_n v_n + q_{n+1} v_{n+1} + \ldots + q_N v_N$

$$= \sum_{i=1}^{N} q_i v_i .$$

When we simply speak of cost we mean the *unreduced* cost. The difference between (13a.2) and (13a.1) is *shadow factor costs*. The case involving continuity factors and the addition of *fixed* costs can be regarded as the very special case involving *one* shadow factor which is a product shadow and even *independent* of the product quantity.

Furthermore let p be the product price, viz. $a = px =$ the sales value of the product, and consequently $r = a - b =$ total profit.

We assume that p is a demand-determined function of x, and every factor price a supply-determined function of the quantity of the factor concerned (cf. (11a.1) and (11a.2)) and on this assumption we undertake a partial variation of the basis factor No. k. As a result a and b and r will be changed. The change in these *economic* magnitudes can be reckoned either per unit of change in the *factor* that is changed, or per unit of change which is caused in the *product* when the factor in question is changed. The first calculation

ECONOMIC ANALYSIS OF LIMITATION LAWS

results in the concepts' marginal intake, marginal outlay, and marginal rentability, and the second calculation results in the concepts' marginal sales, marginal costs, and marginal profit.

These concepts we define more precisely in the following manner. The type of variation we consider is denoted by $d^{pa.k}$. This is the partial increment symbol during a variation, where all basis factors are constant except No. k, while all shadow factors accompany the variation of the basis factor No. k in the way we defined in (12j.1). If there is no risk of misunderstanding we may abbreviate this partial increment symbol to ∂. This leads to:

Marginal intake with respect to factor No. k:

(13a.3) $$a_k = \frac{\partial a}{\partial v_k} = \frac{da}{dx} \cdot \frac{\partial x}{\partial v_k} = p(1+\breve{p}) \cdot x_k' \; ;$$

Marginal outlay with respect to factor No. k:

(13a.4) $$b_k = \frac{\partial b}{\partial v_k} \; ;$$

Marginal rentability with respect to factor No. k:

(13a.5) $$r_k = \frac{\partial r}{\partial v_k} = \frac{\partial(a-b)}{\partial v_k} = a_k - b_k \; ;$$

Marginal sales with respect to factor No. k:

(13a.6) $$a_k' \frac{d^{pa.k} a}{d^{pa.k} x} = \frac{a_k}{x_k'} = p(1+\breve{p}) \; ;$$

Marginal costs with respect to factor No. k:

(13a.7) $$b_k' = \frac{d^{pa.k} b}{d^{pa.k} x} = \frac{b_k}{x_k'} \; ;$$

Marginal profit with respect to factor No. k:

(13a.8) $$r_k' = \frac{d^{pa.k} r}{d^{pa.k} x} = \frac{r_k}{x_k'} \; .$$

We have here used the expression 'marginal outlay with respect to factor No. k' instead of 'of factor No. k', as in the general case it may happen that part of the increase in outlays caused by an increase in factor No. k does not mean something imputed to this factor, but is only occasioned by its variation.

In all essentials (13a.3)–(13a.8) are previously known concepts, merely generalised to fit the case involving shadow factors. Compare e.g. (13a.7) with (10b.13) and (11b.8).

We shall now find an expression for the marginal outlay (13a.4). If No. i is a shadow factor, the derivative of $(q_i v_i)$ with respect to v_i will be equal to $q_i(1+\check{q}_i)$; and consequently the derivative of $(q_i v_i)$ with respect to v_k (v_k being a basis factor) will be equal to $q_i(1+\check{q}_i)$ times the derivative of v_i with respect to v_k, which is the same as the shadow coefficient v'_{ik} defined by (12j.3).

In the general case *all* shadow factor outlays will get an increase of this kind if any one basis factor No. k is increased. This leads to the following expression for the derivative of the shadow factor outlay with respect to the basis factor No. k:

(13a.9) marginal shadow factor outlay with respect to factor No. k

$$c_k = \frac{\partial(q_{n+1}v_{n+1}+ \ldots +q_N v_N)}{\partial v_k} = \sum_{i=n+1}^{N} q_i(1+\check{q}_i)v'_{ik}.$$

Consequently the aggregate marginal outlay with respect to factor No. k — i.e. (13a.4) — will be

(13a.10) $$b_k = q_k(1+\check{q}_k) + c_k$$

(when factor No. k varies and the other basis factors are constant), where c_k is defined by (13a.9). c_k is the *additional term* we now get in the well-known expression (11a.7). With constant factor prices (i.e. $\check{q}_i = 0$) and no shadow factors (i.e. $c_k = 0$) the marginal outlay b_k expressed in (13a.10) is simply reduced to the *factor price* q_k.

In the case where shadow factors are *product shadows*, that is to say, shadow functions of the simple form (12j.5), and consequently shadow coefficients are of form (12j.7), we get

(13a.11) $$c_k = \frac{\partial(q_{n+1}v_{n+1}+ \ldots +q_N v_N)}{\partial v_k} = x_k' \sum_{i=n+1}^{N} q_i(1+\check{q}_i)v_i'$$

(when all shadow factors are product shadows).

Thus in this case the additional term c_k ($k = 1, 2, \ldots, n$) is simply *proportional to the marginal productivity* x_k' (the sum expressed to the right in (13a.11) is independent of k). Concretely we can interpret this as follows: If an increase of factor No. k results in a *large* product increase (i.e. x_k' large), then there will also be a large increase of *outlay* because the large product increase will *entail* a large increase of shadow factors (when these are product shadows). Owing to this proportionality, the condition for economic adaptation will, as we shall see, be particularly simple when the factors are product shadows.

If (13a.10) and (13a.3) are inserted in (13a.5) and (13a.8) we get:

Marginal rentability with respect to factor No. k:

(13a.12) $\qquad r_k = p(1+\check{p})x_k' - [q_k(1+\check{q}_k) + c_k]$;

Marginal profit with respect to factor No. k:

(13a.13) $\qquad r_k' = p(1+\check{p}) - \dfrac{q_k(1+\check{q}_k) + c_k}{x_k'}$.

In the special case of product shadows, (13a.13) reduces to

(13a.14) $\qquad r_k' = \left[p(1+\check{p}) - \sum\limits_{i=n+1}^{N} q_i(1+\check{q}_i)v_i \right] - \dfrac{q_k(1+\check{q}_k)}{x_k'}$

(when all shadow factors are product shadows) and a corresponding reduction takes place in (13a.12).

13b. The substitumal within the confluence region

In exactly the same way as in Section 11d the in-every-respect economic substitution will also now lead to the substitumal as the set of points in the factor diagram where the marginal productivities are proportional to the marginal outlays, viz.

(13b.1) $\qquad \dfrac{x_1'}{b_1} = \dfrac{x_2'}{b_2} = \ldots = \dfrac{x_n'}{b_n}$.

This is graphically illustrated for two factors in Figure (11d.1), where the cost curves are curvilinear. As the ratio between marginal outlay and marginal productivity is the same as *marginal cost*, (13b.1) can also be expressed by saying that all partial marginal costs must be *equal*, i.e.

(13b.2) $\qquad b_1' = b_2' = \ldots = b_n'$.

If we substitute from (13a.10) in (13b.1), we get the following form of the substitumal equations

(13b.3) $\qquad \dfrac{x_1'}{q_1(1+\check{q}_1)+c_1} = \dfrac{x_2'}{q_2(1+\check{q}_2)+c_2} = \ldots = \dfrac{x_n'}{q_n(1+\check{q}_n)+c_n}$.

The difference between these expressions and (11d.2) consists merely in the additional shadow terms c_k.

In the case of product shadows, the substitumal equations are further reduced. This can most easily be seen in the following way. The proportionality between marginal productivities and marginal outlays (i.e., the *equality* between marginal *costs*) can be formulated as follows

(13b.4) $$x_k' = \lambda[q_k(1+\check{q}_k)+c_k],$$

where λ is a proportionality factor independent of k. If the expression for c_k taken from (13a.11) is introduced into (13b.4), we get

(13b.5) $$x_k' = \frac{\lambda}{1-\lambda\Sigma} q_k(1+\check{q}_k),$$

where Σ indicates the sum to the right in (13a.11). This sum is independent of k. In other words, (13b.5) tells us that the form of the substitumal is now *precisely* the same as (11d.2). We can therefore formulate the following proposition:

PROPOSITION (13b.6)
The presence of shadow factors does not change the form of the substitumal, provided that the shadow factors are product shadows.

The substitumal concept, as we studied it in 11d, is therefore applicable to a far more general case than that which we discussed on that occasion. This generalisation has considerable practical interest, as there will generally be numerous factors which for technical reasons can be approximately regarded as product shadows; that is to say, with fabrication coefficients which are single valued functions of the product quantity.

But for the question as to *where* on the substitumal the adaptation is to stop, the presence of shadow factors will, of course, be highly significant. If the purpose is to achieve as big a net profit as possible, the final adaptation will stop at the point on the substitumal where all magnitudes (13a.13) – or in the case of mere product shadows (13a.14) – are zero. Because of the equations defining the substitumal these magnitudes must be zero *simultaneously*. Moreover we can develop an indifference theorem analogous to (10e.8), and in other ways, too, we can carry out the analysis on familiar lines.

13c. Step-by-step adaptation taking marginal rentability and marginal profit into account

In practice it will not always be possible immediately to make an adaptation right up to the substitumal. In such cases it may be necessary to proceed by a small step, and then it is important to proceed in the *right direction* or preferably in the *best direction*. The partial marginal profits (13a.13) will provide information on how one ought to proceed if the direction of the movement is free. The marginal profits (13a.13) indicate, indeed, how much is to be gained per unit of product increase by increasing a single factor. Unless there are special considerations in favour of another approach, it would seem to be natural to endeavour to increase that particular factor for which this marginal profit is greatest. In a way it gauges the strength of the *motive* one will have for increasing (or decreasing) the individual factor, and is therefore a guide during a step-by-step adaptation.

On the other hand, if some kind of *condition* is imposed on the factor variation that can take place from the given factor point, the *marginal rentability* (13a.12) might provide the best guidance. It tells us which part of the factor diagram around the given starting point gives *greater* profit than the starting point.

To investigate this question a little closer, let $dv_1, dv_2, \ldots, dv_n$ be a set of small but otherwise arbitrary factor increases starting from the given factor point. The condition necessary and sufficient for these increases to lead to a point in the profit-increasing region is (provided marginal rentabilities are continuous around the starting point) that

(13c.1) $\qquad r_1 dv_1 + r_2 dv_2 + \ldots + r_n dv_n > 0$.

This follows simply from the marginal increment formula.

We can give a *geometrical* interpretation of the condition (13c.1) which is very handy and a considerable help, e.g. in discussing cases involving complicated factor band conditions in two or three factors. Let (13c.2)

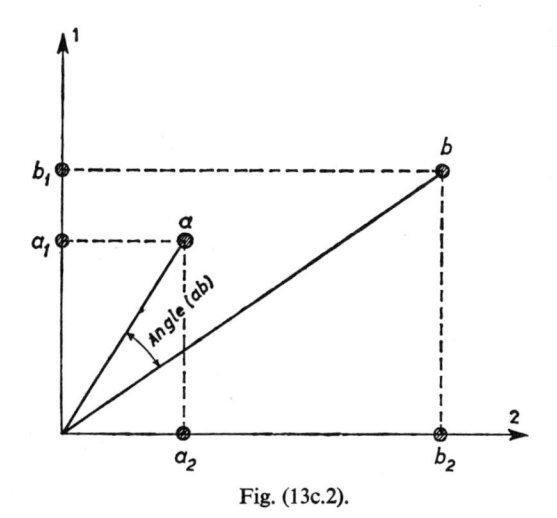

Fig. (13c.2).

be the diagram for any two variables No. 1 and No. 2. Let there be two arbitrary points given, a and b, with coordinates respectively (a_1, a_2) and (b_1, b_2) – see Figure. We draw the rays from a and b to origo, and consider the angle (ab) between these rays. The cosine of this angle is given by

$$(13\text{c}.4) \qquad \cos(ab) = \frac{a_1 b_1 + a_2 b_2}{\sqrt{a_1^2 + a_2^2} \cdot \sqrt{b_1^2 + b_2^2}},$$

where the square roots are taken as positive. In order to remember how the formula is built up, we can regard a and b as two statistic variables and 1 and 2 as the numbers of two observations. (13c.4) is then the formula for the *correlation coefficient*, except that we have taken the observations as they stand, without calculating deviations from the average (*origo correlation* in contrast to correlation around the average).

The correctness of (13c.4) can be seen – as indicated in Figure (13c.3) – by drawing the circle around origin with radius equal to 1 and marking off the points a' and b' where the circle intersects the two rays (or their extensions).

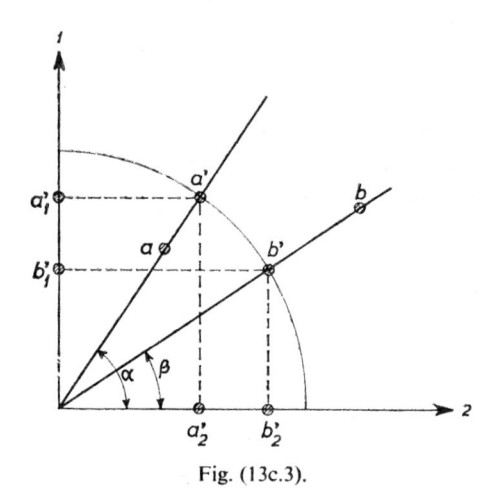

Fig. (13c.3).

In Figure (13c.3) the circle intersects the extension of ray a, but actually intersects the ray b itself. The coordinates for the points of intersection will be

$$(13\text{c}.5) \qquad a_1' = \frac{a_1}{\sqrt{a_1^2 + a_2^2}}, \qquad a_2' = \frac{a_2}{\sqrt{a_1^2 + a_2^2}}$$

and correspondingly for b_1' and b_2'. This simply follows from the fact that the *ratio* between the new coordinates a_1' and a_2' is the same as the ratio between the old a_1 and a_2 (since these lie along the same ray), while only the *lengths* of the new rays are different. The new coordinates a_1' and a_2' are therefore obtained by multiplying the coordinates a_1 and a_2 by a fixed factor (independent of the subscript 1 or 2). This factor is simply the ratio between the length of the new ray and the *length* of the old. For the new ray the length is equal to 1, and for the old it is $\sqrt{a_1^2+a_2^2}$, which gives (13c.5). Similarly for b_1' and b_2'. In the new figure we now consider the angle (ab) as the difference between the angle α which the a-ray forms with the horizontal axis and the angle β which the b-ray forms with the horizontal axis. This gives

(13c.6) $\quad \cos(ab) = \cos(\alpha-\beta) = \cos\alpha\,\cos\beta + \sin\alpha\,\sin\beta = a_2'b_2' + a_1'b_1'$.

If (13c.5) is inserted here, we get (13c.4).

The same rule applies in the case of three variables. Let a and b be two points in the three-dimensional space in Figure (13c.7), and (ab) the angle between the rays leading from origin to respectively a and b.

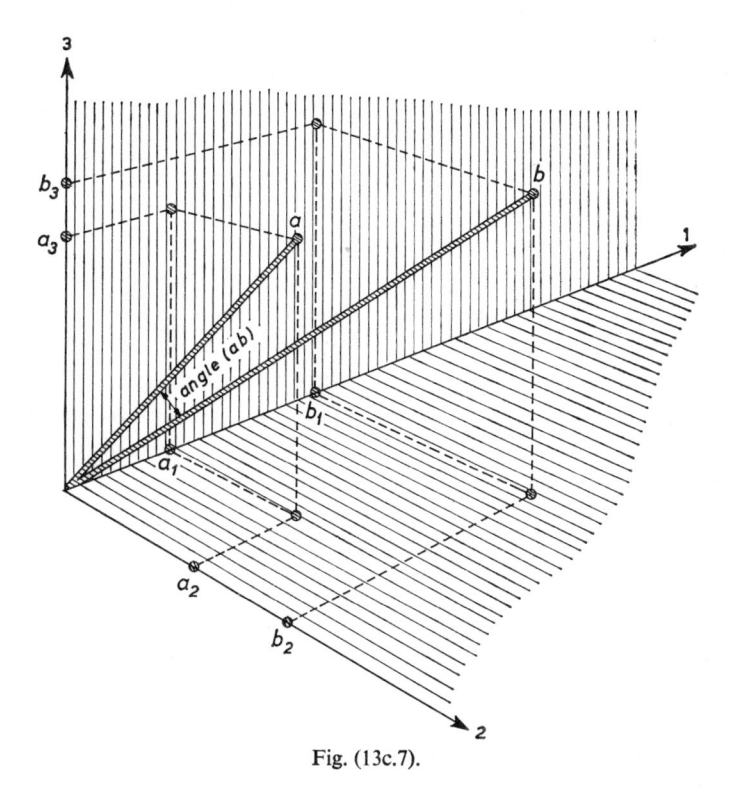

Fig. (13c.7).

Then

(13c.8) $$\cos(ab) = \frac{a_1 b_1 + a_2 b_2 + a_3 b_3}{\sqrt{a_1^2 + a_2^2 + a_3^2} \cdot \sqrt{b_1^2 + b_2^2 + b_3^2}}.$$

Here, too, in fact the analogy with the correlation coefficient (origo correlation) applies. Generally speaking, in n dimensions this correlation expression can be taken as the *definition* of the cosine concept. By classical mathematical facts (13c.8) is always a figure between -1 and $+1$ and it is all the closer to $+1$ the closer the two beams are to lying in the same straight line.

From this geometrical interpretation follows:

(13c.9) *For two beams proceeding from the same point the product sum of the coordinates of the end points (reckoned from this common point) will be positive when and only when the beams form an acute angle with one another.*

This is immediately applicable to (13c.1). It even has a concrete geometrical meaning in the case involving two and three factors. If from the given starting point in the factor diagram we draw an arrow – the arrow of marginal rentability – (whose component in the v_1 direction is the marginal rentability r_1, the component in the v_2 direction is r_2 and so on) we see that:

(13c.10) *Any factor variation which forms an acute angle with the arrow of rentability* (i.e. any factor variation dv_k satisfying (13c.1)) – *and only such factor variations – will lead to a new factor point where profits are greater than at the starting point.*

In Figure (13c.11), for example, the factor displacement PQ, defined by dv_1 and dv_2 (which are read off on the axes in the usual manner) is *at an acute angle* with the arrow of rentability (defined by components r_1 and r_2) and must therefore give an increase in profit. All points – and only those – lying in the shaded portion of the area around P (on one side of the line drawn through P and perpendicular to the arrow of rentability) will give an increase in profits, because here and only here the factor displacement is acute angled to the arrow of rentability. This argument only applies to *small* factor variations, for the criterion (13c.1) only applies to small variations. In a three-dimensional factor diagram the factor points which from a given startingpoint P define a factor variation which is at an acute angle to the arrow of rentability connected with P, will *fill the area* of P on one side of the *plane* passing through P and perpendicular to the arrow of rentability there.

The criterion (13c.10) – illustrated in (13c.11) – leads *inter alia* to an instructive interpretation of the movement that must be carried out assuming that one is to follow a prescribed line (e.g. a particular budgeting line) starting in a given factor point. If, for example, we are at point P in Figure (13c.12), where the arrow of rentability is as shown, and we are com-

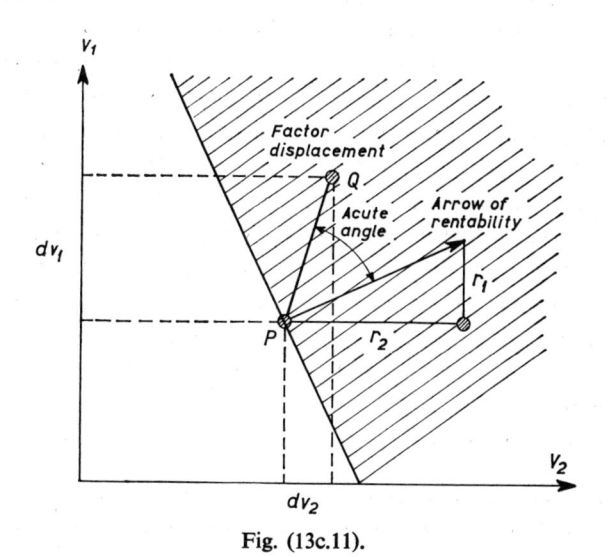

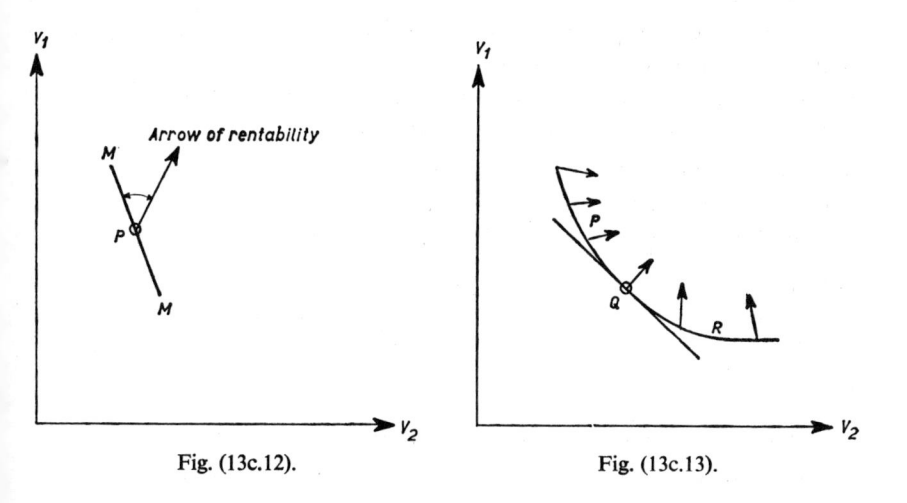

Fig. (13c.11).

Fig. (13c.12).

Fig. (13c.13).

pelled to proceed along line MM, then the movement should proceed in an upward direction towards the north-west. One can imagine the arrow of rentability as representing a *force* pulling the factor point. If the point is compelled to lie on *MM* it will be *drawn* along this line in an upward movement towards the north-west. If a curve is prescribed through a major portion of the factor diagram, and not through a small 'area' around a given starting point, then we can follow the fate of the point as it proceeds along the curve, the rentability arrow changing as we go along. Wherever we are, the factor point will be exposed to the force represented by the arrow of rentability. Everywhere the force will continue to draw the point on, provided it forms an acute angle with the curve that represents the condition imposed on the variation. Thus from *P* in Figure (13c.13) the point will be drawn down towards the south-east, and from *R* it will be pulled in an upward direction towards the north-west. Not till we reach a point where the arrow of rentability is perpendicular to the prescribed curve (more precisely: perpendicular to its tangent) – as at point *Q* – will the movement cease. Point *Q* represents *a stable of equilibrium*; irrespective of whether we start to the left or to the right of *Q*, we shall be led to *Q*. A similar interpretation applies in higher dimensions and for more complicated types of conditions imposed on the movement in the factor diagram.

13d. Further application of the arrow of rentability: adaptation to equivalence factors and to production laws with complicated factor bands

Instances may occur where there is no point within the factor diagram (that part of it where the factor quantities are non negative), where the substitumal condition (13b.3) is fulfilled. A concrete example is the case of equivalence factors. In such cases the method of Section 13c will yield a solution.

Let us as an example take (12f.1). We shall take v_1 and v_2 as basis factors. The production law within this small factor diagram is simply $x = v_1 + v_2$. Thus the two factors are complete equivalence factors; the isoquants are straight lines at 45°, see Figure (13d.4). The total costs are here:

(13d.1) $\qquad b = q_1 v_1 + q_2 v_2 + \gamma q_3 (v_1 + v_2) + q_4 (a v_1 + b v_2),$

hence

(13d.2) $\qquad b = (q_1 + \gamma q_3 + a q_4) v_1 + (q_2 + \gamma q_3 + b q_4) v_2.$

If the prices are dependent on the quantities used, the lines for constant costs might have been curved, e.g. like the dotted curves at bottom left in Figure (13d.4). In this case we shall get a substitumal *SS* which is determined by a reasoning regarding tangency in exactly the same way as in (11d.1) and (11d.2).

But if the prices are *constant* – and the factors are equivalence factors –

we must tackle the question in another way. Since in our example $x_1' = x_2' = 1$, we get

(13d.3) $r_1 = p - (q_1 + \gamma q_3 + aq_4)$; $r_2 = p - (q_2 + \gamma q_3 + bq_4)$.

If $q_1 = q_2$, that is to say the price of standing timber is equally high in both forest areas, then we have always $r_1 > r_2$ (as $b > a$). That is to say, the arrow of rentability points in an upward direction and *more steeply* than 45°.

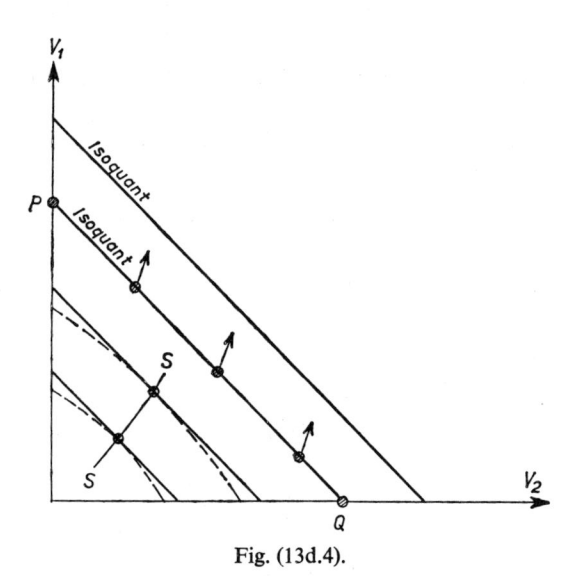

Fig. (13d.4).

This is indicated by the arrows along the isoquant PQ, all pointing in the same direction. If it is given that we have to move along this isoquant, we shall *constantly be drawn in an upward direction towards the north-west* until we arrive at point P. We shall not stop before this point is reached, but we can proceed no further as long as the factor quantities are to be non-negative. If q_1 is so much greater than q_2 that we get $r_1 < r_2$, that is to say that the arrow of rentability is *less steep* than 45°, we shall be drawn along PQ in a downward direction towards the south-east until we stop at point Q. And if $r_1 = r_2$ exactly, we shall be pulled neither in one direction nor the other, but *every* point on PQ will then represent an *indifferent equilibrium* (as long as it is given that we must remain on PQ). The concrete interpretation of these three cases is simply this, that if the price of timber in area A is the same as in area B, and all prices are constant, we shall take all our timber from A, as the transport expenses will be least in this case, but if the price of timber in *A* is so much greater than the price of timber in *B* that the price itself, *including the transport*, is greater for *A*, we shall take all the timber from *B*, and if the price, including the transport, is precisely the same for both areas, then it does not matter which we choose. We can then take all our timber from *A* or all our timber from *B*, or some from *A* and some from *B*, in any proportion whatever (illustrating the fact that in this case the adaptation may take place in any point whatever along the line *PQ*).

In this example the problem is so simple and the solution so obvious that we really do not need to use the arrow of rentability, but it is nevertheless instructive to see how a simple case of this kind, too, can be dealt with in this manner.

Representation by the arrow of rentability comes into its own in more complicated cases. Let us, for example, consider the case represented in Figure (13d.5). The field of arrows – 'the gravitational field' – represents the

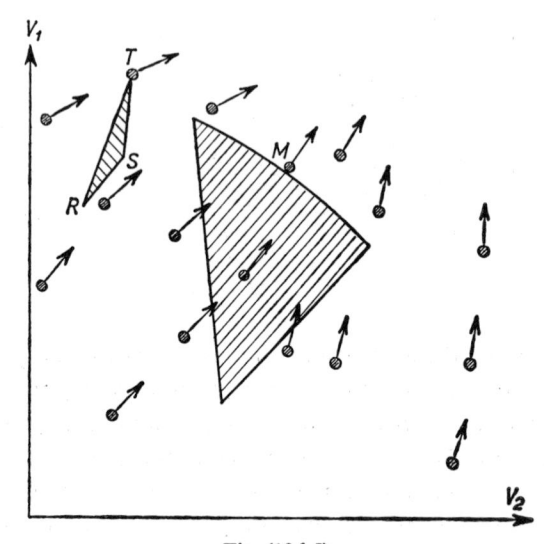

Fig. (13d.5).

'rentability-pull'. In this example the direction of rentability is not the same everywhere, but this is not a necessary assumption for the following argument. Let us assume that we are given a set of *conditions* for the factor-use which can graphically be presented by the small shaded triangle *RST* top left. In other words we must adapt ourselves somewhere within this triangle or along its boundary. Where in this triangle should we stop? The arrow of rentability gives the answer. *No matter where we start*, whether we select a point in the interior of the triangle or on its boundary, we shall in any case be drawn along in such a way that we finally end up at T. If, for example, we start somewhere on the lower line RS, we shall first have to follow it to S and then proceed in an upward direction along line ST until we end up at T. If we start somewhere in the *interior* of the triangle, we shall first be drawn along the direction of the arrow to the right until we reach *some point or other* on the line ST; and from this point, as before, we shall be drawn in an upward direction along the right-hand edge of the triangle to point T. A similar argument shows that if the factor bands are defined by the large shaded triangle in (13d.5), the point of equilibrium will be M.

Point M is determined by a *tangent* condition, while T – in the same way as P, and possibly Q, in Figure (13d.4) – is determined by an *apex condition*, i.e. the point is situated at a *kink* on the boundary of the prescribed factor region. In both cases the condition is a condition of exodus, i.e. we cannot proceed any further, as we should otherwise have to *break out* of the admissible factor region which is prescribed.

The technique of analysis from Figure (13d.5) can be used in a great variety of cases; for in (13d.5) we have only used the arrow of rentability taken as a *datum*, without any assumption as to the reason why the arrow field has acquired its particular structure. Figure (13d.5) and a corresponding figure in higher dimensions therefore provides a very general method. The vast field of modern mathematical programming is essentially built on the kind of reasoning as that exhibited in Figure (13d.5).

If *mixture percentage* are authoritatively prescribed (e.g. butter mixed into margarine, as has been the case in Norway), or bounds for mixture percentages, or *rationing* or *consumption quotas* for the factors, or the like, one will in practice often run into adaptation problems of the kind suggested in Figure (13d.5).

PART FOUR

MULTI-WARE PRODUCTION

CHAPTER 14

TECHNICAL DESCRIPTION OF THE PRODUCTION LAW FOR MULTI-WARE PRODUCTION

14a. Connected products. Assortment and coupling

If there exists some kind of technical connection between several products, e.g. because there are certain production factors which *can* be used or on technical grounds *must* be used *jointly*, or because certain factors can be used *alternatively* for one product or the other, with resultant technical consequences for the production of the other(s), then we say that these products are (technically) connected, or that we are dealing with *multi-ware production*. In this case the production law cannot be studied separately for each separate product, but must be considered simultaneously for all connected products.

We have thus defined the concept-connected products very widely. Within this wide class of production laws we must now distinguish between certain typical special cases. In 1d we have already suggested certain main outlines. We shall now discuss this matter in more detail.

Let m be the number of products and n the number of factors which it is necessary to *analyse simultaneously*. And let the technical conditions for the production be defined by μ production relations, i.e. μ relations where product quantities and/or factor quantities occur. Cf. the general set up (14d.1). The μ equations expressing production relations are assumed to be *independent* of each other. That is to say, none of them can be deduced from the others (identically in all the variables involved).

We can assume that $1 \leq m$ (otherwise the concept of production would disappear).

An important special case is the one where the equations can be solved with respect to the m product quantities and where the m ensuing product functions are single-valued. Cf. Section 14b. Within this case there are again important sub-cases.

We shall base our main classification of the production laws for connected products on the figures m and μ. The difference $\alpha = m - \mu$ we shall call the *degree of assortment* or the degree of *freedom of assortment* for the multi-ware production (mnemonically α may be thought of as the first letter in the word 'assortment').

The case involving single-ware production, which we dealt with in Part two, is $m=\mu=1$, i.e. a degree of assortment $\alpha=m-\mu$ equal to zero.

An important case is $\mu \leqslant m$, that is to say the degree of assortment $\alpha=m-\mu$ is non negative, but we shall not exclude the case $\mu > m$. This latter case, i.e. α negative, is expressed by the existence of one or several *pure factor bands*. Cf. the example in (14d.4) and (14d.5).

Irrespective of the degree of assortment $\alpha=m-\mu$, we can enquire whether, from the given μ relations, it is possible to deduce some, and if so how many, which only link together certain *product quantities*, these relations containing none of the production factors. These relations are *pure product bands*, i.e. they are *factor free*. In other words they hold good, irrespective of what the factor quantities may be. If the number of such relations is κ, we say that the *degree of coupling* – or more precisely the degree of product-coupling for the multi-ware production in question – is κ (mnemonically κ may be thought of as the first letter in the word 'coupling'). It should be clearly recognised that κ is not determined by m, n, μ but represents a new and different aspect of the production structure.

14b. Factorially determined multi-ware production

Let us assume that we have two products produced by means of n factors, and in such a way that if the factor quantities are given, then both product quantities are given. The two product quantities x^1 and x^2 are in this case given *product functions* of the *same* n factor quantities $v_1, v_2, ..., v_n$, i.e.

(14b.1) $\qquad x^1 = x^1(v_1, ..., v_n), \quad x^2 = x^2(v_1, ..., v_n)$.

This is an example of *factorially determined* multi-ware production. In this case there is no assortment, i.e. $\alpha=m-\mu=0$. Similarly in the case where $2 < m$, cf. (14b.9).

As two somewhat different examples of (14b.1) can be mentioned: wool and mutton, or eggs and poultry meat.

In order to enable chickens to live and thrive certain production factors are required – certain materials, certain foods and work. And when these factors are applied, then, *in the same process*, both the products mentioned emerge: not only a certain average quantity of eggs but a certain average quantity of poultry meat. If the factor quantities are given, both one and the other product quantity are thereby determined. In the example $m=\mu=2$, that is to say the degree of assortment α is equal to zero.

The essence of the case (14b.1) is *not* that the ratio between the two product quantities is necessarily fixed. This would be a special case. In general the ratio might be altered, at any rate within certain limits, by means of suitable changes in the factor constellation $(v_1, ..., v_n)$, for instance a change in care and feeding of chickens. By suitable changes in the factor constellation *greater* emphasis may be placed on poultry meat production and *less* on egg production, or vice versa. In this case we say that the products are – to a certain degree – *separable*.[1] The degree of coupling κ (the number of factor free relations between the product quantities) is consequently equal to zero.

The case of coupled (or joint) products is another special case of the factorially determined multi-ware production (14b.1). For example we can assume that the quantity of wool bears a fixed ratio to the quantity of mutton (this can at any rate with a large degree of accuracy be said of a given breed). In such cases the functions in (14b.1) will be of the special form

(14b.1') $\qquad x^1 = c^1 f(v_1, ..., v_n), \quad x^2 = c^2 f(v_1, ..., v_n)$

where c^1 and c^2 are constants and $f(v_1, ..., v_2)$ is the same function in both formulae. In this case the degree of coupling is $\kappa = 1$. And still the degree of assortment is $\alpha = 0$. A change in the factor quantities will in this case mean that breeding is carried on in a different way, perhaps on a larger scale, but – according to the technical circumstances prevailing in this case – always in such a way that the quantity of wool and the quantity of meat change in the *same* proportion.

Coupling can also be somewhat more complicated than in case (14b.1'). The quantity ratio between the two products may not be constant as it is in (14b.1'), but a function of the product quantities x^1 and x^2. This too is a clear case of coupling. The characteristic feature of this case is that x^2 is a *well-defined function* of x^1, where none of the factor quantities occur. We can of course have this case even though x^2 is not simply a constant times x^1. In this case too we have $\kappa = 1$, that is to say the degree of coupling is equal to 1. But still the degree of assortment is $\alpha = 0$.

As another example of coupling between products we may consider that of gas, coke, and coal tar. These three products are linked together in such a way that the quantity of coke is a technically given function of the quantity of gas, and similarly that the quantity of tar is a technically given function of the quantity of gas; while the total product quantity – measured for example by the quantity of gas – is determined by the quantities of the factors.

[1] In other words, separability simply means $x = 0$.

In this case $m=3$, $\mu=3$, $\kappa=2$, viz. the degree of assortment is $\alpha=m-\mu=0$ and the degree of coupling 2.

Graphically the case (14b.1) involving factorially determined bi-ware production with two factors can be represented plotting *two sets* of isoquants in a (v_1, v_2) diagram. Figure (14b.2) illustrates the special case of factorially determined production, which we have termed that of separable products.

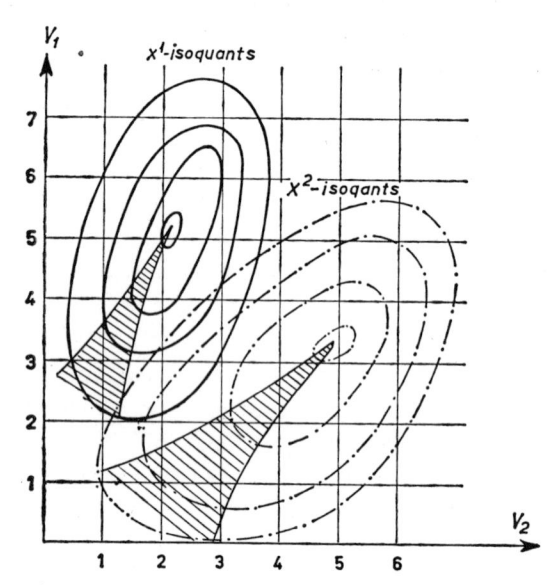

Fig. (14b.2). Factor diagram. Two separable products.

The fully drawn curves in Figure (14b.2) are x^1-isoquants, the dotted ones are x^2-isoquants. The figure illustrates the case of separable products, because we here have *two separate substitution regions* (both shaded). When the composition of the *factor* quantities is about 5:2, the main emphasis in the production is, as one will see, placed on the first product; when it is about 3:5, the main emphasis is on the second product (e.g. feeding hens for increased egg production or for fattening hens). If the substitution regions had been more sharply separated, we should have approached a situation with a clear alternative, i.e. we should now have to make a clear *choice*: we should either have to choose a factor point which entails producing practically speaking only the first product or we should have to choose a factor point which entails producing practically speaking only the second product.

TECHNICAL DESCRIPTION OF THE PRODUCTION LAW 273

In the case of *assorted* production, too, a choice will arise, but in that case it will arise *even though* the factor combination is given. Thus assorted production is in fact not equivalent to the case (14b.2) which we are now considering. Assorted production is definitely an example of alternativity which is different from the one now considered. Cf. Section 14c, especially (14c.2).

If the isoquant systems in Figure (14b.2) *approach* one another, then the possibility of separation between the products becomes less. The extreme case – in Figure (14b.3) – where the isoquant systems coincide completely (and thus the substitution regions coincide completely) illustrates the other extreme case of factorially determined production, viz. *complete coupling*. Proceeding along an x^1-isoquant, that is to say, keeping x^1 constant, will in the case (14b.3) be the *same* as proceeding along an x^2-isoquant, that is to say, keeping x^2 constant. In other words, *at all times*, whenever x^1 has a given magnitude, x^2 must also have a definite magnitude. Figure (14b.3) is therefore the graphic illustration of the case where a definite relation exists between x^1 and x^2, and this relation is independent of the factor quantities.

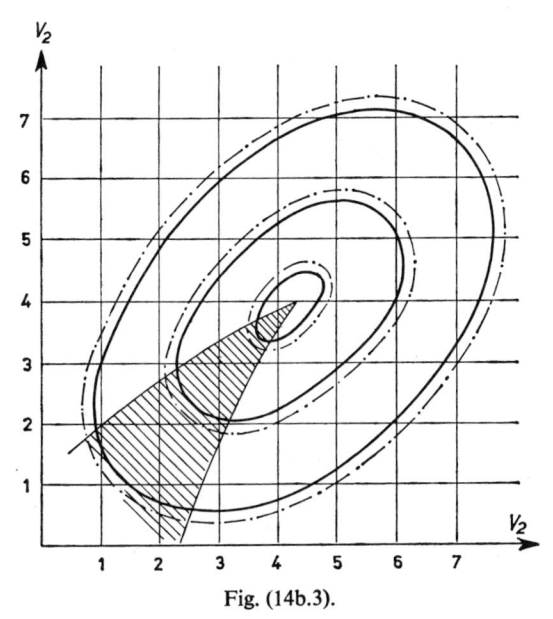

Fig. (14b.3).

To summarise: Figure (14b.3) illustrates the essence of the case we have termed coupling and Figure (14b.2) illustrates separable products. But both cases fall under the general heading factorially determined multi-ware production, and hence under the heading of assortment $\alpha = 0$.

If the situation in Figure (14b.3) furthermore is such that by proceeding from one isoquant to another we change x^2 *in the same proportion* as x^1, then we get the special case of coupling where the quantitative ratio between the two product quantities is constant, i.e. (14b.1′).

The coupling case (14b.3) can also be expressed in a *product diagram*, that is to say, in a diagram whose axes measure the quantities of the two products, not quantities of the factors. We shall then get a curve – a product coupling curve – as suggested in Figure (14b.4). As a general rule this curve will rise outwards in the factor diagram, i.e. an increasing quantity of the first product is associated with an increasing quantity of the second product.

If a mapping of the substitution sectors in the separable-product case (14b.2) is transferred to a diagram with the two product quantities as axes, it will appear as the two shaded regions 1 and 2 in Figure (14b.4). A borderline for a region of this kind is constructed by following a borderline in (14b.2), and for each point on this borderline we can read off on the x^1-isoquants and x^2-isoquants in (14b.2) the values of x^1 and x^2 and plot the corresponding point in (14b.4).

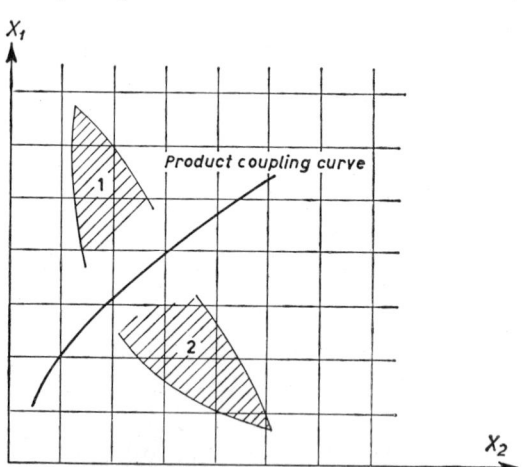

Fig. (14b.4). Product diagram.

The gradual transition from separability to coupling will be illustrated in (14b.4) by a *contraction* of the two fin-shaped shaded areas, and at the same time a tendency for the apexes of these areas to slope towards the north-east or south-west. The two shaded areas will then collapse completely, thus

TECHNICAL DESCRIPTION OF THE PRODUCTION LAW 275

forming the one-dimensional product coupling line. The shape and position of the two substitution regions mapped in the product diagram (14b.4) afford an instructive presentation of the *character* of the technical relationship between two separable products as distinct from the relationship between two coupled products.

With the aid of the marginal productivities it is easy to give a necessary and sufficient criterion for coupling in the case of factorially determined products. Let

$$(14b.5) \qquad x_k{}^i = \frac{\partial x^i(v_1, \ldots, v_n)}{\partial v_k}$$

be the marginal productivity of product No. i with respect to factor No. k. From Figure (14b.3) we see that the coupling criterion can be formulated by saying that the two isoquant systems have a *common tangent* everywhere. This means that the marginal productivities are proportional, in other words that

$$(14b.6) \qquad \frac{x_1{}^1}{x_1{}^2} = \frac{x_2{}^1}{x_2{}^2} = \ldots = \frac{x_n{}^1}{x_n{}^2}.$$

(condition for coupling in the case of factorially determined products).

We can also consider the coupling-situation in another way. The fact that we have coupling in x^1 and x^2 means that there exists a functional relationship

$$(14b.7) \qquad F(x^1, x^2) = 0,$$

which is independent as $v_1, \ldots, v_n$. Let us imagine that the expressions for x^1 and x^2 are taken from (14b.1) and inserted into (14b.7), and let us take the derivative of F with respect to v_k. A partial derivation with respect to v_k then gives $F^1 \cdot x_k{}^1 + F^2 \cdot x_k{}^2 = 0$ where F^1 and F^2 are the partial derivatives of F with respect to x^1 and x^2 respectively. From this follows immediately

$$(14b.8) \qquad \frac{x_k{}^1}{x_k{}^2} = -\frac{F^2}{F^1} = \text{independent of } k,$$

which is the same as (14b.6). The line of reasoning in (14b.7–8) merely shows that (14b.6) is a *necessary* criterion for coupling. In other words, if (14b.7) holds good we must have (14b.6). From the Figure (14b.3) we see that (14b.6) is also a *sufficient* criterion.

If we have m products, the factorially determined case will be characterised by a set of m product functions

$$(14b.9) \qquad x^1 = x^1(v_1, \ldots, v_n), \ldots, x^m = x^m(v_1, \ldots, v_n).$$

In this case too the degree of assortment α will be zero.

The marginal productivities within the system (14b.9) will be defined as in (14b.5).

It is clear that a lack of coupling in the case of multi-ware production must be of great importance in the study of the process of price formation. A change in the price ratio between the two related but to some extent separable products is bound, for example, to result in a quantity adjustment between the two products.

The general criterion for the degree of product coupling κ in the case where all m products are factorially determined and hence $m = \mu$ (i.e. degree of assortment $\alpha = 0$) can be formulated as follows. Form the matrix of the marginal productivities, that is to say the matrix

(14b.10)
$$\begin{pmatrix} x_1^1 & x_2^1 & \ldots & x_n^1 \\ x_1^2 & x_2^2 & \ldots & x_n^2 \\ \ldots & \ldots & \ldots & \ldots \\ x_1^m & x_2^m & \ldots & x_n^m \end{pmatrix}$$

It is necessary and sufficient for the degree of coupling to be κ in the case considered that the matrix (14b.10) is of rank $m - \kappa$; that is to say, at least one of the $(m - \kappa)$-rowed determinants contained in (14b.10) $\neq 0$, while all higher-rowed determinants contained in (14b.10) vanish. The criterion (14b.6) is the special case $m = 2$; (14b.6) tells us, indeed, that all the two-rowed determinants of marginal productivities are equal to zero.

14c. One-dimensional assortment. Single product freedom

Let us assume that there is a choice between raising grain and potatoes on a certain piece of land. A number of patches may concretely be rather *special* to one of these two kinds of cultivation, but let us for a moment ignore them and merely consider those which *according to the free choice* of the farmer can be used either for one or the other product. Similarly for other factors. Not only the land itself but certain types of agricultural machinery can be used generally, and the same applies to unspecialised labour.

Let $v_1, \ldots, v_n$ be the quantities of these generally applicable factors, and let x^1, x^2 be the two product quantities. If $v_1, \ldots, v_n$ are given, we are here obviously faced with a situation which is entirely different from the one we discussed in Section 14b. Now x^1 and x^2 will *not* be given even if $v_1, \ldots, v_n$ are. On the contrary, even if $v_1, \ldots, v_n$ are given, we shall now have a *choice* between x^1 and x^2. Perhaps we shall choose to use the entire given $v_1, \ldots, v_n$ complex to produce x^1, perhaps we shall use all of it to produce x^2, or perhaps we shall divide the given factor complex between the two uses. In other words, when $v_1, \ldots, v_n$ are given, then this only means that a certain *link or band* is determined between x^1 and x^2. In the example this link is *not* a pure product-band (a coupling), i.e. it is not a fixed relation between the two product quantities, which hold good regardless of the *factor* combination that actually prevails. On the contrary, in the example the nature of the relation between the two factor quantities depends on the factor point. This means that the relation now considered will be of the form

(14c.1) $$F(x^1, x^2; v_1, \ldots, v_n) = 0 .$$

This is the only production relation existing in our example. In other words we have $m - \mu = 2 - 1 = 1$, that is to say, a one-dimensional freedom of assortment; or, as we may also more briefly call it, a *one-dimensional assortment*.

Graphically we can express this by drawing the product diagram. See Figure (14c.2). A *curve* in the product diagram is the locus of points where

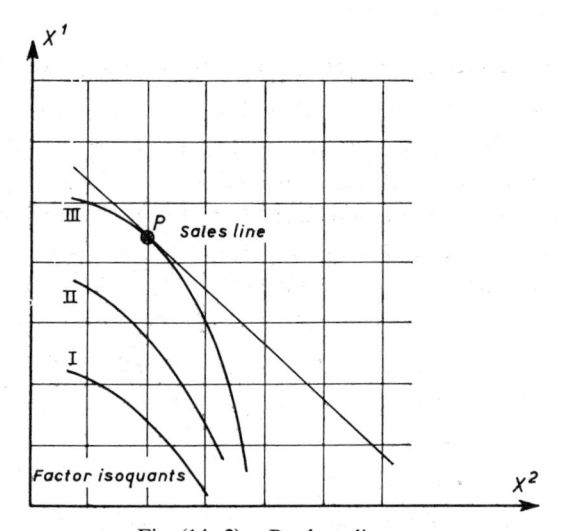

Fig. (14c.2). Product diagram.

all $v_1, \ldots, v_2$ are given. When the factor quantities are given neither x^1 nor x^2 are given, but only a certain *relationship* between x^1 and x^2.

We call a curve of this kind in the product diagram a *factor isoquant*. This is a curve along which all (general) production factors are constant. Three curves of this kind are shown in Figure (14c.2), corresponding to three different choices of the factor point $(v_1, ..., v_n)$. The regular case will be one in which such curves are falling. Cf., as a contrast to this, the coupling curve between x^1 and x^2 in Figure (14b.4). It was a single curve and it was rising towards the north-east.

As we have to fix n magnitudes (n factor quantities) in order to define a factor isoquant, and as the fact that we are choosing a definite point in the product diagram through which the factor isoquant is to pass, only gives one condition in our example, there will as a rule be an $(n-1)$-dimensional infinity of factor isoquants passing through each point in the product diagram (when this is two-dimensional and the freedom of assortment is 1).

Similarly in the case where freedom of assortment exists, we can define marginal productivities, but they will be *conditioned*, e.g.

$$(14c.3) \qquad x_k{}^{1.2} = \frac{\partial x^1}{\partial v_k}$$

(when all factor quantities apart from v_k are constant, and furthermore the product quantity x^2 is constant).

14d. Multi-dimensional assortment. Multiple freedom of products

In practice there will often be *several* kinds of crops between which a choice can be made when the quantities $v_1, ..., v_n$ of the (general) factors are given. And furthermore the production conditions may be such that they will have to be expressed by more than 1, say by μ, production relations. Similar conditions will exist in crafts and to an certain extent in industry. The general systems of production relations now to be considered will therefore be of the form

$$(14d.1) \qquad \begin{aligned} F^1(x^1, ..., x^m \,; v_1, ..., v_n) &= 0 \\ F^2(x^1, ..., x^m \,; v_1, ..., v_n) &= 0 \\ \cdots\cdots\cdots\cdots\cdots\cdots\cdots& \\ F^\mu(x^1, ..., x^m \,; v_1, ..., v_n) &= 0 \,. \end{aligned}$$

In this case the degree of assortment is $\alpha = m - \mu$. No assortment is characterized by $\alpha = 0$, and if α is negative this means that there even exist pure factor bands, i.e. factor quantities $v_1, ..., v_n$ are no longer independent variables.

The degree of coupling – if there is any – will be expressed by the number κ of the equations in (14d.1) that do not containing any of the factor quantities; or, more correctly, by the greatest number of such equations occurring, when the attempt is made to transform the equations (14d.1) in such a

TECHNICAL DESCRIPTION OF THE PRODUCTION LAW   279

way that as many as possible of them are free from factor quantities.

The marginal productivities will now have to be defined by the assumption that not only $(n-1)$ of the factors but also $(m-1)$ of the products are to be kept constant.

As a rule the best picture of the very general situation (14d.1) will be obtained when we use a representation in *parameter-form*. By this I mean the following:

The number of degrees of freedom in (14d.1) is

(14d.2) $$M = n + (m - \mu)$$

We introduce a set of M parameters $t_1, \ldots, t_M$ in such a way that *not only all product quantities but also all factor quantities* can be expressed uniquely in terms of $t_1, \ldots, t_M$; that is to say, in such a way that we have m *product functions* and n factor functions

(14d.3)
$$\begin{aligned}
x^1 &= x^1(t_1, \ldots, t_M) & v_1 &= v_1(t_1, \ldots, t_M) \\
x^2 &= x^2(t_1, \ldots, t_M) & v_2 &= v_2(t_1, \ldots, t_M) \\
&\cdots\cdots\cdots\cdots & &\cdots\cdots\cdots\cdots \\
x^m &= x^m(t_1, \ldots, t_M) & v_n &= v_n(t_1, \ldots, t_M)
\end{aligned}$$

and further in such a way that $t_1, \ldots, t_M$ are *independent* variables. This means that it is impossible from the definition of the parameters and from (14d.1) to deduce any equation which contains only the parameters and holds good identically in the parameters. Any set of parameters $t_1, \ldots, t_M$ satisfying these conditions is called a set of *production parameters*.

The degree of assortment in (14d.1) is $\alpha = m - \mu$. The total number of parameters – as indicated in (14d.2) – is therefore equal to the number n of factors plus the degree of assortment α. In the case involving one product and n factors, $m = \mu = 1$, that is to say, $M = n$. If the degree of assortment α is negative, the number μ of production parameters is *less* than the number n of factors. This is only another expression for the fact that there now exist one or more pure factor bands.

If the M parameters $t_1, \ldots, t_M$ are eliminated from the $m + n$ equations (14d.3), we are left with $m + n - M = \mu$ equations between $x^1, \ldots, x^m$, and $v_1, \ldots, v_n$ and we are thus back again to the form (14d.1).

The parameters $t_1, \ldots, t_M$ merely constitute *a system of coordinates*, thanks to which all the various situations with respect to products and factors may be described in the general case considered. A system of description of this kind can in principle *be selected in many ways*; the important thing is merely to find one which is such that the parameters are functionally independent (within the system (14d.1)) and such that the parameter-form is convenient to handle.

As a very simplified example, let us imagine agricultural production involving a *general* factor, say 'land', which can be used either for product No. 1 or for product No. 2, and in addition two *special* factors, one for each of two products. For the sake of simplicity let us assume that each of the two products requires a fixed area per product unit. We then get an *assortment relation* between the products of the following form

(14d.4) $$\alpha^1 x^1 + \alpha^2 x^2 = v_3,$$

where α^1 and α^2 are constants, x^1 and x^2 the two product quantities, and v_3 the quantity of the general factor 'land'. Let us furthermore assume that the quantity v_1 which is required to produce x^1 and the quantity v_2 required to produce x^2, are determined by

(14d.5)
$$x^1 = a + bv_1$$
$$x^2 = c + dv_2$$

where a, b, c, d are constants, $b \neq 0$ and $d \neq 0$. If we wish to carry out an *analysis* with all three factors v_1, v_2, v_3 as *independent* variables, we should formulate the production conditions as follows

(14d.6) $$\alpha^1 x^1 + \alpha^2 x^2 \leq v_3, \quad x^1 \leq a + bv_1, \quad x^2 \leq c + dv_2$$

and discuss the variation in v_1, v_2, v_3 (and in x^1 and x^2) on the basis of a limitation analysis on lines similar to those we have previously followed. But if we are satisfied with a confluence analysis, then we can immediately put down the three equations (14d.4) and (14d.5). We then have

$$M = n + (m - \mu) = 3 + (2 - 3) = 2.$$

Thus here two parameters t_1, t_2 are required in order to cover the degrees of freedom in the problem. Let us, for example, take the last two terms in (14d.5) as parameters. This gives the following parameter form

(14d.7)
$$\begin{aligned} x^1 &= a + t_1 & v_1 &= t_1/d, \\ x^2 &= c + t_2 & v_2 &= t_2/d, \\ & & v_3 &= (\alpha^1 a + \alpha^2 c) + \alpha^1 t_1 + \alpha^2 t_2. \end{aligned}$$

But we could also have chosen the parameters in an infinite number of other ways. For example, we could have denoted the terms of the extreme right in (14d.5) respectively $t_1 - t_2$ and $t_1 + t_2$. This gives the following parameter form

TECHNICAL DESCRIPTION OF THE PRODUCTION LAW

$$x^1 = a + (t_1 - t_2) \qquad v_1 = \frac{t_1 - t_2}{b},$$

(14d.8) $\quad x^2 = c + (t_1 + t_2) \qquad v_2 = \frac{t_1 + t_2}{d},$

$$v_3 = \alpha^1 a + \alpha^2 c + (\alpha_1 + \alpha_2)t_1 - (\alpha_1 - \alpha_2)t_2.$$

The fact that (14d.7) is a parameter form where t_1 and t_2 may vary as *independent* variables is checked by inserting (14d.7) into (14d.4) and (14d.5). We shall then find that each of the three equations (14d.4) and (14d.5) reduce to $0=0$, no matter what values are attributed to the parameters t_1 and t_2. Similarly in the case (14d.8).

In principle the parameter form in (14d.7) and that in (14d.8) are therefore equally acceptable. In any of these two cases the *covariation* between x^1, x^2, v_1, v_2, v_3 which constitutes the production law, is described by allowing the two parameters t_1 and t_2 to vary freely. But, of course, one of the two parameter forms considered may prove more convenient for special purposes than the other.

If the parameter form is given, then a *parametric marginal productivity* can be defined, viz.

(14d.9) $\qquad\qquad x_{(K)}{}^i = \dfrac{\partial x^i(t_1, \ldots, t_M)}{\partial t_K}$

And we can also define a *parametric factor rate* of increase

(14d.10) $\qquad\qquad v_{j(K)} = \dfrac{\partial v_j(t_1, \ldots, t_M)}{\partial t_K}.$

CHAPTER 15

ECONOMIC ADAPTATION UNDER MULTI-WARE PRODUCTION

15a. Product value and costs under multi-ware production

Let

(15a.1)
$$p^1 = p^1(x^1) \quad q_1 = q_1(v_1),$$
$$p^2 = p^2(x^2) \quad q_2 = q_2(v_2),$$
$$\dots\dots\dots \quad \dots\dots\dots$$
$$p^m = p^m(x^m) \quad q_n = q_n(v_n)$$

be the product demand functions and the supply functions for the factors. For simplicity we shall restrict ourselves to dealing with factors that are independent in supply and products that are independent in demand, but no particular difficulty is involved in writing the corresponding generalised formulae.

The total product value will now be

(15a.2) $$a = p^1 x^1 + p^2 x^2 + \dots + p^m x^m = \sum_i p^i x^i$$

and the total cost of the variable factors will be

(15a.3) $$b = q_1 v_1 + q_2 v_2 + \dots + q_n v_n = \sum_j q_j v_j.$$

The net profit, as before, will be $r = a - b$.

15b. Economic adaptation under factorially determined multi-ware production

The economic adaptation in the case (14b.9) – hence $\alpha = 0$ – can in the main be discussed in a similar way to that followed when we studied adaptation for a single ware. This is due to the fact that in the case now considered any product quantity will be a given function of the factor quantities, and consequently both the total product value a and the total cost b will be given in any factor point. We can plot contour-lines for a and b. For each of them there will be a pencil of curves (in the case of several factors a pencil of surfaces). We can endeavour to find the locus of points of tangency between the two pencils whereby we shall get a *substitumal* in the usual way. This substitumal will be defined by

(15b.1) $$\frac{a_1}{b_1} = \frac{a_2}{b_2} = \ldots = \frac{a_n}{b_n},$$

where

(15b.2) $\quad$ marginal intake $= a_k = \dfrac{\partial a}{\partial v_k} = \sum_i \dfrac{\mathrm{d}(p^i x^i)}{\mathrm{d} x^i} \cdot \dfrac{\partial x^i}{\partial v_k} = \sum_i p^i(1+\check{p}^i) x_k^i$

x_k^i being defined as in (14b.5)

(15b.3) $\quad\quad\quad$ marginal outlay $= b_k = \dfrac{\partial b}{\partial v_k} = q_k(1+\check{q}_k).$

Marginal rentability will, as before, be $r_k = a_k - b_k$.

In the case of several factorially determined products the substitumal in the factor diagram is still of dimensionality 1, but its shape may be a little more complicated than in the case of a single product. It should be noted especially that the tangency-determined substitumal may have *several branches* of which, however, as a rule only one will give the correct and relevant solution under a given set of demand and supply functions (15a.1). At times changes in the price situation obtaining for the products may cause a discontinuous leap from one branch to another (e.g. a transition involving a change of emphasis from the one product to another). Figure (15b.4), for example, gives contour-lines for the total product value a if product No. 1 in (14b.2) is the one that makes a *large* contribution to the product value. The cost lines are assumed to be straight. By determining the tangency we here get two substitumal branches (heavily drawn and shaded), but only the one to the north-west counts, under the price situation illustrated; a is, for example, greater in A than in A' (but the costs are equal) and a is greater in B than in B' (but here, too, the costs are the same), etc. If the price ratio between the products is changed in such a way that No. 2 provides the largest contribution to the total product value, the comparison between A and A', etc., may well, however, have the opposite result. The adaptation point will then jump to the south-east branch of the substitumal (at the same time as the forms of the substitumal branches are somewhat changed).

In order to discuss how the emphasis of production can shift from one product to the other, according to the price situation for the products – and also for other reasons – it will be desirable to study the adaptation also as a movement in the *product diagram*. Let us consider the case involving two products. To a given point in the (x^1, x^2)-diagram corresponds an $(n-2)$-dimensional surface in the factor diagram; the fact that both x^1 and x^2 are to have prescribed magnitudes imposes indeed two conditions on the n factors.

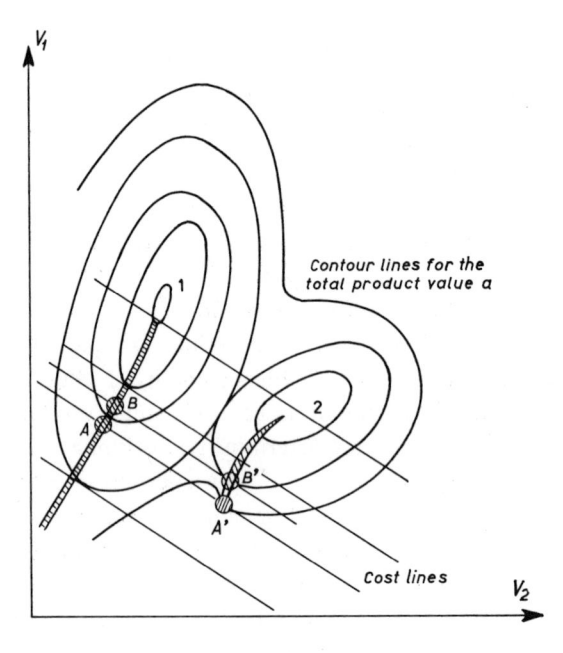

Fig. (15b.4).

We must look for the point along this $(n-2)$-dimensional surface where total costs b are least. The magnitude of total costs thus arrived at will depend on the product quantities (x^1, x^2) which we took as our starting point; in other words this total cost will be a function

(15b.5) $\qquad\qquad \hat{b}(x^1, x^2)$.

We have here supplied the functional symbol b with a 'roof' ^ to indicate that it has emerged after a preliminary adaptation (namely the cost minimalisation under given x^1 and x^2).

The variation of this cost function in the two-dimensional (x^1, x^2)-diagram can be studied. This two-dimensional variation is analogous to the variation along the one-dimensional substitumal in the case involving one single product. From this viewpoint the complete (x^1, x^2)-diagram may be looked upon as a *gross substitumal* (as distinct from the net substitumal considered in the sequel). In the case of a single product with its one-dimensional substitumal we introduced the concept of the isoclinic marginal cost b' (marginality with respect to the product). Now we shall instead have to consider the two *partial* marginal costs in the product diagram (partial marginalities with respect to the two products) defined by

$$(15b.6) \qquad b^1 = \frac{\partial \hat{b}(x^1, x^2)}{\partial x^1}, \quad b^2 = \frac{\partial \hat{b}(x^1, x^2)}{\partial x^2}$$

These two marginal costs must now be compared with the two *marginal sales*

$$(15b.7) \qquad a^1 = \frac{\partial a}{\partial x^1} = p^1(1+\check{p}^1), \quad a^2 = \frac{\partial a}{\partial x^2} = p^2(1+\check{p}^2).$$

The distinction between intake and sales and between outlay and cost is as before. Cf. (13a.3)–(13a.8).

Adaptation within the product diagram can now *formally* be undertaken in the same way as when we investigated the *tension* between the desire for total product and the aversion for total cost within the factor diagram. We can *inter alia* introduce lines for given total cost levels, we can introduce a *net substitumal* in the product diagram, that is to say a line expressing the fact that along it not only *the substitution between factors but also the substitution between products has been carried out* – this will lead to a one-dimensional curve in the two-dimensional (x^1, x^2), and finally we can undertake a movement along *this* net substitumal, thus determining the optimal *scale* for the total production process involving both (or generally all) products.

The treatment of this case of factorially determined products therefore does not in principle involve anything fundamentally new, once we have – by a cost minimalisation under each given (x^1, x^2) combination – determined the cost function (15b.5).

The fact that we have now proceeded in two stages: first varying the factors so as to obtain (15b.5) and secondly varying the combination between the products, does *not* mean that we now have a case of assortment. Indeed, the factor variation leading to (15b.5) was only $(n-2)$-dimensional, not $(n-1)$-dimensional as in the case of a single product where we minimised costs under a given product quantity. The subsequent substitution between x^1 and x^2 is now carried out only to make up for the one dimension we did not use in the cost minimalisation leading to (15b.5).

15c. Two-stage economic adaptation under one-dimensional or multi-dimensional assortment

With freedom of assortment an entirely new situation emerges in the economic adaptation process as compared to the case of no assortment. A complete adaptation has now to take place not only within the factor diagram (factor substitution), but *also* within the product diagram (product substitution). For in this case the problem will still possess a larger or smaller number of degrees of freedom, even if the factor point has been selected.

Often it will prove practical and instructive to think of the adaptation as taking place separately within each of the two diagrams (regions) – that of the factors and that of the products, making within each region a certain assumption regarding the situation obtaining in the other region.

Let us for example take the case illustrated in Figure (14c.2). If the product prices are given, we can, through the product diagram, draw a number of *cost lines*, that is to say, lines along which $a = p^1 x^1 + p^2 x^2$ is constant. These will be straight lines if the product prices are independent of the product quantities, but otherwise they will generally be curved lines. Let us assume that a certain factor combination $(v_1, ..., v_n)$ is given. Corresponding to it, we have a certain factor isoquant in (14c.2); let this be III. What is the greatest sales sum that can be obtained if we have the given factor combination $(v_1, ..., v_n)$? This is clearly determined by proceeding along III in (14c.2), until we reached the highest sales line that can be reached when we have to stick to III. If III has a continuously varying tangent direction (and provided we do not come into conflict with extra conditions such as e.g. that the product quantities must be non-negative) – then the maximum we are looking for will be determined by the point P where III is tangential to a sales line. A tangent condition of this kind will also be arrived at in the case where the sales line is curved. In other words, we now have an adjustment completely analogous to the one we obtained when we endeavoured to determine the smallest possible cost for a given product quantity in the factor diagram for single-ware production. The curve expressing the sacrifice, e.g. curve III, will in all regular cases have a curvature such that it is situated entirely on the south-west side of the curve expressing the result, i.e. the sales line.

Thus point P expresses the greatest total sale a that can result from a given factor combination $(v_1, ..., v_2)$. That is to say, we have thus defined total intake a as a function of $v_1, ..., v_2$. We denote this function

(15c.1) $$\hat{a}(v_1, ..., v_n)$$

The 'roof' ^ over the functional symbol a indicates that it has emerged after a preliminary adaptation (namely sales maximisation under given $v_1, \ldots, v_n$).

But total outlay $b = q_1 v_1 + \ldots + q_n v_n$ is also given as a function of the factor point. In other words, after a *preparatory* analysis of the kind mentioned, in which one attempts to find an adaptation separately in the product diagram, on the assumption of given factor quantities, we can also in *the case involving a one-dimensional freedom of assortment* reduce the problem to one in which a as well as b can be expressed as functions of the factor point. From this point on we can use precisely the same kind of analysis technique as the one used in 15b, where we studied the adjustment problem in the case of factorially determined multi-ware production. If we like, as a last stage in this analysis we can go back to the product diagram and express adaptation for marginal sales and marginal costs just as we did in (15b.5) and (15b.6).

We can also achieve a similar reduction in the case of m products with an arbitrary degree of assortment. As a preparatory step we shall at all times have to introduce as many substitution conditions between the products as necessary, in order to maximate total sales (total product value) under given factor quantities.

The analysis, even of highly general cases, can thus be done by means of a two-stage method similar to the one used in the case of a single product. But it can, if we like, also be carried out *directly*.

15d. Direct analysis of the economic adaptation in the general case

The adaptation in the general case, involving an arbitrary degree of assortment and an arbitrary degree of coupling, can then be discussed in the parameter form, cf. (14d.3). We now introduce:

The parametric marginal intake:

$$(15d.1) \quad a_{(K)} = \frac{\partial a}{\partial t_K} = \sum_i \frac{\partial (p^i x^i)}{\partial t_K}$$

$$= \sum_i \frac{d(p^i x^i)}{dx^i} \cdot \frac{\partial x^i}{\partial t_K} = \sum_i p^i (1 + \check{p}^i) x_{(K)}{}^i.$$

The parametric marginal outlay:

$$(15d.2) \quad b_{(K)} = \frac{\partial b}{\partial t_K} = \sum_j \frac{\partial (q_j v_j)}{\partial t_K} = \sum_j \frac{d(q_j v_j)}{dv_j} \cdot \frac{\partial v_j}{\partial t_K} = \sum_j q_j (1 + \check{q}_j) v_{j(K)},$$

where $x_{(K)}{}^i$ and $v_{j(K)}$ are defined in (14d.9) and (14d.10).

Let us consider a *parameter diagram*, that is to say, a diagram whose axes measure the parameters $t_1, \ldots, t_M$. As these are independent variables and we have now expressed everything through them, both input and output, it will be possible to discuss the adaptation in the parameter diagram in a manner entirely analogous to the one we used in investigating the adaptation in the factor diagram in the case involving a single product. We now get a set of substitumal conditions of the form

(15d.3) $$\frac{a_{(1)}}{b_{(1)}} = \frac{a_{(2)}}{b_{(2)}} = \ldots = \frac{a_{(M)}}{b_{(M)}}.$$

These represent the in-every-respect economic substitution, and they determine a one-dimensional substitumal in the parameter diagram. Corresponding to this is a one-dimensional substitumal through the product diagram $(x^1, \ldots, x^m)$ as well as a one-dimensional substitumal through the factor-diagram $(v_1, \ldots, v_n)$.

Furthermore, a correspondence is determined between the points on the three substitumals, such that a definite point on one of them is equivalent to a definite point on one of the two others.

In order to construct these substitumals, $(n-1)+(m-1)+1$ conditions are obviously required. Thus, after deducting the given production relations, we need

$$(n-1)+(m-1)+1-\mu = n+(m-\mu)-1 = M-1$$

adaptation conditions. These are precisely the conditions of (15d.3). They can be formulated without any further specification of the economic purpose one aims to realise, for the conditions in (15d.3) express an *in-every-respect economic substitution* (both among factors and among products). On the other hand, if we are to fix *a definite point* on the one-dimensional parameter substitumal, the purpose must be specified more accurately. If the purpose is the greatest possible total profit, the extra condition will be that the quantities (15d.3) not only have to be *equal*, but they must all be equal to 1. This follows quite simply from the expression for the parametric marginal rentability, viz.

(15d.4) $$r_{(K)} = a_{(K)} - b_{(K)}.$$

In a point where total profit $r = a - b$ is to be as big as possible, not only must all magnitudes $r_{(K)}$ defined in (15d.4) be equal, but even equal to zero, that is to say all magnitudes (15d.3) equal to 1.

In the parameter diagram, too, the fundamental *indifference theorem* applies saying that marginal costs db/da will be *the same* no matter in what direction it is taken, provided only that the point from which we start is substitumal, i.e. that (15d.3) is fulfilled. Thus let $dt_1, \ldots, dt_M$ be entirely arbitrary small parameter increases. Then to first order approximation

$$da = \sum_K a_{(K)} dt_K \quad \text{and} \quad db = \sum_K b_{(K)} dt_K \;;$$

that is to say, if for a moment we let λ represent the common magnitude (15d.3), we have

(15d.5) $$\frac{db}{da} = \frac{\sum_K b_{(K)} dt_K}{\sum_K \lambda b_{(K)} dt_K} = \frac{1}{\lambda}$$

independent of all the increments $dt, \ldots, dt_M$.

For the sake of simplicity we have based our analysis on multi-ware production with *continuity factors*, but it is equally possible to apply to the multi-ware production the point of view of the limitation theory which we propounded in Part Three.

PART FIVE

ELEMENTS OF A DYNAMIC THEORY OF PRODUCTION

CHAPTER 16

A SURVEY OF THE PROBLEMS OF A DYNAMIC THEORY OF PRODUCTION

In the dynamic theory of production the *time shape* of input and outtake elements is of fundamental importance. This applies to both technical and economic concepts.

As far as *technical concepts* are concerned, a number of dynamic points of view have already been mentioned in Chapter 4. A complete dynamic theory of technical production would have to contain, in addition to these points a thorough discussion, for instance, of the concept of marginal productivity as applied to the *time shapes* of the variable quantities occurring in the theory. We shall, however, not go into these technical questions, in detail, but in the main confine ourselves to what was said in Chapter 4.

Regarding the *economic concepts* we shall have something more to say, particularly regarding two important special problems: that of *depreciation* (a diminution in the value of capital as the result of use or the actual passing of time) and replacement (reinvestment), and that of *varying prices*. Both are closely bound up with certain fundamental questions of principle in the theory of accounting. They belong therefore also to the realm of *business management and administration*. We have here a particularly illustrative example of the close contact which exists on so many points between these two branches of economics: the social and the private. The problem of depreciation – and replacement – and the problem of price variation cannot be properly discussed without coordinating the points of view of both these branches of economics.

Practically all depreciation analysis will in the last resort be based on an economic factor in the form of prices or other value judgment coefficients. The point of time when a concrete capital object may be said to be 'worn out', depends practically always on an economic judgment of this kind. But there are certain aspects of the question which emerge most clearly when it is merely *assumed* that the point of time when each capital object is 'worn out', is given in some way or another, and then consider what consequences this will involve. A *quasi-technical* analysis of this kind, without formally introducing the price concept, can for instance reveal certain fundamental relationships with regard to the replacement process in a large mass of capital objects. It may be a *mixed* mass, as e.g. in the case of a nation's total capital equipment or a mass of *uniform* objects, such as e.g. telephone and telegraph poles. Large firms possessing millions of poles which are in constant need of replacement, such as e.g. The American Telephone and Telegraph Company, need exact knowledge about the regularity involved in this replacement process, and for this reason keep a constant check on it by means of actuarial calculations. The same applies to a number of other objects, such as parts of machinery, apparatus and the like.

If, on the other hand, we are to tackle the question of the most economic lifetime (the scrapping time) of a single capital object, then the analysis must be based *explicitly* on the price concept.

In the sequel we shall consider various problems relating to depreciation and the process of replacement in the various kinds of capital masses.

With regard to the problem of varying prices, we merely note that in cases when production must be planned on a long-term basis (industrial production with big, long-lived capital goods or agricultural production based on long plans for the rotation of crops, etc.) the probable *future* prices, and not the current prices, will be decisive. A full discussion of this factor would involve as deeply in a complete dynamic theory of economics. This would be very much beyond the scope of this book.

CHAPTER 17

THE REINVESTMENT PROCESS IN A MASS WHERE EACH CAPITAL OBJECT HAS A DETERMINED LIFE-TIME

17a. Reinvestment activity as a consequence of a primary investment dose where the distribution of durability is discrete

Let us suppose that at a given point of time, $t=0$, a certain reinvestment takes place, consisting in the first place of a quantity $f(1)$ of the kind of capital object that has to be renewed one year after installation, and secondly a quantity $f(2)$ of the kind of capital object which must be renewed two years after installation, etc. For the sake of brevity, we call them one-year objects, two-year objects, etc. This does not mean that at a point of time $t=0$ these objects were respectively one or two years *old*, but simply refers to the *durability* character of the objects.

The durability x may be determined both on technical and on economical grounds. We presuppose that the concepts 'Quantity of capital' or 'Amount of capital' have been defined – e.g., by means of volume indexes – so that $f(1), f(2)$, etc., can be compared and, if required, added. We shall not take durability category 0 into account, as this would involve specific mathematical difficulties, which are really extraneous to the concrete meaning of the analysis.

If a primary investment dose of this kind is injected at time $t=0$, what *reinvestments* will this occasion in future? We assume that the capital is to be *maintained fully*, and that this will be done in such a way that each capital object taken out of service is replaced by another *of precisely the same durability*. The capital objects with a one-year durability present in

TABLE (17a.1). Primary investment dose

Durability x	Capital amount $f(x)$
1	2
2	5
3	10
4	6
5	3

ELEMENTS OF A DYNAMIC THEORY OF PRODUCTION

TABLE (17a.2).

Primary investment dose (t=0)	Re-investment at following points of time: t =																														
$x = f(x) =$	1	2	3	4	5	6	7	8	9	10	11	12	13	14	15	16	17	18	19	20	21	22	23	24	25	26	27	28	29	30	
1	2	2	2	2	2	2	2	2	2	2	2	2	2	2	2	2	2	2	2	2	2	2	2	2	2	2	2	2	2	2	2
2	5		5		5		5		5		5		5		5		5		5		5		5		5		5				
3	10			10			10			10			10			10			10			10			10			10			
4	6				6				6				6				6				6				6				6		
5	3					3					3					3					3					3					3
Total	26	2	7	13	17	2	12	13	10	2	23	2	7	15	13	2	17	2	16	12	7	2	23	5	7	12	13	2	20

(diagonals labelled $k=1, k=2, k=3, k=4, k=5, k=6$)

the primary dose at $t=0$ will then appear as a reinvestment every single year in the future, the capital objects with a two-year durability will recur every other year, viz. at the points 2, 4, 6, etc. We can illustrate this by means of a numerical example. Let us assume that we have a primary investment dose as in Table (17a.1). From this we derive a reinvestment table as in Table (17a.2).

The figures on the first line of Table (17a.2) are reinvestments of capital objects lasting one year, which, of course, recur annually. The figures on the second line in Table (17a.2) are reinvestments of capital objects lasting two years. They recur every other year. And so on. The figures in the line Total at the bottom of the table give *total reinvestment in each year*. In Figure (17a.3) this total reinvestment is shown graphically by the boldly printed points connected with a broken dotted line. (The fully drawn step-curve in Figure (17a.3) is the result of a moving average which will be explained below.)

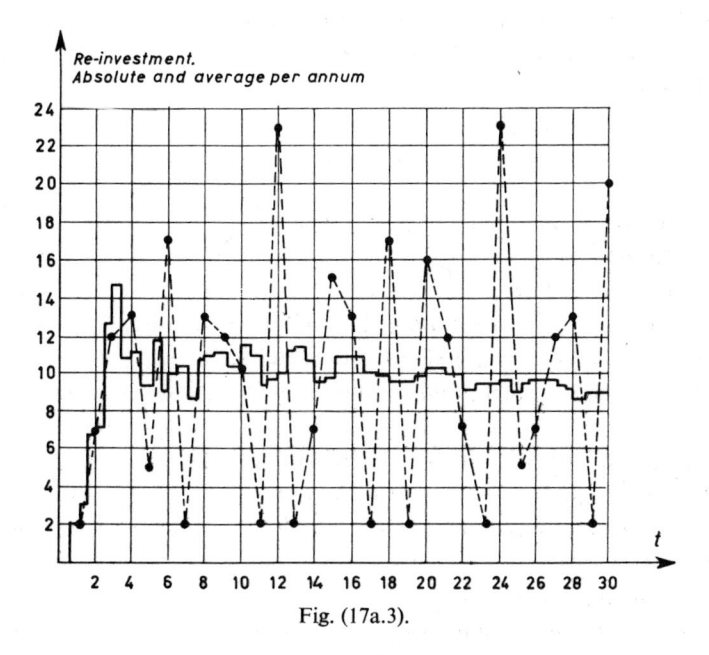

Fig. (17a.3).

Figure (17a.3) shows that total reinvestment considered as a time series is very irregular. There are violent fluctuations from one year to the next. This is, however, – especially for the more distant points on the time axis – simply due to a numerical phenomenon caused by the fact that the example is built on a discrete durability distribution in the primary investment dose. Let us, for example, consider the violent fluctuation in the points where $t=11$, $t=12$, $t=13$. This is due to the fact that $t=11$ and $t=13$ are *prime-numbers* so that here only the one-year capital objects are to be reinvested, while at $t=12$ – which is far from being a prime-number – both the one-year, the two-year, the three-year, and the four-year capital objects are to be reinvested. Similar phenomena occur all along the entire axis.

As we shall in concrete reality always be dealing with capital objects with the most varied durations, and not with durations expressed in integer years, we need not dwell on these extremely fluctuating aspects of reinvestments in the example. Instead we should consider what happens *on the average per annum*.

Let us first consider what the reinvestment will be on the average per annum when we have proceeded a good way along the time axis. Calculated *per annum*, the objects of one-year duration make a contribution to the future reinvestment of $f(1)$, the ones of two-year duration a contribution to future reinvestment of $f(2)/2$, those of three-year duration will give $f(3)/3$, etc. The sum

$$(17\text{a}.4) \qquad \bar{y} = f(1) + \frac{f(2)}{2} + \frac{f(3)}{3} + \ldots, \text{ etc.},$$

is thus the average annual reinvestment when we have proceeded a long way into the future.

If there is a certain *maximum* duration which occurs in the primary investment doses, (17a.4) will only contain a finite number of terms. (17a.4) will then give an exact expression for the future average annual investment, provided we only consider points of time situated far enough in the future for the latest terms (those for very long-duration capital objects) to be included. But even though the ordinate on the distribution curve $f(x)$ does not reach zero for finite values of x, (17a.4) may *converge*, i.e. subsequent terms will make such small contributions that they can be ignored. (17a.4) may therefore nevertheless give a sufficiently accurate expression for the future average annual reinvestment.

Let us next consider a point of time which lies closer to the point of time when the primary dose was injected (closer to $t=0$). Here we can no longer use the asymptotic expression (17a.4). In order to study this *starting* (or *transition* or *initial*) *period* we shall break total reinvestment up into components and consider separately the time series representing all first-time reinvestments, the time series representing all second-time reinvestments, etc. These components are represented by the descending oblique lines in Figure (17a.2). The oblique line $k=1$ gives all first-time reinvestments, $k=2$ gives all second-time reinvestments, and so on. In general we may speak of the kth – component of the time series.

The actual *numbers* along any oblique line whatever, are, as will be seen, the *same* as in the distribution of the primary investment, but in the following respects there is a difference: while the first-time component has an ordinate every year, the second-time component has an ordinate only every other year, the third-time component has an ordinate only every third year, and so on, that is to say generally the k-time component has an ordinate only every k^{th} year. We can express this by saying that the k-time component is all the more *porous*, the larger k is. It is this porosity that produces such violent fluctuations as those seen in Figure (17a.3).

If we are interested in studying the *average* reinvestment per annum at various points of time after the injection of the primary dose, we must in one way or another smooth the various components, so that the effect of the porosity disappears. At the same time we must ensure that everything is included, and that no double counting occurs. Graphically this is taken care of in the following rules below for rectangular presentations.

We take every ordinate in the k-time component and distribute it, apportioning $1/k$ of the ordinate to each of the k-years situated closest to the year to which the ordinate belongs. In the example in Table (17a.2) the smoothed components will then be as shown in Figure (17a.5). In the Figure only the three first components are drawn; the other components can be constructed in a similar way, i.e. by compressing each rectangle down to $1/k$ of the original height and at the same time extending its base line k times, and placing the particular rectangle in such a way that the *middle* of the base line coincides with the exact point of time where the reinvestment in question would have occurred if we had stuck to the original discrete consideration. In this way the total area will be the same before and after smoothing, and there is no undue displacement along the time axis. The average annual reinvestment will in any point of time be the sum of all these components.

Let us find an *analytical* expression for each component and for their sum at any given point of time. We let $f(x)$ indicate the ordinate of the step-function for $k=1$ in Figure (17a.5). This is the same as saying that we let the five discrete numbers 2, 5, 10, 6, 3 in the second column of Table (17a.2) be graphically represented by the rectangles for $k=1$ in Figure (17a.5). The function $f(x)$ is in this interpretation defined not only for the integer values

$x=1, 2, 3, 4, 5$, but for *any* value of x. In the interval $\frac{1}{2} \leq x < 1\frac{1}{2}$ it is equal to 2, in the interval $1\frac{1}{2} \leq x < 2$ it is 5, and so on. Outside of these intervals it is zero.

If we let $y_k(t)$ designate the value at the point of time t of the ordinate

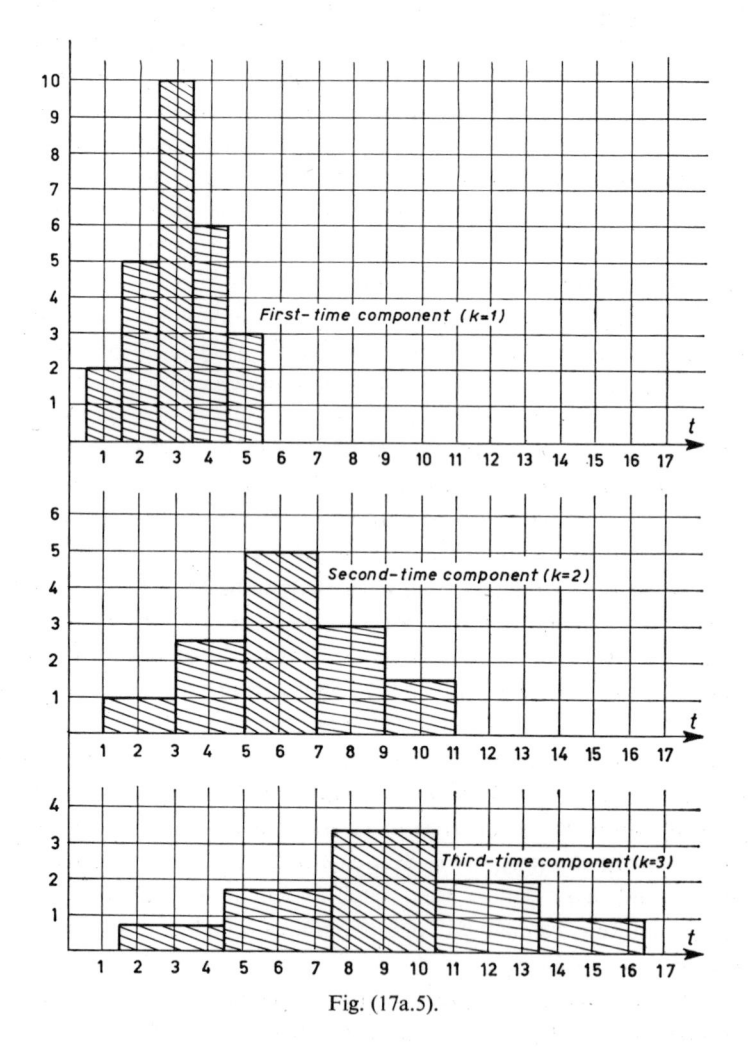

Fig. (17a.5).

of the k-time component – that is to say, defined by the kth rectangular grouping in Figure (17a.5) – we get $y_1(t) = f(t)$. From the way in which the second-time component is formed in Figure (17a.5), we see that the ordinate of this component will be $y_2(t) = \frac{1}{2} f(t/2)$. The ordinate of the third-time component will be $y_3(t) = \frac{1}{3}f(t/3)$, etc. Quite generally we have

(17a.6) $$y_k(t) = \frac{1}{k}f\left(\frac{t}{k}\right) \qquad (t>0\ ;\ k=1, 2, \ldots),$$

where the value of $f(x)$ is defined by the step-function for $k=1$ in Figure (17a.5).

We get the aggregate average reinvestment per annum at the point of time t by adding up all the components (17a.6). This gives

(17a.7) $$y(t) = \sum_{k=1}^{\infty} y_k(t) = \sum_{k=1}^{\infty} \frac{1}{k}f\left(\frac{t}{k}\right) \qquad (t>0).$$

If we apply this formula to the numerical example we have studied above, we get a curve which is plotted as a step-function in Figure (17a.3). As we see, there are still fairly marked fluctuations here – starting fluctuations – in the years immediately following the year when the primary dose was injected. Further along the time axis, however, the fluctuations are damped down. The violent fluctuations which we called the prime-number effect – and which *continued* for a number of years – have now been eliminated.

So far we have assumed that any particle of capital will be *maintained* by reinvestment for all future time. We shall now more generally reckon with a certain *probability* for the maintenance of the particles. Let P_1 be the probability for its being reinvested the first time, P_2 the probability for its also being reinvested the second time, and so on. We can assume $P_1 \geqslant P_2 \geqslant \ldots$ We call the number P_k the *maintenance percentage* for the kth reinvestment.

The kth-time component will now be, not (17a.6) but the mathematical expectation

(17a.8) $$y_k(t) = P_k \frac{f(t/k)}{k}.$$

And the expectation of the aggregate reinvestment will be:

(17a.9) $$y(t) = \sum_{k=1}^{\infty} \frac{P_k}{k} f\left(\frac{t}{k}\right).$$

17b. Reinvestment activity as a result of a primary investment dose where the durability distribution is continuous

In the foregoing subsection we saw that by taking our starting point in a discrete durability distribution in the primary investment dose and calculating the reinvestment in the years to come, we obtained pronounced fluctuations which could not be attributed to any economic reality, but were essentially due to the discrete character of the numerical example, and the assumption that all investment elements are maintained uncurtailed an unlimited number of times. We then undertook a smoothing by calculating what happened on *an average* per annum, by interpreting the function $f(x)$ in a step-function. This did achieve some smoothing, as seen from Figure (17a.3). However, a few small indentations remain. These are due to the fact that we used a step-function, i.e. one representing rectangles. The rectangles contain an element of discontinuity which shows up in the indentations of the smoothed curve in Figure (17a.3).

Let us now see what the reinvestment will be per time unit at the various time points, if we assume that the durability distribution is *continuous*. We express this by assuming that there is a given continuous function $f(x)$ such that in the primary investment dose there is an amount $f(x)dx$ of capital goods with a duration between x and $x+dx$. Furthermore, as above, we designate the kth-time component $y_k(t)$, so that $y_k(t)dt$ is the part of the reinvestment activity in the time interval from t to $t+dt$ which is a k-time reinvestment.

Let us put $t+dt=t'$. The amount of capital to be reinvested for the kth-time in the time interval between t and t' is then clearly equal to the amount of capital in the primary investment dose which had a duration between t/k and t'/k. As the difference between t and t' is infinitesimal this amount can be expressed as

$$f\left(\frac{t}{k}\right) \cdot \left(\frac{t'}{k} - \frac{t}{k}\right) = \frac{1}{k} f\left(\frac{t}{k}\right) \cdot (t'-t) = \frac{1}{k} f\left(\frac{t}{k}\right) dt.$$

According to the definition of $y_k(t)$ this amount must at the same time be equal to $y_k(t)dt$, that is to say, we get

$$y_k(t) dt = \frac{1}{k} f\left(\frac{t}{k}\right) dt,$$

In other words:

$$y_k(t) = \frac{1}{k} f\left(\frac{t}{k}\right) \qquad (t>0\ ;\ k=1, 2, \ldots).$$

This is formally the same expression as the one we got in the preceding subsection by smoothing the discrete example; cf. (17a.6). Aggregate reinvestment will consequently also now be given by (17a.7).

Figure (17b.1) gives a graphic representation of the components and the aggregate reinvestment in a case when we have a continuous durability distribution in the primary investment dose.

Graphically speaking the components can now, as in Figure (17a.5), be described as follows: The first component, that is to say y_1, is simply the durability distribution curve in the primary dose, the argument of the function now being interpreted as the *time-variable* proceeding beyond $t=0$, instead of as the durability-variable in the distribution curve for the primary dose at $t=0$. If the durability distribution curve is unimodal, we get a component such as y_1 in the upper portion of Figure (17b.1). The second component, that is to say y_2, emerges from the durability distribution curve by doubling the abscissae and at the same time reducing the ordinate to half. This gives the curve y_2 in the upper portion of Figure (17b.1). Corresponding-

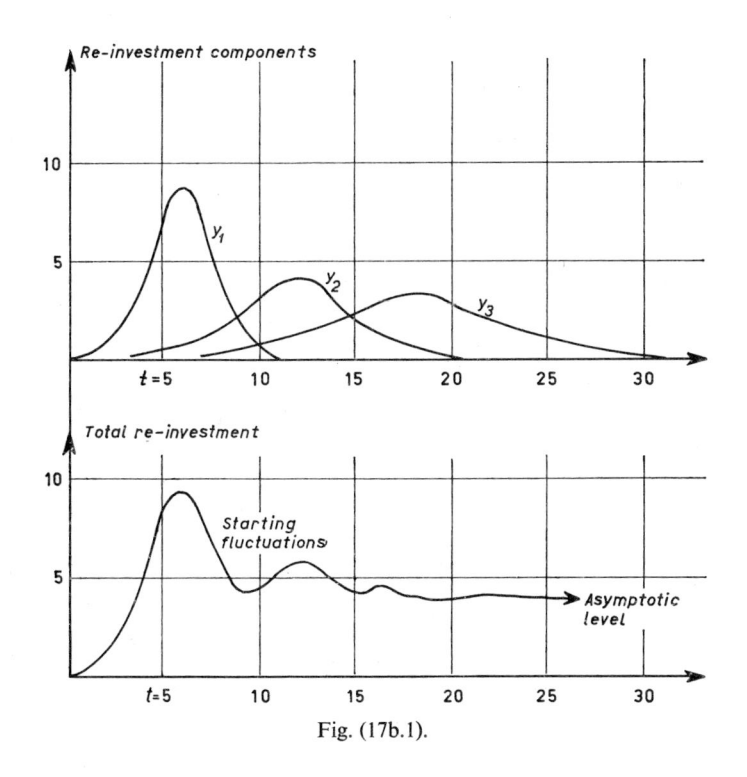

Fig. (17b.1).

ly for y_3, and so on. If the primary dose has a clearly unimodal shape, y_1 will cause a *peak* in the total reinvestment curve. The component y_2 will also produce a peak but a weaker one, and so on. Altogether we shall get a curve of the shape suggested in the lower portion of Figure (17b.1).

After these *initial fluctuations* the curve approaches a constant *asymptotic level*, which in the continuous case is given by

(17b.2) $$\bar{y} = \int_0^\infty \frac{1}{x} f(x) \, dx.$$

Provided this integral in (17b.2) converges, $y(t)$ will approach the constant asymptotic level given by this integral.

As we see, formula (17b.2) is analogous to (17a.4) for the discrete case.

The proof of (17b.2) can be given as follows: Let us define the figures δ and x_k by

(17b.3) $$t = \frac{1}{\delta} \quad \text{and} \quad x_k = k\delta = \frac{k}{t} \qquad (k=1, 2, \ldots, \infty).$$

Then

$$x_{k+1} - x_k = \frac{k+1}{t} - \frac{k}{t} = \frac{1}{t} \qquad (k=1, 2, \ldots, \infty).$$

If we substitute this in the expression to the right in (17a.7) we shall get

(17b.4) $$y(t) = \sum_{k=1}^\infty \frac{1}{k\delta} f\left(\frac{1}{k\delta}\right) \delta = \sum_{k=1}^\infty \left[\frac{1}{x_k} \cdot f\left(\frac{1}{x_k}\right)\right] (x_{k+1} - x_k).$$

When here $t \to \infty$, then $\delta = 1/t = (x_{k+1} - x_k) \to 0$. According to the definition of the integral term, the sum to the right above will then tend to the integral

(17b.5) $$\int_0^\infty \frac{1}{x} f\left(\frac{1}{x}\right) dx$$

By replacing the variable of integration x in (17b.5) by $x = 1/\xi$ and afterwards writing x instead of ξ we get (17b.2).

If we drop the assumption of complete maintenance of all capital objects, and instead assume a maintenance percentage P_k, we get also in the continuous case formulae exactly similar to (17a.8–9).

17c. Reinvestment when new primary investment doses are injected at various points of time

We have so far considered the result of a single primary investment dose. Let us now see what the result will be if the *primary* investment varies with time in a certain way. Let us first consider the discrete case. Let $F(x, T)$ be the amount of x-durable capital which is injected as a primary investment at the point of time T ($x = 1, 2, 3, \ldots; T = 0, 1, 2, \ldots$).

For every value of T we can use the same reasoning as in Section 17a, that is to say we can find how great average annual reinvestment will be caused by the primary investment injected at T. A subsequent summation over T will then give the total reinvestment.

Let as before $y_k(t)$ be the amount of kth-time reinvestment that takes place in the year t. Previously this reinvestment was only due to a primary investment at the point of time $t=0$; it will now be supplemented by various primary investment doses, viz.: In the *first* place from the $1/k$-annuals which were primary investments at $t-1$ (they recur for the kth time at the point of time t). The amount of these capital objects was $F(1/k, t-1)$. At the kth reinvestment this ordinate must be reduced to $1/k$ in order to give figures reckoned per annum. Thus the first contribution to $y_k(t)$ – if everything is to be maintained – is

$$\frac{1}{k} F\left(\frac{1}{k}, t-1\right).$$

In the *second* place there is a contribution from the primary investment at $t-2$, viz. from the $2/k$ annuals (they are reinvested for the kth time at the point of time t). Reduced to terms of reinvestment per annum this is

$$\frac{1}{k} F\left(\frac{2}{k}, t-2\right).$$

There are corresponding contributions from the point of time $t-3$, and so on. All in all we therefore get

(17c.1) $$y_k(t) = \frac{1}{k} \sum_{s=1}^{\infty} F\left(\frac{s}{k}, t-s\right) = \frac{1}{k} \sum_{T=-\infty}^{t-1} F\left(\frac{t-T}{k}, T\right).$$

If, as a special case, primary investment is zero except for $T=0$, viz.

(17c.2) $$F(x, T) = 0 \quad \text{except for} \quad T=0,$$

(17c.1) will reduce to (17a.6); for in this case in the summation (17c.1) there is only one term left, namely for $s=t$, that is to say, for $T=0$.

The aggregate reinvestment at the point of time t, taking into consideration the maintenance percentages, will then be

(17c.3) $$Y(t) = y_1(t) + y_2(t) + \ldots = \sum_{k=1}^{\infty} \frac{P_k}{k} \sum_{s=1}^{\infty} F\left(\frac{s}{k}, t-s\right).$$

This is a general formula which shows the composition of the aggregate reinvestment in the discrete case. It can be applied to a varying primary investment, to an arbitrary durability distribution of each single primary investment dose, and for an arbitrary maintenance percentage curve P_k.

In the special case where durability distribution in the primary investment doses is constant over the time, i.e. when all primary investment doses have the *same* relative durability distribution, the primary investment at the point of time T with duration x may be written in the form

(17c.4) $$F(x, T) = f(x) \cdot h(T),$$

where $f(x)$ is the durability distribution curve (assumed constant) and $h(T)$ the size of the primary investment dose at T (including all durability categories).

In the partition (17c.4) an arbitrary constant factor can be transferred from f to h or vice versa. This means that $f(x)$ can be normalized in a conventional way, for instance in such a way that

(17c.5) $$\sum_{x=1}^{\infty} f(x) = 1.$$

Inserting (17c.4) into (17c.3) we then immediately get

(17c.6) $$Y(t) = \sum_{s=1}^{\infty} y(s) \cdot h(t-s) = \sum_{T=-\infty}^{t-1} y(t-T) \cdot h(T),$$

where $y(t)$ is the same as in (17a.9), that is to say, the future time-curve for total investment which would result if we undertook a *one-time* primary investment with the given durability-distribution $f(x)$.

(17c.6) expresses a process – a *linear accumulation* – which in its form is very general and which is often encountered in other fields, too, of the dynamic theory; the time-function h is a *replenishment function* (a stimulant) which brings new elements into the system (adding 'energy'), y is an *absorption function* (a weight system) which expresses *how* the added elements are accumulated. And Y is the *resultant*.

The x-durable capital objects are those that will vanish when they have remained x years in the mass. The total mass of such objects which are of x-durability and were primarily invested at T is $F(x, T)$. How much of this amount – or of its corresponding reinvestments – will *still be left* at the subsequent arbitrary point of time t? From and including $t = T$ and to, but not including, $t = T + x$, this amount is constant, and equal to $F(x, T)$. And generally: at any point of time $t \geq T$ it is equal to

(17c.7) $$P_{\text{int}(t-T)/x} \cdot F(x, T),$$

where the symbol 'int' means 'the greatest integer which is contained in' and P_0 is conventionally put equal to 1. Indeed, if k is a given non-negative integer and t runs from and including $T+kx$ and to, but not including, $T+(k+1)x$, then clearly the amount of x-durable goods which were primarily invested at T and are present at a given t in the interval considered, will be equal to $P_k \cdot F(x, T)$, that is to say, equal to (17c.7).

The total amount of x-durable capital objects present at any given point of time t – no matter when they were primarily invested – is consequently

(17c.8) $$K(x, t) = \sum_T P_{\text{int}(t-T)/x} \cdot F(x, T) \qquad (T \leqslant t, 0 < x),$$

where the summation T is extended to all the points of time *prior to t*, where primary investment took place, cf. the analogy with (17c.1), which was, however, a formula that only expressed annual reinvestment.

The *total* capital mass – irrespective of durability – which is present at any given point of time t is by (17c.8)

(17c.9) $$K(t) = \sum_{x=1}^{\infty} \sum_T P_{\text{int}(t-T)/x} \cdot F(x, T) \qquad (T < t).$$

If all first-time primary invested elements are maintained all the way through, factor P in (17c.8) and (17c.9) merely has to be replaced by 1.

Formula (17c.3) may be interpreted as telling us what the average aggregate *annual reinvestment* will be when the initial situation is not given in the form of a certain amount of new capital objects primarily invested at a given moment, but in the form of a known *evolution* of primary investments in the past. This is the same as assuming that we start with a certain collection of capital objects which need not consist only of zero-age objects. Formula (17c.8–9) tells us – under the same assumptions – what the total *capital mass* and its *durability* distribution will be at a subsequent arbitrary point of time.

If we have a set-up involving *continuous* distribution of primary investments both according to durability and time of injection, that is to say, if $F(x, T)$ is a function such that $F(x, T) \, dx \, dT$ is the total amount of primary investment in the interval of time from T to $T+dT$, which has a durability between x and $x+dx$, then instead of (17c.1) we will get

(17c.10) $$y_k(t) = \frac{1}{k} \int_{s=0}^{\infty} F\left(\frac{s}{k}, t-s\right) ds$$

$$= \int_{s=0}^{\infty} F(s, t-ks) \, ds = \frac{1}{k} \int_{T=-\infty}^{t} F\left(\frac{t-T}{k}, T\right) dT$$

and instead of (17c.3)

(17c.11) $$Y(t) = \sum_{k=1}^{\infty} \frac{P_k}{k} \int_{s=0}^{\infty} F\left(\frac{s}{k}, t-s\right) ds = \sum_{k=1}^{\infty} P_k \int_{s=0}^{\infty} F(s, t-ks) ds$$
$$= \sum_{k=1}^{\infty} \frac{P_k}{k} \int_{T=-\infty}^{t} F\left(\frac{t-T}{k}, T\right) dT.$$

CHAPTER 18

THE REINVESTMENT PROCESS IN A MASS WHERE THERE IS A PROBABILITY LAW FOR THE LIFETIME OF EACH CAPITAL OBJECT

18a. Departure gauges

In a mass of uniform capital objects such as e.g. telegraph poles, or a specific kind of machine component (cf. the examples given in Chapter 16) it will as a rule be possible to draw up on the basis of statistics a *mortality curve (retirement curve)* for such objects. It would then be plausible to assume that *every new unit* which is added to the mass is subjected to a probability distribution of this kind as long as it is in existence. We assume that it is the *same* curve for all units. This assumption that the durability is subject to a probability law is in *one* way more general than the assumption that the life-time for each object is a *given* number (determined by the durability of the old object which the new one is to replace). But on the other hand, we now make the more restrictive assumption that all units are *alike*. Thus we do not now have a possibility of distinguishing between *different typical sorts* of objects as we had in Chapter 17. For this reason the analytical schema we are now considering cannot be used for studying the movement in a very complex mass of capital objects (e.g. that of a country); but it provides a useful point of departure for discussing the movement in a fairly uniform mass of capital objects. If a mass with a few different types of object is involved, it is of great assistance to undertake an analysis *separately* for each part of the total mass. Analyses of this kind are of considerable interest from the point of view of *business management*.

We shall express the retirement conditions in our mass of uniform capital objects by the same symbols as those we use to describe the *mortality situation* in a human population.[1] Let l_x be the number of objects still existing in the mass (i.e., alive) x years after entry (birth); l_x can be expressed in relation to a conventional size of the initial mass (batch born at a given

---

[1] For a precise interpretation, on the lines of probability theory, of such concepts, see for instance Erling Sverdrup: 'Basic concepts in life assurance mathematics' *Skandinavisk Aktuarietidsskrift* 1952.

date), e.g. $l_0 = 100\,000$. For our purpose it is most practicable to let l_x be expressed *per unit*, i.e. to put $l_0 = 1$. The number of objects from this mass (batch) retiring (dying) in the xth year of age, that is to say between the ages of x and $x+1$, is denoted

(18a.1) $$d_x = l_x - l_{x+1} = \text{departure effect.}$$

When $l_0 = 1$, (18a.1) expresses the departure in the year x calculated in relation to the initial mass (the original batch). We can, however, also express it in relation to the mass present at the beginning of the year of departure, which gives

(18a.2) $$q_x = \frac{d_x}{l_x} = \frac{l_x - l_{x+1}}{l_x} = \text{departure probability.}$$

We call (18a.1) the departure *effect* in order to emphasise that figure d_x is reckoned in relation to what in a way is the *cause* of the whole process, viz. the existence of the initial mass (the original batch). And we call (18a.2) the departure *probability* in order to emphasise that q_x expresses the chance existing at any point of time for the departure of a capital object of age x.

The complementary probability to (18a.2), viz.

(18a.3) $$p_x = 1 - q_x = \frac{l_{x+1}}{l_x} = \text{probability of non-departure (persistence probability)}$$

expresses the chance of an object of age x which is present at the beginning of the year also being present at the end of the year.

Generally speaking there will be a certain maximum age ω beyond which we can assume that no object can continue to function (live). That is to say

(18a.4) $\quad l_x = 0$ for $x > \omega \quad$ and consequently $\quad d_x = 0$ for $x > \omega$.

For the sum of the d's we have

(18a.5) $$d_0 + d_1 + \ldots + d_\omega = l_0 = 1.$$

18b. Maintenance equation and calculation of maintenance investment as a time series

Let z_t be the total accretion (addition) of new objects in the year t, that is to say, in the year running from t to $t+1$. We assume that this accretion occurs at the beginning of the year. z_t can thus be conceived as an accretion taking place exactly at the point of time t. Let us assume that at the points of time $T, T+1, ..., t$, accretions $z_T, z_{T+1}, ..., z_t$ have occurred. What *departure effect* will this produce in the immediately following year, that is to say, the year extending from t to $t+1$? The accretion z_t will obviously produce departure effect $d_0 z_t$ in the year between t and $t+1$; z_{t-1} will cause $d_1 z_{t-1}$; z_{t-2} will cause $d_2 z_{t-2}$, and so on. If the *new* accretion, that is to say, z_{t+1}, which occurs at the beginning of year $t+1$, is to neutralise exactly the departure effect in the year that has just elapsed, i.e. in the year t, it must be equal to

(18b.1) $\qquad z_{t+1} = d_0 z_t + d_1 z_{t-1} + d_2 z_{t-2} + ... + d_{t-T} z_T \qquad$ (for $t \geq T$).

This is a fundamental equation for all the following analysis. We call it the *maintenance equation*. That it is fulfilled for every $t \geq T$, is the necessary and sufficient condition for a capital mass *produced* by the investment series z_T to be able to *subsist* from year to year at a constant size; that is to say, that it is to the necessary and sufficient condition for the mass to be *stationary* (apart from the small irregularities which might occur if departure was spread over the year while accretion took place only *once* a year).

We can also deduce (18b.1) in another way. Let K_t be the *capital stock* existing at the beginning of year t, that is to say, at the point of time t. It consists of objects that have been invested at various points of time. First there are a number of objects which have been invested at precisely the moment t. The amount of them is z_t, or to express it more explicitly, it is $l_0 z_t$ (as $l_0 = 1$). Secondly it consists of some objects that were introduced a year previously. The amount of these was z_{t-1} and of these $l_1 z_{t-1}$ are left at the point of time t, etc. Thus all in all the capital stock at t, when no accretion occurred before T, is equal to

(18b.2) $\qquad K_t = l_0 z_t + l_1 z_{t-1} + l_2 z_{t-2} + ... + l_{t-T} z_T \qquad (t \geq T)$.

The *increase* in this stock from t to $t+1$ is
$K_{t+1} - K_t = (l_0 z_{t+1} + l_1 z_t + ... + l_{t-T+1} z_T) - (l_0 z_t + l_1 z_{t-1} + ... + l_{t-T} z_T)$.
If we rearrange the terms we get

(18b.3) $\qquad K_{t+1} - K_t = z_{t+1} - (d_0 z_t + d_1 z_{t-1} + ... + d_{t-T} z_T)$.

The condition under which this increase in the capital stock is equal to zero leads immediately to (18b.1).

If in (18b.1) the subscript on the last term d is equal to or greater than ω, then $t = T + \omega$, and the summation will automatically be interrupted, so that we get

(18b.4) $\quad z_{t+1} = d_0 z_t + d_1 z_{t-1} + \ldots + d_\omega z_{t-\omega} \quad$ (for $t \geq T+\omega$),

where T is the earliest moment when investment took place.

In (18b.4) the number of terms on the righthand side is constant, *that is to say independent* of t. And the coefficients d are also independent of t. For any point of time t which lies *at or after* $T+\omega$ the right side of the maintenance equation (18b.4) is thus simply a *moving average* of the z-series. The d weights are non-negative, and the sum of the weights is 1, according to (18a.5).

As soon as we have passed the initial period, the investment needed to keep the capital mass unchanged will thus be given by a time series which *builds itself up forwards* merely by virtue of the fact that the *next* ordinate is the average of the preceding ones. The weights in this moving average are the departure effects d_x.

During the initial period, on the other hand, we must use the maintenance equation in its *complete (unabbreviated)* form (18b.1). In this latter form a new term is added every year. We can write this more explicitly as follows:

(18b.5)
$$\begin{aligned}&\text{First year} \quad : \; z_{T+1} = d_0 z_T, \\ &\text{Second year}: \; z_{T+2} = d_0 z_{T+1} + d_1 z_T, \\ &\text{Third year} \quad : \; z_{T+3} = d_0 z_{T+2} + d_1 z_{T+1} + d_2 z_T, \\ &\qquad \text{etc.}\end{aligned}$$

Using (18b.5) – which is merely another method of writing (18b.1) – the investment series required to maintain the capital stock unchanged can *be calculated step by step*, from the point of time $T+1$, provided merely that the departure effect curve d_x is given (or the departure probability curve q_x is given, from which d_x can easily be calculated).

If we continue the calculation by (18b.5) after the lapse of the initiation period it will *automatically* change into the calculation of a moving average, that is to say a summation with a *constant* number of terms, as given in (18b.4). The time curve z_t, which from and including the point of time $T+1$ is calculated in this way, – first by (18b.5) and subsequently by (18b.4) – we call the *maintenance investment*.

18c. Breaking maintenance investment down into its component parts

Not all the terms in (18b.1), or – which is the same thing – (18b.5) will be of equally great importance. Let us assume, for example, that the first d's are nearly equal to zero. In practice they will often be; for as a rule there is little probability of *newly installed* objects requiring to be replaced during the first few years. The first maintenance investments z_{T+1}, z_{T+2}, etc., will therefore be almost equal to zero, according to (18b.5). But this being so the maintenance investments situated a *little* further out will mostly be influenced by the *last term* $d_{t-T}z_T$ in (18b.5); for the terms just preceding the last one will be small, owing to the fact that z_{T+1}, z_{T+2}, etc., are small, and the terms at the beginning of the expression will be small, because d_0, d_1, etc., are small. The initial investment z_T may naturally remain large, even though z_{T+1}, z_{T+2}, etc., are small. In a sense we may consider z_T as a *primary* investment and the subsequent values of z as *re*investment.

During the initial period after T the departure from the *original* stock, i.e. $d_{t-T}z_T$, will practically speaking alone determine how much we have to invest every year in order to compensate for the departure. Thus, apart from the multiplicative constant z_T, the time series for the necessary investment will – in the period immediately following T – be the same as the given series for departure effect d_x. In other words we now get approximately $z_{t+1} = d_{t-T}z_T$.

Thus during this period the picture presented is a very clear one; we are now for the time being free from the complications which subsequently arise because the capital objects first installed in order to compensate for departure, will themselves begin to deteriorate and must be replaced. Because of these complications the other terms in (18b.1) will gradually become significant.

Even when this time comes, however, it would appear to be an advantage to consider separately *that* portion of the maintenance investment which is due to the departure from the original mass. This in turn makes it appropriate that we should also consider separately *that* part which is due to the departure from those objects which we *first* dealt with separately, and so forth. The result of this is that we shall split the combined maintenance investment into *generations*. The *first* generation consists of those renewals which have been made necessary because the original stock z_T loses some of its units, the *second* generation consists of those renewals which are necessary because the first generation gradually loses some of *its* units, and so forth.

It is easy to indicate what these *generation-components* $z_{1,t}$, $z_{2,t}$, etc., will be. In the first place it is clear that $z_{1,t}$ is zero for $t=T$, and does not commence to acquire effective ordinates until at the very earliest at $t=T+1$, as it has to replace some of what disappears between T and $T+1$. Since $z_{1,t}$ does not start until $t=T+1$, its first units will themselves depart between $T+1$ and $T+2$, and consequently $z_{2,t}$ cannot obtain effective ordinates until at the very earliest at $T+2$, and so on. In other words[1]

(18c.1) $\quad z_{k,t}=0 \quad$ for $\quad t<T+k, \quad$ that is to say for $\quad k>t-T$.

In building up the formulae for generation-components it is however most convenient to include all terms prior to $t>T$, with the understanding that some of them may be equal to zero in accordance with (18c.1).

The first-generation-component, that is to say, the departure from the initial mass z_T, will, in view of what has just been said, simply be equal to

(18c.2) $\quad\quad\quad\quad\quad\quad z_{1,t+1}=d_{t-T}z_T \quad\quad\quad\quad$ (for $t \geqslant T$).

Of these first-generation objects, the following disappear during year t (that is to say, between t and $t+1$): $d_0 z_{1,t}$ of those that were introduced at the beginning of the year, $d_1 z_{1,t-1}$ of those that were introduced at the beginning of the previous year, and so on. In other words, the second-generation-component will be

(18c.3) $\quad\quad z_{2,t+1}=d_0 z_{1,t}+d_1 z_{1,t-1}+\ldots+d_{t-T}z_{1,T} \quad$ (for $t \geqslant T$)

and generally

(18c.4) $\quad z_{k+1,t+1}=d_0 z_{k,t}+d_1 z_{k,t-1}+\ldots+d_{t-T}z_{k,T} \quad$ (for $t \geqslant T, k \geqslant 1$).

Let us add up all the equations (18c.2–4). In so doing we note that for $t>T$ (but not for $t=T$) the total investment is the sum of the component investment components that is to say

(18c.5) $\quad z_t = z_{1,t}+z_{2,t}+\ldots$ ad infinitum $\quad$ (for $t>T$, but not for $t=T$).

In the case of discrete summation (which we have used) (18c.5) will for a fixed value of t, owing to (18c.1), only contain a finite number of terms, and the sum will therefore certainly converge. For $t=T$ definition (18c.5) will not apply; i.e. the sum $z_{1,T}+z_{2,T}+\ldots$ does not indicate the given amount z_T. The sum in (18c.5) for $t=T$ contains according to (18c.1) only zero terms. Therefore the addition of all equations (18c.2–4) gives

(18c.6) $\quad z_{1,t+1}+z_{2,t+1}+\ldots = d_{t-T}z_T+d_0(z_{1,t}+z_{2,t}+\ldots)$
$\quad\quad\quad\quad\quad\quad\quad\quad\quad\quad\quad + d_1(z_{1,t-1}+z_{2,t-1}+\ldots)+\ldots$
$\quad\quad\quad\quad\quad\quad\quad\quad\quad\quad\quad + d_{t-T-1}(z_{1,T+1}+z_{2,T+1}+\ldots)+d_{t-T}\cdot 0$.

If this equation is rearranged we shall get back to (18b.1). This provides a check that our component break down is correct.

---

[1] If we imagine that departure takes place *continuously* and commences *immediately* we shall not accept any limitation such as (18c.1).

(18c.4) clearly expresses how the generation-components are built up: each of them is formed simply by taking the *product sum* of the preceding component and the d-row. As from and including the point of time $t = T + \omega$ this product addition – in accordance with (18b.4) – will automatically be reduced to a moving average, viz.

(18c.7) $\quad z_{k+1,t+1} = d_0 z_{k,t} + d_1 z_{k,t-1} + \ldots + d_\omega z_{k,t-\omega} \quad$ (for $t \geq T+\omega$).

When we operate with discrete observations, the work will be simplified as a result of the fact that a larger and larger part of the terms will vanish for the higher components on account of (18c.1).

Graphically the generation components and their summation for the total investment curve will be represented as in Figure (17b.1), but the *reason* why the successive components gradually become flatter and flatter is now a different one. The flattening-out is now due to the fact that each component – as soon as we have proceeded beyond the initial period – is a moving average of the preceding one. Cf. (18c.7).

Moreover, this circumstance also explains why the successive components gradually become more and more *regularly bell-shaped*. In probability theory it is shown that a repeated process of this kind of moving averages finally leads to the normal (Gaussian) distribution curve, almost irrespective of whatever distribution one starts with. The student should set out graphically a few simple examples and verify this.

The structure of the maintenance is in an illuminating way revealed by drawing these generation components. In practice one should always begin by constructing at any rate the first of them. In many cases it may be practical to carry out an analytical smoothing of the d-curve, that is to say introduce a known mathematical function for it. If, for example, one uses exponential functions, the formulae for the generation-components can be explicitly deduced. This gives, in effect, an approach which to a large extent recalls analytical smoothing of mortality tables and insurance calculations.

The case which involves starting with a capital mass consisting not only of new objects (as in z_T) but of objects with a certain age distribution, can largely be reduced to the above. Let $K_{x,T}$ be the given initial capital distribution, i.e. $K_{x,T}$ is the number of x-year-old capital objects present at T. How can this mass have arisen? If the departure effects d_x, and consequently also the numbers l_x, are known, we can immediately calculate from $K_{x,T}$ what the investment must have been at $T-x$. It must obviously have been z_{T-x}, determined by

(18c.8) $\quad\quad\quad\quad K_{x,T} = l_x z_{T-x}$

For $x=0, \ldots, \omega$ this gives a determination of the investment curve backwards to the point of time $S=T-\omega$. When these investment figures are given, (18b.1) and (18b.4) can be used to determine the maintenance investment forwards in time from T on. We now only have to calculate with a whole row of known initial magnitudes z instead of a single one. The breakdown into generation-components can also be carried out practically as before. The difference is only that the first generation will now be

(18c.9) $\qquad z_{1,t+1} = d_{t-T} z_T + d_{t-T+1} z_{T-1} + \ldots + d_{t-T+\omega} z_{T-\omega}$ (for $t \geqslant T$)

instead of (18c.2).

18d. The segment method

The course of the maintenance process, during the initial period from T on can also be studied by splitting the course of time up into *segments*, i.e. by looking first at the time from $(T+1)$ to $T+\omega+1$, then at the time from $T+\omega+2$ to $T+2(\omega+1)$, etc. In the first segment we can use (18b.1), but not (18b.4). If we do this, z will be calculated up to and including $T+\omega+1$, and these values can then be taken as *data* for calculating the next segment with the aid of (18b.4), and so on.[1]

This method is justified when the d-row is given by an analytical expression, which is such that (18b.1) can be summed up in explicit form. This is, for example, the case with a *rectangular* distribution, i.e. all the d's are equal, that is to say $d_0 = d_1 \ldots = d_\omega$ equal to a common number d (which on account of (18a.5) must be equal to $1/(\omega+1)$), and otherwise $d_x = 0$. (This corresponds to the much-used depreciation rule that the value of a newly acquired capital sum ought to be divided up into equally large annual amounts over a given period.) In this case (18b.5) gives

$$z_{T+1} = d z_T \qquad z_{T+2} = d(z_T + z_{T+1}) = d(1+d) z_T ,$$
$$z_{T+3} = d(z_T + z_{T+1} + z_{T+2}) = d[1 + d + d(1+d)] z_T = d(1+d)^2 z_T$$

and generally

$$z_{T+n} = d(1+d)^{n-1} z_T .$$

This applies as long as we remain within the first segment, that is to say,

---

[1] This method is used *inter alia* by Harald Schulthess, *Mitth. d. Vereinigung Schweizerischer Versicherungsmathematiker* 1937, see especially p. 75, and by Gabriel Preinreich, *Econometrica*, July 1938, especially p. 223, and *The Present Status of Renewal Theory*, Baltimore, 1940, especially pp. 17–21.

THE REINVESTMENT PROCESS

for $n \leqslant \omega+1$. If we let $_1z_t$ denote the total maintenance investment in this first time-segment, we consequently get

(18d.1) $\qquad _1z_t = d(1+d)^{t-(T+1)} z_T \quad$ (for $\quad T+1 \leqslant t \leqslant T+\omega+1$).

Thus in the first segment the maintenance investment now increases in the same way as a capital sum with an interest rate of $d = 1/(\omega+1)$.

The exponential expression (18d.1) can of course be calculated for any magnitude of t, but outside the first segment it will *not* give the magnitude of the maintenance investment. The method we used to deduce (18d.1) will in fact be invalid outside the first segment, because there we shall have to use some of the d_x-magnitudes which are not equal to the common number d, but are equal to 0.

In the first point of time in the second segment, that is to say for the point of time $T+\omega+2$, the maintenance investment according to (18b.4) will be equal to

$$z_{T+\omega+2} = d(z_{T+1} + z_{T+2} + \ldots + z_{T+\omega+1}).$$

All magnitudes on the right side are here given by (18d.1), consequently we get

$$z_{T+\omega+2} = d^2[(1+d)^0 + (1+d)^1 + \ldots + (1+d)^\omega]z_T$$
$$= d[(1+d)^{\omega+1} - 1]z_T.$$

At the next point of time we get

$$z_{T+\omega+3} = d(z_{T+2} + z_{T+3} + \ldots + z_{T+\omega+2}).$$

All magnitudes are here given by (18d.1), except for the last, and that one we have just determined. That is to say, we get

$$z_{T+\omega+3} = d^2[(1+d)^1 + (1+d)^2 + \ldots + (1+d)^{\omega+1} - 1]z_T$$
$$= d[(1+d)^{\omega+2} - (1+2d)]z_T.$$

At the subsequent point we similarly get

$$z_{T+\omega+4} = d(z_{T+3} + z_{T+4} + \ldots + z_{T+\omega+3})$$
$$= d^2[(1+d)^2 + (1+d)^3 + \ldots + (1+d)^{\omega+2} - (1+1+2d)]z_T$$
$$= d(1+d)[(1+d)^{\omega+2} - (1+3d)]z_T.$$

And furthermore

$$z_{T+\omega+5} = d^2\{(1+d)^3 + (1+d)^4 + \ldots + (1+d)^{\omega+3}$$
$$- [1 + 1 + 2d + (1+d)(1+3d)]\}z_T.$$

318   ELEMENTS OF A DYNAMIC THEORY OF PRODUCTION

The subtraction term inside the square brackets can be reduced to $3(1+d)^2$, so that we get

$$z_{T+\omega+5}=d(1+d)^2[(1+d)^{\omega+2}-(1+4d)]z_T.$$

The general rule is now clear: everywhere in the second segment we have

(18d.2) $z_{T+(\omega+1)+n}=d(1+d)^{n-2}[(1+d)^{\omega+2}-(1+nd)]z_T$

with $n=1, 2 \ldots (\omega+1)$. If we denote the arbitrary point of time by $t(=T+(\omega+1)+n)$, we thus get inside the second segment

(18d.3) $_2z_t=d(1+d)^{t-(T+1)}z_T-d[1+(t-T-\omega-1)d](1+d)^{t-T-\omega-3}z_T$

(for $T+\omega+2 \leqslant t \leqslant T+2(\omega+1)$).

We can continue in this way for the third segment, too, and so on. For later segments the formulae prove somewhat unwieldy, but it is particularly for the first segments that this method is of interest.

In all cases where the departure effect curve d_x terminates or commences *steeply*, as it does in the rectangular distribution we are now discussing, the maintenance investment will make a jump in moving from the first to the second segment. In our example this jump is expressed in the last term in (18d.3). Indeed, the first term in (18d.3) expresses what the maintenance investment *would have been* if in the second segment, too, it had followed the same law as it follows in the first segment, viz. (18d.1). At the *first point of time* in the second segment, that is to say at $t=T+\omega+2$, the jump will be equal to dz_T, that is to say, as great as the entire maintenance investment which we had at the first point of time in the *first* segment. At the next change of segment there is no jump in the ordinate, but the curve shows a break in the direction of the *tangent*. Breaks of this kind will also occur at later changes in segment, though they will be smaller. The course of affairs will appear from the upper portion of Figure (18d.4).[1]

It is constructive to compare this segment method with the generation-component method applied to the same case of a rectangular d-curve. The first generation component will now according to (18c.2) be a *rectangle*, with the following ordinates: first $z_{1,T}=0$, then $z_{1,t}=$ constant $=dz_T$ for $t=T+1$, $T+2, \ldots, T+\omega+1$, and then once again zero. This sequence is represented by 1 in the lower part of Figure (18d.4). The second generation component will according to (18c.3) be a *triangle* with the following ordinates: first $z_{2,T}=z_{2,T+1}=0$, then rising for every time-unit by d^2z_T up

[1] The curves are constructed by using various calculations carried out in the work of Preinreich.

to the maximum magnitude dz_T for $t=T+\omega+2$, and then falling correspondingly, and finally again equal to zero. We can write this

for
$$(\omega+1-|T+\omega+2-t|)d^2z_T$$

$$t=T+2, T+3, \ldots, T+2(\omega+1)$$

($\|$ indicate numerical value). The third generation component will be more bell-shaped (three jointed second-degree curves which have a common tangent at the joints), and so on. Cf. the lower curves in Figure (18d.4).

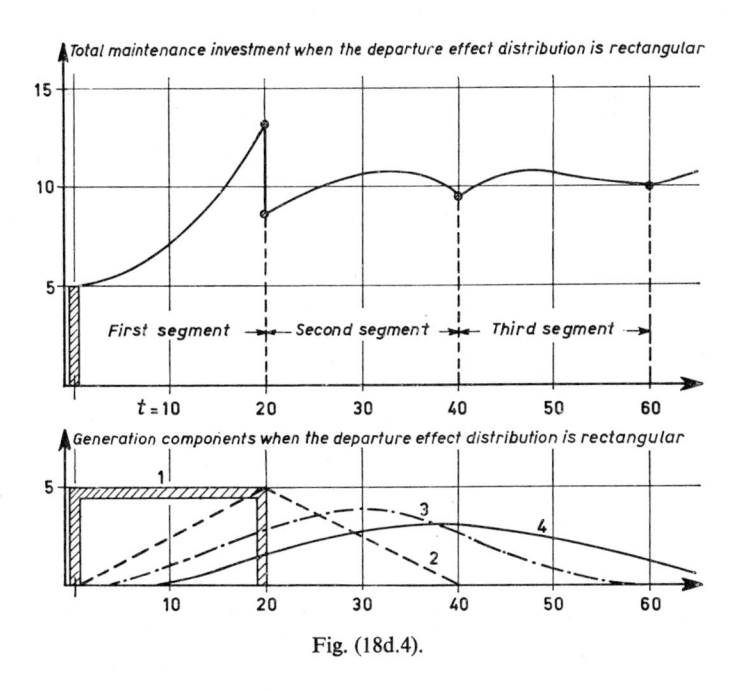

Fig. (18d.4).

Every generation component of the kind studied in Section 18c applies for the *whole* time range, but none of them will separately give the maintenance investment. In order to find *this* at a given point of time we must add up all the generation components at this point. And circumstances may be such that we must include *a very large number of components* in order to obtain a sufficiently accurate expression of total investment. With the segment components it is the other way round: each of them applies only to a certain segment of the time axis, but on the other hand immediately provides a *complete and exact* expression of total maintenance investment. Especially at the beginning of the maintenance process and at the segment transitions, where discontinuities or other extraordinary curve forms may arise, the segment method will provide the best information on the nature of the maintenance process. (But a weak point in the form of the segment method that was presented above, is of course the very special assumption of a rectangular form of the d-curve.)

18e. Maintenance investment when a considerable period of time has elapsed since starting

In the upper part of Figure (18d.4) it will be seen that the maintenance investment after a lapse of time approaches a certain level around which the curve remains practically constant. This phenomenon is similar to what we observed in Figure (17b.1). The height of this asymptotic level can be determined by considering the magnitude of the capital stock. It is given by (18b.2). When we have moved so far from the start that the situation is practically *stationary*, that is to say, with both K and z independent of t, we must according to (18b.2) have

(18e.1) $$K = (l_0 + l_1 + \ldots + l_\omega) z .$$

The l's can be expressed by the d's as follows:

$$\begin{aligned} l_0 &= d_0 + d_1 + d_2 + \ldots + d_\omega , \\ l_1 = l_0 - d_0 &= d_1 + d_2 + \ldots + d_\omega , \\ l_2 = l_1 - d_1 &= d_2 + \ldots + d_\omega , \\ &\ldots\ldots\ldots\ldots\ldots\ldots\ldots \\ l_\omega &= d_\omega . \end{aligned}$$

If we add together all these equations we get

(18e.2) $$l_0 + l_1 + \ldots + l_\omega = d_0 + 2d_1 + 3d_2 + \ldots + (\omega+1)d_\omega = \sum_x (x+1) d_x .$$

The expression to the right here is the average *lifetime* when the departure of the capital objects is taken as concentrated around the *end* of each year; that is to say, immediately before a new influx. The sum of the weights, that is to say, $\Sigma_x d_x$, is equal to 1 according to (18a.5). If (18e.2) is introduced into (18e.1), we get

(18e.3) $$z = \frac{K}{\Sigma_x (x+1) d_x}$$

(when the state has become stationary).

If the start took place in the way that a certain amount of new capital objects z_T was suddenly invested at the point of time T, and this stock subsequently maintained by a never failing influx of maintenance investment – as assumed in 18b, c and d – then the stationary level K in (18e.3) will obviously be none other than z_T. Thus in this case we have

$$(18\text{e}.4) \qquad z = \frac{z_T}{\Sigma_x (x+1) d_x}$$

(when the state has become stationary).

This formula gives the height of the asymptotic level which the maintenance investments approach after the initial fluctuations have been overcome. Cf. e.g. (18d.4).

If a problem should arise where $\Sigma_x d_x$ is >1 (not in conformity with the wear-and-tear problem we have dealt with above), then the asymptotic development of the reinvestment would not be a constant level but a *rising exponential trend*. This is understood intuitively: every element joining the mass gives rise to a total departure which is greater than the element itself. But in (18b.1) the new accretion is determined by the departure in the preceding time, and thus it will in this case be greater than a previous accretion. The newly introduced elements will in turn have to be replaced by a still greater influx at a subsequent time, and so on. If conversely $\Sigma_x d_x$ is <1, the asymptotic development of the reinvestment will be a declining exponential trend. Cf. also the argument in connection with (18f.9).

18f. The method of curve fitting. Maintenance investment when the departure distribution is almost normal (Gaussian)

When the departure effect distribution shows a marked bell-shape – something like a normal (Gaussian) form – the initial fluctuations around the asymptotic level (18e.4) will be *very regular*. In this case one is tempted to try to approximate the investment curve z_t by the sum of a constant or a (say linear) trend and one or more damped sine functions, that is to say, functions of the form

$$(18\text{f}.1) \qquad v_t = A\, e^{\beta t} \sin(a + \alpha t).$$

In (18f.1) the amplitude A, the phase a, the damping exponent β and the frequency α are *constants*. In special cases, however, there may be reasons for allowing A to be a real polynomial in t, cf. the discussion of the roots in (18f.6) and the end of the section.

The curve representing (18f.1) will have a shape as suggested in (18f.2)

In order to give actual damping β must be negative. The greater the negative β is in numerical value, the more marked is the damping, that is to say, the quicker the fluctuations will fade out. The student may choose a few numerical examples and draw the curves by means of figures from a sine table and an exponential table.

We shall indicate how a curve of this kind can be determined so that it *fits* in the best possible way the investment curve which is actually observed in a given concrete case. The theory setting this out is simplest when, as an approximation, we assume that the investment is carried out in a *continuous* manner. In such cases equation (18b.1) will have to be replaced by the following integral equation

(18f.3) $$z(t)=f(t-T)K+\int_{x=0}^{t-T} f(x)z(t-x)\,dx \quad (\text{for } t>T),$$

where $f(x)$ indicates the departure, that is to say, what we previously denoted d_x. It will frequently be convenient to use a normalization factor so that

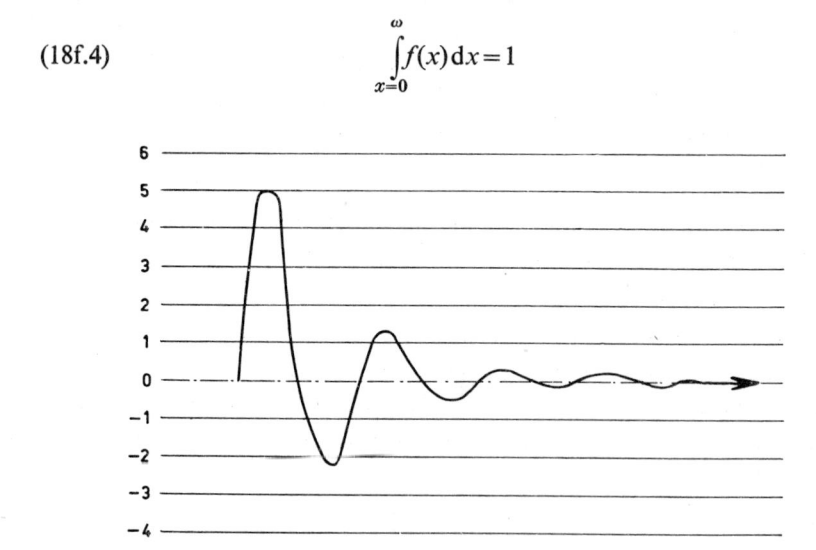

(18f.4) $$\int_{x=0}^{\omega} f(x)\,dx = 1$$

Fig. (18f.2).

but this is not necessary in principle. K in (18f.3) indicates the stock of *new* capital objects introduced at T. In a discrete treatment of the problem this mass might be considered simply as *a particular one of the z-ordinates*, viz.

z_T. Cf. the argument in connection with (18c.8). But this is not possible now, as maintenance investments will now occur all the way down to T, and these will have to be designated z_T. Furthermore, the initial input K at T will as a rule be of a *different order of magnitude* than the z's (or more correctly of a different dimension, as z is calculated per time unit, but K is not). For this reason, too, K should now be dealt with separately as a distinct term[1].

The term $f(t-T)K$ in (18f.3) also possesses a special significance with respect to the break-down into *generation components*. Reinvestments caused by K represent the *first* reinvestment generation, while the integral represents the total effect of *all the other* generations.

After the lapse of the initial period, (i.e. after the point of time t which is so late that $(t-T)$ becomes larger than the largest argument x for which $f(x)$ is different from zero, the formula (18f.3) will be simplified to,

$$(18\text{f}.5) \qquad z(t) = \int_{x=0}^{\omega} f(x) z(t-x) \, dx \quad (\text{for} \quad t > T+\omega) .$$

If we try to fit components of the type (18f.1) to the solution $z(t)$ of the integral equation (18f.5) it is most convenient to write the component in a complex exponential form. In other words the question is now whether one – or more – functions of the form $A\,e^{\gamma t}$, with γ (and A) complex, satisfies (18f.5). When we insert this function into (18f.5), we shall see that the equation can be divided by $A\,e^{\gamma t}$, so that we are merely left with the following equation, which is *independent of t*

$$(18\text{f}.6) \qquad \int_{x=0}^{\omega} e^{-\gamma x} f(x) \, dx = 1 .$$

This is the *characteristic* equation for determining γ. As a rule it will have a number of roots $\gamma_1, \gamma_2, \ldots$. The aggregate

$$(18\text{f}.7) \qquad A_1 e^{\gamma_1 t} + A_2 e^{\gamma_2 t} + \ldots$$

with *arbitrary* A's will then satisfy (18f.5). This can easily be seen by inserting (18f.7) for $z(t)$ in (18f.5).

We have to choose the A's in such a way that (18f.7) reproduces in the

---

[1] By interpreting (18f.3) as a Stieltjes or Lebesgue integral we can *formally* permit the last term in (18f.3) to be included in the integral, but it is much simpler to keep it separate. If we do, the integral can be assumed to be an ordinary Riemann integral.

best possible way that particular one among all the functions satisfying (18f.5) which is the reinvestment curve in our case. In a moment we shall see how this determination of coefficients $A_1, A_2, \ldots$ can be carried out. But first let us look a little more closely at the characteristic roots.

It is easy to see that the characteristic equation (18f.6) – provided all $f(x)$ ordinates are non-negative – must have *one and only one real root*, and that this is positive, zero, or negative, accordingly as the integral (the sum) of the departure ordinates is greater, equal to, or less than 1. Let us in fact consider the function

(18f.8) $$F(\gamma) = \int_{x=0}^{\omega} e^{-\gamma x} f(x) dx .$$

The derivative of this is

(18f.9) $$F'(\gamma) = -\int_{x=0}^{\omega} x\, e^{-\gamma x} f(x) dx .$$

The integral in (18f.9) is positive, consequently $F(\gamma)$ is monotonically decreasing with an increasing real γ. Thus at the most there can only be one real value of γ for which $F(\gamma) = 1$. If

$$\int_{x=0}^{\omega} f(x) dx = 1$$

then $\gamma = 0$ is a root – and consequently the only real root. If

$$\int_{x=0}^{\omega} f(x) dx > 1 ,$$

then $F(0) > 1$, and consequently – on account of F's monotonic decrease – we must turn to positive γ values in order to find one that makes $F = 1$; if a γ of this kind exists at all. Conversely, if

$$\int_{x=0}^{\omega} f(x) dx < 1 .$$

That a real root exists, follows from the fact that by making γ sufficiently large in numerical value, we can diminish (when γ is positive) or enlarge (when γ is negative) the integrand in (18f.8) as much as we like. (Cf. furthermore the reasoning at the end of Section 18e.) A positive real γ means a rising exponential trend; $\gamma=0$ means an asymptotic level, and a negative real γ means a falling exponential trend.

One question that will arise when we fit an expression of the form (18f.7) to $z(t)$ is *whether the roots* $\gamma_1, \gamma_2, \ldots$ are *simple or multiple*. For a root γ_i to be a multiple root, it is necessary and sufficient that $F(\gamma_i)=1$ and at the same time that $F'(\gamma_i)=0$. By means of this we can easily see that the *real root must be simple*. Indeed, when γ is real, the integrand to the right in (18f.9) will be non-negative throughout the entire interval of integration and effectively positive in an interval of measure greater than zero. The fact that the real root is always simple, also follows from the remark above that $F(\gamma)$ is *monotonically* decreasing for an increasing real γ.

In the case of complex roots the question of multiplicity is not so easy to clarify. Attempts at the Oslo University Institute of Economics to construct cases which give multiple complex roots, have failed. On the other hand we have failed to prove that all complex roots must always be simple.

If in any given case one were confronted with an equation (18f.6) which gives a p-double complex root $(p>1)$, then one merely has to consider the coefficient A in question as a $(p-1)^{\text{th}}$ degree polynomial in t, and in the subsequent fitting procedure take the p coefficient in this polynome – instead of a simple constant A – as the linearly involved unknowns, which are to be determined from the observational material.

For the numerical calculation of the complex roots a distinction between the real and the imaginary part in (18f.6) must be made. When the real part of γ is designated β and the imaginary part α, that is to say, if we put

(18f.10) $$\gamma = \beta + i\alpha ,$$

where

$$i = \sqrt{-1}, \quad \alpha \text{ and } \beta \text{ real},$$

we get

$$e^{-\gamma x} = e^{-(\beta+i\alpha)x} = e^{-\beta x} e^{-i\alpha x} = e^{-\beta x}(\cos \alpha x - i \sin \alpha x) ,$$

that is to say

(18f.11) $$\int_{x=0}^{\omega} e^{-\gamma x} f(x) dx = \int_{x=0}^{\omega} e^{-\beta x} \cos \alpha x f(x) dx - i \int_{x=0}^{\omega} e^{-\beta x} \sin \alpha x f(x) dx .$$

If this is to be equal to the real number 1, we must have separately

(18f.12) $\quad \int\limits_{x=0}^{\omega} e^{-\beta x} \cos\alpha x f(x) dx = 1 \quad$ and $\quad \int\limits_{x=0}^{\omega} e^{-\beta x} \sin\alpha x f(x) dx = 0$.

These are two real equations for determining the two real unknowns α and β. The complex roots can only occur in conjugated couples. For if (α, β) form a root, then as will be seen from (18f.12) $(-\alpha, \beta)$ must also be a root. If the departure effects distribution $f(x)$ is bell-shaped, almost normal (Gaussian), and with (18f.4) fulfilled, an approximation to the root can be determined by

(18f.13) $$\alpha^2 - \beta^2 + 2\frac{\bar{x}}{\sigma^2}\beta = 0,$$

$$\alpha\left(\beta - \frac{\bar{x}}{\sigma^2}\right) = \frac{2\pi n}{\sigma^2},$$

where

(18f.14) $$\bar{x} = \int\limits_{x=0}^{\omega} x f(x) dx, \quad \sigma^2 = \int\limits_{x=0}^{\omega} (x - \bar{x})^2 f(x) dx,$$

and n is successively made equal to 1, 2, 3, ... ; $n=1$ corresponds to the first fluctuation component (the one with the smallest α), $n=2$ corresponds to the second, and so on.[1]

The best use one can make of (18f.13) will as a rule be to take the roots here as *approximate magnitudes*, which are then successively improved by some iteration method or other applied directly to (18f.6). If the roots of (18f.13) are sufficiently good, the first round of an iteration method applied to (18f.6) will already make this clear. If they are not good enough, the iteration method will provide the first step towards an improvement of the values.

Once the characteristic roots have been determined with sufficient accuracy, the aggregation coefficients, that is to say the coefficients $A_1, A_2, \ldots$ in (18f.7) must be determined from observation. If part of the reinvestment curve is *known* (e.g., calculated numerically by direct recursion from the given starting point T, or calculated analytically by the segment method) the most logical step is to determine the constants A by *statistical fitting*, (e.g., by the method of least squares) to the known portion of the reinvestment

---

[1] A graphic representation from which the solutions of (18f.13) can be read off approximately, is given by Lotka, *Annals of Mathematical Statistics*, March 1939.

curve. The most natural approach would be to use an interval from the *same* time range for which the exponents γ are determined, that is to say, the time *after* the initial period (the characteristic equation is based on (18f.5), and this equation is only applicable after the initial period). Especially when we restrict ourselves to the use of a small *number* of components (which means that the method is to a marked degree an approximation method), a determination of the A's by statistical fitting procedure will be plausible.

In the case where all the roots in the characteristic equation are simple, we can also proceed in another way.[1] In (18f.3) z occurs at all points of time between the initial point T and t. In this interval *we choose an arbitrary fixed point of time* $S(>T)$ and consider the values of z at points *before* S as *initial values*, while equation (18f.3) is to apply for $t>S$. We split the integration in (18f.3) at the point S, and consider the following two expressions which then arise

(18f.15)
$$P(t) = z(t) - \int_{x=0}^{t-S} f(x) z(t-x) \, dx$$
$$= \int_{x=t-s}^{t-T} f(x) z(t-x) \, dx + Kf(t-T).$$

The first expression to the right here contains z-ordinates after S, and to these ordinates we shall fit the aggregate (18f.7). The last expression in (18f.15) contains z-ordinates (and K) at the points of time *before* S. With the help of these we can in principle calculate the function $P(t)$ – the *trial function* – for any $t>S$. This expression for $P(t)$ can also be written

(18f.16)
$$P(t) = Kf(t-T) + \int_{s=T}^{S} f(t-s) z(s) \, ds.$$

This form expresses more clearly the character of P: the function P arises when we allow the weight system f to slide across a conventionally determined section of the z-series, namely the interval between S and T – *the trial region* – and for every position of the weight system note the magnitude of the moment (the product sum) of f and z. After having defined $P(t)$ in this way,

---

[1] The procedure to be considered is a modification of the method of P. Hertz, *Mathematische Annalen* 1908 and Alfred J. Lotka, *The Annals of Mathematical Statistics* 1939, especially p. 9. In the latter article the method is used without raising the question of the multiplicity of the roots in the characteristic equation.

328   ELEMENTS OF A DYNAMIC THEORY OF PRODUCTION

we multiply it by $\exp(-\gamma_k t)$, where γ_k is a root in (18f.6), and we integrate between S and $S+\omega$. This operation, applied to the first expression in (18f.15) – after the aggregate (18f.7) has been inserted for z – gives

$$(18f.17) \quad \sum_j A_j \left[\int_{t=S}^{S+\omega} \exp[(\gamma_j-\gamma_k)t]\,dt - \int_{t=S}^{S+\omega} dt \int_{x=0}^{t-S} dx \, \exp[(\gamma_j-\gamma_k)t - \gamma_j x]f(x) \right]$$

An interchange of the order of the integrations in the double integral gives

$$\int_{x=0}^{\omega} dx \int_{t=S+x}^{S+\omega} dt.$$

For a term where $\gamma_j = \gamma_k$, we get after carrying out the integrations

$$A_j \left[\omega - \int_{x=0}^{\omega} \exp(-\gamma_k x) f(x) \cdot (\omega - x)\,dx \right]$$

which on account of (18f.6) can be reduced to

$$(18f.18) \qquad A_j \int_{x=0}^{\omega} x \, \exp(-\gamma_k x) f(x)\,dx.$$

If $\gamma_j \neq \gamma_k$ we get

$$A_j \left[\frac{\exp[(\gamma_j-\gamma_k)(S+\omega)] - \exp[(\gamma_j-\gamma_k)S]}{\gamma_j-\gamma_k} \right.$$

$$\left. - \int_{x=0}^{\omega} \exp(-\gamma_j x) f(x) \, \frac{\exp[(\gamma_j-\gamma_k)(S+\omega)] - \exp[(\gamma_j-\gamma_k)(S+x)]}{\gamma_j-\gamma_k}\,dx \right]$$

Here the first term in the first fraction will cancel against the first term in the second fraction, on account of (18f.6). Similarly the second term in the first fraction will cancel against the second term in the second fraction. Thus after integration we are only left with a magnitude such as (18f.18) in the term or terms for which $\gamma_j = \gamma_k$. If we assume that all the roots in the characteristic equation are simple, that is to say, all magnitudes $\gamma_1, \gamma_2, \ldots$ are *different*, then there is one and only one term where $\gamma_j = \gamma_k$, namely the term $j=k$. Thus the preceding integration will in this case give an *unambiguous* determination of the constant A_k, viz.

THE REINVESTMENT PROCESS

(18f.19)
$$A_k = \frac{\int_{t=S}^{S+\omega} \exp(-\gamma_k t) P(t) \, dt}{\int_{x=0}^{\omega} x \exp(-\gamma_k x) f(x) \, dx}.$$

Let us consider especially the *numerator* in this expression. It is dependent on S both through its upper and lower integral limits, and because $P(t)$ by (18f.16) depends on S. We designate this numerator

(18f.20)
$$p(S) = \int_{t=S}^{S+\omega} \exp(-\gamma_k t) P(t) \, dt.$$

The derivative of $P(t)$ with respect to S is

$$\frac{dP(t)}{dS} = f(t-S) z(S) ;$$

consequently

(18f.21)
$$\frac{dp}{dS} = \int_{t=S}^{S+\omega} \exp(-\gamma_k t) f(t-S) z(S) \, dt$$
$$+ \exp[-\gamma_k(S+\omega)] P(S+\omega) - \exp(-\gamma_k S) P(S).$$

The integral here reduces to $\exp(-\gamma_k S) z(S)$ on account of (18f.6). The term with $P(S+\omega)$ vanishes. This will be seen by inserting $S+\omega$ for t in (18f.16), and noting that $f(x) = 0$ for $x > \omega$. Inserting $t = S$ in (18f.16) we see that $P(S)$ is equal to the function $z^*(S)$ defined by

(18f.22)
$$z^*(S) = K \cdot f(S-T) + \int_{S=T}^{S} f(S-s) z(s) \, ds.$$

That is to say

(18f.23)
$$\frac{dp}{dS} = \exp(-\gamma_k S)[z(S) - z^*(S)].$$

This shows under what circumstances the coefficient A_k determined by (18f.19) is *affected* by the choice of S. Let us imagine that S rises from T. If the investment ordinates $z(S)$ which are gradually passed in this process, *are not arbitrarily given* but are determined as the *maintenance investments* necessary to maintain the stock K of *new* objects installed at T, then the coefficient A_k will *not* be affected by the increase of S, that is to say, by pushing forward the integration interval which serves to determine A_k. For in this case $z(S)$ will all the time remain equal to the expression to the right in (18f.22), that is to say, equal to $z^*(S)$, consequently (18f.23) will constantly be equal to zero. Cf. (18f.3). But if the $z(S)$-values we pass are given more or less arbitrarily (as initial conditions), then A_k will be affected by the change in S, as we then get a contribution to (18f.23) which is different from zero. *A_k will therefore be constant from and will include the point S where we have passed all the arbitrarily given z-values, and thus from then on we only have z-values determined as maintenance investments based on the preceding maintenance investments.* From that point on it makes no difference whether S is pushed further forward or not. This clarifies what is contained in the method for determining the A-coefficients which is given in (18f.19).

The function $p(S)$ can be expressed by integrating (18f.23) between T and S. The constant term which emerges in this integration can be determined by noting that $p(T) = \exp(-\gamma_k T) \cdot K$, as will be seen by putting $S = T$ in (18f.20) and (18f.16) and using (18f.6). We thus get

$$(18\text{f}.24) \qquad p(S) = \int_{t=T}^{S} \exp(-\gamma_k t)[z(t) - z^*(t)] dt + K \cdot \exp(-\gamma_k T)$$

or after insertion from (18f.22)

$$(18\text{f}.25) \qquad p(S) = \int_{t=T}^{S} \exp(-\gamma_k t)\left(z(t) - \int_{s=T}^{t} f(t-s) z(s) ds\right) dt$$

$$+ \exp(-\gamma_k T) K \left(1 - \int_{x=0}^{S-T} \exp(-\gamma_k x) f(x) dx\right).$$

If the investments z are made as maintenance investments already *immediately* from the point of time T when the mass K of new capital objects was installed, we can in (18f.25) put $S = T$. There will then, as we have seen, be no point in making S bigger. If we put $S = T$, then the large integral in the beginning of (18f.25) and the little one at the end will both disappear, so that we are left only with $\exp(-\gamma_k T)K$. In other words, when the investments are made as maintenance investments right from the beginning, the aggregation coefficient A_k will simply be equal to

(18f.26) $$A_k = \frac{K \exp(-\gamma_k T)}{\int_{x=0}^{\omega} x \exp(-\gamma_k x) f(x) \, dx}.$$

If arbitrarily given investments occur, e.g. throughout the whole period ω after T, then in (18f.25) we insert $S = T + \omega$. This means that the last term disappears, leaving us only with the first integral between the limits T and $T+\omega$.

The amplitude A for the real exponential trend (which takes the form of a horizontal asymptotic level when we have (18f.4)), is immediately determined by (18f.26), as it stands. For by inserting a real γ everything in (18f.26) becomes real. In case (18f.4), that is to say with the real root equal to zero, (18f.26) will express the same as (18e.3).

When inserting a complex γ in (18f.26), we shall have to split (18f.26) into a real and an imaginary part for the purpose of numerical calculation. If this is done simultaneously for the two complex values γ which form a conjugated pair (as we have seen, the complex roots γ can only occur in conjugated pairs), then the result arrived at can always be combined so as to give a real expression of the form (18f.1). *All the components* – apart from the real exponential trend, which may take the form of an asymptotic level – *must therefore – when the roots in the characteristic equation are simple – be real components of the form* (18f.1).

If multiple roots occur, we can not apply the method set out in (18f.15–26). In order to achieve the general solution we must then let the A's be polynomials of t, as mentioned above.

It is not to be *expected* that the method of curve fitting will give particularly good results, except for the interval for which the characteristic equation (18f.6) is valid, viz. the interval *after* the initial period. But if the departure effect curve is regularly bell-shaped, the adaptation will frequently be fairly good even for a certain part of the initial period. For the very first part, however, it will nearly always be poor; here we shall get wilder and wilder fluctuations, the closer we approach the starting point T (a general phenomenon – the Gibbs phenomenon – which occurs near joins in the fitting with trigonometric functions). And if the departure effect function $f(x)$ terminates somewhat abruptly at $x=\omega$, the fit will be poor *even further out*. In such cases the fit will be particularly bad at each of the first segment changes. For this reason a case such as (18d.4) is quite unsuited to treatment by the method of curve fitting; at any rate this method cannot be used until we have moved a *considerable distance* from the starting point. We must proceed so far that the maintenance investment begins to move in a fairly narrow band around the asymptotic level. And once we have got so far, it might not even be necessary to do anything else than to calculate the height of the asymptotic level.

In order to form a well founded opinion on the *point of time from which* one can start relying on the result given by the method of curve fitting, one may for *a certain interval after the start* calculate the investment curve by direct numerical recursion, using the maintenance equation (or the segment method) and comparing the result thus arrived at with the result of the method of curve fitting.

CHAPTER 19

DEPRECIATION ANALYSIS

We have discussed the time shape which the reinvestment curve in a large capital mass will acquire, given various assumptions with regard to the composition of the capital stock and given various requirements with regard to its maintenance. We shall now consider more closely the process which is responsible for the fact that the problem of reinvestment occurs at all, that is to say, the actual *depreciation* – i.e. the *decline in the ability to produce output* or the *decline in value* of the capital objects, which results from wear and tear or simply from becoming out of date.

Let us first consider those aspects of the question of depreciation which can be expressed as a function of the *age* alone of the capital objects. This procedure is in keeping with the discussion in preceding chapters. If we can assume a certain *normal* intensity of use, and a certain *normal* probability of the means of production becoming out of date, then the essence of the problem will be covered if we consider age as a descriptive variable.

19a. Technical depreciation defined by the principle of remaining services

Let us consider a mass of uniform new capital objects invested at the point of time $T=0$. That is to say, the primary investment dose is of the same kind as the one we took as our starting point in the preceding chapter. We shall *not*, however, now assume that the mass is maintained; we shall now, in fact, assume that *no* reinvestment is undertaken. The process that takes place will then be a *pure depreciation process*. How large a portion of the capital will then remain x years after the start?

If we only consider the *number* of objects still *functioning*, then the answer is simply l_x (cf. the definitions of l_x, d_x, etc., at the beginning of (18a)). But this does not provide the correct expression for the *depreciation* which has taken place, since every single one of the objects still functioning has been subject to wear and tear and, from the capital point of view, is no longer comparable with what was originally installed. In order to obtain an expression of the depreciation we must not consider the *number* of capital objects, but *the sum of the productive services which the capital still contains*. If we assume a constant intensity of use (a constant stream of services per time unit from every capital object), then the sum of the remaining services can simply be measured by *the number of years' work remaining*. If we assume that departure takes place at the end of each year, then at the beginning of age x this number is equal to

(19a.1)   Remaining years' work $= l_x + l_{x+1} + \ldots + l_\omega$.
(remainder of services)

For there are l_x objects functioning during the year between x and $x+1$, l_{x+1} functioning between $x+1$ and $x+2$, and so on. Thus the sum of the number of years' work will be (19a.1).

If we take the ratio of this sum to the *number* of objects functioning at the beginning of the year x, we get

(19a.2)   Average remaining effective time $= \dfrac{l_x + l_{x+1} + \ldots l_\omega}{l_x}$.

And if we take the ratio of (19a.1) to the sum of the remaining years of work we had at the start of the whole process

(19a.3)   The remaining fraction $H_x = \dfrac{l_x + l_{x+1} + \ldots + l_\omega}{l_0 + l_1 + \ldots + l_\omega} =$
(service fraction)
$= \dfrac{l_x + l_{x+1} + \ldots + l_\omega}{\bar{x}}$,

where

(19a.4) $\bar{x} = l_0 + l_1 + \ldots + l_\omega = \sum\limits_{x=0}^{\omega}(x+1)d_x =$ average duration life expectancy of capital objects

(when departure takes place at the end of every year). The remaining fraction (19a.3) is obviously 1 at the start and 0 when the last capital object is no longer functioning, that is to say,

(19a.5) $H_0 = 1$, $H_{\omega+1} = 0$ and generally $H_x = 0$ for $x > \omega$.

The way in which H_x decreases with increasing x gives an expression of the *speed (velocity) at which the capital is drained of its content of productive services*. H_x is the survival curve – not of the *number* of capital objects (for this role is played by the survival curve l_x) – but of *the sum of the services* in the capital objects.

The remaining fraction H_x can be used as a gauge of depreciation. The depreciation in the year between x and $x+1$ (when the capital amount is measured per unit of the original capital invested) is simply equal to the decline in the remaining fraction H_x in the course of this year, that is to say, equal to

(19a.6)   Depreciation (under normal use) $h_x = H_x - H_{x+1}$.

We say that the depreciation here is defined by *the principle of remaining services*.

No matter how the l_x series runs, provided (19a.5) is fulfilled, we shall always have

(19a.7) $$h_0 + h_1 + \ldots + h_\omega = 1,$$

that is to say, the sum of the depreciations is equal to the capital stock (the service-producing stock) with which we started. For if an insertion is made from (19a.6) into the left member of (19a.7), we get

$$(H_0 - H_1) + (H_1 - H_2) + \ldots + (H_\omega - H_{\omega+1}) = H_0 - H_{\omega+1} = 1.$$

If an insertion is made from (19a.3) into (19a.6), the expression for depreciation will be

(19a.8) $$h_x = \frac{l_x}{l_0 + l_1 + \ldots + l_\omega} = \frac{l_x}{\bar{x}}.$$

Graphically (19a.3) and (19a.4) can be illustrated as in Figure (19a.9). First the l_x-curve is drawn. Then a vertical is drawn in such a position that the two shaded regions are equal. The point at the foot of the vertical will then give the average lifetime $\bar{x}$. For this point will then be such that, if we take the rectangle with $\bar{x}$ as the base line and 1 as the height, then in area this rectangle will be equal to the area below the l_x-curve, and according to the left expression in (19a.4) this is precisely the definition of $\bar{x}$.

The H_x-curve must be constantly curving, with its hollow side upwards, since the rate of growth of the ordinate (viz. $(-h_x)$) will according to (19a.8) be constantly decreasing in numerical value. To summarise: The course of the H_x-curve is as indicated in Figure (19a.9).

For the sake of simplicity we have drawn all the curves in Figure (19a.9) continuous.

If the intensity of use (the intensity with which the capital objects are used) *varies* over a period of time so that it occasionally lies over and occasionally lies under the *normal* intensity of use which we assumed when constructing the l_x-curve, then in the complete expression for depreciation we must calculate with an *intensity term* as an expression of this deviation. Let its magnitude x years after the point of time when the new capital objects were installed be denoted by $\delta_x{}^*$. The actual depreciation in the year lying between the point of time x and $x+1$ will then be

(19a.10) $$\delta_x = h_x + \delta_x{}^* .$$

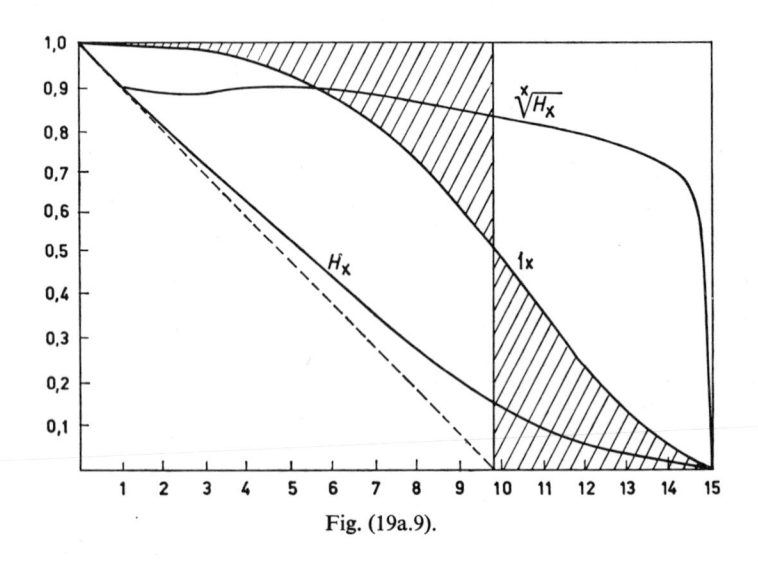

Fig. (19a.9).

Taking a more general viewpoint, $\delta_x{}^*$ can be interpreted as including not only direct *technical* wear and tear, but also such things as capital objects becoming *out of date* owing to new inventions or becoming *useless* owing to changes in demand conditions. As a rule the last-mentioned will usually take the form of *price or value changes* for the capital objects.

Formula (19a.10) gives depreciation per unit of the original capital stock that is to say, calculated as though originally there was only one single new capital object. If the original number of new objects was K_0, the total depreciation on these would be equal to

(19a.11) $$D_x = \delta_x K_0 .$$

This is the depreciation which occurs when originally a certain number of new capital objects was invested, and no supplementary investment was subsequently made. Should a supplementary investment be carried out (maintenance, repairs, or complete replacement of single machines), then this can be dealt with in the same way as the original investment, by including a certain curve which describes the depletion speed for the services originally comprised in this new investment. This curve may perhaps be somewhat different from the one applicable to the original capital stock, and in this case the composition of the total depreciation will be a little more complicated, although in principle the same. Nor is any new principle involved if a capital stock is composed of *partial stocks*, each of which consists of a larger number of uniform objects.

If specific information is available on the lifetime of every single one of a large number of uniform capital objects, then the series for d_x and l_x can be determined by a calculation technique which is essentially the same as that used in constructing a mortality table for a human population. Consequently the h_x-series, too, can be determined, and thus depreciation can be defined exactly for *a stock of this kind taken as a whole*. Since we assume that these calculations are based on *factual* observations, the result will be a departure effect curve influenced by all the conditions, and circumstances, technical and economical, which in practice determine depreciation.

If a concern has only one or a few capital objects of a definite kind, it is still possible to carry out a depreciation calculation based on this principle, provided only that the departure effect curve for *this sort* of capital objects is known on the basis of experience available from any outside source, e.g. joint statistics for several concerns or published by official authorities. The calculation of depreciation within the single concern will, however, in such cases contain a large degree of uncertainty, as special conditions within each concern may result in depreciation proceeding more quickly or more slowly than on an average within the stock on which these calculations are based.

19b. Writing-off plan and actual writing-off

By *writing-off* is meant an item in the books of a concern (of a person, or of a company) which aims to give a bookkeeping expression for the actual concrete process which has taken place in the depreciation. Thus writing-off is something that takes place in the accounts, and depreciation is something that takes place with the concrete objects.

Writing-off, however, aims to *express* the depreciation and to give a *true* expression of it. Its purpose is to express what 'has actually taken place'. Consequently, if writing off and depreciation are both expressed in terms of money, and if for the time being we assume that prices are constant and that accurate information can be obtained, *then in principle writing off and depreciation will be equally big* (the principle of truth).[1]

Both in theoretical economics and from the point of view of bookkeeping the writing off (the depreciation) is a cost item which must be taken into account if *net interest and net property (capital)* are to be arrived at. No matter what system of special accounts is used for the purpose of writing-off, the point will always be that net income in the year the writing-off takes place decreases by the writing-off amount, and net property (capital) at the end of the year is reduced by the same amount. We can therefore say that the actual terms income and property (capital) are *insolubly linked to* the term writing-off (depreciation). The fact that we have a depreciation phenomenon creates a main difficulty which is common to the definition of *all* the terms with which we are here concerned. Once one of the terms has been fixed, the others will follow suit without much difficulty, but before any of them can be definitely fixed, depreciation – and with it writing-off – must be defined. We may therefore say that writing-off, income and property (capital) are basically only three aspects of one and the same fundamental problem of definition.

Writing off involves two phases: first the writing-off plan is set up. This is done – or should be done – at the same time as the (for this particular concern) *new* capital objects are acquired. For a certain period of time this plan is adhered to. Subsequently, on the basis of new experience gained, it may prove necessary to *correct* the plan or, to put it differently, *adjust* the plan. At the latest when the capital object is *discarded* (by the concern), that is to say, when it is sold as used or is scrapped, an adjustment of this kind is necessary, and then it is not only temporary but definitive. These two kinds of writing-off – those that are carried out according to plan and those which might be described as adjustments – should be kept apart. Cf. 19a.10).

If precise l_x-data are available for every single *kind* of capital object included in the accounts of a concern, and assuming that no complication will arise owing to price variations, then these data will determine the writing-off plan. If at the point of time 0 a large number K_0 of uniform capital objects are acquired, then in effect the writing-off plan must assume

---

[1] As a rule this is also the assumption of the tax laws. In this respect the American tax laws are very explicit: 'The capital sum to be recovered shall be charged off over the useful life of the property. ... such ratable amount as may reasonably be considered necessary to recover during the remaining useful life of the property the unrecovered cost.' *Revenue Act of 1936*. Regulations 94. Art. 23(1)–5.

that that year $h_0 K_0$ is written off, next year $h_1 K_0$, and so forth, assuming that intensity of use is normal. If there are grounds for believing that super- or sub-normal use will occur, or other special depreciation elements will enter, then these must be taken into consideration. Cf. (19a.10). If the Bookkeeping Department is required to present a correct expression of *what is actually happening* and the data are available, then the writing-off is determined. There will be no room for any other considerations. It would, for example, be impossible to establish a principle to the effect that the writings-off in the account should show a certain smoothness throughout the successive account periods, or the like. Whether they are smooth or not depends on the l_x-curve and possibly the $\delta_x{}^*$-curve and cannot be imposed as an independent principle.

Nor can it be said that the question of writing off is the same as the question of how the concern will enter the capital expenses in the 'self-cost' calculations it sets up as the basis for its *sales policy*. The form these calculations take will *inter alia* depend on the sales strategic type to which the concern conforms. If the necessary concrete depreciation data are available, there will thus be a definite writing-off plan which in principle will be the only correct one independent of all other considerations.

In practice, however this is not what happens. Even if we ignore complications introduced by price variations and the like, there are few types of capital objects for which exact l_x-calculations exist. The reason is in the first place that calculations of this kind demand comprehensive statistic observations of *uniform* objects, and in the second place that the time of departure of every single object of this kind depends partly on *economic* conditions, so that *different* l_x-curves for the same kind of object under varying market conditions would be needed, and perhaps even under other more specialised conditions. The last-mentioned might as an alternative be read into $\delta_x{}^*$. To a certain extent it will be a matter of convention just how much one reads into the l_x-curve and how much into $\delta_x{}^*$. In any case, the point is that an accurate writing-off *plan* can be set up only if one has fairly advanced information about the total δ_x-curve.

All these considerations mean that in practice one must as a rule be satisfied with a – sometimes very crude – *approximation method* for the writing-off plan. Nevertheless it is important to bear in mind the solution in principle by means of (19a.8) and (19a.10). Only by taking account of these formulae one can decide whether a given approximation method is good or bad.

A few of the approximation methods that are in vogue may be mentioned.

THE AMOUNT-CONSTANT METHOD (THE AMOUNT- AND TIME CONSTANT METHOD)

This is the simplest writing-off plan. It consists of assessing the probable lifetime ξ of a capital object and then writing off $1/\xi$ of the total value every year in the ξ years. In the course of ξ years the object will thus have been written down to 0. If one can reckon with a probable *scrapping* after ξ years, then the method should only be applied to the *difference* between the value on acquisition and the value on scrapping. The remainder fraction and the annual writing-off will according to this method be

(19b.1) The remainder fraction $= H_x^{AC} = 1 - (x/\xi)$.

Annual writing-off $= h_x^{AC} = 1/\xi$ during year.

The topscript AC indicates 'the amount-constant method'. Graphically H_x^{AC} is represented by the dotted line in Figure (19a.9) if the probable lifetime ξ has been correctly assessed as x.

If a large mass of uniform capital objects is written off according to this method, the writing-off *will all this time proceed at a swifter rate than the actual depreciation*. Since $l_x > 1$ (except $l_0 = 1$), if $\xi = \bar{x}$, h_x^{AC} must according to (19b.1) be greater than h_x according to (19a.8). A consequence of this is that writing down according to this method will always be completed before its time, provided no extraordinary depreciation phenomena of the type δ_x^* occur. This is illustrated in Figure (19a.9), where the H_x-curve in its entirety lies above the dotted line (and has this line as its tangent at the point $x=0$). The *total writing-down amount* according to this method will be right, even though the speed of writing-off is made too big.

THE PERCENT-CONSTANT METHOD

In this method a fixed percentage of the amount *remaining* at all times is written off. The remainder fraction will then decrease like a capital placed at a negative rate of interest, that is to say as an exponential function with a negative exponent. We therefore put

(19b.2) The remainder fraction $= H_x^{PC} = e^{-\nu x}$.

Annual writing-off $= h_x^{PC} = (1-e^{-\nu})e^{-\nu x}$ in ν years.

The superscript PC indicates 'the percent-constant method,' ν is a certain fixed time – the writing-off time – such that after its lapse no more writing-off occurs, that is to say

(19b.3) $h_x^{PC} = 0$ for $x > \nu$.

The constant γ – *the writing-off exponent* – can be determined by stating that the remainder fraction, after a certain conventionally fixed time (which can be selected as ν or as some other number) has been reduced to a certain size. If the remainder fraction after n years is to be reduced to α percent, γ must be made equal to

$$(19\text{b}.4) \qquad \gamma = \frac{-\ln \alpha}{n}.$$

Calculated as a fraction per annum the writing-off will be

$$(19\text{b}.5) \quad p = \text{Annual writing-off fraction} = \frac{H_x^{PC} - H_{x+1}^{PC}}{H_x^{PC}} = 1 - e^{-\gamma}.$$

When writings-off at this rate have taken place x times, the remainder fraction will be precisely as given in (19b.2). For after the first writing-off we are left with

$$1 - (1 - e^{-\gamma}) = e^{-\gamma}.$$

If this is written down once again, then we are left with

$$e^{-\gamma} - e^{-\gamma}(1 - e^{-\gamma}) = e^{-2\gamma},$$

and so on.

Whether this method will give a quicker or less quick writing-off than the actual depreciation depends on the course of the l_x-curve, and on the magnitude chosen for γ, and the point of time in the writing-off period we have reached. It is always possible to choose a γ of such magnitude that *to start with* writing-off is as strong or stronger than actual depreciation. In order to do this we have merely to ensure that $h_0^{PC} > h_0$, that is to say that

$$(19\text{b}.6) \qquad 1 - e^{-\gamma} \geq \frac{1}{\bar{x}}, \quad \text{i.e.} \quad \gamma \geq -\ln\left(1 - \frac{1}{\bar{x}}\right),$$

where $\bar{x}$ is the average durability for the capital objects. We assume $\bar{x} > 1$ (as otherwise it would in all circumstances be impossible to cover actual depreciation by a writing off undertaken at the end of the first year). (19b.6) tells us that if the annual writing-off fraction $p = 1 - e^{-\gamma}$ is made equal to or greater than unity divided by the average durability of the capital objects, then *to start with* writings-off will be equal to or greater than actual depreciation.

Even though in choosing the writing-off fraction p – or the writing-off exponent γ – we make p so great that this is fulfilled, we are (provided merely we do not have $p = 1$, that is to say $\gamma = \infty$) bound sooner or later to reach a point of time when writing-off begins to be *less* than actual depreciation. In fact, there must even come a point of time when the *total* writing-off carried out according to this method, becomes less than the total actual depreciation. This follows simply from the fact that the remainder fraction according to (19b.2) – for finite γ – does not fall to zero in the course of a finite time, while the actual remainder fraction H_x, according to the assumption (19a.5), does.

We might also put the matter like this: the fact that we choose a *large* writing-off exponent γ (a large writing-off fraction per annum) will certainly make the first annual writings-off big, but it will make subsequent annual writings-off *small*. These later writings-off will be less than they would have been if we had chosen a smaller writing-off fraction (because with a larger fraction the amount remaining, on which writings-off will be based, will be so much the less). And this under-rating of writing-off per annum in later years must finally – no matter how γ has been chosen – have a cumulative effect, so that the non-written-off portion according to the percent-constant method will be greater than the actual services remaining in the capital objects.

It is of interest to know *when* the non-written-off remainder according to the percent-constant method catches up with the actual remainder percentage, and *how* γ is to be selected in order that the point of time of overtaking is to be as late as possible, that is to say so that the remainder percentage we have at the moment of overtaking is as small as possible. The answer to the first question is provided merely by putting $H_x{}^{PC} = H_x$, that is to say

(19b.7) $$e^{-\gamma x} = H_x, \quad \text{hence} \quad \gamma = \frac{-\ln H_x}{x},$$

hence $p = 1 - \sqrt[x]{H_x}$, where $H_x = $ (19a.3).

This equation defines x – the durability for which overtaking takes place – as a function of γ (or of p). Or we may say, γ (and p) as functions of x. The latter mentioned view is most convenient when x is only defined in terms of integers while γ, as likewise p, are allowed to vary continuously.

The most complete picture is obtained by drawing one of the expressions written in (19b.7) as functions of x. We can, for example, draw the curve $1 - \sqrt[x]{H_x}$. This curve can be directly derived from the H_x-curve, that is to say derived directly from the depreciation-determined l_x-curve. And the ordinate on this curve tells us directly how large the annual writing-off percentage, using the percent-constant method, must be made in order for the overtaking durability to be x. The starting point of the curve, that is to say $x = 0$, gives us

$$p = 1 - \sqrt[0]{H_0} = 0,$$

DEPRECIATION ANALYSIS

and tells us that if nothing is written off, the actual depreciation will already immediately have overtaken writing-off. The terminal point $x = \omega + 1$ gives $1 - 0 = 1$, and merely tells us that the only way we can get the remainder fraction down to zero by the percent-constant method is to make the annual writing-off equal to 100 per cent, that is to say, write down the *whole* capital value the very first time a writing-off is carried out. This is a trivial case, as it ignores the whole point of writing-down, which is to *distribute* the amount over several bookkeeping periods.

In all other cases an overtaking age is bound to occur, and the writing-down fraction which makes the overtaking age equal to a given figure between 0 and ω is given by the ordinate of the $1 - \sqrt[x]{H_x}$ curve. We know from (19a.9) that the H_x-curve falls. As a rule $\sqrt[x]{H_x}$, too, will fall, hence $1 - \sqrt[x]{H_x}$ will rise. But it is not certain that this will apply everywhere. Cf. the course of the $\sqrt[x]{H_x}$-curve in (19a.9). The criterion can be expressed as follows: We have

$$\log \sqrt[x]{H_x} = \frac{\log H_x}{x}.$$

Both logarithms are negative (as H_x is less than 1 and x is not negative). In numerical value $\log H_x$ is rising (because H_x is sinking). If the numerical value of $\log H_x$ is rising at a *greater rate* than x – that is to say, *the elasticity of $\log H_x$ with respect to x is greater than 1 in numerical value* – then $\log H_x/x$ will rise in numerical value, that is to say $\log \sqrt[x]{H_x}$ will rise in numerical value, and $\sqrt[x]{H_x}$ will sink, and consequently $1 - \sqrt[x]{H_x}$ will rise.

The fact that the $\sqrt[x]{H_x}$ curve may rise can also be seen in the following way. The condition

$$\sqrt[x]{H_x} < \sqrt[x+1]{H_{x+1}}$$

can be written

$$\sqrt[x]{\frac{l_x + A}{\bar{x}}} < \sqrt[x+1]{\frac{A}{\bar{x}}},$$

i.e.

(19b.8) $$l_x < A \left(\sqrt[x+1]{\frac{\bar{x}}{A}} - 1 \right),$$

where $A = l_{x+1} + l_{x+2} + \ldots + l_\omega$.

An example of (19b.8) being fulfilled can be constructed by first selecting two arbitrary numbers $\bar{x}$ and A, such that

$$0 < A \leq \bar{x} - 1$$

and an arbitrary integer $x > 0$, and thereafter choosing a number l_x which satisfies (19b.8) and also satisfies

(19b.9) $$l_x \leq \frac{\bar{x} - 1 - A}{x}.$$

When (19b.9) is fulfilled the figures $l_0, l_1, \ldots, l_{x-1}$ can always be chosen in such a way that $l_0, l_1, \ldots, l_x$ is a non-rising series of non-negative figures and with $l_0 = 1$ and l_x non-negative so, that

$$l_0 + \ldots + l_x + A = \bar{x}.$$

That is to say the example is a real l_x-series. And in this example, moreover, (19b.8) is fulfilled for the special selected x-value.

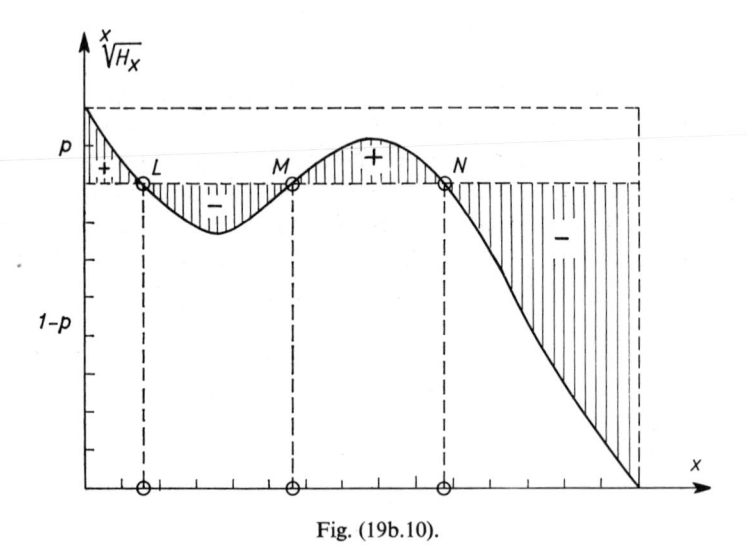

Fig. (19b.10).

In the figure it is unnecessary to draw the $1 - \sqrt[x]{H_x}$ curve separately; we need only read off the ordinates of $\sqrt[x]{H_x}$ *from above*, from the line 1. If the $\sqrt[x]{H_x}$-curve first sinks and then rises, subsequently sinking again (it cannot *start* by rising, as the ordinate will never be greater than 1, and it must *conclude* its course by sinking, as it has to reach 0 by passing through positive values) – then, as suggested in Figure (19b.10), a given horizontal level representing a selected p will be able to cut the curve at three points, L, M, and N. In the first and third regions the $\sqrt[r]{H_x}$-curve will lie above the given horizontal level, and thus the writing off carried out up to that point according to the percent-constant method be more than sufficient to cover the actual depreciation that has taken place. These areas are marked $+$ in the figure. In the second and fourth regions the opposite will take place, they are marked $-$. By lowering the horizontal line, that is to say, increasing the annual writing-off fraction p, point M will move to be left while L and N will move to the right.

It is primarily the point where the writing-off *for the first time* is overtaken by depreciation that is of interest, that is to say, point L. This is the point one should aim to postpone as far as possible. And, as will be seen, this can be done by selecting an annual writing-off percentage which is as *big* as possible, that is to say, by placing the *centre of* gravity of writings-off as soon after the point of time of installation as possible. But in return, one must then be prepared for the possibility of writings-off to start by being *much too great* compared with actual depreciation. This is inevitable; it merely means that the percent-constant method in this case is a highly unsuitable method of representing the actual course of depreciation.

We have assumed above that a capital object has a value equal to zero at the end of its lifetime. As a rule, however, the object will still possess a certain scrapping value even after it has been discarded, e.g. a scrapping value in the form of scrap-iron, when we are dealing with machinery. This is – as we have already mentioned above – simply taken account of by writing-off the *difference* between the original value and the probable scrapping value, instead of writing off the whole original value of the whole machine.

ANALYTICAL SUMMARY

PART ONE / BASIC CONCEPTS OF PRODUCTION

CHAPTER 1 / WHAT IS PRODUCTION?

1a. *Production in the technical sense. Production factors and products*

Technical production: any transformation process which can be directed by human beings, or which human beings are interested in. Loss of identity by the production factors. Movement, selection, conservation. To a certain extent the distinction between production factors and products is conventional, depending on the particular aspect of the problem in question.

1b. *The distinction between a scientific statement and a value judgement*

Science seeks results which can be subjected to the criterion of false or correct in an objective way. On the other hand a practical-political rule of conduct presupposes the taking of a standpoint in a human conflict of interests. The first is a question of 'scientific statement', the second implies also a 'value judgement'. In a scientific analysis the choice of presuppositions introduces sometimes – perhaps unconsciously – some element of value judgement.

1c. *Production in the economic sense. Evaluation coefficients*

Production in the economic sense: the attempt to create a product which is more highly valued than the original input elements.

1d. *Single production, assorted production, and joint production*

Single production: only one kind of product. Assorted production: a given set of production factors can be used optionally for either one kind of product or for another. Joint production: a given set of production factors will – if used – necessarily produce more than one kind of products simultaneously.

1e. *The technical, financial, and political organisation of production. Horizontal and vertical concentration. State control*

CHAPTER 2 / PRODUCTION FACTORS

2a. *Specified and implied factors. Controllable and non-controllable, economic and free factors*

In reality the production factors are infinite in number, but only a limited number of them can be *specified* and made the subject of analysis. Some of the factors can be controlled, others not. Some are economic (i.e. have value), others are free.

2b. *Fixed and variable factors. Capacity. Short-term and long-term factors*

Fixed factors: their quantity remain constant independent of the quantity of the product. Variable factors: their quantity will be changed with the quantity of the product. Short-term factors: may be changed even in the short run. Long-term factors: can *only* be changed in the long run. Reversible and irreversible factors.

2c. *Special and general factors. The problem of association between given input elements and given output elements*

Special factors (special costs): can be classified into categories according to their place in the production process. General factors (general costs): cannot be so classified.

2d. *Definition of the term factor quantity and product quantity. Elementary factors*

Unless the quantity concept is properly established, a great deal of the theory of production will have no valid foundation. Elementary factors: the quantity can be technically defined.

2e. *Factor complexes. Equivalence factors and aggregate factors. Shadow factors*

There are two cases in which it is possible to aggregate several elementary factors on a purely technical basis: in the case of equivalence factors, and in the case of coupled factors. Equivalence factors: one can be substituted for another in a *technically* given ratio. Shadow factors: their quantity must follow certain other factor quantities.

CHAPTER 3 / PRODUCTION TECHNIQUE, CONSTANT TECHNIQUE AND VARIABLE TECHNIQUE

3a. *Definition of constant technique*

It is impossible to achieve a theoretically precise definition of the concept of constant technique by proceeding to a detailed description of the technical forms in the production. We say that the technique is constant as long as the functional relation(s) expressing the dependence of the product quantity(-ies) on factor quantities remain(s) the same. Otherwise we say that the technique is changed.

3b. *Changes in the nature of factors*

A transition from certain kinds of production factors to others is a change in technique.

3c. *Changes in the production function (changes in the production table)*

The law connecting the factors and the product is changed. According to the definition in 3a this is a change in technique even if the kinds of production factors remain the same.

3d. *Changes in the factor quantities under a constant production function (production table)*

According to the definition in 3a this will not be a change in technique.

CHAPTER 4 / VARIOUS TYPES OF PRODUCTION THEORY

4a. *Momentary production and time-shaped production. Static and dynamic theory of production*

Momentary production: can be studied *as though* it takes no time. Time-shaped production: here the time shapes of input- and output streams will be essential.

4b. *Number of stages and stage tempo. Input curves and step diagram*

Under momentary production the variation of the factors is characterised by two things, the *relation* between the factor quantities and the production *scale*. Under time-shaped production a third characteristic is a factor's *concentration* in time. Step diagram. Stage tempo. Number of stages. Stage interval.

ANALYTICAL SUMMARY   349

4c. *The stage interval. Time-rigid and time-elastic production process*

In agriculture the *time lapse* between the production stages is fairly fixed, while in industry it can to a certain extent be changed.

4d. *Mean production period and average liquid capital in a closed production process*

The production period: a weighted average of the figures showing the length of time since the individual inputs were made.

4e. *Risk and anticipation in the theory of production*

PART TWO / MOMENTARY SINGLE PRODUCTION USING ONLY CONTINUITY FACTORS

A. TECHNICAL SECTION

Technical presuppositions in Part Two: single-ware production, momentary production, technical measurability, constant technique, continuity factors.

CHAPTER 5 / VARIOUS METHODS OF DESCRIBING A CONTINUOUS PRODUCTION LAW

5a. *Production function, product table, and isoquants*

The product function is the function showing the technical relationship of dependence between the product quantity on the one side, and the factor quantities on the other. In a given case its form can be represented either by an analytically formed product function, numerically by a product table, or graphically by a product curve, a product surface or isoquants. Several numerical examples, both concrete as well as constructed.

5b. *Marginal productivities*

The marginal productivity with respect to a factor: the partial derivative x_k' of the product function with respect to the factor. We say that factor No. k is sub-maximal, maximal, or super-maximal, according to whether x_k' is positive, zero, or negative. Calculation of the marginal productivity by the help of finite (as opposed to infinitesimal) increments. A continuity factor is a factor whose marginal productivity in any point is a continuous function of all factor quantities. The substitution region consists of those – and only those – points in the n-dimensional factor diagram where all n marginal productivities are non-negative. The substitution fraction. An isocline: a curve in the factor diagram along which the ratios between the marginal productivities (the substitution fractions) keep constant.

5c. *Product accelerations*

The product accelerations: the partial derivatives of the second order of the product function. Direct accelerations. Cross accelerations. The marginal productivity of a certain factor is increasing or decreasing according to whether the relevant direct acceleration is positive or negative. Two factors are complementary, independent, or alternative according to whether the relevant cross acceleration is positive, zero, or negative.

5d. *Average productivities*

The average productivity for a factor: the product quantity divided by the factor quantity. If the average productivity for factor No. i increases (decreases) when the quantity of factor No. i increases, we say that there exists an increasing (decreasing) average return of factor No. i. Proposition (5d. 6): increasing average return when, and only when, $x_i' > \bar{x}_i$, decreasing average return when, and only when, $x_i' < \bar{x}_i$.

5e. *Marginal elasticities*

The marginal elasticity of a factor: the partial elasticity of the product function with respect to the quantity of the factor. Proposition (5e.4): if, and only if, $\varepsilon_i > 1$, there exists an increasing average return for factor No. i; if, and only if, $\varepsilon_i < 1$, there exists a decreasing average return for factor No. i. The virtual product share. The substitution region can also be defined as the region where all marginal elasticities are non-negative.

5f. *The passus coefficient*

The passus coefficient: the elasticity of the product quantity with respect to an arbitrary of the factors when all the factors vary proportionally. (It will be independent of which factor we look at.) Elasticity

ANALYTICAL SUMMARY 351

with respect to scale. Calculation by the help of finite (as opposed to infinitesimal) increments.

5g. *Further consideration on proportional factor variation*

A proportional factor variation is equivalent to a movement along a factor beam, i.e. a straight line through origin. In a factor point where $\varepsilon > 1$, all the average productivities will increase if we make an infinitely small movement out along the factor beam. And *vice versa*. In a factor point where $\varepsilon = 1$ (and where $\varepsilon > 1$ before the point and $\varepsilon < 1$ after the point) the production scale is technically optimal. (5g. 12) gives the first and (5g. 16) the second form of the beam variation equation.

5h. *The passus equation*

Three methods of deriving the passus equation (5h.3): (1) by the help of the marginal increment formula, (2) by the help of the scale factor μ, (3) by the help of the first form of the beam variation equation. The passus equation in the form of elasticities: the passus coefficient is equal to the sum of the marginal elasticities.

5i. *Further details concerning isoquants and isoclines*

In a case involving two factors the isoquants are on the decrease in the interior of the substitution area. The slope of the tangent to the isoquant through a given factor point expresses the substitution ratio (the substitution relationship) in the factor point concerned. The construction of isoclines when the isoquant map is known. The condition for the isoquant being curved towards origin in the interior of the substitution region (5i.10) for two factors, (5i.11) generally.

CHAPTER 6/THE TECHNICAL OPTIMUM LAW WHEN CONSIDERING PARTIAL VARIATION OF A FACTOR OR A GROUP OF FACTORS

6a. *History of some basic concepts*

Ricardo and von Thünen. The quantitative formulation of the regularities of production. The marginal approach. The diminishing return. The marginal and the residual principle of reward. The agricultural chemists. Example from Mitscherlich about the effect of lime fertilizer.

Multi-dimensional variation and the optimum law. Economists round the turn of the century.

6b. *Detailed analysis of the technical optimum law as it appears when we consider the partial variation of a factor*

If a factor varies while the others are kept constant, we usually get a typical optimum law as indicated in Figure (6b.1). Both the optimum properties as well as the properties of maximality can be described by the marginal elasticity.

6c. *The technical optimum law for variation of a partial factor complex*

CHAPTER 7 / THE PARI-PASSU LAW

7a. *Definition of a pari-passu law*

A pari-passu law is a production law in which the passus coefficient is equal to 1 for every factor combination. This is tantamount to the product function being homogeneous to degree 1, cf. (7a.2).

7b. *Special properties of the pari-passu law*

By multiplying all factor quantities by m (a proportional factor variation) in a pari-passu law, the marginal productivities, the average productivities, and the marginal elasticities will remain constant, while the product accelerations will be reduced to the mth part. In the pari-passu law the isoclines will be straight lines through the origin. In a pari-passu law $\sum_{i=1}^{n} v_i x'_{ik} = 0$. In the pari-passu law for two factors the direct accelerations always have the same sign, and the cross-accelerations always have the opposite sign of the direct accelerations.

7c. *Further observations on the pari-passu law in two factors*

The assumption that a production law has a pari-passu character does not necessarily imply the existence of an optimum law in every factor or in any single factor. If we have a pari-passu law in two factors and one factor is applied technically optimally, then the other factor must be applied technically maximally, and *vice versa*. In a pari-passu law in two factors, the interior of the substitution region coincides with the region where there exists a diminishing *average* return for both factors. This common region lies within the region of complementarity. This latter region coincides with the region where there exists a diminishing *marginal* return for both factors. Reflexive property of the optimum law: in a pari-passu law in two factors, we can derive from the optimum effect in one factor an optimum effect in the other factor. A generalisation to several factors and to the ultra-passum law is not very simple.

7d. *The pari-passu law in three factors*

The substitution region becomes a sort of triangular 'dunce's cap' in the three-dimensional factor diagram.

7e. *The substitution region in a pari-passu law of n factors*

In the pari-passu law in n factors every factor is super-optimal in the interior of the substitution region. If any factor is suboptimal the point must lie outside the substitution region. If all factors except one are maximal, the remaining one must be optimal. Thus in a pari-passu law not all the factors can simultaneously be applied technically optimally. If one factor is optimal in the substitution region of the pari-passu law then all the others must be maximal. I.e.: in the substitution region of the pari-passu law the technical optimalisation is alternative, not simultaneous. In a pari-passu law in n factors where a technical optimum law prevails for every factor, there exists in the substitution region a diminishing marginal return for every one of the n factors.

CHAPTER 8/THE ULTRA-PASSUM LAW

The regular ultra-passum law

The ultra-passum law: a production law in which the passus coefficient is *not* equal to 1 in every factor point. The *regular* ultra-passum law: by a movement along an arbitrary rising curve in the factor diagram the passus coefficient will gradually diminish steadily from values in excess of 1, through 1 and 0 and to negative values, cf. (8.1). The substitution region lies in the with respect to the scale technically pre-optimal region. In the with respect to the scale technically post-optimal part of the substitution region there exists both a diminishing average return and a diminishing marginal return with respect to every single factor. The regular ultra-passum law in n factors can be imagined to have emerged by, in a pari-passu law in $n+m$ factors, keeping m factors constant while varying the other n factors. In practice we must often be prepared to meet the regular ultra-passum law.

B. ECONOMIC SECTION

CHAPTER 9 / THE STRATEGIC TYPES AND THE AIMS OF ECONOMIC ADJUSTMENT

9a. *The necessity of taking into consideration other forms of market than free competition and absolute monopoly*

Fixation strategy. Negotiation strategy. Autonomous and conjectural fixation strategy.

9b. *Quantity adjustment*

The price is assumed to be given from the outside.

9c. *Stochastic price adjustment*

9d. *Elasticity-influenced price-quantity adjustment*

The price is assumed to be dependent on the quantities bought or sold by the enterprise in question.

9e. *Option fixation*

The supplier determines both price and quantity.

9f. *Option reception*

The option receiver can answer only yes or no.

9g. *Aims and conditions for an adjustment process*

Both aims and conditions must be stated precisely before anything can be said about what is 'best possible'.

CHAPTER 10 / ECONOMIC ADJUSTMENT TO FIXED PRICES

10a. *Introduction*

It is presupposed that the producer acts as a price-fixed quantity adjuster in all markets. The cost equation. Graphic representation: in two factors a cost line, in three factors a cost plane.

10b. *Cost minimisation under a given product quantity*

Graphically in two factors: find the factor point where the given isoquant is tangential to one of the cost lines. Analytically in n factors with the help of Lagrange's method. In the adjustment point the marginal productivities are proportional to the factor prices, or in other words: all the partial marginal costs are equal. The second-order condition: the isoquants must be curved towards the origin in the vicinity of the equilibrium point.

10c. *Product maximisation with given total cost*

Graphically in two factors: find the factor point where the given cost line is tangential to one of the isoquants. Analytically in n factors with the help of Lagrange's method. The tangential conditions are the same as in Section 10b, but the side-condition is now a different one.

10d. *The in-every-respect economic substitution. The substitumal*

Both the problem of cost minimisation and that of product maximisation lead to one and the same curve: the substitumal. More generally: the in-every-respect economic substitution also leads to this same curve. The parameter representation of the substitumal with the product quantity as parameter: (10d.9). The substitumally marginal fabrication coefficients. These satisfy the aggregation equation (10d.11). Under fixed factor prices the substitumal is one specific of the isoclines. In the pari-passu law, under fixed factor prices, the substitumal is therefore simply a factor beam. Under the ultra-passum law the substitumal will not necessarily be a factor beam, but as a rule it will be a rising curve in the factor diagram.

10e. *Co-variation between costs and product quantity along the substitumal. The economic optimum law*

The substitumal cost function and the concepts connected with it: the substitumal marginal cost, the substitumal piece cost, and the substitumal cost flexibility. In the case with fixed factor prices the substitumal marginal cost is equal to the ratio between the price of an arbitrary factor and the marginal productivity of this factor. – The indifference proposition for the general marginal cost is given in (10e.8). The passus proposition for total cost: in a substitumal point, factor prices being fixed and given, total cost is equal to the product of the passus coefficient, the substitumal marginal cost, and the product quantity. In a substitumal point, factor prices being fixed and given, the passus coefficient has precisely the same significance in relation to total costs as marginal elasticities have for every single factor. Under the pari-passu law and fixed factor prices, we get no economic optimum law along the substitumal, for then both the substitumal marginal cost and the substitumal piece cost have the same constant size. If the fundamental rule regarding the variation of ε along the substitumal (10e.20) applies, we will, under the ultra-passum law, get an economic optimum law along the substitumal as indicated in Figure (10e.21). Fixed factors and fixed costs. The global cost. The global piece cost.

10f. *Profit Maximisation*

Total profit is the difference between the total intake (total turnover) and the total cost. Apart from possible terminal maxima, total profit has a maximum in a point where the substitumal marginal cost is equal to the product price, and the substitumal marginal cost curve is rising. Graphic representation in Figure (10f.7). The condition for positive total profit is that the product price is greater than the substitumal average cost. The deviation of the passus coefficient from unity in the adjustment point is a measure of how great a part the gross profit constitutes of the total intake. Profit maximisation adjustment can also be discussed directly in one stage, that is to say, without going via the substitumal. Disregarding possible terminal maxima, total profit is greatest at a point where, for every single factor, there is equality between its price and its marginal productivity calculated in money. The second-order conditions derived by the direct method. For certain questions the direct method is the simplest, but the argument via the substitumal gives a better understanding of several questions. Under the pari-passu law, given fixed factor prices, there is either no point or infinitely many points which satisfy the condition of profit maximisation.

10g. *Profit optimisation*

The profit rate r/b is greatest at a point where the substitumal marginal cost is equal to the substitumal average cost, i.e. in the substitumal point where the scale is technically optimal.

10h. *The general demand functions for the factors and the general supply function for the product*

10i. *The effect of a change in the product price*

The direct supply elasticity for the product (10i.1). The direct supply

ANALYTICAL SUMMARY   357

curve for the product is rising. The short-term supply curve (10i.4) and the long-term supply curve (10i.5). A change in the product price also affects the demand for factors. The effect depends on whether the substitumal is rising or declining with respect to the factors.

10j. *The effect of a change in one of the factor prices*

The direct (ordinary) demand elasticity for a production factor. The cross-demand elasticities. The direct demand curve will be declining for all factors (disregarding possible terminal maxima). This applies in the general case with n factors. In the case involving two factors complementarity in the technical sense implies complementarity in demand (disregarding possible terminal maxima). Corresponding proposition for alternativity. Generalising these propositions to the case involving several factors is not very simple. A partial change in one of the factor prices also affects the quantity supplied of the product.

10k. *Capacity adjustment*

Maximum capacity. Optimum capacity. The latter must as a rule be calculated on an index basis. It is only in the vicinity of the technically optimal scale that piece cost can be reduced by building a plant with large capacity.

CHAPTER 11 / ECONOMIC ADJUSTMENT UNDER ELASTICITY-INFLUENCED PRICE-QUANTITY ADJUSTMENT

11a. *Introduction*

It is here assumed that the concern is functioning as an elasticity-influenced price-quantity adjuster in all markets. The marginal outlays: the partial derivatives of the total cost with respect to the individual factor quantities. The marginal outlay for a factor is equal to the corrected factor price. In two factors the cost lines will now not necessarily be straight lines, but they are still falling. As a rule they are curved from origin.

11b. *Cost minimisation under a given product quantity and variable factor prices*

Graphically in two factors: find the factor point where the given isoquant is tangential to one of the cost lines defined by the given factor supply functions. Analytically in n factors with the help of Lagrange's method. At the adjustment point the marginal productivities are proportional to the corrected factor prices, or, in other words: all the partial marginal costs are equal.

11c. *Product maximisation under a given total cost and variable factor prices*

Graphically in two factors: find the factor point where the cost line, defined by the given factor supply functions and the given size of total cost, is tangential to one of the isoquants. Analytically in n factors with the help of Lagrange's method. The same tangent conditions as in 11b, but the side-condition is now a different one.

11d. *The in-every-respect economic substitution under variable factor prices. The substitumal under variable factor prices*

As in the case with fixed factor prices, both the problem of cost minimisation and that of product maximisation lead to one and the same curve: the substitumal. More generally: the in-every-respects economic substitution also leads to this same curve. The parameter representation of the substitumal with the product quantity as parameter: (11d.3). The substitumally marginal fabrication coefficients. Under variable factor prices, regardless of whether the production law is pari-passu or ultra-passum, the substitumal will not necessarily be one of the isoclines, but as a rule it is a rising curve in the factor diagram.

11e. *The co-variation between costs and product quantity along the substitumal corresponding to the given factor supply functions. The economic optimum law under variable factor prices*

The substitumal cost function and the other substitumal cost concepts. In the case involving variable factor prices, the substitumal marginal cost is equal to the ratio between the marginal outlay (the corrected price) for an arbitrary factor and the marginal productivity of this factor. The indifference proposition for the marginal cost also applies in the general case with variable factor prices. At a substitumal point under variable factor prices the total cost is equal to the product of the flexibility-corrected passus coefficient, the substitumal marginal cost, and the product quantity; thus we get complete agreement with the case of quantity adjustment, excepting that the passus coefficient ε now is substituted by the flexibility-corrected passus coefficient $\varepsilon/(1 + q_0)$. If rule (11e.13) applies, we shall, in a regular ultra-passum law, get an economic optimum law along the substitumal also in the case with variable prices. – Some examples showing how one can make a comparison between the cost curves under variable factor prices and under fixed factor prices.

11f. *Profit maximisation under variable product price*

The marginal intake: the derivative of the total intake with respect to the product quantity. The marginal intake can be interpreted as a corrected product price. Disregarding any terminal maxima, the total profit is greatest at a point where the substitumal marginal cost curve intersects the marginal intake curve from its lower side. The appurtenant product price is found by inserting the value we have found for x into the demand function. The adjustment point must lie on a superelastic part of the demand curve. Under price-variable (i.e. elasticity-influenced) adjustment the enterprise will achieve greatest profit (apart from possible terminal maxima) by operating in such a way that every factor acquires a price which is *less* than its marginal productivity calculated in terms of money. Under such an adjustment the profit can be positive even if the adjustment takes place in the with respect to the scale technically pre-optimal region. By elasticity-influenced adjustment in the product market there exists no supply curve for the product.

PART THREE / MOMENTARY SINGLE PRODUCTION WITH LIMITATION FACTORS

CHAPTER 12 / TECHNICAL ANALYSIS OF LIMITATION LAWS

12a. *The simple minimum law*

No substitution possibilities between the factors. Confluence line. Limitation line. Minimum factor. The limitation-fabrication coefficients. The product function under the simple minimum law: (12a.2).

12b. *Marginal definition of minimum, maximum, and limitation factors. General definition of the limitation law*

If from a given factor point it is impossible to increase the product quantity without increasing factor No. k, we say that the latter is an (effective) *minimum* factor at this point. A minimum factor which is further such that the product quantity does not increase when this factor alone is increased, is said to be an (effective) *limitation* factor or limitational at this point. (I) A complete substitution law. (II) A limitation law in the wider sense. (III) A complete limitation law.

12c. *The production law in the case of technically given but not constant limitation-fabrication coefficients. Independent limitation factors*

The factor functions (12c.1). The limitation functions (12c.2). The general expression of the product function in a direct minimum law (the case with directly limiting factors).

12d. *Separate factor rings*

12e. *Mixed factor rings*

12f. *Confluence analysis, all-region analysis, and delimitation analysis. Basis variables*

In an all-region analysis the production law is studied for a free variation of the factors in the entire factor diagram. An important part of the all-region analysis is the delimitation analysis, i.e. the demonstration of the special form possessed by the confluence region. An analysis limited to the study of what happens in the confluence region is called a confluence analysis.

12g. *The marginal productivity concept when the production law contains limitation factors*

Forward, the rate of increase of the total product is equal to the rate of increase for the minimum function which has the least forward rate of increase. Backwards, the rate of increase of the total product is equal to the rate of increase for the minimum function which has the greatest backward rate of increase.

12h. *The delimitation definition of the confluence region. The relationship with the substitution region. The limitation law as an extreme case of the optimum law*

Outside the confluence region there is everywhere at least one factor which is such that its quantity can be decreased (while the others are constant), without the product quantity being decreased. But in the confluence region no factor will be of this kind. The confluence region consists of those and only those factor points where all the generally defined backward marginal productivities are positive, not zero.

12i. *The delimitation problem. A method of constructing the confluence region*

12j. *Basis factors and shadow factors. Product shadows and factor shadows*

The reduced product function. The reduced marginal productivity. The shadow functions and the shadow coefficients.

CHAPTER 13 / ECONOMIC ANALYSIS OF LIMITATION LAWS

13a. *The economic production concepts within the confluence region*

The reduced cost. The unreduced cost. The shadow factor costs.

13b. *The substitumal within the confluence region*

The presence of shadow factors does not change the form of the substitumal provided that the shadow factors are product shadows. But for the question as to *where* on the substitumal the adaptation is to stop, the presence of shadow factors is significant.

13c. *Step-by-step adaptation taking marginal rentability and marginal profit into account*

The marginal rentability decides whether a given direction is profit increasing. The arrow of rentability.

13d. *Further application of the arrow of rentability: adaptation to equivalence factors and to production laws with complicated factor bands*

PART FOUR / MULTI-WARE PRODUCTION

CHAPTER 14 / TECHNICAL DESCRIPTION OF THE PRODUCTION LAW FOR MULTI-WARE PRODUCTION

14a. *Connected products. Assortment and coupling*

If there exists some kind of technical connection between several products, we say that these products are (technically) connected, or that we are dealing with multi-ware production. A production relation: an equation making a connection between product quantities or between these and the factor quantities. – The degree of assortment (the degree of freedom of assortment) is equal to the number of products minus the number of production relations. A pure factor band is a production relation which only connects certain product quantities. The degree of coupling is equal to the number of pure factor bands.

14b. *Factorially determined multi-ware production*

Factorially determined multi-ware production: a production law where the product quantities are given provided the factor quantities are given. Coupled production: there exists a certain state of dependence between the product quantities regardless of how large the factor quantities are. If the ratio between the product quantities can be changed by changing the factor quantities, the products are separable. Two sets of isoquants in cases with factorially determined bi-ware production. With coupled production the two sets of isoquants coincide completely.

14c. *One-dimensional assortment. Single product freedom*

Even if the factor quantities are given, the producer will have a choice between the two products. To a given *point* in the factor diagram, there is an equivalent *curve* in the product diagram (a factor isoquant). Conditioned marginal productivities.

14d. *Multi-dimensional assortment. Multiple freedom of products*

Representation in parameter-form. The number of parameters introduced is equal to the number of production factors plus the degree of assortment. Parametric marginal productivity. Parametric factor rate of increase.

CHAPTER 15 / ECONOMIC ADAPTATION UNDER MULTI-WARE PRODUCTION

15a. *Product value and costs under multi-ware production*

15b. *Economic adaptation under factorially determined multi-ware production (hence $d = 0$)*

In the case of several products the substitumal in the factor diagram will be a little more complicated than in the case of a single product. It should be noted especially that the tangency determined substitumal may have several brances of which, however, as a rule only one will give the correct solution.

15c. *Two-stage economic adaptation under one-dimensional or multidimensional assortment*

In cases with freedom of assortment an adaptation has to take place not only within the factor diagram (factor substitution), but also within the product diagram (product substitution). It will often be practical to think of the adaptation as taking place separately within each of the two diagrams (regions).

15d. *Direct analysis of the economic adaptation in the general case*

The adaptation in the general case, involving an arbitrary degree of assortment and an arbitrary degree of coupling, can best be discussed in parameter form. In a point where the total profit is to be as big as possible, the parametric marginal intake must for any parameter be equal to the parametric marginal outlay.

PART FIVE/ELEMENTS OF A DYNAMIC THEORY OF PRODUCTION

CHAPTER 16/A SURVEY OF THE PROBLEMS OF A DYNAMIC THEORY OF PRODUCTION

In the dynamic theory of production the time shape of input and outtake elements is of fundamental importance. Depreciation. Varying prices.

CHAPTER 17/THE REINVESTMENT PROCESS IN A MASS WHERE EACH CAPITAL OBJECT HAS A DETERMINED LIFETIME

17a. *Reinvestment activity as a consequence of a primary investment dose where the distribution of durability is discrete*

If a primary investment dose is made at a certain time, what reinvestment will this occasion in future? The smoothed reinvestment components. The rectangular presentation.

17b. *Reinvestment activity as a result of a primary investment dose where the durability distribution is continuous*

After some starting fluctuations the time-curve for the aggregate reinvestment approaches a constant asymptotic level.

17c. *Reinvestment when new primary investment doses are injected at various points of time*

The primary investment is assumed to vary with time in a certain way. In the special case where durability distribution in the primary investment doses is constant over the time, the aggregate reinvestment can, at a certain point in time, be interpreted as the result of a linear accumulation. The replenishment function (the stimulant). The absorption function (a weight system). The resultant.

CHAPTER 18 / THE REINVESTMENT PROCESS IN A MASS WHERE THERE IS A PROBABILITY LAW FOR THE LIFETIME OF EACH CAPITAL OBJECT

18a. *Departure gauges*

In a mass of uniform capital objects it will as a rule be possible to draw up on the basis of statistics a mortality curve (retirement curve) for such objects. The retirement conditions in a mass of uniform capital objects can therefore be expressed by the same symbols as those we use to describe the mortality situation in a human population.

18b. *Maintenance equation and calculation of maintenance investment as a time series*

That the maintenance equation is fulfilled for every $t \geq T$ is the necessary and sufficient condition for a capital mass produced by the investment series z_T to be able to *subsist* from year to year at a constant size, that is to say, be stationary. As soon as we have passed the initial period, the investment needed to keep the capital mass unchanged will be given by a time series which builds itself up forwards simply by virtue of the fact that the next ordinate is the average of the preceding ones. The weights in this moving average are the departure effects d_x.

18c. *Breaking maintenance investment down into its component parts*

The combined maintenance investment can be split into generation-components. The first generation consists of those renewals which have been made necessary because the original stock loses some of its units, the second generation consists of those renewals which are necessary because the first generation gradually loses some of its units, and so forth. The graphic pictures of the successive generation-components gradually become more and more regularly bell-shaped.

18d. *The segment method*

The course of the maintenance process during the initial period can also be studied by splitting the course of time up into *segments*. Especially at the beginning of the maintenance process and at the segment transitions where discontinuities or other extraordinary curve forms may arise, the segment method will provide the best information on the nature of the maintenance process.

18e. *Maintenance investment when a considerable period of time has elapsed since the starting*

After a certain lapse of time the maintenance investment approaches a certain level around which the curve remains practically constant.

18f. *The method of curve fitting. Maintenance investment when the departure distribution is almost normal (Gaussian)*

When the departure distribution shows a marked bell-shape, something like a normal (Gaussian) form, the initial fluctuations around the asymptotic level (18e.4) will be very regular, and the investment curve can then approximately be described by the sum of a constant or a trend and one or more damped sine functions. It is not to be expected that the method of curve fitting will give particularly good results, except for the interval following after the initial period.

CHAPTER 19 / DEPRECIATION ANALYSIS

Depreciation: the decline in the ability to produce output or the decline in value of the capital objects, which results from wear and tear or simply from becoming out of date.

19a. *Technical depreciation defined by the principle of remaining services*

Remaining years' work. Average remaining effective time. The remaining fraction (the service fraction).

19b. *Writing-off plan and actual writing-off*

By writting-off is meant an item in the books of a concern which aims to give a bookkeeping expression for the actual concrete process which has taken place in the depreciation. Writing-off plan. Adjustment of the writing-off plan. If precise l_x-data are available for every single kind of capital object included in the accounts of a concern, then these data will determine the writing-off plan (provided that no complication will arise owing to price variations). But in practice this is not what happens. Even ignoring complications with varying prices and the like, there are only a few types of capital objects for which exact l_x-calculations exist. This means that in practice one must as a rule be satisfied with some approximation method or other for the writing-off plan. The amount-constant method. The percent-constant method.

INDEX

Aarum, T. 44
accelerations; direct 58f, 89–91, 97, 105, 108, 118, 191
action parameter 136
adjustment; – in the case of variable prices 140, 196–222; aim of – 141–143, 147, 151, 159, 175, 217; capacity – 194; complete – 142; elasticity-influenced price-quantity – 138, 196–222; general – under conditions 140; group – 142; quantity – 135, 138f, 144–195; quantity – in the case of variable prices 144–195; single factor – 142; stochastic price – 137; substitution – 160, 173, 175, 180, 228; volume – 160, 175, 180
age of the capital 333
all-region analysis 235f, 280
alternative optimalisation 117
amount-constant method 340
anticipation 38
arrow of rentability 260–265
assortment; – relation 280; degree of – 269f, 286f, 293; freedom of – 269, 277, 286f
autonomous fixation strategy 137
availability box 226
average cost (piece cost) 166, 168f, 176f, 186, 189, 208, 211–217; global – 173–175, 179, 188f; substitumal – 167, 169–171, 173, 176, 188, 205–208, 211, 243f, 255f
average remaining effective time 334
average return (when considering partial variation of a factor) 61–64, 83, 91f, 94, 107, 116, 127f; decreasing – 61–63, 83, 92, 94, 107f, 118, 127f; increasing – 61–63, 94, 116, 123
average return (when considering a proportional variation of a factor) 66, 70f, 123; decreasing – 66, 70f, 123; increasing – 66, 70f

Basis factor 249–254, 262
beam variation equation (first form) 72f, 76; – (second form) 73, 100

Clark, J. B. 89
Cobb-Douglas function 42, 52, 65, 78, 97, 105
combined factors 21–23
competition; cut-throat – 174; free – 135f
complementarity; – in demand 192; – production factors 60, 104, 106, 119, 128, 192
concentration, horizontal and vertical 12f, 135f
confluence; – analysis 235–237, 280; – line 225, 230f, 235, 244; – region 232, 235, 237, 242–245, 247–252, 255
constant technique 24–28, 40f, 100f
continuity factors 40, 54, 60, 105, 118, 144, 196, 227–230, 236, 241, 243, 252, 289
cost 83, 141, 143–147, 164–175, 198–201, 208–217, 242, 255, 282f; – equation 145, 152, 164, 198, 205f; – flexibility 167–169, 208, 210; – function 284; – line 145–148, 152, 154–159, – minimisation 141, 147–152, 154–156, 159, 162, 201–207; – plane 145f; general –s 17; global – 173; reduced – 252
coupling; complete – 273
cross accelerations 58f, 105, 108, 119, 191

Delimitation; – analysis 235, 251; – problem 244; – table 245–247
demand curve; – of a production factor 186–194; forced – 141
demand elasticity; – of a product 141, 197, 217–222; – of a production factor 191–195; cross – between the factors 191
demand function for a production factor 186–194
departure; – of capital objects 309; – effect of capital objects 310–313; – effects distribution of capital objects 319, 326; – probability of capital objects 310, 312
depreciation 293f, 333
discontinuity factor 228
Douglas, P. 42
duopoly 137
Durability (lifetime) of a capital object 295, 320, 334f, 340

Economic factor, 15
economic law along the substitutimal 171–173, 175, 211–212
elasticity; – of the passus coefficient 168–172, 190; – of the substitumal average cost 168–170, 211; – of the substitumal marginal cost 168f, 172 189, 210–212

elementary factor: absolute – 20
equivalence factor 21, 262
evaluation coefficient 8–10, 37, 228, 293

Fabrication coefficient 29, 62, 225, 230f, 251, 256
factor; – band 270; – beam 69–71, 74, 105–113, 163, 168; – complex 21f, 98, 131; – diagram 49f, 277, 284, 288; – function 230, 279; – point 49f; – price 58, 144–146, 149f, 160f, 166, 180, 190–194, 196, 199f, 206, 211, 219–221, 228, 243f, – price flexibility 198, 202, 210, 221f; – price function 243; corrected – price 198, 201–203, 206–209, 213–215, 217–222, 254; – quantity 18–21, 26f, 30, 41, 78, 162, 186, 196; – relation 237, 264, 266f, 275; – ring 231; mixed – ring 232, 237; separate – ring 244; – shadow 249, 251; partial – variation 51, 62, 83–98, 150, 198, 203, 243
fixation parameter 136f
fixation strategy 136; conjectured – 137
fixed cost 173–175, 178f
fixed factor 15–18, 131, 169, 173, 185f
fixed price 138f, 144–195
free factor 15, 162, 164

General costs 17
general factor 17
generation component 312–316, 318–320, 323
graphic method of presentation (of a production law) 47–51

Implied factors 14f, 101, 131
independent factor 60
indifference proposition for the general marginal cost 166, 209, 288
initial fluctuations 303, 321
input curve 30f, 36f
intake; total – 175, 179, 217, 286
interest 83
investment; primary – 293, 333
irreversible factor 16
isocline 56–58, 80, 102, 163, 168, 175, 207
isoquant 44, 47, 49–51, 78–82, 147–149, 151–160, 195, 210f, 203–205, 262f, 272, 275

Johnson, A. 88, 152
joint production 10f

Langrange's method 149, 153, 202, 204
Liebig, J. von 86
limitational factor 60, 118, 228f, 230–232, 237
limitation-fabrication coefficient 226
limitation; – function 230; – law 227–231, 252; – line 225f
long-term factor 16
long-term supply curve 188f

Macro analysis 10, 18, 86
macro-cosmos 12
maintenance; – equation 310–312; – investment 310–313, 315–323, 329–332; – percentage 301, 304
managing (other's work) 20
marginal; – analysis 83; – cost 165–167, 169–172, 174, 185f, 188, 207, 209, 212, 219, 255f, 285, 288; general – cost 166, 209; indifference proposition for – cost 166, 209, 288; partial – cost 150, 203, 255, 285; – determination of working wages 83–86; – efficiency 52; – elasticity 62–65, 77, 90, 93–98, 102f, 105–108, 111–113, 115f, 124–127, 168, 173 – fabrication coefficient for shadow factor 251; – intake (– sales) 217–220, 253, 285–287; parametric – intake 287; – low point 90f, 94f, 97; – outlay 198, 253–255, 283, 285; parametric – outlay 287; – principle of wage 83–86, 180, 22; – productivity 51–63, 74–76, 80, 83–85, 89–91, 94, 102, 116–118, 128, 148, 153, 161, 163, 166, 180, 201–203, 205f, 208f, 221, 227–230, 235–238, 240–242, 244, 247, 250f, 254f, 278, 293; parametric – productivity 281; reduced – productivity (basis form) 250; relative – productivity 56; – profit 176, 219, 253, 256; – rentability 253, 255, 257, 259, 283; parametric – rentability 288; – return 59, 84, 88, 104, 108, 118, 128; decreasing return (when considering partial variation) 59f, 84, 88, 104, 107, 115, 118; increasing – return 59f; – top point 48, 89–91, 94f
maximum 244; – capacity 194f; – factor 87, 92–94, 106, 113–117, 124–126, 130, 164, 229; – of product quantity at a partial variation 88–90; absolute – point 125, 194
mean production period 35–38
micro-cosmos 12
micro point of view 86

INDEX

minimal; – factor 225, 227, 231; – form 249; – ring 236, 244f
Mitscherlich 86f
monopoly 135, 140, 197, 217, 220, 222
multi-ware 11–13; 269f, 282, 289; factorially determined – production 270f, 275, 282 286f

National income 83f, 135
negotiation strategy 136
net profit 142, 176f, 256, 282

Optimality coefficient; individual – 244
optimal factor 92, 94, 106, 113–119, 124–126, 130, 164
optimum 7, 90–96, 170–173, 186, 243; – capacity 194f; – law 42, 88–98, 171–173, 212, 243f; technical – law 42, 88–98; reflexive property of the – law 95, 109–113; economic – 10, 170–173, 196
option fixation 140
option reception 140f

Parametric factor rate of increase 281
Pareto 102
pari-passu law 56, 95, 99, 119, 125–127, 163, 169, 173, 195f, 208
passus; – character 98, 101, 190; – coefficient 65–78, 86, 99, 120–127, 130, 167–173, 179, 190, 209, 222, 244; flexibility-corrected – coefficient 210–212; fundamental rule regarding the variation of the – coefficient 170–173, 211; – equation 73–78, 86, 103, 106, 117, 125–127, 130, 167, 209
percent constant method 340, 342, 345
piece cost; global – 173–175, 179, 188f
poly-poly 137
post-maximal region with respect to the scale 123f, 126, 164
post-optimal region with respect to the scale 123f, 126, 130, 170–175, 177–179, 195
pre-maximal region with respect to the scale 123f, 125f, 164
pre-optimal region with respect to the scale 123f, 126, 131, 170–172, 211, 222
price-flexibility; – for a factor 201; – for a product 139, 198, 217–222
principle of remaining services 333, 335
probability of non-departure (of capital objects) 310

product 3f; – accelerations 58f, 80–82, 90f, 97, 102–105, 108, 111, 117, 150f, 154, 180f, 184, 191; – coupling curve 274f; – curve 47–51, 90f; – demand curve 138, 196f, 217, 222; – demand function 138, 196f, 217, 282; – diagram 274, 277, 283–287; – price 141, 171–177, 187, 196, 217f, 286; corrected – price 217–222; – price flexibility 218; – quantity 18–21, 25–28, 40f, 50, 61, 65, 90, 99, 109, 123, 150, 162, 164f, 187, 196, 208, 220; – shadows 249–252, 254, 256; – surface 49; – table 42–46; degree of – coupling 269–272, 276, 278, 287; reduced – function 252; ring-constructed – 234
production; – factor 3f, 14–21; – function 21, 25–27, 41–51, 55, 62, 95, 109, 162, 188, 227, 234, 279; – in the economic sense 8–11; – in the technical sense 3f; graphic method of presentation of a – law 47–51; numerical method of presentation of – law 42–46; analytical method of presentation of a – law 42; – period 29, 35–38; – process 34f; – relation 269f, 278, 288; – scale 66, 70, 121, 156; – technique 24–28; – maximisation 142, 151–154, 159, 162, 203f; alternative – 60, 119; changes in the – (in the – table) 25f; demand curve of – 186–194; joint – 10f; organisation of – 11–13, 26;
products; connected – 269f; coupled or joined – 271–275; separable – 271, 275–276
profit; – maximisation 142, 175–195, 217–222; – optimisation 142, 186; net – 142, 176f, 256, 282; rate of – 142, 186; total – 142, 175, 178f, 219, 221f
proportional variation of a factor 65, 68–73, 98–102, 121–124
productivity, average – 61–63, 66, 70, 90–92, 103

Quality of the product 30
quasi-rent 15, 195
quasi-technical 10

Rectangle of availability 226
region of complementarity 108, 115
region of possibility (for an in all respects economic situation) 159
reinvestment 295, 321, 333
remainder of services 334, 342

INDEX

remaining fraction 334, 340–342
remaining year's work 334
rent 83f,
residual determination of working wages 83–86
reversible factor 16
Ricardo 83f
ring function 231–241, 243–247, 250
risk 38

Sales line 286
scale condition 160, 175, 179
segment method 316, 332
service fraction 334
shadow; – coefficient 249–251, 254; – factor 22, 249–256; – function 250f
short-term factor 16, 169, 173
simple minimum law 227, 230–232
special cost 17
special factor 17
specified factor 14f, 20, 101, 131, 173, 185
stage; – interval 34f; – tempo of production 31f, 34; number of –s 30–33
starting (or transitional, or initial) period 298, 312, 315, 323, 331
step diagram 30–33
strangulation point 89–91
strategic types 135–140
submaximal factor 89, 93f, 130
sub-optimal factor 89–91, 93f, 117
substitumal 58, 154–164, 166f, 169f, 173, 176, 188, 205–208, 211, 243f, 255f, 262, 283–285, 288f; – condition 160–162, 206, 262, 288; –cost flexibility 167f, 208, 210; –cost function 165–175, 208–217; – equation 215; – factor function 162, 165, 171, 207f; – marginal cost 165–167, 169–171, 174f, 182, 185, 207, 210–212, 219, 284
substitumally marginal fabrication coefficients 162–165, 190, 207
substitution 55, 154–164, 205–208, 243, 285–287; – adjustment 160, 173, 175, 180, 228; – between products 285; – factor 227; – law 244; complete – law 227; – ratio 55f, 79; – region 55, 64, 79, 81, 106–109, 113–119, 125–130, 147, 149, 162, 195, 242–244, 272, 296; – relationship between factors 55, 60, 79, 227, 229; the in-every-respect economic – 154–164, 205–208, 243f, 255, 288
super-maximal factor 88f, 92
super-optimal factor 90, 91–94, 116, 128

supply; – curve of a production factor 142, 196f, 206, 213; – curve of the product 138, 186f, 222; direct – curve of the product 197–189, 222; forced – curve 141; – function of the product 138f, 186–189, 222; direct – elasticity of a product 187–189
survival curve 334

Technically; – maximal (when considering a partial variation) 89, 92–94, 106, 113–117, 124–126, 130, 164; – maximal production scale 123f, 131; – submaximal (when considering a partial variation) 89, 92–94, 106, 113–117, 124–126, 130, 164; – supermaximal (when considering a partial variation) 89, 92–94, 106, 113–117, 124–126, 130, 164; – optimal (when considering a partial variation) 92, 94, 106, 113–119, 124–127, 130, 164; – optimal production scale 71, 122–125, 130, 170–172, 186, 195; – suboptimal (when considering a partial variation) 92, 94, 106, 113–119, 124–127, 130, 164; – superoptimal (when considering a partial variation) 92, 94, 106, 113–119, 124–127, 130, 164
technical unit of measurement 18, 40, 144, 196
technique; change in – 24f
tender 139
theory of production; dynamic – 30, 293f; static – 30

Ultra-passum law 101, 120–131, 169, 173, 175, 208, 211; regular – 120–131, 169, 173, 175, 185f, 211
unreduced cost 252

Value on scrapping 340, 345
variable; – cost 173–175; – factor 15–18, 131, 144, 169, 175, 179, 185; – price 140, 196–222
virtual, product share 64
volume condition 160, 175, 180
Von Thünen 83, 180

Wage 83–85
Walras, L. 88
Weber, M. 8
Wicksell, K. 88, 102
Wicksteed, P. H. 88
writing-off 337
writing-off plan 337–339, 345